JERUSALEM AND PAROUSIA

CONCORDIA ACADEMIC PRESS

JERUSALEM
AND PAROUSIA

JESUS' ESCHATOLOGICAL DISCOURSE
IN MATTHEW'S GOSPEL

JEFFREY A. GIBBS

Concordia Academic Press
A Division of
Concordia Publishing House
Saint Louis, Missouri

Copyright © 2000 Jeffrey A. Gibbs
Published by Concordia Publishing House
3558 S. Jefferson Avenue, St. Louis, MO 63118-3968
Manufactured in the United States of America

Library of Congress Cataloging-in-Publication Data

Gibbs, Jeffrey A.
    Jerusalem and Parousia : Jesus' eschatological discourse in Matthew's Gospel / Jeffrey A. Gibbs.
        p.   cm.
    Includes bibliographical references.
    ISBN 0-570-04288-7
    1. Bible. N.T. Matthew—Criticism, interpretation, etc. 2. Eschatology—Biblical teaching.
I. Title.
    BS2575.2 .G53   2001
    226.2'06—dc21   00-011891

1 2 3 4 5 6 7 8 9 10   09 08 07 06 05 04 03 02 01 00

For Renée
γυναῖκα ἀνδρείαν τίς εὑρήσει;
τιμιωτέρα δέ ἐστιν λίθων πολυτελῶν ἡ τοιαύτη.

CONTENTS

ABBREVIATIONS

AB	Anchor Bible
ABD	*Anchor Bible Dictionary*. Edited by D. N. Freedman. 6 vols. New York, 1992
AsTJ	*Asbury Theological Journal*
AThR	*Anglican Theological Review*
BAGD	Bauer, W., W. F. Arndt, F. W. Gingrich, and F. W. Danker. *A Greek-English Lexicon of the New Testament and Other Early Christian Literature*. 2d ed. Chicago: 1979
BDF	Blass, F., A. DeBrunner, and R. W. Funk. *A Greek Grammar of the New Testament and Other Early Christian Literature*. Chicago, 1961
BibLeb	*Bibel und Leben*
BJRL	*Bulletin of the John Rylands Library*
BT	*The Bible Translator*
BTB	*Biblical Theology Bulletin*
BZ	*Biblische Zeitschrift*
CBQ	*Catholic Biblical Quarterly*
CTQ	*Concordia Theological Quarterly*
ED	Eschatological Discourse
ET	English translation
ExpTim	*Expository Times*
FoiVie	*Foi et vie*
GTJ	*Grace Theological Journal*
HBT	*Horizons in Biblical Theology*
IBC	Interpretation: A Bible Commentary for Teaching and Preaching
Int	*Interpretation*
JBL	*Journal of Biblical Literature*
JES	*Journal of Ecumenical Studies*
JSNT	*Journal for the Study of the New Testament*
JSNTSup	Journal for the Study of the New Testament Supplement Series
JSOTSup	Journal for the Study of the Old Testament Supplement Series
JTS	*Journal of Theological Studies*
LSJ	Liddell, H. G., R. Scott, and H. S. Jones. *A Greek-English Lexicon*. Oxford, 1953

LXX	Septuagint
MT	Masoretic Text
NA[26]	Nestle, E. and E., K. and B. Aland, et al. *Novum Testamentum Graece*. 26th ed. Stuttgart, 1979
Neot	*Neotestamentica*
NovT	*Novum Testamentum*
NTS	*New Testament Studies*
RefR	*Reformed Review*
RSV	Revised Standard Version of the Bible
RTR	*Reformed Theological Review*
SBLDS	Society of Biblical Literature Dissertation Series
SBLSP	*Society of Biblical Literature Seminar Papers*
SJT	*Scottish Journal of Theology*
ST	*Studia Theologica*
Str-B	Strack, H. L., and P. Billerbeck. *Kommentar zum Neuen Testament aus Talmud und Midrasch*. 6 vols. Munich, 1922–1961
TDNT	*Theological Dictionary of the New Testament*. Edited by G. Kittel and G. Friedrich. Translated by G. W. Bromiley. 10 vols. Grand Rapids, 1964–1976
TS	*Theological Studies*
TynBul	*Tyndale Bulletin*
USQR	*Union Seminary Quarterly Review*
WBC	Word Biblical Commentary
WMANT	Wissenschaftliche Monographien zum Alten und Neuen Testament
WTJ	*Westminster Theological Journal*
ZNW	*Zeitschrift für die neutestamentliche Wissenschaft*
ZTK	*Zeitschrift für Theologie und Kirche*

PREFACE

This monograph is a slightly revised version of my doctrinal dissertation at Union Theological Seminary in Virginia, completed in 1995 under the guidance of Jack Dean Kingsbury. With rare exceptions, the revisions entailed removal or shortening of material in the notes. As is probably often the case, this author of a now-published dissertation is acutely aware of many places where this work could be improved. Such is the nature of scholarship.

I am most grateful to Concordia Academic Press and specifically to the Editorial Committee for accepting this volume for publication.

1

INTRODUCTION
AND METHODOLOGY

RECENT STUDY OF THE ESCHATOLOGICAL DISCOURSE

The Eschatological Discourse (ED) in Matthew's Gospel (Matt 24:1–26:2) cries out to the reader, drawing attention to itself and demanding interpretation. Everyone agrees that all five major discourses in the Gospel of Matthew (chs. 5–7, 10, 13, 18, 24–25) are significant. But the ED is unique by virtue of its concluding position and the summarizing addition of "all" to its transitional formula ("And it came about that when Jesus had finished *all* these words," 26:1). In addition, whereas Jesus' words in the other four major discourses speak in part regarding events beyond the temporal boundaries of Matthew's Gospel and focus on eschatological events and meaning, the ED is completely dedicated to "future" events and the proper understanding of those events. Accordingly, an in-depth examination of Matthew's ED possesses an intrinsic value for those who wish to understand the eschatological perspective and message of the first canonical Gospel.

Somewhat surprisingly, the amount of attention that recent scholarship has devoted to the ED in Matthew is not large.[1] To date, the two major studies are those of Viktor Agbanou, which treats the whole of Matthew 24–25, and Fred Burnett, which addresses only Matt 24:1–31.[2] There are, of course, other studies of the ED on a much smaller scale, as well as major studies of Matthean eschatological perspective as a whole.[3]

To introduce the approach and goals of this monograph, this chapter shall note briefly some characteristics of the recent study of Matthew 24–25, as well as some of its more prominent results. Brief critique will suggest that redaction-critical study of Matthew's ED often has not respected the character of this discourse as a part of the larger whole of Matthew's Gospel. The methodology with which this present work will study Matt 24:1–26:2 will then be presented.

Most of the study of Matthew's Gospel in the last forty years has been redaction-critical study, and the study of the ED has been no exception. Three assumptions have tended to characterize this work, with direct implications for the conclusions reached. Those assumptions have been (1) Markan priority, (2) a relatively late date in the mid 80s or early 90s for Matthew's Gospel, and (3) the understanding that the Gospel is to be read as a "window" into the community of the redactor. This third assumption has had special influence because scholars have understood the "disciples" in Matthew's Gospel as transparent "stand-ins" for the members of Matthew's own church. Jesus' words in the ED, by implication, are really words spoken directly to Matthew's own community.[4]

Certain results emerge naturally from these assumptions, two of which may be highlighted here. First, redaction critics tend strongly towards reading Matthew's ED in Markan terms. Mark 13 thus becomes the primary grid through which Matt 24:4–25:46 (the ED minus its narrative framework) is read,[5] and the very real danger exists that Matthew's own material will not serve as the primary interpretive framework for the ED.

Second and more importantly, interpretations that simply do violence to the narrative context of Matt 24:4–25:46 are considered viable options because the discourse is not taken seriously as a speech by Jesus to his disciples on the Mount of Olives (24:3). For example, it is common to assert that "this generation" of Matt 24:34 refers not to the generation of those who oppose Jesus in the story of the Gospel but rather to the community of the evangelist, an interpretation that has no support whatsoever from within the text of the Gospel.[6] Moreover, some interpreters combine the view of a late date for the Gospel's composition with the concept of the disciples' "transparency" to assert that, despite that fact that the disciples clearly ask Jesus about the time when the temple would be destroyed (24:3), Jesus' discourse never answers that question because "Matthew is not concerned with the question as to how far Jesus' predictions were fulfilled in the events of A.D. 70; for his generation that problem was no longer valid."[7] Regardless of what one thinks of a later date for Matthew or of the concept of the disciples' "transparency," it is evident that these very assumptions create problems that can be resolved only by ignoring either the plain sense of words ("this generation") or obvious and important features of the text (Jesus' direct answer to his disciples' question). I do not wish to cast aspersions on the entire enterprise of redaction-critical study of Matthew's Gospel. I only wish to suggest that a method other than the redaction-critical approach might prove more amenable to reading Matt 24:4–25:46 in a way that allows it to retain its character as a speech of Jesus to his disciples within the narrative that is the First Gospel.

This study will proceed, as its title indicates, to interpret Jesus' ED *in Matthew's Gospel*, that is, giving full weight to its specific location in a particular narrative. In so doing, I shall be offering a narrative-critical reading of Matt 24:4–25:46, interpreting it in context as part of a Gospel narrative. Such holistic narrative-critical interpretation has become popular in recent years, so a full-fledged defense of the method is not necessary. I will, however, offer a brief summary of some of the more important concepts of narrative-critical study with special attention to problems created by the Gospel's extensive use of direct discourse.

A NARRATIVE-CRITICAL APPROACH TO THE ESCHATOLOGICAL DISCOURSE

I have suggested that the chief failure of recent scholarship on Matthew 24–25 has been the lack of a holistic treatment of the discourse. This has been true regarding the place of the ED within the *context* of the Gospel, and within the *narrative* of the Gospel. It is with special attention to the Gospel as a narrative that I may describe the methodology for this present narrative-critical approach to Matthew's ED.

GENERAL FEATURES OF A NARRATIVE-CRITICAL APPROACH

The Gospel of Matthew (as well as the other canonical Gospels) is a "story," that is, a narrated series of events that is linked by temporal and causal connections.[8] When a story is told by a text, a story-world is created for the real reader to experience.[9] To read a story as a story is to attend to this story-world and not to treat it as a means to another end. That is to say, the story offered by the text is a mirror and not a window.[10] As Susan Lanser puts it, "The ur-convention of novelistic discourse is that the text will permit the creation of a coherent and human, if hypothetical world."[11] Take note of the term "coherent" in Lanser's words. In order for a story to be a story it must be coherent, that is, it "should make sense in narrative terms" and "fulfill in some logical (although perhaps unexpected) way the expectations it arouses; it should satisfactorily resolve the implications of the situation it displays."[12]

There can be no doubt that, for centuries, the Gospel of Matthew was read as a coherent story, narrating events that were related by temporal and causal sequence.[13] It was only in the wake of the advance of modern critical studies that the character of Matthew's Gospel as a narrative was swallowed up by other hermeneutical debates and concerns.[14] But Matthew's Gospel is a coherent story, or narrative, and it is in the light of this foundational conviction that this study of the place and function of the ED will proceed.[15]

Thus, by implication, this study will be text-based, formal, descriptive: an attempt to describe features of the text as it stands, and the interrelationships between parts of that text. Though I am personally committed to the personal, faithful, Christian appropriation of the Gospel of Matthew's message by real human readers, I shall not take up that issue. To use the categories of E. D. Hirsch, as echoed by Thomas Wolthuis, I shall focus on "meaning" instead of "significance."[16]

Interpreting Matt 24:1–26:2 in light of its setting in the narrative of Matthew's Gospel, I shall be engaging in "narrative criticism" as it has been clearly and succinctly described by Mark Allan Powell.[17] As is common among narrative-critical studies, this study draws upon the distinctions of Seymour Chatman[18] that describe "story" (the "what" of the narrative; characters, events, and settings) and "discourse" (the "how" of the narrative; with special attention to the "persons" of the implied author, narrator, and implied reader). Brief discussion of some of these features will now follow. I shall devote my chief attention in this methodological discussion, however, to the ways that the narrative, and especially the discourses of Jesus in the narrative, act to inform and shape the "implied reader" of the story of Matthew's Gospel.

Matthew's Gospel is, as we have seen, a story. That means it has a "plot" in the classic sense of a sequence[19] of events, linked temporally and causally, that have a beginning, middle, and end.[20] The plot of Matthew's Gospel, as is so often the case with stories, is advanced most significantly through the device of conflict, especially through the conflict between Jesus and the religious leaders.[21]

If attention to the "story" of the Gospel means attention to the plot, and especially to the conflict that helps to move the plot forward, attention to the "discourse" of the Gospel means attention to "how" the story is told. Important in this regard are the narrative-critical concepts of "implied author," "narrator," and "implied reader."

The "implied author" of the Gospel of Matthew is not the real author, Matthew. Rather, the implied author is a reconstruction, based on the text itself, that represents the perspective from which the story is told and ought to be interpreted.[22] Although it is valid to note that there is no effective difference between the "implied author" as perspective and the "narrator" of the Gospel as the actual voice that tells the story,[23] I shall preserve the terminological difference. The reason for this is that at least once in the ED ("Let the reader understand," 24:15), the "implied author" bypasses completely the characters in the narrative (Jesus and the disciples) and directly addresses the "implied reader." Referring to the "narrator" throughout the discussion of the paper will permit the distinctive use of "implied author" at a very few, but decidedly crucial, points.

Briefly described, the narrator of Matthew's Gospel is a third person, heterodiegetic (i.e., not a character within the story) narrator.[24] The narrator is "reliable" in that his evaluative point of view (i.e., the norms according to which all characters and events in the narrative are judged[25]) agrees with that of the implied author, whose point of view is also equated with that of God.[26] The importance of the narrator in Matthew's Gospel, or in any story with a narrator, may be illustrated with this observation. The narrator rules and governs all the characters, events, and settings in the story: all of them. In Matthew's story, even the "characters" of God and Jesus are, in a sense, "at the mercy" of the narrator. In the words of Norman Petersen, the narrator is "the external voice that tells the whole narrative and therefore governs the narration from beginning to end."[27]

If the narrator is the "voice" that tells the story, the implied reader is a construct completely within the text of Matthew's Gospel, "the audience presupposed by the narrative itself."[28] In a way that corresponds to the virtual identification of "implied author" and "narrator" in Matthew's Gospel, the "implied reader" and the "narratee" are virtually indistinguishable.[29]

The implied reader, then, is a construct in the text itself. The importance of the implied reader may be quickly understood by describing him or her as the target audience of the narrative. The implied reader observes the entire movement of the plot, sees all the interaction of the characters, accepts the evaluative point of view of the narrator, and makes deductions and value judgments based on all of these textual data. The implied reader is "the one in whom the intention of the text achieves its realization."[30] Indeed, the importance of identifying the ways that the implied reader is to respond to the narrative can be seen in Powell's summary description of the purpose of narrative-critical study of the Bible: "The goal of narrative criticism is to read the text as the implied reader."[31]

At this point, let me emphasize that the implied reader of the Matthew's Gospel is not to be identified with the figure of the disciples in the Gospel. The importance of this point will become evident in the treatment of the ED and, specifically, in understanding the disciples' question in 24:3. Several recent writers have made it clear that the implied reader is not the same as "the disciples."[32] Since the implied reader is not to be equated with the disciples, the implied reader will also be free "to 'draw near' or 'distance' himself or herself from any given character(s) as signaled by the implied author or narrator."[33] Also, because the implied reader is not to be equated with the disciples in the Gospel, the temporal perspective and location of the implied reader of Matthew can be clearly identified. Noting the indications of 27:8 and 28:15, Kingsbury concludes that "the phrase 'to this day' points to a place in time that lies beyond the resurrection, and the 'distance' between the Jews and the implied reader to which the latter comment [28:15] attests suggests that the implied reader is to be regarded as a disciple of Jesus."[34] The importance of thus locating the implied reader of Matthew's Gospel is underlined by the fact that, whereas only some portions of the other great discourses in Matthew seem to refer to a time beyond the story-time of the Gospel (e.g., 7:15–23; 10:17–23), in the case of Matthew 24–25, the entire discourse applies to the time beyond the temporal boundaries of the Gospel. The whole of the ED will "make sense" to the implied reader, since it speaks directly to the time period in which the reader is located. The mission to the nations has already begun (24:14; 28:19). The importance of knowing the "location" of the implied reader will be most significant in the interpretation of Matt 25:31–46.

THE NARRATOR'S INSTRUCTION OF THE IMPLIED READER

If, then, the goal is to read the text as the implied reader would, how is the implied reader addressed, informed, and influenced in his or her understanding of the story?[35] First of all, and most obviously, the narrator guides the implied reader of the Gospel. This occurs first of all through the use of "telling," that is, explicit commentary of various types.[36] Most importantly, the narrator quotes from the OT, thus offering the authoritative, divine[37] interpretation of events that take place in the story: "This whole thing happened so that what was spoken by the Lord through the prophet might be fulfilled, saying, 'Behold the virgin will be pregnant' " (1:22–23).[38] The narrator also gives explanations of the meaning of words in languages other than Greek (1:23; 27:3; 27:46), thus guiding the implied reader.[39] Three times, the narrator actually gives way to the implied author, who bypasses the characters in the story and makes direct address to the implied reader (24:15; 27:8; 28:15).

In addition to offering explicit commentary, the narrator of Matthew's Gospel uses "compositional techniques," such as concatenation or inclusion, to guide and inform the implied reader of the Gospel in "the way he/she should go."[40] Examination of the effects of primacy or recency and the use of redundancy further aid in determining the effect of the story on the implied reader.[41] Also, the very arrangement and juxtaposition of events in the narrative can at times reveal information to the implied reader of the Gospel.[42]

Apart from the guidance that the narrator of Matthew's Gospel offers to the implied reader, the character of Jesus is the most significant source of information and interpretation in the story. Because he is so closely aligned with the narrator,[43] Jesus is a completely reliable character, that is, the implied reader can trust as true the things that Jesus, by word or deed, indicates are true.[44]

The Implied Reader and Jesus' Great Discourses

In Matthew's Gospel with its great discourses, the words of Jesus are extremely significant in guiding the implied reader of the Gospel. These events[45] are important because they reveal Jesus' (and therefore the narrator's and God's) evaluative point of view with respect to characters and events both within the plotted story and beyond its temporal boundaries.[46] The reference to "future" events and their meaning is significant for several reasons. First, as noted above, the entire ED in Matthew projects into the time beyond the end of the plotted story, that is to say, after Jesus' resurrection from the dead and the commissioning of the eleven disciples. Second, this "future" time is also the time in which the implied reader of the Gospel is located. Third, unlike Jesus, the narrator does not address the nature and meaning of these future events. Only through the words of Jesus does the implied reader learn about them and their meaning.

If it is granted that the implied reader of Matthew's Gospel is informed through the words of Jesus, and especially through his extended discourses, precisely how does this informing take place? This is an area of criticism that has not been marked by sufficient precision. The following discussion will give some grounding and specification to the general truth that the reader of Matthew's Gospel is effectively addressed and informed by the great discourses of Jesus found in that Gospel.

To begin with, it must be asserted that, to whatever extent the implied reader of the Gospel is addressed through the discourse material, the characters within the story to whom the discourse material is ostensibly addressed are also the "target" of the speeches of Jesus. There can be no return to the "transparency" position described above in the critique of recent research on the ED.[47] Rather, at times Jesus' direct speech to a character in the story of Matthew's Gospel will directly address only that character, although the implied reader will overhear the conversation. At other times, the implied reader of the Gospel will also be addressed. How is it possible to tell when that "double" addressing of "character in the story" and "implied reader of the Gospel" is taking place?

It must also be stated that direct, second person speech in the Gospel does not automatically address the implied reader. Although this statement goes contrary to the assertion of some,[48] it is the only logical position to hold. The only means by which "Jesus" can address the other characters in the story of Matthew's Gospel—"the disciples," "the crowds," or "the leaders"—is second person address. To use Susan Lanser's terms, when Jesus gives his great discourses (and other speech material) in the Gospel, he is acting as a "private narrator" whose speech is directed to a character or group within the story.[49]

Second person address in the speeches of Jesus does not, in itself, force the conclusion that the implied reader of the Gospel is being "included" in the speech. However, to the extent that lengthy, uninterrupted direct discourse material occurs, the implied reader is addressed "alongside of" the characters internal to the story. This is true because, as Vorster comments, the extended action of "imitation" gives a much more powerful impression of "directness" than the action of "simple narration."[50] When direct speech is *extended* in a narrative, the narrative framework around the speech tends to fade and the impression of direct address to the implied reader is created. Dramatic deceleration of story-time, which is an inevitable byproduct of extended direct discourse, also functions to focus attention on the conversations or speeches given in detail and thus also works to include the implied reader of the Gospel.[51]

Another specific technique that includes the implied reader in the speech of Jesus is Matthew's use of the historic present tense. Anderson notes that, of the eighty uses of the historic present, most of them occur with third person verbs of "saying" and, in thirty-seven of those instances, λέγει introduces the speech of Jesus.[52] In this way, emphasis is placed on the speech of Jesus and the implied reader is brought more closely into contact with that speech.[53]

Again, the speeches of Jesus function to include the implied reader of the Gospel along with the character(s) to whom the speeches are addressed when the direct discourse refers to events that will occur only in the time that extends beyond the temporal boundaries of the Gospel's plotted story. Although such references have been called "anachronisms" and "alien to the immediate situation"[54] of the characters in the story to whom they are spoken, it must be maintained that these "future" events make sense when understood as speaking to the "future" of the characters in the story. Thus it is proper, as Kingsbury carefully states, to note that units such as 7:15–23 are meant "only *in part* for the first disciples, and that they therefore have in view still other persons," namely the implied reader of the Gospel.[55] Because these "looks" beyond the temporal boundaries of the Gospel's plotted story speak to the time in which the implied reader of the Gospel stands, that implied reader is addressed by means of such "future" speech.

"INCLUSIVE" TECHNIQUES IN THE DISCOURSES OF JESUS

Another category of speech that can be said to address both the character(s) and the implied reader of the Gospel is that of "timeless," "impersonal," or "inclusive" expressions.[56] Since scholars who mention this type of speech have not described it more precisely, I shall do so. The following examples of such speech are taken from the extended discourse material of Matthew's Gospel, including chapters 11 and 23 along with the five larger speeches.

1. Expressions with πᾶς ὁ + participle (5:22, 28, 32; 7:8, 21, 26; 11:28); πᾶς ὅστις (7:24; 10:32); πᾶς + noun (13:52)

2. Personal relative clauses, with or without the particle of unreality: ὃς ἐάν (5:19, 22, 22; 18:5); ὃς ἄν (10:42; 18:6); ὅς (10:38, 42); ὅστις ἄν (10:33); ὅστις (5:39, 41; 13:12, 12; 18:4; 23:12)

3. The use of substantized participles (5:21; 7:22; 10:22, 37, 37, 39, 39, 40, 40, 41, 41; 23:11; 24:13)

4. The use of πολλοί with the future indicative (7:22; 24:5, 10, 11, 12)

5. The use of rhetorical questions (6:27; 7:9; 18:12; 23:17; 24:45)

By means of "inclusive" devices such as these, the implied reader of the Gospel is addressed and affected by the discourses of Jesus in line with their intended effect as information, exhortation, or encouragement.

On a larger syntactical level, generalized proverbial speech in Jesus' extended discourses addresses both the implied reader and the character(s) in the story to whom it is spoken. Because "proverbs" are, by their nature, generally applicable, those that occur in the extended discourses also address, inform, or guide the implied reader of Matthew. Examples of proverbial speech would include the general beatitudes in Matthew's Gospel (5:3–10; 11:6; 24:46), numerous (but not all) second person imperatives (5:25–26, 29–30; 6:3, 19–20, 26–34; 7:2, 3–5, 6, 7, 12, 13–14; 10:16, 27, 28b, 29–31; 23:36), and other proverb-like teaching by Jesus (5:13, 14–16, 45; 6:22–23, 24; 10:24–25, 26; 18:18; 23:8b, 9b, 10, 24; 24:27–28). In addition, there are three identical occurrences of third person imperatival speech[57] that constitute an especially powerful means of addressing the implied reader: ὁ ἔχων ὦτα ἀκουέτω (11:15; 13:9, 43).[58]

On the largest level of pertinent material, story-like speech and story-parables[59] also function to inform and guide both the character(s) internal to the story as well as the implied reader of the Gospel. Story-like speech and story-parables in Jesus' lengthy discourses blur the boundary between levels of narration. In so doing they bring the implied reader close to the material being presented.

The final class of devices by which the implied reader of the Gospel is included in the discourses of Matthew's Gospel is, in a sense, in a class of its own. Along with two statements that occur in narrative portions of the Gospel (27:8; 28:15), Matt 24:15, "Let the reader understand," effectively bypasses the characters who are in the context, while it speaks directly to the implied reader of the Gospel. This is a statement that, in effect, does not apply at all to any character within Matthew's story, but only to the implied reader. Along with this unambiguous and noteworthy example of direct address to the implied reader, I will argue below that Jesus' words in Matt 24:25, "Behold, I have told you in advance," ἰδοὺ προείρηκα ὑμῖν, apply to the implied reader in a very dramatic way. Owing to the perfect tense and the lexical meaning of the verb, "to foretell, tell or proclaim beforehand,"[60] Jesus' words in 24:25 only "activate" in the future time in which the implied reader finds himself or herself. By means of these words, which Jesus formally addresses to the figure of the disciples, he "projects" the warning against confusion over the time of his Parousia into the time period beyond the end of the plotted story of the Gospel. The words of 24:25 are not a warning about future events that is given to the "present" time of "the disciples." Rather, these words are a warning that is activated, so to speak, only in the "future" time of the implied reader, who only then is able to know that he or she has been "told beforehand." Thus the words "See, I have told you beforehand" speak directly to the implied reader. Along with the address to the implied reader in 24:15, 24:25 acts powerfully to focus the attention of the implied reader on the statements being made in the immediate context. The reason why this much attention is directed to the implied reader will have to be determined from the context. But the fact of the address is noteworthy.

This completes the list of "inclusive" devices by which the extended discourses in Matthew's Gospel act to address and inform the implied reader. In the succeeding chapters, I shall offer my analysis of how the implied reader is informed regarding the eschatological kingdom connected to Jesus and the issue of conflict with Jesus. The analysis will follow the contours of the Gospel's plot, building up to the ED itself and including the part of the story that lies after the discourse.

I shall not be attempting a "naive," or first-time, reading of the Gospel story.[61] However, since the Gospel is a story, and that story does have a shape, a holistic appreciation of the ED in its literary setting logically will be preceded by a description of the prior material and an analysis of how the prior story-line contributes to the understanding of the material in the discourse itself. Because the narrative-critical implied reader is the "imaginary person for whom the intention of the text always reaches its fulfillment,"[62] at any given point in the narrative the implied reader is able, for the purpose of understanding that particular aspect of the narrative, to draw on all the information available in the Gospel.[63]

After the analysis of the Gospel's story, which reaches its story-time conclusion at 28:16–20, the analysis of the ED itself will take place. It is only in light of both the plot and the eschatological point of view of the narrator and Jesus, as shown in the whole of Matthew's story, that the ED can be properly understood.

The focus will be holistic. I shall attempt to allow Matt 24:4–25:46 to be interpreted in light of the overall eschatological point of view of Jesus and the narrator of the Gospel. Furthermore, I am seeking to understand the role that the ED plays within the entire narrative of the Gospel. The goal is to read the discourse of Matt 24:1–26:2 as the implied reader does.

NOTES

[1] Viktor K. Agbanou, *Le Discours Eschatologique de Matthieu 24–25: Tradition et Rédaction* (Paris: Libraire Lecoffre, 1983), 11. Agbanou contrasts the paucity of research on Matthew 24–25 with that concerning both Mark 13 and Luke 21. He suggests that the Matthean discourse has not been studied as extensively because it is assumed that its theology is fundamentally the same as that of Mark 13. The best single description of the study of Mark 13 remains the older work of George Beasley-Murray, *Jesus and the Future* (London: Macmillan, 1954). For an updated survey of work in Mark 13, see George Beasley-Murray, *Jesus and the Last Days: The Interpretation of the Olivet Discourse* (Peabody, Mass.: Hendrickson, 1993), 162–349. The most prominent redaction-critical study of Mark 13 is perhaps Rudolf Pesch, *Naherwartungen: Tradition und Redaktion in Mk.13* (Düsseldorf: Patmos-Verlag, 1968).

[2] Agbanou, *Discours;* Fred W. Burnett, *The Testament of Jesus-Sophia: A Redaction-Critical Study of the Eschatological Discourse in Matthew* (Washington, D.C.: University Press of America, 1979). One additional work, an unpublished dissertation, exists: S. Vandakumpadar, *The Parousia Discourse Mt.24–25: Tradition and Redaction* (Ph.D. diss., Pontifical Biblical Institute, 1976). I was not able to gain access to this work for the writing of this monograph.

[3] See, for instance, David C. Sim, *Apocalyptic Eschatology in the Gospel of Matthew* (Cambridge: Cambridge University Press, 1996); Kathleen Weber, *The Events of the End of the Age in Matthew* (Ph.D. diss., Catholic University of America, 1994).

[4] See, for instance, the consistent and direct application of this principle in Robert H. Gundry, *Matthew: A Commentary on His Literary and Theological Art* (Grand Rapids: Eerdmans, 1982). Gundry's overall "title" for the section 23:1–25:46 is "The Rejection of Falsely Professing Jewish Christian Leaders as Portrayed in the Rejection of Israel's Leaders" (p. ix). Early presentations of the concept of the "transparency" of the disciples in Matthew include Gerhard Barth, "Matthew's Understanding of the Law," in *Tradition and Interpretation in Matthew* (ed. Günther Bornkamm, Gerhard Barth, and Heinz Joachim Held; London: SCM Press, 1963), 58–164; Ulrich Luz, "The Disciples in the Gospel according to Matthew," in *The Interpretation of Matthew* (ed. Graham Stanton; Philadelphia: Fortress, 1983), 98–128.

[5] Rudolf Schnackenburg, *Matthäusevangelium 1,1–16,20* (Würzburg: Echter-Verlag, 1985), 232, presents five reasons why Matthew's eschatological near-expectation is

much less urgent than Mark's. The five reasons are all redactional changes that Matthew has made to Mark's text in incorporating it into his own discourse. Cf. Francis W. Beare, "The Synoptic Apocalypse: Matthean Version," in *Understanding the Sacred Text* (ed. John Reumann; Valley Forge, Pa.: Judson, 1972), 117; Ferdinand Hahn, "Die Eschatologische Rede Matthäus 24 und 25," in *Studien zum Matthäusevangelium: Festschrift für Wilhelm Pesch* (ed. Ludger Schenke; Stuttgart: Verlag Katholisches Bibelwerk, 1988), 110–11.

6 Thus Rudolf Pesch, "Eschatologie und Ethik: Auslegung von Mt 24,1–36," *BibLeb* 11 (1970): 235, writes, "Matthäus denkt hier gewiß an die eigene Generation." See also Georg Strecker, *Der Weg der Gerechtigkeit: Untersuchung zur Theologie des Matthäus* (Göttingen: Vandenhoeck & Ruprecht, 1962), 43.

7 David Hill, *The Gospel of Matthew* (London: Oliphants, 1972), 317. For similar comments, see Rudolf Schnackenburg, *Matthäusevangelium 16,21–28,20* (Würzburg: Echter-Verlag, 1987), 234; Wolfgang Trilling, *The Gospel according to St. Matthew*, vol. 2 (New York: Crossroad, 1981), 185; John P. Meier, *The Vision of Matthew: Christ, Church, and Morality in the First Gospel* (New York: Paulist, 1978), 167–68.

8 Shlomith Rimmon-Kenan, *Narrative Fiction: Contemporary Poetics* (London: Methuen, 1983), 3, prefers to make a distinction between "story" as "the narrated events, abstracted from their disposition in the text and reconstructed in their chronological order," and the narrated text itself. With regard to the Gospel of Matthew, the events, with few exceptions (cf. Matt 14:3–12) occur in the text in chronological order. Thus her distinction is not necessary.

Even with regard to Matt 14:3–12, the most commonly offered example of "narrative incoherence" in Matthew's Gospel, its narrative coherence can be argued. See O. Lamar Cope, "The Death of John the Baptist in the Gospel of Matthew; or, the Case of the Confusing Conjunction," *CBQ* 38 (1976): 515–19; R. V. G. Tasker, *The Gospel according to St. Matthew* (Grand Rapids: Eerdmans, 1961), 141; Thomas R. Wolthuis, "Experiencing the Kingdom: Reading the Gospel of Matthew" (Ph.D. diss., Duke University, 1987), 220.

9 Narrative-critical "story" readings have been criticized by some for being "ahistorical" readings. As will become evident in the discussion of the implied reader below, this charge is not completely accurate. It is true, however, that a narrative critic temporarily sets aside his or her view of the correspondence between the story-world and the real world of human experience in order to perceive and describe the world created by the narrative. If the narrative critic does not think that the story-world corresponds to the real world, then the significance of the narrative for the critic's own life may be minimal or nonexistent. If, on the other hand, the narrative critic (on other grounds) regards the story-world as a faithful representation of historical events (as do I), then the narrative-critical description of the "story-world" becomes normative for life and for faith.

10 Cf. Wolthuis, "Experiencing," 32–38.

11 Susan S. Lanser, *The Narrative Act: Point of View in Prose Fiction* (Princeton: Princeton University Press, 1981), 113; cf. R. M. Frye, "The Jesus of the Gospels: Approaches through Narrative Structures," in *From Faith to Faith: Essays in Honor of Donald G. Miller on His Seventieth Birthday* (ed. Dikran Hadidian; Pittsburgh: Pickwick, 1979), 77; Jack D. Kingsbury, *Matthew as Story*, 2d rev. and enl. ed. (Philadelphia: Fortress, 1988), 2.

12 Thomas M. Leitch, *What Stories Are: Narrative Theory and Interpretation* (University Park, Pa.: Pennsylvania State University Press, 1986), 117. Leitch calls these two statements "the rule of coherence" and "the rule of closure." Consider also the comments of Leopold Sabourin, " 'You Will Not Have Gone through All the Towns of

Israel, before the Son of Man Comes' (Mat 10:23b)," *BTB* 7 (1977): 10: "It is particularly necessary to admit from the beginning that Matthew, a careful redactor, does not harbor in his text flagrant incoherencies, even though his desire to incorporate in it various traditions has not always allowed him to pursue without some 'arrangement' the basic orientation of his work."

[13] Mark A. Powell, *What Is Narrative Criticism?* (Minneapolis: Fortress, 1990), 42, notes that historical critical study of the Gospels did not tend to seek closer relationships between the Gospel pericopes.

[14] The magisterial work of Hans Frei, *The Eclipse of Biblical Narrative: A Study in Eighteenth and Nineteenth Century Hermeneutics* (New Haven: Yale University Press, 1974), sets forth this development in biblical studies.

[15] Cf. Stephen D. Moore, "Are the Gospels Unified Narratives?" *SBLSP, 1987* (ed. Kent Richards; Atlanta: Scholars Press, 1987), 443–58, for a dissenting voice.

[16] Wolthuis, "Experiencing," 41, 63. In passing, I may note my own conviction that the story related in Matthew's Gospel is, in fact, historical.

[17] Powell, *Narrative.*

[18] Seymour Chatman, *Story and Discourse: Narrative Structure in Fiction and Film* (Ithaca: Cornell University Press, 1978).

[19] Leitch, *What Stories Are,* 4.

[20] Cf. Frank J. Matera, "The Plot of Matthew's Gospel," *CBQ* 49 (1987): 235–36, for a helpful discussion of the concept of plot.

[21] Kingsbury, *Matthew as Story,* 3; Wolthuis, "Experiencing," 167. Rejected is the attempt of Powell, *Narrative,* 46–49, to show that the real conflict that drives the plot of Matthew's Gospel is the conflict between God and Satan.

[22] Cf. Powell, *Narrative,* 5. On the issue of the relationship of the "implied author" and the real author, Wolthuis, "Experiencing," 81–82, says this:

> One looks for what is written, not what was intended to be written. Although a text, as well as a speech, may be freed from the intention of the discourser, it cannot be freed from what it actually did when spoken or written.... One begins with the text itself. What the writer did or said in a text, intended or unintended, is synonymous with what the text does or says when it is written.

These comments respond to charges of "subjectivity" that might be leveled against narrative criticism's focus on the text as story instead of the attempt to bring to light the real author of the text or his *Sitz im Leben.* Narrative criticism in itself is no more subjective than any other methodology in biblical studies.

[23] Lanser, *Narrative Act,* 49; cf. Janice Cappell Anderson, "Over and Over and Over Again: Studies in Matthean Repetition" (Ph.D. diss., University of Chicago Divinity School, 1985), 37.

[24] Powell, *Narrative,* 25; cf. Anderson, "Over and Over," 37.

[25] For a thorough theoretical discussion of "point of view," see Boris Uspensky, *A Poetics of Composition,* trans. Valentina Zavarin and Susan Wittig (Berkeley: University of California Press, 1973). For a succinct discussion of evaluative point of view as used in narrative criticism, see Powell, *Narrative,* 23–25.

[26] Jack D. Kingsbury, "The Figure of Jesus in Matthew's Story: A Rejoinder to David Hill," *JSNT* 25 (1985): 65.

[27] Norman R. Petersen, " 'Point of View' in Mark's Narrative," *Semeia* 12 (1978): 107. The failure to understand the importance of the narrator's point of view fuels other

misunderstandings of the Gospel. The objection of David Hill, "The Figure of Jesus in Matthew's Story: A Response to Professor Kingsbury's Literary-Critical Probe," *JSNT* 21 (1984): 39, to Kingsbury's insistence on "Son of God" as the dominant christological title in Matthew's Gospel, arises from the observation that Jesus nowhere calls himself the Son of God. But, as Kingsbury rightly notes, "Within the world of his story, *Matthew* establishes God's system of values as normative" (*Matthew as Story*, 11; emphasis added). Thus, since God's view of Jesus is that he is the Son of God (3:17; 17:5), the view of Kingsbury is validated.

28 Chatman, *Story and Discourse*, 149–50. The concept of the "implied reader" receives greatest attention in the work of Wolfgang Iser, *The Implied Reader: Patterns of Communication in Prose Fiction from Bunyan to Beckett* (Baltimore: Johns Hopkins University Press, 1974). However, see Powell, *Narrative*, 18–20, for the difference between Iser's "interaction" model and the narrative-critical "implied reader."

29 Jack D. Kingsbury, "Reflections on 'The Reader' of Matthew's Gospel," *NTS* 34 (1988): 455. Kingsbury calls the narratee a "stand-in" for the implied reader.

30 Kingsbury, "Reflections," 456.

31 Powell, *Narrative*, 20.

32 See especially Kingsbury, "Reflections," 456–59. Also see David B. Howell, *Matthew's Inclusive Story: A Study in the Narrative Rhetoric of the First Gospel* (JSNTSup 42; Sheffield: Sheffield Academic Press, 1990), 8, 53, who notes that the reader knows far more than any character in the story.

33 Kingsbury, "Reflections," 457–58.

34 Kingsbury, "Reflections," 456.

35 Powell, *Narrative*, 23, calls this "a central question" for narrative-critical study.

36 Howell, *Inclusive*, 213, notes that as the story progresses, the reader of the Gospel of Matthew comes to depend on the information and evaluative point of view that is afforded through the commentary of the narrator.

37 Kingsbury, "Rejoinder," 65; cf. Howell, *Inclusive*, 168, 186; Richard A. Edwards, "Reading Matthew: The Gospel as Narrative," *Listening* 24 (1989): 254. For a discussion of the implied reader's knowledge of OT Scripture, see Mark A. Powell, "Expected and Unexpected Readings of Matthew: What the Reader Knows," *AsTJ* 48 (1993): 41–43.

38 Fred W. Burnett, "Prolegomena to Reading Matthew's Eschatological Discourse: Redundancy and the Education of the Reader in Matthew," *Semeia* 31 (1985): 96, writes concerning 1:23: "The reader is thus informed *by the most authoritative voice in the text* who Jesus is, and the reader of a classical text like Matthew will align himself or herself with the position of the omniscient narrator."

39 Howell, *Inclusive*, 105.

40 For an extensive listing of these techniques, see David Bauer, *The Structure of Matthew's Gospel: A Study in Literary Design* (JSNTSup 31; Bible and Literature Series 15; Sheffield: Almond Press, 1998), 13–19.

41 On the primacy/recency effect, see Howell, *Inclusive*, 115. See Rimmon-Kenan, *Narrative Fiction*, 120.

42 Dorothy Sayers, *The Man Born to Be King: A Play-Cycle on the Life of Our Lord and Saviour Jesus Christ* (New York: Harper & Row, 1943), 4–5, writes:

Accordingly, it is the business of the dramatist not to subordinate the drama to the theology, but to approach the job of truth-telling from his own end,

and trust the theology to emerge undistorted from the dramatic presentation of the story. This it can scarcely help doing, if the playwright is faithful to his material, since the history and the theology of Christ are one
thing: His life is theology in action, and the drama of His life is dogma
shown as dramatic action.

43 See Kingsbury, *Matthew as Story*, 46; Petersen, "Point of View," 102; Burnett,
    "Prolegomena," 97.

44 On Jesus' reliability, see Kingsbury, "Rejoinder," 65; Anderson, "Over and Over," 62;
    Mark A. Powell, "The Religious Leaders in Matthew: A Literary-Critical Approach"
    (Ph.D. diss., Union Theological Seminary in Virginia, 1988), 28.

45 See Powell, *Narrative*, 35, for the "speeches" of Jesus as "events."

46 The concept of "evaluative point of view" may be defined as "a particular way of
    looking at things which also entails rendering some judgment on them in terms of
    the degree to which they are good or bad, right or wrong" (Kingsbury, *Matthew as
    Story*, 34).

    The evaluative point of view of the narrator of the Gospel, and of Jesus in the
    Gospel, is thoroughly "eschatological," especially with regard to the meaning of
    Jesus' present ministry within the boundaries of the story-world of the Gospel. In
    using the term "eschatological" I mean what George B. Caird, *The Language and
    Imagery of the Bible* (Philadelphia: Westminster, 1980), 244, calls "historical eschatol-
    ogy," that is, the discussion that "deals with the goal of history." In Matthew, such
    eschatology also may be described in the words of Donald Hagner, "Apocalyptic
    Motifs in the Gospel of Matthew: Continuity and Discontinuity," *HBT* 7 (1985): 56,
    as having "an apocalyptic orientation; it contains not simply an expectation of 'end
    things,' but also of a radical transformation of the present order by supernatural
    agency in the near future. It is furthermore deeply rooted in Old Testament prophe-
    cy." More definition of "eschatology" will be offered in the next chapter.

47 Cf. Günther Bornkamm, "End-Expectation and Church in Matthew," in *Tradition
    and Interpretation in Matthew* (ed. Günther Bornkamm, Gerhard Barth, and Heinz J.
    Held; London: SCM Press, 1963).

48 Kingsbury, *Matthew as Story*, 110; cf. Andrew T. Lincoln, "Matthew—A Story for
    Teachers?" in *The Bible in Three Dimensions: Essays in Celebration of Forty Years of
    Biblical Studies in the University of Sheffield* (ed. David J. A. Clines, Stephen E. Fowl,
    and Stanley E. Porter; Sheffield: Sheffield Academic Press, 1990), 116.

49 Lanser, *Narrative Act*, 138.

50 W. S. Vorster, "Literary Reflections on Mark 13:5–37: A Narrated Speech of Jesus,"
    Neot 21 (1987): 208; cf. Howell, *Inclusive*, 174; Rimmon-Kenan, *Narrative Fiction*,
    109–10.

51 Rimmon-Kenan, *Narrative Fiction*, 56; Powell, *Narrative*, 45.

52 Anderson, "Over and Over," 72–73.

53 Howell, *Inclusive*, 173.

54 Howell, *Inclusive*, 218; Kingsbury, *Matthew as Story*, 107.

55 Jack D. Kingsbury, "The Place, Structure, and Meaning of the Sermon on the
    Mount," *Int* 41 (1987): 135; emphasis added.

56 Kingsbury, *Matthew as Story*, 110; Howell, *Inclusive*, 221.

57 Noted and emphasized also by Howell, *Inclusive*, 221, and Anderson, "Over and
    Over," 102.

58 Note also the very similar statement of Jesus, not found in one of the extended discourses, at 19:12: "Let the one who is able to accept, accept."

59 I distinguish between "story-like speech" and "story-parables" on formal grounds. Story-parables (examples of which would include 7:24–27; the seven parables of chapter 13; 18:23–34; 25:1–13; and 25:14–30) are actually "narratives" told by Jesus. In relating them, Jesus uses third person, past tense verbs, at times aided by historic present tenses. By means of these story-parables, the character Jesus acts as an intradiegetic narrator (i.e., a narrator within the story-world of the Gospel). In this capacity as the one character in the Gospel story who himself regularly functions as a storyteller, Jesus possesses an ability to address and persuade the implied reader of the Gospel in a way that only the narrator of the Gospel shares. The implied reader of the Gospel is able, alongside of the character(s) in the story to whom the story-parable is addressed, to enter into the "world within the world" and view its reality and be affected by its values and message.

In formal distinction to story-parables, story-like speech occurs three times in the extended discourses of Jesus in Matthew's Gospel (11:16–17; 18:12–13; 24:45–51). Each of these sections is introduced with a rhetorical question, and the material employs present tenses, future tenses, and conditional sentences. Jesus does not tell a story so much as he describes a situation.

60 BAGD, 708.

61 For a balanced discussion of the concept of a "naive" reading of Matthew's Gospel, see Powell, "Expected," 33–35.

62 Powell, "Expected," 32.

63 Powell, *Narrative*, 20; Kingsbury, "Reflections," 456. A comparison might be drawn to the experience of the Christian liturgy. The liturgy has, in part, the shape of a narrative. It is sequential. During its course, things really take place. The fact that the individual worshiper might have "read" this "story" hundreds of times before does not detract from the "flow of the story." Rather, the repeated "reading" enables the worshiper to more fully understand and appreciate any given part of the liturgy in light of the whole.

2

"IN THOSE DAYS":
THE NARRATOR'S ESCHATOLOGICAL
POINT OF VIEW OF JESUS

The central task of narrative criticism is to enable the real-life reader to under-stand the story of Matthew's Gospel as the implied reader would understand it.[1] In order to discover how the implied reader approaches the ED of Matthew's Gospel, it is first necessary to sweep in broad strokes the entire story of the Gospel. Beginning with this chapter, the purpose of this survey of Matthew's Gospel will be to take note of the textual data throughout the Gospel that reveal one aspect of the evaluative point of view of the implied author, namely, the "eschatology" of Matthew's Gospel. A sweep of the entire Gospel (chapters 2–5 of this book) will set the stage for the examination of the ED, thus preventing an exegesis that does not take adequate account of the place of ED in the whole of the story of Matthew's Gospel.

In Matthew's Gospel, the implied author's eschatology finds expression pri-marily through the reliable narrator and Jesus, the reliable protagonist. It may bear repeating that "eschatology" here is used in a specific manner, that is, as referring to "apocalyptic eschatology." Apocalyptic eschatology is part of the evaluative point of view of Matthew's Gospel regarding history and time. It asks and seeks to answer questions such as these: "What is history's goal? Who is in control of history? How does the present time relate to the final goal of history?" These kinds of questions are central to the evaluative point of view of the implied author of Matthew's Gospel.[2]

When I speak of the "eschatology" or "eschatological point of view" in Matthew's Gospel, I include the following aspects of what in NT studies is currently called "apocalyptic eschatology." First, Matthew's Gospel shares an historical dualism with the historical context in which the Gospel was com-posed. This present sinful age will be overtaken and supplanted by the new age to come. Second, this new age will come with effects for the entire cosmos; the whole creation will be affected. Further, there is a strong emphasis in Matthew's Gospel upon the coming day of universal judgment. The point of view of Matthew's Gospel shares much in common with the general context in which it was written.[3]

In this chapter, I will survey the first large division of the Gospel of Matthew, Matt 1:1–4:16.[4] As will become clear, in this division it is the narrator's own commentary that shapes the implied reader's understanding of eschatology in the story of the Gospel. Through the narrator's own phraseology and through the use of authoritative scriptural quotations, the narrator leads the implied reader to see the eschatological implications of the origin of Jesus. With the one important exception of the testimony of John the Baptist, it is exclusively the narrator himself who reveals the eschatological point of view regarding the story he has to tell. Also, with the exception of the testimony of the Baptist, the focus in the first large division of the Gospel of Matthew is on the significance of the present time, beginning with the birth of Jesus. This focus of the narrator on the eschatological meaning of Jesus' present life and ministry will be maintained throughout the Gospel. By contrast, it is exclusively through the voice of the protagonist, Jesus, that the implied reader receives information and understanding about the future events that reach outside the time of the events in the Gospel itself, even to the consummation of the age (28:20). The speech of Jesus dealing with these "future" events has special significance for the implied reader, for, like the narrator, the implied reader stands in the time between the end of the Gospel and the consummation of the age.[5]

THE NARRATOR'S POINT OF VIEW OF THE PRESENT TIME OF THE STORY: JESUS IS "THE CHRIST"

To begin the examination of the narrator's eschatological point of view concerning Jesus' earthly life and ministry, one need go no farther than the first verse of the Gospel: "Book of the origin of Jesus Christ, son of David, son of Abraham" (1:1). The appellation "Christ" (χριστός) connected to the name of the protagonist, Jesus, draws attention to itself. Likewise, the repetition of "Christ" in the near context, with varying degrees of "connectedness" to the proper name "Jesus,"[6] serves to emphasize that this Jesus, the story's protagonist, is the Christ.[7] The term, however, is not explicitly explained by the narrator. It will, however, possess an inevitable eschatological meaning for the implied reader. That this is so can be demonstrated on two fronts that augment each other. First, exploration of the term's meaning in the "social and historical context of the real author of the narrative"[8] will show that eschatological components of meaning attend the use of the term. Second, the way that the narrator characterizes Jesus as "the Christ," already in the first chapter of the story, makes it clear that, in agreement with the social context, the term carries eschatological meaning.

That "Christ" entails eschatological connotations in the social and historical context of the real author of the narrative cannot be a matter of doubt. It is true that the use of the term "Messiah" (מָשִׁיחַ) in the OT to refer to a true "eschatological Savior-Messiah" is generally denied.[9] Also, in the Greek texts of the pseudepigraphical literature "Christ" (χριστός) is limited to *Pss. Sol.* 17:32; 18:1, 5, 7.[10] However, the use of the concept of a "Messiah figure" is more widespread, especially in the Pseudepigrapha,[11] than this paucity of usage might indicate.[12] Thus, the literature speaks of "the Elect One" (*1 En.* 39:6; 40:6; 45:3–5), "the Righteous/Wise One" (*1 En.* 91:10; 92:3–4), "the Chosen One" (*1 En.* 48:6), as well as "God's Son" (*4 Ezra* 7:28; 13:32, 37, 52; 14:9). Although caution in formulating a general "Jewish messianic expectation" is enjoined upon the interpreter by the data of the contemporary sources themselves,[13] the comment of Beasley-Murray is justified: "The evidence we have reviewed cannot be said to indicate that the messianic hope was of secondary importance in the apocalyptic movement."[14] It is clear that the use of the title "Christ" in the social and historical context of the real author of the First Gospel would entail eschatological meaning.

That the narrator of Matthew's Gospel agrees with the social and historical background in understanding the term "Christ" in eschatological terms can be quickly shown. It is evident in the narrator's genealogical recapitulation of Israelite history. The generations since Abraham, by way of King David and the Babylonian captivity and exile, find their fulfillment in this one who repeatedly is called "Christ." For the narrator, and thus also for the implied reader who accepts the narrator's point of view, "Christ" is the one who brings the expectation of the OT to realization. Although attestation of "Son of David" as an eschatological messianic title in the social and historical context in which the story of Matthew's Gospel arose is limited,[15] such an understanding of "Son of David" certainly would fit into the presentation of Jesus already given through the use of "Christ," and through the genealogy's recapitulation of Israelite history, which reached its former apex in the career of "David the king" (1:6). The entrance of this Jesus onto the stage of the history of the Jewish people brings this history to its fulfillment. Through the genealogy, as the narrator moves to the actual description of the "origin" (γένεσις, 1:1, 18) of Jesus, the narrator signals the implied reader to expect a radical shift in categories of salvation-history.

Already with Jesus' birth, the time of fulfillment has arrived. For Matthew's Gospel, the decisive juncture in the history of God's dealings with Israel and all the nations has arrived with the birth of Jesus, the Christ. Jesus' birth, life, and ministry have a significance that extends past the discourse-time of the story and beyond the temporal position of narrator and implied reader ("to this day," 27:8; 28:15), even to the consummation of the age (28:20).[16] Thus, from the very outset of the Gospel, through the use of the designation "Christ," the narrator informs the implied reader that the appearance of Jesus has eschatological implications. For the "Christ" is "God's Anointed, the King and Shepherd of Israel."[17]

As the narrator moves to describe the actual birth of Jesus, the implied reader again is informed, in eschatological terms, of the significance of that birth. The birth of Jesus is announced and interpreted by means of angelic mediation.[18] Jesus' birth serves the eschatological function of salvation of the people from their sins (1:21);[19] the child's very name, "Jesus," shows this to be so.[20] Jesus' birth fulfills the prophecy of Isaiah 7 regarding "Emmanuel" (Matt 1:23). Here the narrator, by thus evaluating the supernatural conception and the birth of Jesus, informs the implied reader that Jesus brings "an eschatological expectation to fulfilment."[21] In addition, one might also conjecture that the narrator has attempted to meld two diverse strands of eschatological expectation that may be assumed to be known to the implied reader. That is to say, some first-century "eschatological groups" awaited the arrival and action of a Messiah. On the other hand, others apparently expected God to act directly, without aid of a personal messianic instrument.[22] At 1:23, the narrator of Matthew's Gospel merges the two views. Yes, Jesus is "the Christ" (1:1, 16, 17, 18), awaited as part of the eschatological salvation envisioned by some. At the same time, it is precisely in the person of the Christ that one sees "God with us," the abiding presence of God himself with his people.

This early, controlling[23] description of Jesus' significance underscores the narrator's portrayal of Jesus as the eschatological Savior from sin (1:21) and, by implication, the view that the time of Jesus' present life and ministry are eschatological in nature. In Jesus, God "in the person of his Son resides even now with those who live in the sphere of his eschatological rule (1:23)."[24]

As the narrator continues to present the significance of Jesus, the Christ, a new element explicitly emerges in the account of the magi's arrival in Jerusalem. Even as the fulfillment theme, begun in chapter 1 (1:23), is continued and heightened throughout chapter 2 (2:6, 15, 18, 23), the theme of "royalty" comes to expression as Jesus is presented as the eschatological King through the authoritative interpretation of Scripture. For the magi arrive to ask about a "king": "Where is the one who has been born King of the Jews? For we saw his star in the East, and we have come to worship him" (2:2). However, the narrator describes the response to this troubling question in terms of "the Christ": "And [Herod] gathered all the chief priests and scribes of the people and inquired from them where the Christ was to be born" (2:4).

Who is this King, newly born? The implied reader knows that he is Jesus, the Christ. How shall the Christ be understood? He is the King of the Jews. The equating of "Christ" and "King of the Jews" performs two anticipatory functions in Matthew's story. First, it looks forward to the explicit announcement that "the kingdom/reign of heaven is at hand" (3:2; 4:17; 10:2) and links Jesus the King with the coming of the reign.[25] Second, the phrase "King of the Jews" will occur again, but not until 27:11, 29, 37. There in chapter 27, the narrator, in the account of Jesus' torment and death, portrays with strong irony[26] the tormentors and opponents of the suffering and crucified Jesus as unwittingly yet clearly declaring the truth of his identity.[27] Accordingly, already at 2:4, through the magi's naming of Jesus as "King of the Jews," the implied reader first learns of the goal or direction of the eschatological ministry of Jesus. He will accomplish the task of saving his people from their sins (1:21) through his death and resurrection as the true King of the Jews.

Before leaving the narration of chapter 2, let one other significant aspect of the implied reader's education emerge. The narrator describes the disturbed reaction of Herod and "all Jerusalem with him" (2:3) at the arrival of the magi. This reference to "Jerusalem" prepares the implied reader for the coming conflict of Jesus with both "Jerusalem" and the religious leaders whose seat of power is there located. The conflict with the religious leaders will not assume full-blown, murderous proportions until the second half (11:2–16:20) of the second major division of the Gospel (4:17–16:20). This conflict, however, is a major device through which the plot of the Gospel moves forward,[28] and, as I shall show, comes to assume a strong eschatological dimension. Neither will the related theme of conflict with Jerusalem become obvious until the third major section of the Gospel's story (16:21–28:20). But already at this point in the Gospel's story, the implied reader has received a hint of what lies ahead.[29]

As the implied reader moves farther into the first major division of the Gospel at 3:1, he or she is informed that, although the entire period of Jesus' life from infancy to adulthood is glossed over, there is still an unbreakable connection between what has begun in the origin of Jesus, the Christ, and what is now related through the ministry of John the Baptist. The narrator makes this connection through the use of "and in those days" (ἐν δὲ ταῖς ἡμέραις ἐκείναις) at 3:1. It is possible that there is an end-time nuance to the phrase, as argued by some.[30] From a literary standpoint, however, the most significant aspect of the phrase is the use of the demonstrative pronoun "those." The time in which the origin, birth, and infancy of Jesus, as well as the ministry of John, take place, are "those days." From the standpoint of the narrator and the implied reader, after the end of the discourse-time and before the Parousia, the gap of several decades in the life of Jesus has little significance. Joseph, Mary, and God's Son[31] flee to Egypt, return from Egypt, and settle in Nazareth, all in fulfillment of the prophecy of Scripture. Then, without any distinction or note of passage of time, the narrator continues the retrospective narration, "And, in those days [also] John the Baptist appeared, preaching in the desert." The sense imparted to the implied reader is that all of "those days" are of a piece.[32] They deal with the origin of the person of Jesus, the Christ. John, as forerunner, will also serve to introduce and reinforce Jesus to the implied reader.

With the appearance of John, the narrator introduces a major new emphasis on the eschatological character of the events that have begun with the origin of Jesus. For the message of John the Baptist in those days of Jesus' birth, flight to Egypt, and residence in Nazareth is this: "Repent, for the reign of heaven has come near" (μετανοεῖτε· ἤγγικεν γὰρ ἡ βασιλεία τῶν οὐρανῶν, 3:2). There are several important interpretive questions that cluster around the appearance of John the Baptist in Matthew's story. The most important questions are three in number. First, what is the narrator's evaluative point of view of John? Second, what is John's own eschatological point of view? This second question can be divided into two smaller, yet vital areas of widespread exegetical debate: (1) What is the meaning of "has come near" (ἤγγικεν, 3:2)? And (2) what, in light of the social and historical context in which the narrative that is Matthew's Gospel arose, would be in the mind of the implied reader when he or she encounters the expression "the reign of heaven"? The third question is, What is the relationship of John the Baptist to Jesus with regard to eschatological point of view?

THE NARRATOR'S POINT OF VIEW: JOHN THE BAPTIST

What is the narrator's evaluative point of view of John the Baptist? It is, on one very important level, thoroughly positive. This is clear from both the commentary of the narrator and that offered later by Jesus. The narrator specifically identifies John as the one who was spoken of by Isaiah the prophet (Isa 40:3). Especially in light of the way in which the narrator has similarly used Scripture to evaluate events in the conception, birth, and life of Jesus, such evaluation of John underscores his importance.[33] John is part of God's eschatological plan, the fulfillment of which began with the birth of Emmanuel.

The narrator of Matthew's Gospel further shows his positive evaluation of the Baptist by describing him in terms that, in light of Jesus' later identification of John with eschatological Elijah (11:14; 17:9–13), are strongly reminiscent of Elijah the Tishbite's appearance in 2 Kgs 1:8. There, in the LXX, Elijah is described to Ahab as "a hairy man, being girded about his loins with a leather belt" (ἀνὴρ δασὺς καὶ ζώνην δερματίνην περιεζωσμένος τὴν ὀσφὺν αὐτοῦ). Here in Matt 3:4, John "had his coat out of camel's hair, and a leather belt around his loins" (εἶχεν τὸ ἔνδυμα αὐτοῦ ἀπὸ τριχῶν καμήλου καὶ ζώνην δερματίνην περὶ τὴν ὀσφὺν αὐτοῦ). Already through the physical description of the Baptist, the narrator prepares the implied reader for understanding John in terms of eschatological Elijah, as the speech of Jesus will later make explicit (11:14; 17:9–13).[34]

Furthermore, the fact that Jesus, the eschatological Christ, willingly comes to John for baptism serves to underscore John's "reliability" for the implied reader. Jesus, the protagonist, shows that John has a part to play in what Jesus himself must do and experience. It is also in the context of Jesus' baptism by John that God directly enters the story of the Gospel as a character in order to speak. Here God offers the climactic evaluative point of view regarding Jesus: "This is my beloved Son, in whom I am well-pleased" (3:17).[35]

Yet another way the narrator indicates a positive evaluation of the Baptist is by placing John's words and ministry in parallel with those of Jesus, God's Son. This motif is well established by scholars and needs to be noted. John Meier presents the data well, noting parallels between John and Jesus in the use of "appear" (παραγίνεται, 3:1, 13); the "united front" of opposition of both Pharisees and

Sadducees (3:7; 16:1–12); the common epithet "brood of vipers" in the mouths of John and Jesus (3:7; 12:34; 23:33); the common image of judgment against "every unfruitful tree" (3:10; 7:19); and Jesus' words to the Baptist in 3:15: "It is fitting for *us* to fulfill all righteousness."[36]

It is undeniably true that the narrator's view of John the Baptist positions the implied reader to hear the preaching of John in a favorable manner. John is a reliable character who can be trusted to reveal the narrator's "true" evaluative point of view.[37] This leads us to the consideration of the second question regarding John's role in Matthew's Gospel, namely, what is the evaluative point of view that is revealed through the phraseology of the Baptist?

John the Baptist's Eschatological Point of View

To begin with, the obvious may be stated. John's point of view is thoroughly eschatological and, indeed, apocalyptic.[38] John stands in the prophetic tradition that emphasizes judgment. He links the coming of the reign of heaven inseparably with coming judgment.[39] John probably differs from any significant strand of apocalypticism in early Judaism in that he announces the impending wrath over Israel at large, and not over a portion of Israel or over the Gentiles as such.[40] But his speech does share the common imagery of Jewish apocalyptic eschatology. The image of "threshing as judgment" occurs in *4 Ezra* 4:30–32.[41] Box notes the image of the axe laid to the tree's root at Isa 10:34 and Jer 46:22.[42]

Moreover, the fire of judgment is eschatological because it is unquenchable.[43] This fire-judgment of God is the main theme in John's preaching of the reign of heaven.[44] As portrayed by Matthew, the reliable character of John reveals himself as "a preacher of repentance with a strong near-expectation of divine punishing judgment."[45] He expects the reign of heaven to manifest itself in divine, final judgment upon the present order.[46] The extent to which John sees an immediate manifestation of the reign of heaven is determined by the interpretation of his declaration that "the reign of heaven has come near" (ἤγγικεν ... ἡ βασιλεία τῶν οὐρανῶν, Matt 3:2). Two issues are involved in interpreting these words. First, what are the implications of the perfect indicative active, ἤγγικεν? Second, what is the general meaning of ἡ βασιλεία τῶν οὐρανῶν as a "symbol of cultural range" derived "from the social and historical context of the real author of the narrative"?[47]

The Meaning of ἤγγικεν (3:2)

The meaning of "has come near" has, of course, long ago been caught up in the debate over "consistent" versus "realized" eschatology.[48] Without making any attempt to canvass the debate of the meaning of ἤγγικεν ("has come near"), one can note the three major views: (1) that ἤγγικεν expresses virtual arrival of the reign of heaven;[49] (2) that ἤγγικεν expresses the reign of heaven that is near but not present;[50] and (3) that ἤγγικεν is ambiguous enough to encompass both senses.[51]

The chief objection to taking the Baptist's speech as reference to an already present reality arises from the natural lexical sense of ἐγγίζω, which is correctly given as "approach, come near,"[52] "to move nearer to a reference point ... to approach, to come near, to approximate,"[53] "to bring near, draw nigh, be at hand."[54] At the risk of oversimplification, however, usage in the LXX as well as in Matthew's Gospel reveals that this verb's lexical meaning can, by means of context, be "stretched" to the equivalent of "arrive" or "begin."

One can begin, for instance, with Ps 118:169 (MT 119:169): "Let my prayer come near before you, Lord; according to your word understand me" (ἐγγισάτω ἡ δέησίς μου ἐνώπιόν σου, κύριε· κατὰ τὸ λόγιόν σου συνέτισόν με). Now, no one would contend that the translator of the psalm intended to say, "Let my prayer approach, but not reach as far as you, Lord." The contextual sense of the aorist imperative active, "draw near," is "get close enough to do some good" or simply "reach, arrive." One might note also the usage in LXX Lam 4:18, where the triple parallelism supports the meaning for ἐγγίζω of "to arrive." The translator wrote: "We caught our little ones, that they might not go into our streets; our time has arrived [ἤγγικεν], our days have been fulfilled [ἐπληρώθησαν], our time is present [πάρεστιν]." The parallelism is likely to be "synonymous" owing to the threefold repetition of "our time ... our days ... our time" (ὁ καιρὸς ἡμῶν ... αἱ ἡμέραι ἡμῶν ... ὁ καιρὸς ἡμῶν). The sense of the perfect indicative active, the aorist indicative passive, and the present indicative active (ἤγγικεν, ἐπληρώθησαν, πάρεστιν) would then be roughly the same: "It has happened; time is up." These two examples from the LXX should, I think, refute any claim that ἐγγίζω (in the perfect indicative at Lam 4:18!) cannot "mean" something like "to arrive." Given the proper context, it can mean just that.

This only shows, of course, that John's phraseology at Matt 3:2 *could* mean "the reign of heaven has arrived." It will require data from Matthew's Gospel itself to show that it likely does have the sense of actually impinging on, and occurring in, the present time of the story in which John is speaking. Those data are found in Matthew's Gospel as follows, under three parts.

First, a major aspect of the eschatological point of view of the Gospel's narrator and of Jesus himself is that the present ministry of Jesus is eschatological in character. With the coming of Jesus into world as "God with us," as Christ promised of old, God's end-time reign has come into the present in a real, yet hidden, manner. I shall show this extensively as our overview of the Gospel's plot continues. For now, we might simply observe the material already reviewed in this chapter: Jesus is, from the time of his origin, the eschatological Christ (1:1, 16, 17, 18); he is the end-time King of the Jews, whose birth fulfills the prophecy of Micah (2:5–6). Note also material elsewhere in the Gospel, especially the point made by Jesus himself regarding the ministry of exorcisms: "But if I myself am casting out the demons by the Spirit of God, then the reign of God has come upon you" (Matt 12:28).

In showing that the present time of Jesus' ministry is eschatological in nature, I do not wish to deny the strong presence of a future, yet-to-be-fulfilled dimension to the concept of "the reign of heaven" in Matthew's Gospel.[55] Indeed, I will insist on it. But neither can it be denied that, because Jesus the Christ, is present, so also is the reign of heaven already present in some real, powerful sense.

Second, and more specifically, at 26:45–47 the narrator joins his own words with the words of Jesus in a way that shows that it is indeed probable that the perfect indicative ἤγγικεν in 3:2; 4:7; and 10:2 has the sense "has arrived."[56] In the Garden of Gethsemane, Jesus speaks to the disciples and says, "Behold, the hour has arrived [ἤγγικεν ἡ ὥρα], and the Son of Man is being betrayed into sinners' hands. Get up, let us go. Behold, the one who is betraying me has arrived [ἤγγικεν]" (26:45–46). The narrator continues with these words: "And while he was still speaking, behold, Judas, one of the Twelve, came" (26:47). In 26:47, there are not one, but two specific indicators that show that the time of Jesus' speaking in 26:45–46 is the same time as that of Judas' arrival in the garden. The "times" overlap. The first indicator is the particle, "yet, still" (ἔτι, 26:47). The second indicator is the genitive absolute, using the present participle active, "while he was speaking" (αὐτοῦ λαλοῦντος). Following the natural understanding of the relative time of participles,[57] the present participle expresses a time coincident with the main verb.[58] Hence the narrator, quite forcefully, has Jesus twice using the term ἤγγικεν while the thing of which he is speaking (his "hour," the coming of "the betrayer") has actually begun to take place. An additional support is found in the probable parallelism[59] between the use of ἤγγικεν at 26:45–46 and at 3:2; 4:17; and 10:2. Accordingly, the Baptist's words at 3:2, ἤγγικεν ... ἡ βασιλεία τῶν οὐρανῶν, must be understood to say that the reality for which "the reign of heaven" is the signifier has already, in some real sense, entered into the present time of the story of Matthew's Gospel.[60]

As noted above, not everything that pertains to the reign of heaven is a reality with the initial coming of the Christ. There is a major emphasis on a future consummation beyond the boundaries of the story. But in the view of the narrator and of the Baptist, it can nevertheless be said that "the reign of heaven has arrived."

The third support for translating the phrase as "the reign of heaven has arrived" is found in the following observation. Later in the story, Jesus teaches that John belongs in the "new time" that has begun with the coming of Jesus, the Christ.[61] A more thorough discussion of Matt 11:12–13 will take place in the next chapter. At this point, however, it may be noted that, whatever other difficulties arise in the understanding of these words of Jesus in Matthew's Gospel, this much is clear. "All the Prophets and the Law prophesied until John"[62] (11:13) supports the view that John is included in the era that stands in contrast to the time of the Prophets and the Law.[63]

Thus, John's eschatological point of view is this: he announces the present (though hidden) reality of the "reign of heaven." John himself is an eschatological figure and his call to repentance is a call to escape the eschatological judgment that is impinging on the present moment because in a real sense "the reign of heaven" has, through the Coming One (3:11), arrived.[64]

THE MEANING OF "THE REIGN OF HEAVEN" IN THE FIRST CENTURY

To continue the discussion of John's own eschatological point of view, it is necessary to assess the impact of the expression "the reign of heaven" (3:2). I shall proceed by surveying what is known about the meaning of this concept in the social and historical milieu in which the real author composed Matthew's Gospel.

In the twentieth century, the focus of study on "the reign of heaven (or God)"[65] has been oriented toward the historical Jesus and the meaning of the expression in his mouth.[66] The literature on this question is enormous.[67] This debate regarding the historical Jesus provides insight regarding the use and meaning of the expression "the reign of heaven" in the context in which Matthew's Gospel was written.[68]

The enduring contribution of Albert Schweitzer (and Johannes Weiss) has been the insight that in a first-century Palestinian Jewish historical context, "the reign of heaven" was an eschatological concept. Yet the fundamental error in these groundbreaking treatments was the assumption that there existed in Palestinian Judaism at the turn of the eras something approaching a monolithic "eschatological expectation." By making this assumption a circular argument resulted. These early proponents of "consistent" eschatology posited an identifiable, well-defined Jewish eschatological expectation that could be summed up by the phrase "the reign of heaven," and then they placed that expectation in the mouth of Jesus because Jesus' preaching was centered on "the reign of heaven." Schweitzer, for instance, insisted on the use of the Similitudes of Enoch (*1 Enoch* 37–71) for the understanding of "the Son of Man" in the Gospels. Schweitzer felt this reliance on *1 Enoch* was justified because he thought *1 Enoch* expressed "*the* Jewish eschatology."[69] With regard to the figure of "Messiah," Schweitzer stated that "eschatology" pictured "Messiah" as "a heavenly being in a world which was already being transformed into something supra-mundane."[70] Schweitzer assumed that there was a general notion of "Jewish eschatology" and then found it wherever the expression "the reign of heaven" occurred in authentic sayings of Jesus.

More recent study has shown the complexities of the task of understanding "the reign of heaven" in its first-century milieu. The task begins with study of the OT texts that speak either directly or indirectly of Yahweh as King.[71] Use of the intertestamental literature has become more sophisticated, as scholars have realized the diversity and (at times) dearth of material regarding the reign of God, or eschatological issues at all.[72] Some even doubt whether the intertestamental literature can yield a broad perspective on first-century beliefs at all.[73]

Nor is the situation different with regard to "rabbinic literature."[74] Enough warnings have been issued to produce an attitude of extreme caution when seeking data in the later rabbinic writings that might reflect first-century Palestinian beliefs and attitudes.[75] Confident statements to the effect that "the rabbis" taught such and such seem to be out of order. Further, while the study of the Targums as "a bridge between the Bible and later rabbinic literature"[76] has emerged as a field in its own right, Targumic studies contain their own inherent complexities.[77]

All of these caveats effectively prevent dogmatic statements about what "the reign of heaven" certainly and always meant in the milieu in which the real author of Matthew's Gospel wrote. Nevertheless, a brief summary of the results of current studies can reveal the probable outlines of understanding, which then can be assumed to have been present in the mind of the implied reader of Matt 3:2, "Repent, for the reign of heaven has arrived (or begun)."

The first issue to be considered is the element of temporal reference. What are the temporal implications of "the reign of heaven"? On this point, a shift has occurred in how scholars understand the temporal reference of "the reign of heaven." The older view posited a dichotomy between "present" and "future." "The reign of heaven" could refer to one or the other, but not to both.

On the one hand, it was widely recognized that the present kingship of Yahweh is assumed as an eternal fact in the pertinent literature.[78] It was central to the faith of the Israelites and of early Judaism to state this eternally present and valid fact: Yahweh is always and already King, and his reign is already a present reality.

On the other hand, other scholars have emphasized that other texts in the OT and Jewish literature expressed the sense of "the reign of God" arriving or taking place in a way that had not yet arrived. In the future, God the King would act decisively in history, even (in the expectation of some) to bring history to its end. This view of "the reign of God" as future expectation of God's royal action occurs, for example, in the OT,[79] in the pseudepigraphical literature,[80] the Qumran materials,[81] and the Targum to Isaiah.[82] In light of these two different ways that the pertinent literature understood "the reign of heaven," scholars formerly tended to view the temporal reference of "the reign of heaven" as either present or future, but not both.[83]

The tendency in more recent scholarship is not to posit a dichotomy between speaking of "God's reign" as an extant eternal reality or as an awaited inbreaking of "God's reign" in history. Rather, they are both valid components of the same meaning. It is perhaps true that one temporal connection will be more dominant than another, as in the case of the OT.[84] But once it is admitted that "the reign of heaven" has no predetermined, limited, specific, temporal reference, then the way is clear to acknowledge that "the reign of heaven" in the first century context of Matthew's Gospel could have both a present experiential and a future end-time dimension.[85]

The second issue in understanding "the reign of heaven" follows on the heels of the question of temporal reference. This is the view, not new, but newly emphasized, that "the reign of heaven" is a dynamic concept that involves the understanding of God's "sovereignty" (*Herrschaft*) more fundamentally than it does the notion of God's "kingdom" (*Reich*).[86] The latter understanding can be, of course, a natural consequence of the former.[87] When God acts in power, there results a sphere over which he rules that may be entered, as one enters a "kingdom," or *Reich*. But rather than thinking first in spatial or temporal terms, one should adopt an understanding of God's powerful manifestation of himself, along with the blessing or judgment that flows from that manifestation.[88] "The reign of heaven" is understood in terms of God's activity.

A third issue with regard to the contextual meaning implicit in the expression "the reign of heaven" relates to the concept of the Messiah. As we have seen, the understanding of the "Messiah" in first-century eschatological expectation is complex and varied. This is true also with regard to the relationship of a "Messiah" to the concept of the "reign of heaven."[89] It should not be assumed that expectation of the manifestation of the reign of heaven always included a role for a "Messiah" as part of that expectation. In Matthew's Gospel, however, the eschatological reign of heaven announced by John is associated with "the one coming after me" (ὁ ... ὀπίσω μου ἐρχόμενος, 3:11), who is mightier than John. In the context of Matthew's story, the reader knows that this can only be a reference to Jesus, the Christ.[90] Already the narrator has revealed that Jesus is the Christ (1:1, 16, 17, 18), the eschatological King of the Jews (2:2, 4), whose origin is from God and whose birth and life in "those days" (3:1) fulfills both the history of the Israelite nation as well as specific references from the Holy Scriptures.

In light of the current understanding of "the reign of heaven" in a less rigid framework,[91] one final assertion should be made. Even with all the possible understandings that this concept apparently had in the first century, a strong "eschatological" tone was still fundamental to the proclamation that "the reign of heaven" was something to be expected in the future, whether near or far off.[92] "The reign of heaven" could be understood as a manifestation of the present reality of God's kingship, or of a future manifestation of God's royal power to judge and to save. "The reign of heaven" tended to be seen as a "dynamic" concept, with a focus on God's action, rather than on a "realm" or "sphere" in which God's righteous rule prevailed. The role of a "Messiah" in thinking about "the reign of heaven" could be a major one, or "Messiah" could be completely absent.

John the Baptist's Point of View:
The Reign of Heaven Is a Present Eschatological Reality

In light of this discussion, it is clear that the "background" use of "the reign of heaven" in no way contradicts or renders unlikely to the implied reader John's message of eschatological judgment. Rather, John's message is a consistently final, eschatological one. It is oriented altogether around the eschatological judgment through "the Coming One."[93] And John announces that, in some real way, the reign of heaven has already arrived. Those who fail to repent in light of the reign of heaven that he announces will be like chaff in the fire. Like the OT prophets,[94] John announces the Day of the Lord. This is the eschatological point of view of the Baptist in the story of Matthew's Gospel as he proclaims, "The reign of heaven has arrived."

John the Baptist's Point of View as "Insufficient"

The third important interpretive question that clusters around the appearance of John the Baptist in Matthew's Gospel is the question of the relationship of John the Baptist to Jesus, the protagonist. As noted above, on one level the narrator has a thoroughly positive view of John. The way in which the Baptist is paralleled, with regard to actions and with regard to his utterance, with Jesus is not the least way in which the narrator shows John to be a "reliable" character.

Another facet of the narrator's presentation of John comes to light in chapter 3, and it is a crucially important one. For, as is more directly apparent in the second major section of Matthew's story (4:17–16:20), especially at 4:17–23 and 11:2–6, there is a certain tension between the Baptist's eschatological point of view and that of Jesus himself. But here in chapter 3, the implied reader already learns that there is an "insufficiency"[95] about the Baptist's conception of the reign of heaven that has begun already in the person of the Coming One. For John predicts the appearing of the Coming One, and the Coming One, in fact, abruptly appears on the scene of the story.[96] But when Jesus, the royal eschatological Christ and Coming One, appears, John immediately shows that he [partially] misunderstands the nature of the reign of heaven that Jesus has come to bring. The narrator offers an inside view of Jesus' mind by means of an articular infinitive of purpose[97]: "Then Jesus appeared to John from Galilee at the Jordan in order to be baptized by him" (τοῦ βαπτισθῆναι, 3:13). The narrator then reveals the Baptist's misunderstanding or insufficient point of view: "But John tried[98] to prevent him, saying, 'I need to be baptized by you, and you are coming to me?' " (3:14). John's understanding of Jesus' stated purpose is defective. If it were otherwise, John would have agreed with the purpose of Jesus' coming to him, as explicitly stated by the narrator.

Jesus, of course, prevails in the end, but not without the narrator's subtle evaluation of John's opposition as ultimately satanic in origin. For of John, it is said, "Then he permitted him" (τότε ἀφίησιν αὐτόν, 3:15d). And it does not seem accidental, after Jesus overcomes the temptation of Satan in chapter 4, that the narrator writes of Satan, "Then the devil left him" (τότε ἀφίησιν αὐτόν, 4:11a).[99]

Thus, although the theme of the Baptist's insufficient eschatological point of view will be more fully developed as the plot of Matthew's Gospel progresses, the implied reader knows that it is the eschatological point of view of Jesus that must take precedence over that of John the Baptist. Certainly, John is not rejected, for the narrator has announced him as the fulfillment of Scripture (3:3), and Jesus calls him to join in fulfilling all righteousness.[100] But Jesus is the Christ (1:1, 16, 17, 18), the messianic King of the Jews (2:2, 4), and it is his evaluative point of view that flawlessly mirrors that of God and of the narrator. For, as the story now reveals, God himself, in apocalyptic revelatory fashion,[101] declares Jesus to be God's Son. In addition, if it is true that this visual and auditory revelation is given to Jesus and not to the Baptist,[102] this underscores the priority of Jesus all the more.

Thus, the relationship of John to Jesus is marked by a certain tension. This tension between the points of view of the "reliable" Baptist and Jesus, the protagonist, centers on the eschatological character of Jesus' present ministry, which will begin with his own public proclamation at 4:17, "Repent, for the reign of heaven has arrived." There is a "gap" in the story here, for the implied reader surely will be puzzled at the revelation that John's point of view is insufficient. But this "gap" in the narrator's story does not call upon the implied reader to reject John's eschatological point of view entirely. For Jesus himself later echoes John's very phraseology (12:34; 23:33). Rather, the implied reader will understand that, although Jesus will certainly bring eschatological judgment on the last day, his present ministry brings with it eschatological salvation, for Jesus is the Christ who has come to save his people from their sins (1:21). What John has not adequately expressed is the salvific nature of the presence of "God with us" in the eschatological "now" time of the story.[103]

At this point, let us summarize this lengthy discussion of the importance of John the Baptist in communicating the eschatological point of view of Jesus' ministry in the present story-time of the Gospel. First, the narrator himself gives a positive view of John and therefore of his phraseology. John is the one spoken of by the prophet (3:3), the one whom the reader understands and will understand as eschatological Elijah (3:4; 11:14; 17:9–13). Second, John's own words reveal his reliable evaluation of the present time. The "now" time of the story is the time of the arrival (though not the consummation) of the eschatological reign of heaven, which will bring the fire of judgment against the chaff of those who do not bring forth the fruits of repentance (3:7–12). John knows that the agent of this judgment will be the Coming One, and the implied reader knows that this surely refers to Jesus. Third, at the same time that the implied reader accepts John's "reliable" point of view, he or she is led also to question it, in view of the tension between John's understanding of Jesus' purpose and Jesus' own understanding (3:13–15). As will become evident when Jesus' initial preaching of the reign of heaven (4:17) is followed by the gathering of disciples and the proclamation of eschatological blessings in the present time to the community of the disciples (5:3–10), the implied reader knows most emphatically that the eschatological Christ has come in the "now" time of the story primarily to offer salvation, to save his people from their sins (1:21).

Informed by the appearance and preaching of the Baptist, the implied reader continues, in this first major section of the story (1:1–4:16), to receive information from the narrator regarding the eschatological nature of the reign of heaven that Jesus is bringing. In the story of Jesus' temptation by Satan, there is a foreshadowing of later "satanic" struggles with Peter (16:23) and with the religious leaders (27:40). But the very conflict with Satan itself helps to underscore the eschatological nature of the present time of Jesus' life and ministry, for such conflict with and defeat of Satan was part of the eschatological expectation in first-century Judaism.[104]

In the final pericope (4:12–16) of the first major section of the Gospel, the narrator again shows Jesus' actions to be the fulfillment of Scripture. Following the handing over of John into prison, Jesus departs to Galilee and dwells in Capernaum, thus fulfilling the prophecy of Isa 8:23–9:1.

It is also well to review what the implied reader has learned regarding the correct eschatological point of view with which to read the story of Matthew's Gospel. On the basis of the narrator's commentary, the evaluation of Jesus, beginning with his very origin, is an eschatological one. The categories employed by the narrator in relating the person and origin of Jesus are understood by the implied reader as end-time, eschatological categories. Jesus is the Christ. He fulfills Scripture, indeed, brings the entire period of OT waiting to its completion. He is the prophesied King, the Christ foretold.

In addition to the narrator, John the Baptist, who also appeared "in those days" (3:1), instructs the implied reader. John's preaching underscores the eschatological nature of the times in which the Christ has appeared. Particularly John's words "Repent, for the reign of heaven has arrived" (3:2) are important for the implied reader. The implied reader will know that the eschatological reign of heaven is expected. And now it is announced by John, in terms of judgment by the coming Christ.

Moreover, the implied reader also comes to see that John's point of view, while correct, is nevertheless insufficient. For John does not give adequate expression to the salvific character of the origin, life, and ministry of Jesus. The implied reader observes John's own misunderstanding in action in the unit on the baptism of Jesus (3:13–15). The implied reader thus expects and awaits further clarification regarding the eschatological character of this present ministry of Jesus, the Christ. In other words, he waits for Jesus himself to begin to speak. It is with the discourses of Jesus that the implied reader will gain further understanding of the correct eschatological point of view regarding both the present time of Matthew's story and the times that follow the resurrection.

NOTES

[1] Powell, *Narrative*, 20.

[2] Note the happy turn of phrase of O. Lamar Cope, " 'To the Close of the Age': The Role of Apocalyptic Thought in the Gospel of Matthew," in *Apocalyptic and the New Testament* (ed. Joel Marcus and Marion L. Soards; JSNTSup 24; Sheffield: Sheffield Academic Press, 1989), 113, when he writes from a redaction-critical perspective: "The point of view of the Gospel of Matthew is powerfully shaped by a doctrine of the coming judgment."

[3] In using the phrase "apocalyptic eschatology," I am largely following standard scholarly usage. There is, however, one necessary point of clarification regarding this phrase. It is commonly held that apocalyptic eschatology necessarily includes a true "near-expectation" (*Näherwartung*). Yet, as I shall attempt to show, there is in Matthew a strong theme of "delay" or "time between Jesus' resurrection and Parousia." While rejecting a "near-expectation" in Matthew's Gospel, I do agree that two other "basic" themes of apocalyptic eschatology are certainly present in Matthew. That is, Matthew's point of view sees a historical dualism between "this age and the age to come"; cf. Paul J. Achtemeier, "An Apocalyptic Shift in Early Christian Tradition: Reflections on Some Canonical Evidence," *CBQ* 45 (1983): 241. Also present in Matthew's point of view is a strong emphasis on a future coming day of universal judgment; cf. Cope, "To the Close," 115–16.

[4] I postpone discussion of the structure of Matthew's Gospel until chapter 3, which will begin with Matt 4:17.

[5] Kingsbury, *Matthew as Story*, 38.

[6] Thus, twice the anarthrous noun "Christ" is joined directly to the name "Jesus," 1:1, 18, while at 1:16 the narrator writes, "Jesus, the one who is called Christ," thus indicating the nature of "Christ" as a title. Moreover, at 1:17, in summing up the genealogy, the narrator writes, "And from the deportation to Babylon until *the* Christ, fourteen generations." It becomes clear, then, from this varied usage, that Jesus, the protagonist, is being titled as "the Christ." For the "messianic content" of "Christ" at 1:1, see also W. C. Davies and Dale C. Allison, *A Critical and Exegetical Commentary on the Gospel according to Saint Matthew*, vol. 1 (Edinburgh: T. & T. Clark, 1988) 155.

[7] Jack D. Kingsbury, "The Figure of Jesus in Matthew's Story: A Literary-Critical Probe," *JSNT* 21 (1984): 8.

[8] Powell, *Narrative*, 29, in brief description of Wheelwright's "categories of symbols," speaks thus concerning "symbols of cultural range." For further discussion, see Powell, "Expected," 35–41.

[9] William S. Green, "Introduction: Messiah in Judaism: Rethinking the Question," in *Judaisms and Their Messiahs at the Turn of the Christian Era* (ed. J. Neusner, W. S. Green, and E. S. Frerichs; Cambridge: Cambridge University Press, 1987), 8, claims that "Messiah" in OT texts "denotes one invested, usually by God, with power and leadership, but never an eschatological figure." Cf. Friedrich Hesse, "מָשַׁח and מָשִׁיחַ in the Old Testament," *TDNT* 9:496–505.

10   Str-B 1:10–11 lists *Pss. Sol.* 17:32; 18:5; *1 En.* 48:10; 52:4; *4 Ezra* 7:28; 12:32; *2 Bar.* 29:3; 39:7; 40:1; 72:2 as the oldest overt uses of "Messiah" to mean "der erwartete Heilskönig."

11   The term "Pseudepigrapha" is used with reference to the documents contained in James H. Charlesworth, ed., *The Old Testament Pseudepigrapha* (2 vols.; Garden City, N.Y.: Doubleday, 1983). Citations from pseudepigraphical writings will all come from this work.

12   Some, of course, such as Joachim Becker, *Messianic Expectation in the Old Testament* (trans. David E. Green; Philadelphia: Fortress, 1980), would argue that there is scarcely a trace of "the Messiah" concept in all the OT. Becker writes: "A distinction, however inadequate, must be made between the hopes of eschatology and those of eschatological messianism. Essential to messianism is the figure of a savior, more specifically a royal figure of Davidic lineage. Until the second century B.C. one searches in vain for such a figure" (p. 79). Becker also argues that "a genuine messianic expectation" exists for the first time in the Judaism of the second and first centuries B.C. (p. 83). Others, such as George Beasley-Murray, *Jesus and the Kingdom of God* (Grand Rapids: Eerdmans, 1986), 146, take a more balanced view toward messianic expectation in the OT. Beasley-Murray writes that while the Messiah is present at times in OT texts, he is depicted not "as the agent through whom the kingdom comes, but rather as the agent of the kingdom after God has established it." See also Joseph Klausner, *The Messianic Ideal in Israel* (translated from the third edition by W. F. Stinespring; New York: Macmillan, 1955), 236–43; G. F. Moore, *The Age of the Tannaim* (vol. 2 of *Judaism in the First Centuries of the Christian Era*; New York: Schocken, 1958), 323–76; Hesse, *TDNT* 9:505–9.

13   James Charlesworth, "The Concept of the Messiah in the Pseudepigrapha" in vol. 19.1 of *Aufstieg und Niedergang der Römischen Welt*, part 2: *Principat* (ed. Wolfgang Haase; Berlin: Walter de Gruyter, 1979), 217.

14   Beasley-Murray, *Jesus and the Kingdom of God*, 61.

15   Leopold Sabourin, *L'Évangile selon Saint Matthieu et ses Principaux Parallèlles* (Rome: Biblical Institute, 1978), 290, cites *Pss. Sol.* 17:21–23. Str-B 1:525 says that this is the only reference to the Messiah as the Son of David before the turn of the eras.

16   As is evident, I hold to a two-stage division of salvation-history in Matthew's Gospel, nicely expressed by Perry Kea, "The Sermon on the Mount: Ethics and Eschatological Time," *SBLSP, 1986* (Atlanta: Scholars Press, 1986), 91: "The *arrival* of Jesus into Matthew's narrative world marks the beginning of a new epoch in world time" (emphasis added). For the understanding of a three-stage salvation-historical schema, see John P. Meier, *Law and History in Matthew's Gospel: A Redactional Study of Mt. 5:17–48* (Rome: Biblical Institute, 1976), 25–40; John P. Meier, "John the Baptist in Matthew's Gospel," *JBL* 99 (1980): 403–5. Chris C. Caragounis, "Kingdom of God/Kingdom of Heaven," in *Dictionary of Jesus and the Gospels* (ed. Joel B. Green, Scot McKnight, and I. Howard Marshall; Downers Grove, Ill.: InterVarsity, 1992), 417–30, sees Jesus' ministry as only "the preliminaries, not the kingdom of God itself."

17   Kingsbury, *Matthew as Story*, 46–47.

18   Hagner, "Apocalyptic," 60, notes dreams, astronomical happenings, and fulfillments as "apocalyptic-like" features.

19   Note well that, according to U. Luz, *Matthew 1–7: A Commentary* (trans. Wilhelm Linss; Minneapolis: Augsburg, 1989), 121, Jewish texts never speak of the Messiah as forgiving sins. Here, perhaps, already at 1:21 the implied reader is informed that this eschatological Christ is different from expectations current in the contemporary milieu.

20 Noted again recently by Sheila A. Klassen-Wiebe, "Matthew 1:18–25," *Int* 46 (1992): 394: "The name "Jesus" ... means 'Yahweh saves.' "

21 Davies and Allison, *Matthew*, 1:217–18, who go on to note the expectation that God would be especially "with" his people "in messianic times (Isa 43.5; Ezek 34.30; 37.27; Zech 8.23; 11QTemple 29.7–10; Jub. 1.17, 26; Rev 21.3)."

22 Cf. Charlesworth, "Concept," 217.

23 Burnett, "Prolegomena," 96, argues that because this is how Jesus is first presented to the reader by the omniscient narrator, this view of Jesus will inform and color the entire narrative. For a recent attempt to read the entire Gospel in this way, see David D. Kupp, *Matthew's Emmanuel: Divine Presence and God's People in the First Gospel* (Cambridge: Cambridge University Press, 1996).

24 Kingsbury, *Structure, Christology, Kingdom*, 138.

25 Meier, "John the Baptist," 404: "The birth of the King necessarily involves a fuller coming of the kingdom, from the birth of Jesus onward." Cf. Francis W. Beare, *The Gospel according to Matthew: Translation, Introduction and Commentary* (San Francisco: Harper & Row, 1981), 35.

   Sverre Aalen, " 'Reign' and 'House' in the Kingdom of God in the Gospels," *NTS* 8 (1961–1962): 215–40. Aalen, 217, discerns a "tension" between Jesus as King in the Gospels and the phrase "kingdom of God/heaven." He comments on the basis of Matt 12:25–28 that "if there is a king in the kingdom of God, it must be Jesus. But if he is king, then the translation 'reign of God' is no longer adequate" (p. 229). In Matthew's view, Jesus himself is both the King (2:2; 25:34, 40) and the abiding presence of God himself with his people (1:23).

26 Note Dorothy Jean Weaver's fine study of irony, "Power and Powerlessness: Matthew's Use of Irony in the Portrayal of Political Leaders," *SBLSP, 1992* (Atlanta: Scholars Press, 1992): 454–66.

27 Cf. Jack D. Kingsbury, "The Developing Conflict between Jesus and the Jewish Leaders in Matthew's Gospel: A Literary-Critical Study," *CBQ* 49 (1987): 65.

28 Kingsbury, "Developing Conflict," 57.

29 Wolthuis, "Experiencing," 240; Jack D. Kingsbury, "The Plot of Matthew's Story," *Int* 46 (1992): 348.

30 Cf. Kingsbury, *Structure, Christology, Kingdom*, 28–31; Joachim Gnilka, *Das Matthäusevangelium*, part 1 (Frieburg: Herder, 1986), 65. Davies and Allison, *Matthew*, 1:288, say that an eschatological nuance is "quite possible."

31 Kingsbury, *Structure, Christology, Kingdom*, 45–47, has shown that the repeated use of the phrase "the child and his mother" (2:11, 13, 14, 20, 21) emphasizes that the child Jesus is in no true sense the son of Joseph. He is the Son of God; cf. Gundry, *Matthew*, 31.

32 Cf. Luz, *Matthew 1–7*, 166.

33 Note the use of "the one spoken of" (ὁ ῥηθείς) and "through Isaiah the prophet" (διὰ Ἠσαΐου τοῦ προφήτου) with reference to John (3:3) and "that which was spoken of" (τὸ ῥηθέν) and "through the prophet" (διὰ τοῦ προφήτου) with reference to Jesus (1:22; 2:5, 15, 18, 23).

34 Many agree in seeing John's appearance described in terms of 2 Kgs 1:8; cf. George E. Ladd, *The Presence of the Future: The Eschatology of Biblical Realism* (Grand Rapids: Eerdmans, 1974), 106; Henry Alford, *Matthew-Mark*, vol. 1, part 1 of *Alford's Greek Testament: An Exegetical and Critical Commentary* (Grand Rapids: Guardian, 1976), 20; G. H. Box, *St. Matthew* (New York: Henry Frowde, 1922), 91.

[35] Kingsbury, "Probe," 21.

[36] Meier, "John the Baptist," 387–91; cf. Walter Wink, *John the Baptist in the Gospel Tradition* (Cambridge: Cambridge University Press, 1968), 33.

[37] Powell, "Religious Leaders," 49; Kingsbury, "Probe," 6.

[38] That is, John's evidences a belief in (1) historical dualism, (2) a universal cosmic expectation of judgment, and (3) an expectation of the imminent judgment and the end of the world. As the discussion shall demonstrate, in this expectation of imminent final judgment the Baptist's eschatological point of view is shown to be "insufficient."

[39] Donald A. Carson, "Matthew" in volume 8 of *The Expositor's Bible Commentary* (ed. Frank E. Gaebelein; Grand Rapids: Zondervan, 1984), 103–4.

[40] Cf. R. T. France, *Jesus and the Old Testament: His Application of Old Testament Passages to Himself and His Mission* (London: Tyndale, 1971), 228; Str-B 1:180; Frederick D. Bruner, *The Christbook: A Historical/Theological Commentary (Matthew 1–12)* (Waco: Word, 1987), 76.

[41] "For a grain of evil seed was sown in Adam's heart from the beginning, and how much ungodliness it has produced until now, and will produce until the time of threshing comes.... O sovereign Lord, but all of us also are full of ungodliness. And it is perhaps on account of us that the time of threshing is delayed for the righteous."

[42] Box, *Matthew*, 59.

[43] Ladd, *Presence*, 107.

[44] T. W. Manson, *The Sayings of Jesus* (Grand Rapids: Eerdmans, 1979), 40.

[45] Schnackenburg, *Matthäusevangelium 1,1–16,20*, 30: "ein Bußprediger mit starker Naherwartung des göttlichen Strafgerichts."

[46] Ladd, *Presence*, 108.

[47] Powell, *Narrative*, 29.

[48] For an excellent series of essays dealing with the entire twentieth-century debate regarding eschatology and the kingdom of God, see Wendell Willis, ed., *The Kingdom of God in 20th-Century Interpretation* (Peabody, Mass.: Hendrickson, 1987).

[49] C. H. Dodd, *The Parables of the Kingdom* (rev. ed.; New York: Charles Scribner's Sons, 1961), 29; Robert Berkey, "ΕΓΓΙΖΕΙΝ, ΦΘΑΝΕΙΝ, and Realized Eschatology," *JBL* 82 (1963): 177–87.

[50] J. Y. Campbell, "The Kingdom of God Has Come," *ExpTim* 48 (1936–1937): 91–94. Barclay M. Newman and Philip C. Stine, *A Translator's Handbook on the Gospel of Matthew* (New York: United Bible Societies, 1988), 61; Strecker, *Der Weg*, 165.

[51] Bruner, *Matthew 1–12*, 123.

[52] BAGD, 213.

[53] Johannes P. Louw and Eugene A. Nida, eds., *Greek-English Lexicon of the New Testament Based on Semantic Domains* (2d ed.; 2 vols.; New York: United Bible Societies, 1989), 1:192, 632.

[54] *A Lexicon Abridged from Liddell and Scott's Greek-English Lexicon* (Oxford: Clarendon Press, 1972), 189.

[55] Cf. Strecker, *Der Weg*, 169–70.

[56] The other uses of "draw near" in Matthew's Gospel are 21:1, 34. In each of these places the aorist indicative active does mean "draw near but not yet arrive." For Matthew's use of ἐγγύς, "near," see 24:32, 33; 26:18.

[57] Cf. BDF, § 339; Nigel Turner, *Syntax*, vol. 3 of *A Grammar of New Testament Greek* by James Hope Moulton, Wilbert Francis Howard, and Nigel Turner (Edinburgh: T & T Clark, 1963), 79; James W. Voelz, *Fundamental Greek Grammar* (St. Louis: Concordia, 1986), 131, 140; C. F. D. Moule, *An Idiom Book of New Testament Greek* (2d ed.; Cambridge: Cambridge University Press, 1959), 99.

[58] Donald Verseput, *The Rejection of the Humble Messianic King: A Study of the Composition of Matthew 11–12* (Frankfurt am Main: Peter Lang, 1986), 282.

[59] Eduard Schweizer, *The Good News according to Matthew* (trans. David E. Green; Atlanta: John Knox, 1975), 494, although translating 3:2, 4:17, 10:2 with "is near," admits the parallelism between these verses and 26:45–46.

[60] Cf. Herbert Preisker, "ἐγγύς, ἐγγίζω, προσεγγίζω," *TDNT* 2:331; Bruner, *Matthew 1-12*, 123; Berkey, "Realized Eschatology," 183.

[61] For Sabourin, *L'Évangile*, 32, John's position in the "new economy" is adequately proven by virtue of the fact that John's speech matches that of Jesus (3:2; 4:17). In affirming that John's ministry belongs in the "new time" of fulfillment, I do not intend to deny that John also has links to the old era of prophecy as well. For a fuller discussion of this twofold character of John and his ministry, see the discussion of 11:7–15 in chapter 3.

[62] Gundry, *Matthew*, 211.

[63] Davies and Allison, *Matthew*, 2:257; Meier, "John the Baptist," 396, and Schnackenburg, *Matthäusevangelium 1,1–16,20*, 101–2; Schweizer, *Good News*, 261.

For those who place John in the period of the "prophets and the law," see Floyd V. Filson, *A Commentary on the Gospel according to St. Matthew* (London: Adam & Charles Black, 1960), 138; Box, *Matthew*, 193; Beare, *Matthew*, 260; Carson, "Matthew," 268; Gottlob Schrenk, "βιάζομαι, βιαστής," *TDNT* 1:610.

[64] Kingsbury, *Matthew as Story*, 50.

[65] The majority view, as noted by Ron Farmer, "The Kingdom of God in the Gospel of Matthew," in *The Kingdom of God in 20th-Century Interpretation* (ed. Wendell Willis; Peabody, Mass.: Hendrickson, 1987), 120, understands the two phrases to be "synonymous." Margaret Pamment, "The Kingdom of Heaven according to the First Gospel," *NTS* 27 (1980–1981): 211–32, has argued unsuccessfully that in Matthew's Gospel the "kingdom of heaven" is purely future and otherworldly, whereas "kingdom of God" refers to God's sovereignty.

[66] Cf. Johannes Weiss, *Jesus' Proclamation of the Kingdom of God* (ed. and trans. R. H. Hiers and D. L. Holland; repr., Chico, Calif.: Scholars Press, 1985), and Albert Schweitzer, *The Quest of the Historical Jesus: A Critical Study of Its Progress from Reimarus to Wrede* (repr., New York: Macmillan, 1968).

[67] The reader may find an excellent volume of survey essays in Willis, *The Kingdom of God*.

[68] Scholarship has proceeded by studying the concept of "Yahweh's kingship," rather than only the phrase, "the kingdom of God"; cf. Michael Lattke, "On the Jewish Background of the Synoptic Concept 'The Kingdom of God,' " in *The Kingdom of God in the Teaching of Jesus* (ed. Bruce Chilton; Philadelphia: Fortress, 1984), 73; John Bright, *The Kingdom of God: The Biblical Concept and Its Meaning for the Church* (New York: Abingdon, 1953), 7; Dale Patrick, "The Kingdom of God in the Old Testament," in *The Kingdom of God in 20th-Century Interpretation* (ed. Wendell Willis; Peabody, Mass.: Hendrickson, 1987), 67.

[69] Schweitzer, *Quest*, 267 (emphasis added).

[70] Schweitzer, *Quest*, 348.

71 Cf. Patrick, "Kingdom of God"; Hermann Kleinknecht et al., "βασιλεύς κτλ.," *TDNT* 1:564–93; Beasley-Murray, *Jesus and the Kingdom of God*, 18–20.

72 Bruce Chilton, "Introduction," in *The Kingdom of God in the Teaching of Jesus* (ed. Bruce Chilton; Philadelphia: Fortress, 1984), 9; cf. Lattke, "Jewish Background," 78; John Collins, "The Kingdom of God in the Apocrypha and Pseudepigrapha," in *The Kingdom of God in 20th-Century Interpretation* (ed. Wendell Willis; Peabody, Mass.: Hendrickson, 1987), 88.

73 Bruce Chilton, *A Galilean Rabbi and His Bible: Jesus' Use of the Interpreted Scripture of His Time* (Wilmington: Michael Glazier, 1984), 35. For the contrary understanding, see Charlesworth, "Concept," 194.

74 For survey and bibliography on the recent study of "rabbinic literature," see Anthony Saldarini, "Reconstructions of Rabbinic Judaism," in *Early Judaism and Its Modern Interpreters* (ed. Robert A. Kraft and George W. E. Nickelsburg; Philadelphia: Fortress, 1986), 437–77. On the relationship of this literature to the NT, see the general work of Martin McNamara, *Palestinian Judaism and the New Testament* (Wilmington: Michael Glazier, 1983).

75 The caution was sounded long ago by Samuel Sandmel, "Parallelomania," *JBL* 81 (1962): 1–13. See especially the work of Jacob Neusner, including the following: *Judaism without Christianity: An Introduction to the System of the Mishnah* (Hoboken, N.J.: Ktav, 1991); "The Formation of Rabbinic Judaism: Yavneh (Jamnia) from A.D. 70 to 100," in vol. 19.2 of *Aufstieg und Niedergang der Römischen Welt*, part 2: *Principat* (ed. Wolfgang Haase; Berlin: Walter de Gruyter, 1979), 3–42; "The Modern Study of the Mishnah," in *Mishnah, Midrash, Siddur*, vol. 1 of *The Study of Ancient Judaism* (ed. Jacob Neusner; Hoboken, N.J.: Ktav, 1981), 3–27; "The Use of the Later Rabbinic Evidence for the Study of First-Century Pharisaism," in *Approaches to Ancient Judaism: Theory and Practice* (ed. William Scott Green; Missoula: Scholars Press, 1978), 215–28; "The Use of Rabbinic Sources for the Study of Ancient Judaism," in *Text as Context in Early Rabbinic Literature*, vol. 3 of *Approaches to Ancient Judaism* (ed. William Scott Green; Chico, Calif.: Scholars Press, 1981), 1–18. See also Chilton, *Galilean Rabbi*, 30; McNamara, *Palestinian Judaism*, 40–41; Charlesworth, "Concept," 194.

76 Renee Bloch, "Methodological Note for the Study of Rabbinic Literature," in *Approaches to Ancient Judaism: Theory and Practice* (ed. William Scott Green; Missoula: Scholars Press, 1978), 60–61. Cf. Chilton, *Galilean Rabbi*, 38; Neusner, "Modern Study," 9.

77 Bruce Chilton, *The Glory of Israel: The Theology and Provenience of the Isaiah Targum*, JSOTSup 23 (Sheffield: JSOT Press, 1982), 48.

78 Gerhard von Rad, "βασιλεύς," *TDNT* 1:568, notes the "timeless" aspect of Yahweh's kingship in the OT at Exod 15:18; 1 Sam 12:12; Pss 145:11; 146:10. In the "intertestamental" literature, note *1 En.* 9:4; 12:3; 25:5, 7; 27:3; 84:2, 5; 91:13; *2 En.* 39:8; *Sib. Or.* 1:7; 3:617, 717; 5:499; *2 Bar.* 21:6. For Qumran, see B. T. Viviano, "The Kingdom of God in the Qumran Literature," in *The Kingdom of God in 20th-Century Interpretation* (ed. Wendell Willis; Peabody, Mass.: Hendrickson, 1987), 97–108. With regard to the rabbinic literature, see Chilton, "Introduction," 18; cf. Joachim Jeremias, *New Testament Theology: The Proclamation of Jesus* (New York: Charles Scribner's Sons, 1971), 32; Karl G. Kuhn, "βασιλεύς," *TNDT* 1:572–73. On the Targums, see Bruce Chilton, *God in Strength: Jesus' Announcement of the Kingdom*, Studien zum Neuen Testament und seiner Umwelt, series B, vol. 1. (Freistadt: Plöchl, 1979), 87; *Galilean Rabbi*, 60.

79 Von Rad, *TDNT* 1:569, notes Isa 24:23; 33:22; Zeph 3:15; Obad 21; Zech 14:16. Lattke, "Jewish Background," 79, refers to Dan 2:44; 3:33; 4:31.

80 Note *1 En.* 25:3; *T. Naph.* 8:2–3; *Sib. Or.* 3:46; 3:767; and the oft-cited passage *T. Mos.* 10:1–10.

81 Viviano, "Kingdom of God," 105–6.

82 Chilton, *Galilean Rabbi*, 60, says: "The kingdom is something that is to be 'revealed,' which implies ... that the kingdom is a reality which awaits disclosure."

83 The favorite tactic in this debate was, of course, to discount all the opposing party's evidence as "inauthentic." This is noted by Schweitzer, *Quest*, 333, citing W. Wrede, regarding the developments in "life of Jesus" research in the nineteenth and early twentieth century.

84 See Patrick, "Kingdom of God," 76–77.

85 It is interesting at this point to note the alignment of the work of Bruce Chilton and Norman Perrin, who arrive at a similar place via different paths; cf. Chilton, *God in Strength*, 89, 284; Norman Perrin, "Jesus and the Language of the Kingdom," in *The Kingdom of God in the Teaching of Jesus* (ed. Bruce Chilton; Philadelphia: Fortress, 1984), 96. See also W. Emory Elmore, "Linguistic Approaches to the Kingdom: Amos Wilder and Norman Perrin," in *The Kingdom of God in 20th-Century Interpretation* (ed. Wendell Willis; Peabody, Mass.: Hendrickson, 1987), 62; Farmer, "The Kingdom of God," 119–30; Reginald Fuller, "Jesus, Paul, and Apocalyptic," *AThR* 71 (1989): 135–37, 141–42. For a critique of Perrin's dependence on the distinction between "steno" and "tensive" symbols, see Dale C. Allison, *The End of the Ages Has Come: An Early Interpretation of the Passion and Resurrection of Jesus* (Philadelphia: Fortress, 1985), 107–12.

86 R. Hiers and D. Holland, introduction to *Jesus' Proclamation* by Johannes Weiss, 46; Strecker, *Der Weg*, 170.

87 Karl L. Schmidt, "βασιλεία," *TDNT* 1:579; Jeremias, *New Testament Theology*, 98; Lattke, "Jewish Background," 73; Str-B 1:173–74.

88 Str-B 1:173–74; Davies and Allison, *Matthew*, 1:389; Lattke, "Jewish Background," 73; Kingsbury, *Structure, Christology, Kingdom*, 133–37.

89 Cf. Beasley-Murray, *Jesus and the Kingdom of God*, 20–22.

90 See Davies and Allison, *Matthew*, 1:312–14, on the question of the meaning of "the one coming after me" for the *historical* John. See also J. A. T. Robinson, "Elijah, John, and Jesus" in *Twelve New Testament Studies* (London: SCM Press, 1962), 28–52.

91 Julius Schniewind, *Das Evangelium nach Matthäus* (Göttingen: Vandenhoeck & Ruprecht, 1964), 24; Donald Guthrie, *New Testament Theology* (Downers Grove, Ill.: InterVarsity, 1981), 411.

92 Collins, "The Kingdom of God," 95; Allison, *End of the Ages*, 103.

93 Kingsbury, *Matthew as Story*, 50. Schnackenburg, *Matthäusevangelium 1,1–16,20*, 30.

94 Carson, "Matthew," 103.

95 Kingsbury, *Matthew as Story*, 50, says: "John's conception of Jesus' ministry, though it is correct, is also insufficient."

96 Note in 3:12–13 the presence of a narrative technique that is used elsewhere by the narrator of the Gospel. The technique is one of predicting a future event, and then immediately introducing a partial fulfillment of the prediction. So John, in effect, says, "The Coming One will come after, with judgment in his hand, and he will cleanse his threshing floor, gather his grain, and burn the chaff" (3:11–12). And in the next verse, the narrator says, "Then Jesus appeared from Galilee." The other passages where this technique occurs are 9:38 / 10:1; 26:2 / 26:3–4; 16:28 / 17:1.

[97] Turner, *Syntax*, 141.

[98] The conative sense of the imperfect, διεκώλυεν, is encouraged by the context. At first John objected, but unsuccessfully. The desire of Jesus to be baptized prevails in the end.

[99] For other "satanic" opposition to Jesus, see 16:23 and 27:40; cf. Ronald Witherup, "The Cross of Jesus: A Literary-Critical Study of Matthew 27" (Ph.D. diss., Union Theological Seminary in Virginia, 1985), 260–65.

[100] Note 3:15: "For thus it is fitting for *us* to fulfill all righteousness." Later, of course, Jesus' words again give high position to the Baptist in the salvation-historical scheme of the reign of heaven's arrival (11:7–15; 17:9–13; 21:23–27; 21:28–32).

[101] Schnackenburg, *Matthäusevangelium 1,1–16,20*, 35; Davies and Allison, *Matthew,* 1:329.

[102] Cf. Jack D. Kingsbury, "The Parable of the Wicked Husbandmen and the Secret of Jesus' Divine Sonship in Matthew: Some Literary-Critical Observations," *JBL* 105 (1986): 643. Davies and Allison, *Matthew*, 1:330, while not fully endorsing Kingsbury's position, admit the singular form of the verb, "he saw," and they find "noteworthy" that "there is no remark on the amazement or awe of others present."

[103] Cf. Bruner, *Matthew 1–12*, 81; Ladd, *Presence*, 108.

[104] *T. Naph.* 8:4: "If you achieve the good, my children, men and angels will bless you; and God will be glorified through you among the Gentiles. The devil will flee from you; wild animals will be afraid of you, and the angels will stand by you"; cf. *T. Mos.* 10:1. Tremper Longman, "The Divine Warrior: The New Testament Use of an Old Testament Motif," *WTJ* 44 (1982): 303, may be correct in seeing a backdrop concept of "holy war," with Jesus as the figure of the "divine warrior."

3

"LET THE ONE WHO HAS EARS HEAR": RESPONSE TO JESUS' END-TIME MINISTRY OF WORD AND DEED

In the first major section of Matthew's Gospel (1:1–4:16), the narrator of the story has informed the implied reader regarding the eschatological character of the time of the story. With the coming of Jesus, the Christ, into the story-world of the Gospel, God has begun to act, in a hidden manner to be sure, to establish the end-time rule of the reign of heaven. By means of OT fulfillment quotations, by means of the narrator's own commentary and arrangement of events, and by means of the characterization and speech of John the Baptist, it has been the narrator who has shown the implied reader that the eschatological reign of heaven has begun with the coming of the Christ. Our previous discussion has carried us to this point.

The discussion now turns to address the second major section of Matthew's Gospel, 4:17–16:20.[1] In this section, the goal remains that of narrative-critical method in general, namely, to read the story as the implied reader would. Specifically, the aspect of the implied reader's "instruction" that is in focus is the eschatological point of view of the Gospel's narrator. As the story unfolds, how is the implied reader to evaluate the events depicted and predicted with respect to the final goal of history and God's great triumph in and over history?

Matt 4:17–16:20 has many features that inform the implied reader about the goal of history. Yet there is one innovation of overarching importance. In the first major section of the story, it was the narrator's own voice that guided and informed the reader. By dramatic contrast, in the Gospel's second major section the character of Jesus becomes the chief source of information and insight. And although the deeds of Jesus communicate eloquently, it is chiefly the direct speech of Jesus that instructs, and Jesus' speech often addresses the implied reader as the story unfolds.

Jesus begins to teach, both in lengthy direct discourse and in shorter segments of direct speech. For the first time, the implied reader learns things about the judgment day and events beyond the temporal boundaries of the story-world of the Gospel. In addition, the implied reader realizes the implications of the end-time character of Jesus' present ministry for the other characters. Along with these characters, the implied reader learns that one's present response to this

Jesus also has an end-time character. Those who respond in discipleship receive eschatological blessing now and will be saved on the last day. Similarly, those who respond in hostility and opposition to Jesus seal for themselves the terrible fate of judgment. In this second major section of the Gospel, the implied reader himself or herself hears the crucial call and knows of its end-time implications: "Let the one who has ears hear" (11:15; 13:9, 43).

THE IMPLIED READER AND MATTHEW 4:17: JESUS BEGINS TO SPEAK

At 4:17, Jesus, the protagonist, speaks in a public manner for the first time in Matthew's Gospel. This feature alone, in light of the importance of Jesus' direct speech in the story from this point onward, makes 4:17 a notable structural turning point.[2] As David Howell points out, the implied author of Matthew has aligned the speech of Jesus with that of the narrator in order to indicate that "Jesus' speech thus shares the ideological point of view of the narrator, and is, in fact, the primary vehicle by which the author expresses his ideological point of view."[3] The implied reader knows that crucial new direction is forthcoming. Even though the implied reader has not "heard" from Jesus up to this point, the identity of Jesus as God's only Son makes certain that what Jesus says (and does) will reliably reflect the evaluative point of view of the reliable narrator.

As Jesus, the protagonist, begins to speak publicly for the first time in Matthew's story, his speech has an eschatological content: "Repent, for the reign of heaven has arrived!" (4:17). These opening words of Jesus have a decisive impact on what the implied reader expects from Jesus' speech as the story continues.[4]

Jesus' words are identical in form to the words of John the Baptist (3:2). This verbatim repetition recalls for the implied reader the "tension" between John and Jesus that was evident at Jesus' baptism. There, as a result of John's objection to Jesus' approach for baptism, the implied reader learned that there was some "insufficiency" about John's understanding of the reign of heaven that has already begun in the person of the Coming One. John's proclamation of the reign of heaven was dominated by the expectation of end-time judgment, but there was an "insufficiency" in John's own point of view. Here in 4:17, when Jesus begins to speak by repeating the words of the Baptist, that repetition focuses and intensifies the reader's anticipation of what Jesus will say and do next.[5]

How will the tension between John's view of the reign of heaven and Jesus' view of that same reality[6] be resolved? Why did John not see more accurately? What is the significance of Jesus' opening words, "Repent, for the reign of heaven has arrived"?

When John said, "The reign of heaven has arrived," his words gained meaning in large part through what came next. In that case, the implied reader learned that one aspect of the reign of heaven involves end-time judgment. Those who were baptized and confessed their sins would escape the judgment (3:6). But those who refused John's message heard only more of the threat of eschatological judgment (3:7–12).

When the same words come from Jesus' mouth, their meaning is in large part determined by what Jesus says and does next. What comes next is the calling of disciples (4:18–22); a ministry of teaching, proclaiming, and healing (4:23); and the response of crowds from throughout the area to Jesus' end-time ministry (4:23–25). The fact that, in the story of Matthew's Gospel, the reign of heaven has broken into the present time[7] means that Jesus has come to bring an eschatological salvation, that is, a salvation that will avail at the last day. Although the reign of heaven surely will mean the end-time judgment depicted so fiercely by John's preaching, in the present time of the story the inauguration of the reign of heaven connotes a ministry on the part of Jesus of outreach and salvation. Simply put, it means the activity of the Christ who has come to save his people from their sins (1:21).[8] It is not that John's message was wrong. Neither is it the case that when John preached, the reign of heaven was not "present" as it is here at 4:17 with the preaching of Jesus. John is able, in fact, to proclaim the "arrival" of the reign of heaven precisely because the end-time Christ (2:4), the King of the Jews (2:2), has already appeared "in those days" (3:1).[9] Nor is it the case that John and Jesus proclaimed two different realities under the same expression "the reign of heaven." The "flexibility" of meaning of the concept "the reign of heaven" in Matthew's Gospel allows John and Jesus to speak of aspects of the same reality.[10] But the implied reader has known already from 1:21 that the end-time ministry of Jesus[11] will be first and foremost a ministry of salvation: "For he will save his people from their sins."

For the implied reader, here is the answer to the question of how John's own understanding of the reign of heaven is insufficient. Jesus' end-time ministry first means salvation, proclamation, healing, and mission to the lost sheep of the house of Israel (15:24). That this is the nature of Jesus' present ministry is highlighted all the more for the implied reader because it functions as a partial "corrective" to John's own understanding.[12]

Thus, as the implied readers understand the end-time ministry of Jesus Christ, the Son of God, they understand the primary purpose and activity of that ministry to be salvation. This salvation is offered as Jesus summons people to repentance and discipleship, that is, to enter into "the sphere of God's end-time rule."[13] And, although "the crowds" are present (5:1), overhear, and react with astonishment to Jesus' claim of authority (7:28–29), it is principally to his disciples that Jesus directs the Sermon on the Mount, the first of the great discourses in Matthew's Gospel.

THE SERMON ON THE MOUNT

The Sermon[14] is, within the story-world of Matthew's Gospel, directed to Jesus' disciples.[15] According to the principles outlined in chapter 1 of this book, the implied reader of the Gospel is more or less fully addressed or "included" by the Sermon according to the rhetorical techniques utilized.[16] The combination of extended direct discourse[17] and various "generalizing" ways of speaking ensure that the Sermon addresses the implied reader along with the disciples.[18] My brief comments on the Sermon at this point will only focus on the extent to which "eschatological point of view" is revealed through the authoritative words of Jesus. As is the case with all of the major discourses,[19] Jesus' Sermon on the Mount has an "eye" toward the relationship of Jesus' present activity and the last day. More specifically, it contains the first explicit teaching on the end-time significance of one's response to Jesus' present ministry. Those who respond to Jesus in discipleship gain end-time salvation, both now and on the last day. Those who fail to respond thus to Jesus' ministry will receive final condemnation on that day.

The Beatitudes (5:3–12) are Jesus' opening words of the Sermon and both the disciples and the implied reader are addressed by these generalized[20] sayings of Jesus. These "eschatological blessings"[21] from the mouth of Jesus, couched in terms strongly reminiscent of Isaiah's prophecy of end-time salvation,[22] bless the disciples and the implied reader.[23] By means of them, both the disciples in the story and the implied reader understand that, whereas God's[24] final act of deliverance still lies in the indefinite and undefined future[25] (cf. the future tenses in 5:4, 5, 6, 7, 8, 9), nevertheless the disciples of Jesus experience, and indeed are said to possess, the reign of heaven itself already beginning with the time of Jesus' ministry in Israel.[26] The Beatitudes promise God's eschatological salvation and blessing to Jesus' disciples and do so in a way that shows the tension between the "already" and the "not yet."[27]

In addition to the Beatitudes, other portions of the Sermon on the Mount present the eschatological realities involved in the story of Matthew's Gospel. The Lord's Prayer (6:9–13) in general, and the Second Petition ("Let your reign come," 6:10a) in particular, direct the attention of Jesus' disciples to eschatological realities.[28] Also, the implied reader is addressed by virtue of the Prayer's position in the middle of this extended direct discourse of Jesus.

The first three petitions of the Lord's Prayer (6:9c; 6:10a; 6:10b–c) are generally seen as parallel in meaning.[29] All beseech the action of God[30] to hallow his own name, to cause his reign to come, to cause his will to be done. In light of the significance of "the reign of heaven" in Matthew's story, the Second Petition, "Let your reign come," deserves special consideration. What is being asked of God in this petition? For what are the disciples of Jesus commanded to pray? Since this petition requests a "coming" of the reign of God in a time future to the moment when Jesus gives the prayer, toward what future does the prayer direct the disciples and the implied reader to look?

It seems beyond question that, in one sense, the Second Petition (as well as the First and Third) directs the attention and faith of the ones who thus pray to the consummation of the reign of heaven. It is true that, as disciples of Jesus, those who pray have already entered into the end-time reality of God's reign.[31] The consummation and full victory of God's end-time reign, however, await the last day, and the faith of the one who prays, "Let your reign come" is directed toward that day. A final, fully-realized eschatological sense probably underlies the Second Petition of the Lord's Prayer.[32] The use of aorist imperatives (as opposed to "ongoing" or "repeated" present imperatives) would also more naturally support this interpretation of all three of the first petitions in the prayer.[33]

Nevertheless, in the context of Matthew's story, it should also be noted that there is a future application of the Second Petition of the Prayer that does not look exclusively at the consummation and end of the age. Indeed, the reign of heaven is already at hand and has already arrived (3:2; 4:7). Those interpreters are correct who see a dual reference in this petition, as Donald Carson notes: "The reader of Matthew's Gospel ... perceives that the kingdom has already broken in and prays for its extension as well as for its unqualified manifestation."[34] This fits in with our observation that the reign of heaven in Matthew's Gospel is a flexible, broadly applicable concept. In John's preaching, it primarily means future judgment. In Jesus' preaching and activity, its primary meaning is present opportunity for salvation in light of the future consummation.

Other "eschatological" features of the Lord's Prayer can also be seen to have "future" applications which are not directly concerned with the consummation at the end of the age. The hallowing of God's name can be seen with the same duality of temporal reference.[35] Likewise, the doing of God's will, and the danger of "temptation," point forward to the development of Jesus' earthly ministry[36] and specifically to Jesus' agony in the garden.[37] As will be more fully developed in chapter 5 of this book, the narrator views Jesus' agony in Gethsemane as an answer to the Prayer's Third Petition, "Let your will be done," as well as being a manifestation of the Second Petition, "Let your reign come."[38]

Thus, in the Lord's Prayer the disciples learn to ask for God to continue to accomplish his purposes that are now operative in Jesus' words and deeds, and, furthermore, to pray for the final eschatological salvation that will be manifested fully only on the day of judgment. In turn, the implied reader, who also awaits that judgment day, will observe the story of Matthew's Gospel in anticipation of "upcoming" manifestations of God's action through Jesus' ministry. As the Sermon continues, the implied reader will watch and learn as the disciples are urged to turn away from worry over mundane concerns (6:25–32) and continue to seek after the reign and righteousness of God that, though hidden, are nonetheless a present reality, operative in the "here and now" of the story of the Gospel.[39]

In the concluding section of the Sermon on the Mount (7:13–27) the disciples (the principal recipients of the Sermon within the story-world of the Gospel) are exhorted to enter by the narrow gate that leads to life (7:13–14)[40] and to beware of the deadly teaching[41] of false prophets (7:15–20). Also, the disciples are warned concerning their own standing at the temporally indeterminate final judgment on "that day," when some will finally "enter into the reign of heaven."[42] Those who enter will be the ones who have done the will of Jesus' Father in heaven (7:21–22).

Finally, the disciples learn clearly and forcefully that both end-time opportunity and crisis have entered into the present time because of the ministry of Jesus, the Christ. The story-parable in 7:24–27 refers to the day of judgment: "Everyone ... will be compared (ὁμοιωθήσεται, 7:24, 26)."[43] Yet one's present response to the words of Jesus forms the basis for the contrast between the fate of the wise and the fate of the foolish: "Everyone who hears these words of mine and does/does not do them...." The disciples in the story learn not only that Jesus' present activity is of an eschatological nature, but also that response to Jesus, whether of discipleship ("hearing and doing") or of opposition ("hearing and not doing"), also possesses an end-time character.[44]

Although human opposition to Jesus thus far in the story has scarcely come to expression (cf. 2:1–18), the disciples here receive that paradigm by which all response may be properly viewed from an eschatological point of view. All who respond in obedient discipleship receive eschatological blessing now (5:3, 10) and will be saved on the last day; their house will stand because of its unshakable foundation (7:25). But those who respond in disobedience, hostility, and opposition to Jesus also seal for themselves an eschatological fate, that of the terrible judgment on the last day; great will be the fall of their crumbling house (7:27).

This much the disciples, as characters in the story, learn through the conclusion of the Sermon on the Mount. That the implied reader is also included in this "eschatological instruction" is evident from the following data. The exhortation to enter by the narrow gate or way (7:13–14) extends beyond the temporal boundaries of the story of the Gospel and so is addressed to the time in which the implied reader is also situated. This is true also of the warning against the false prophets (7:15–20).[45] Further, in 7:21–23 the implied reader is, by means of the generalizing function of πᾶς ὁ λέγων (7:21a), ὁ ποιῶν (7:21d), and πολλοί (7:22a) "included" and addressed by the warning about entering the reign of heaven on the last day.[46] Most significantly, the theme of "eschatological response to Jesus" in 7:24–27 also addresses the implied reader. The implied reader is included in this section by virtue of generalizing speech (πᾶς ὅστις, 7:24; πᾶς ὁ + participle 7:26).

Moreover, as Jesus creates the story-world of the parable of the Two Builders, the implied reader is included in this "story within the story" and is thus addressed as fully as are "the disciples" in the story.[47] This instruction allows the implied reader to understand the proper eschatological point of view regarding both the present of the story-world and the final judgment, toward which the implied reader also looks.[48] In view of the importance of conflict between Jesus and his opponents as a driving force in the story of Matthew's Gospel,[49] this motif of "eschatological response" to Jesus will help to steer the way for the implied reader as he or she continues to observe and learn from the story, and specifically from Jesus' words[50] in the story.[51]

The words of Jesus in the Sermon on the Mount have addressed and informed the implied reader of the Gospel of Matthew regarding the valid end-time point of view of the Gospel's narrator. Both the present events of the story and the consummation of the age have been illumined. At 7:28–29, the Sermon concludes by means of its narrative framework. The formulaic conclusion "And it happened when Jesus completed these words" is one of the most obvious structuring features of Matthew's story, occurring as it does after each of the five largest discourses (7:28; 11:1; 13:53; 19:1; 26:1).[52] With regard to the concluding formula, two observations are in order. First, one ought not forget that the repeated concluding formulae of the great discourses in Matthew emphasize the importance of the speeches. By means of the words of Jesus, the implied reader is informed and guided in his or her understanding of the story and the events therein.[53] Second, from the perspective of literary function, the concluding formulae might better be called "reintegrating" formulae. By the end of each of the lengthy discourses, the implied reader has been away from the basic "line" of the story for some time.

The reintegrating formulae in general, and specifically 7:28, function to ease the implied reader back into the narrator's description of the story.[54] Here, at 7:28–29, the implied reader is "brought back" from contemplation of the last day and returned to the narrative that is describing the significance of the words and deeds of Jesus. Having listened to the authoritative teaching of Jesus of Nazareth, the Christ, the implied reader is prepared to observe the course of the story as Jesus continues about the work of offering end-time salvation to his people Israel. Of especial interest will be the way that characters in the story respond to Jesus' end-time ministry. In the narrative conclusion, the crowds express amazement at Jesus' claim to authority,[55] which is unlike the shallowness and self-understanding of their teachers. The implied reader acknowledges this authority of Jesus because he or she knows that Jesus speaks and acts with divine authority as the Son of God.[56] But the implied reader waits to see whether or not the crowds will respond to Jesus in discipleship, for only that response will suffice on the last day.[57]

Jesus' Ten Deeds of Power in Matthew 8 and 9

The story of Matthew's Gospel proceeds in chapters 8–9 with a series of miraculous deeds by Jesus. Although various attempts to describe a purposeful structure for these ten works of power have been offered,[58] for our purposes it is enough to see the ten miracles as evidence that in Jesus the end-time reign of heaven is functioning in the present time of the story. I will proceed to note briefly the ways that the narration of chapters 8–9 acts to reinforce and broaden the eschatological understanding of the implied reader of the Gospel.

In 8:1–4, Jesus cures a person of his leprosy, thus performing one of the miracles that was to accompany the messianic age.[59] At 8:5–13, the faith of the Gentile centurion, which so fully acknowledges and trusts the authority of Jesus to heal his servant, calls forth from Jesus words that contrast such faith with those in Israel who will not respond thus to Jesus. The centurion believes in Jesus' authority as God's Son. Those who will dine with the patriarchs in the messianic banquet will be like the centurion. Those in Israel who, also in the present, do not receive Jesus in faith will be cast into the outer darkness on the judgment day. In the past, Israelites had a natural claim to be the "sons of the reign."[60] But with the coming of the reign of heaven in Jesus, even Israelites, if they do not respond in faith to Jesus, will be rejected,[61] while Gentiles will be received[62] as "true" sons of the reign of heaven.[63] The theme of "eschatological response," so strongly presented in 7:24–27, is here reinforced.

Following the healing of Peter's mother-in-law (8:14–15) and a summary of exorcisms and healings that fulfill the prophecy of Isa 53:4, Jesus is engaged in conversation by two men. In Jesus' response to the "eager scribe," the implied reader encounters Jesus' first use of the phrase "the Son of Man." Because "the Son of Man" has, to date, figured so prominently in the scholarly discussion of the eschatological view of Jesus,[64] a brief digression here at its first occurrence in the Gospel's story will examine how the implied reader of the Gospel reacts to the expression.

The meaning of "the Son of Man" in the historical setting in which the story was written by the flesh-and-blood author of the Gospel is important for understanding the implied reader's reaction to "the Son of Man" in Matthew's Gospel. Although the discussion on the linguistic and theological background of "the Son of Man" has many permutations, there are two main positions. The first position holds that, in the first century, "the son of man" was a well-known eschatological "title" with its roots in the interpretation of Daniel 7 and with connections of some sort to *1 Enoch* 37–71.[65] The second position denies the existence of an established "titular" use of the phrase, holding rather that the Greek ὁ υἱὸς τοῦ ἀνθρώπου is the rendering of an Aramaic phrase that is understood as something of a circumlocutionary way of referring to oneself, to the speaker.[66] My position is this: While there can be no doubt that "one like a son of man" in Dan 7:13 was a concept that was developed and given eschatological meaning in Judaism after the time of the writing of the Danielic visions,[67] it cannot be established that such an influence was so widespread that it was able to impart an automatic, "eschatologically titular" sense to the phrase ὁ υἱὸς τοῦ ἀνθρώπου itself.[68]

It is clear that certain passages in Matthew's Gospel in which Jesus calls himself "the Son of Man" do make reference to the vision of Daniel 7. Interaction with Daniel 7 will be required in order to understand those texts as the implied reader would understand them. It is not, however, the presence of the mere phrase "the Son of Man" in those texts that establishes the connection with Daniel 7, but rather additional markers that so function. The phrase in and of itself can be assumed to be no more than a reference, indirect in some fashion, to the speaker himself and in the Gospel of Matthew, always as a self-reference of Jesus.

Our discussion of "the Son of Man" thus far has focused on questions of history and background. Of even greater importance, however, are observations of how the phrase itself functions within the story of Matthew's Gospel. Background can only tell us what the implied reader might assume. The understanding of the implied reader is informed and shaped as he or she reads the story of Matthew itself. We now turn, therefore, to pertinent observations of the use of "the Son of Man" in Matthew's Gospel.

With regard to this first usage[69] of "the Son of Man" at 8:20, the implied reader is somewhat puzzled. Jesus has not been hesitant to refer to himself directly, using personal pronouns since he began his outreach to Israel at 4:17.[70] Why does he now refer to himself, in conversation with the scribe, as "the Son of Man"? The answer lies in Kingsbury's conclusion that "the Son of Man" can be described as Jesus' way of referring to himself with reference to unbelieving "outsiders," or in contexts in which conflict and/or vindication for Jesus are present.[71] In Matthew's story, "the Son of Man" cannot be understood as a "title," either in the sense that it carries automatic "freight" of meaning or in the sense that it identifies "who Jesus is."[72] In light of this feature of Matthew's Gospel, I will adopt the translational equivalent of "this man" when rendering the Greek phrase ὁ υἱὸς τοῦ ἀνθρώπου.[73]

Equipped in this way with data from throughout the Gospel's story,[74] the implied reader will discern the significance of Jesus' use of "this man" in 8:20. It is one of several markers that show that the eager scribe does not come as a disciple, nor does Jesus here invite him into discipleship. Rather, Jesus speaks to him as to an outsider, in contrast with the reluctant disciple of 8:21–22, to whom Jesus sternly says, "Follow me, and allow the dead to bury their own dead."

As the story continues, the disciples experience the authority of Jesus over the winds and the sea (8:23–27). Although the implied reader knows that Jesus has called the people in the boat to be his disciples (4:18–22) and to experience already the reality of end-time blessings (5:3), the inadequate questioning and response of the disciples ("Who is this one?" 8:27) shows that the implied reader is more fully informed than the disciples themselves. The implied reader knows who this one is. The implied reader knows that God's end-time reality and reign have entered the time of the story, because Jesus is the Christ, the Son of God.

The implied reader's understanding of the eschatological nature of Jesus' ministry is reinforced as the story proceeds. Jesus exorcises two demoniacs (8:28–34). Before the exorcism, the demons cry out, "Have you come here to torment us before the time?" Already, before the day of the demons' final rejection and torment (25:41),[75] Jesus' ministry means the presence of "eschatological conflict with the kingdom of Satan."[76]

In addition to conflict with Satan, the first direct indications of conflict with Israel occur in Matthew 9. The scribes who accuse Jesus of blasphemy (9:3), the Pharisees who grumble that Jesus is eating with societal outcasts (9:11), and the Pharisees who interpret Jesus' exorcism as occurring by means of the ruler of the demons (9:34) all serve to introduce and foreshadow the greater conflict between Jesus and Israel and, in particular, Israel's religious leaders.[77] The implied reader knows that response to Jesus has an eschatological "cast" to it (7:24–27). At this point in the story, the conflict between Jesus and Israel and its leaders is only presaged.[78] It will open up into full and lethal flower in chapters 11 and 12, in the second half of the second major section of the Gospel's story.

By contrast with those who now begin to come into conflict with Jesus, the implied reader accepts and understands Jesus' own eschatological evaluation of his words and deeds at 9:15: "The sons of the bridegroom are not able to mourn as long as the bridegroom is with them. But days will come when the bridegroom will be taken away from them, and then they will mourn." In what seems to be a "development" of eschatological thinking for the first-century culture in which the story was written,[79] Jesus plainly reveals to the disciples of John (and reinforces for the implied reader) that the present time is a time of eschatological joy and feasting, not a time for fasting and mourning.[80] That the present is not the consummation of eschatological joy is made fully clear, for "days will come when ... they will mourn."[81] The reign of heaven is present, but in a hidden manner. Nevertheless, the use of the "bridegroom" and "wedding" imagery is significant. The implied reader learns that this is an image that Jesus uses with reference to his Parousia at the consummation of the age (25:1–13). But once again, as with the very term "the reign of heaven" itself, the eschatological point of view revealed through the speech of Jesus has a flexible quality that allows application in more than one way.[82]

With the matching summary statement of 9:35 (cf. 4:23), the narrator acts to bind together the entire section that includes the Sermon on the Mount and the "ten miracles" section of chapters 8–9. The statement of David Bauer is pertinent:

> Matthew underscores the eschatological nature of the ministry of Jesus
> by references to Galilee, to the Gospel of the kingdom (4:23; 9:35), and to
> the kingdom of heaven.... To sum up: in 4:23–9:35 Matthew presents Jesus
> as one who performs an eschatological ministry of teaching and healing in
> Galilee to all Israel within the context of his proclamation that the kingdom
> of heaven is at hand. These acts point to the transcendent authority of Jesus

and draw forth reactions of two types: amazement; and the accusation that Jesus is in league with the devil.[83]

To underscore Bauer's last point, the implied reader has learned that the reactions to Jesus' eschatological ministry also have end-time implications. Those who follow as disciples are blessed now and will be finally blessed. Those who reject and oppose will be judged. Present, end-time response determines final, end-time fate.

THE IMPLIED READER AND THE MISSIONARY DISCOURSE

At 9:36, the story of Matthew's Gospel reaches the narrative framework of the second of the great discourses, the Missionary Discourse of chapter 10. Here the implied reader, who already has learned of the eschatological implications of discipleship in terms of end-time blessings, learns that Jesus' disciples, or at least the inner group of the Twelve, share also in the end-time work of Jesus. His ministry offers salvation to those who receive him and brings judgment upon those who reject him. The mission entrusted to the Twelve at this point in the Gospel's story does the same.[84]

A number of important eschatological markers occur in the narrative framework that introduces the discourse (9:36–10:4). The crowds whom Jesus sees are described as "like sheep without a shepherd." The implied reader knows that, as the eschatological royal Christ foretold in prophecy, Jesus has come to "shepherd" his people Israel (2:6).[85] Also, when Jesus sees the crowds in need of shepherding, he himself describes the situation thus: "The harvest [ὁ ... θερισμός] is great, but the workers [οἱ ... ἐργάται] are few."

This companion metaphor to that of "shepherding" also carries end-time connotations for the implied reader of Matthew's Gospel, for in the parable of the Wheat and the Tares, Jesus explicitly says in 13:39, "The harvest [ὁ ... θερισμός] is the consummation of the age."[86] Note that here in 9:37–38, "harvest" is not the action of reaping, but rather the crop that someday will be reaped.[87] Also, the prayer to the Lord of the harvest is not for "reapers" (θερισταί), but for "workers."[88] Thus, the present time of mission for Jesus' disciples does not imply an immediate action of "harvesting." This activity is reserved for the angels on the last day (13:30, 39).[89] The prayer to the Lord of the harvest for workers in the harvest does mean that the work of offering end-time salvation to Israel has been extended to the Twelve. This, the implied reader knows, is the first concrete outworking of the call to "mission" contained in the first calls to discipleship ("I will make you to be fishers of persons," 4:19).

Discipleship with Jesus means mission. Thus informed, the implied reader knows not only to view Jesus' own ministry of salvation as eschatological in character but also to view similarly the mission that is abruptly[90] entrusted to the Twelve here in the present time of the story of Matthew.

It is, of course, the end-time character of the mission of the Twelve that touches upon our purpose. This end-time character is made clear in the address of Jesus to the Twelve, 10:5–42. I shall briefly examine the discourse and note especially the portions that address and inform the implied reader even as the character of the disciples is being addressed.

The opening words of Jesus are of interest to the implied reader. Jesus specifically limits the mission of the Twelve to the lost sheep that are[91] the house of Israel. This limitation, which has been so troubling for redaction-critical study of Matthew,[92] poses no real problem for the implied reader. He or she knows that, with the conclusion of the story, the mission of the Eleven will be extended to encompass all the nations (28:18–20).[93] A more difficult problem is encountered at 10:23, but to that the discussion will come in short order.

After limiting the "target" of the mission of the Twelve, Jesus empowers them for specific forms of mission. First and foremost, they are to preach that the reign of heaven has entered into the present, just as John and Jesus before them had so announced: "Preach, and say, 'The reign of heaven has arrived' " (10:7).[94] This alone establishes the end-time nature of the mission.[95] In addition, however, the Twelve are commanded at 10:8 to perform mighty acts of power which have already characterized Jesus' own eschatological ministry of salvation: healings (4:23, 24; 8:7, 16; 9:35); raising of the dead (9:23–26); cleansing of lepers (8:2–4); and exorcisms (8:16, 28–34; 9:32–34).

As the discourse progresses, the implied reader is not surprised to discover teaching regarding the theme of "eschatological response," this time to the mission of the Twelve. Jesus grounds (γάρ) his explicit prohibition against taking "gear" for the trip (10:9–10a) with the axiom "The worker is worthy of his food" (10:10b). On their mission, there will be some who respond favorably, by receiving the messengers and offering them shelter and life's necessities (10:11). These are "worthy" persons, "worthy" houses, who will "hear the Gospel and act as host"[96] to the messengers who proclaim the reign of heaven. On such houses, the Twelve's eschatological blessing of peace[97] will remain. Favorable response to the end-time mission of the Twelve results in end-time blessing.

There will, however, be those persons and houses that will neither offer hospitality to the messengers nor receive their message (10:14). After departing those places, the disciples are to give a sign of rejection (10:14). Jesus solemnly declares what the end-time consequences of this rejection of the mission of the Twelve will be: "It will be better for the land of Sodom and Gomorrah in that day than for that city" (10:15). On the temporally indeterminate day of judgment, those who reject the present end-time mission of the Twelve reap for themselves end-time judgment.

The implied reader of the Gospel has learned all of this (10:5–15) regarding the end-time mission being entrusted to the Twelve. Yet the discourse has not directly included or addressed the implied reader. He or she is still only "eavesdropping" on the discourse of Jesus to the Twelve within the story. The relation of the implied reader to the Missionary Discourse does change in 10:17–23. But it does not change in that the discourse ceases to address the Twelve and only addresses the implied reader. Jesus' words in 10:17–23 still do speak to the disciples within the story. Because they describe and predict events that will take place only after the end of the Gospel's story, however, the implied reader also is included along with the Twelve.

The implied reader knows of no evidence that the persecutions that are described beginning at 10:17 happened during the story-time of the Gospel.[98] These events project beyond the Gospel's story-time, into the time after the resurrection of Jesus and before the consummation of the age. Owing to the almost complete absence of "generalizing" language[99] and the consistent second person address, the implied reader understands that the events described in 10:17–23 can be expected to occur during the lifetime of the Twelve, in the time after the resurrection of Jesus.[100] The persecutions experienced by the Twelve will be primarily at the hands of Jewish opponents (10:17),[101] for it seems that even when the persecution takes places in Gentile contexts, the ones who are leading (ἄγω, 10:18) and delivering over (παραδίδωμι, 10:19a) the Twelve will be Jewish opponents. Even when all hate them a proverbial word of encouragement sustains the Twelve: "the one who endures to the end will be saved" (10:22).[102] Because he or she stands in the time between Jesus' resurrection and Parousia, the implied reader might perhaps be expected to share the experiences predicted in 10:17–23. But this point is clear. These verses also remain a natural part of the commission to the Twelve, as that commission extends into the time beyond the temporal boundary of the Gospel.

In view of the persecution that the Twelve are destined to experience, Jesus commands them to hasten through the cities of Israel. When persecution arises in this city, leave and flee to the next (10:23a). For the disciples will certainly not finish going through the cities of Israel until this man comes (10:23b). Jesus thus puts a temporal limitation on the mission that is to be directed only to the lost sheep of Israel (10:5–6).

We arrive at one of the most difficult sayings in the Gospel of Matthew. How will the implied reader of Matthew's Gospel understand 10:23?

THE IMPLIED READER'S UNDERSTANDING OF MATTHEW 10:23

From a narrative-critical perspective, there are, indeed, a number of possible answers to this question.[103] The best answer will take into account the data, available to the implied reader from the entire story,[104] that address the following questions: (1) Who is Jesus, the speaker of the saying? (2) Is there, in Matthew's story, the expectation that the end of the age is coming very soon, indeed, within the life span of the characters within the story itself? (3) What does the implied reader know about the mission of the Twelve to the nation of Israel? (4) What other passages speak about Jewish persecution of the Twelve in the time after the resurrection and before the consummation of the age? Finally, (5) since every one of the interpretive options put forward during the history of interpretation of 10:23 requires some "figurative" or "flexible" reading of aspects[105] of the saying or its context,[106] which of these readings will be most consistent with what the implied reader knows from other material in the Gospel's story?

On the basis of these questions, we may search for the best solution to the implied reader's problem. Because of the length of the discussion here offered, allow me to state in advance my own conviction. The implied reader does not understand the temporal limitation of 10:23b, "until this man comes," as a reference to the Parousia of Jesus at the end of the age. Rather, data from within the narrative enable the implied reader to know that the event referred to by the words "until this man comes" is the destruction of the temple and the city of Jerusalem that Jesus elsewhere predicts. With this in mind, we now turn to the five questions listed above.

WHO IS JESUS?

The first question is this: Who is Jesus, the speaker of 10:23? In light of this question, one may quickly dismiss the view, common to some redaction critics, that sees a simple contradiction between this verse (and related verses such as 16:28 and 24:34) and other features in the Gospel such as the "long delay" found in the parables of the Wise and Faithful Servant ("my master is delaying," 24:48); the Ten Maidens ("because the bridegroom was delaying," 25:5); and the Talents ("after a long time," 25:19).[107] The implied reader of the Gospel knows that the character of Jesus is reliable and espouses the point of view of the narrator and the implied author. As the Christ, the Son of God, Jesus would not be capable of blatant self-contradiction.[108]

DOES MATTHEW'S STORY CONTAIN A NEAR-EXPECTATION OF THE CONSUMMATION OF THE AGE?

This is the second question: Does Matthew's story contain a near-expectation of the consummation of the age, limited in fact to the life span of the *disciples* in the story of the Gospel?[109] The three passages that are adduced in favor of this view are 10:23; 16:28; 24:34. The second two, and especially 24:34, also will be treated at length. But let it be noted that, in the view of the implied reader, it is very unlikely that such a near-expectation of the consummation in the life span of the disciples is part of the Gospel's eschatological point of view. There is a wealth of material that teaches the implied reader otherwise. Already mentioned is the thrice-repeated, deliberate emphasis on a delay of the Parousia at 24:48; 25:5; and 25:19. Note especially that these three passages, embedded as they are in story-like speech (24:45–51) and story-parables (25:1–13, 14–30), speak the message of the long-delayed consummation *to the time and situation of the implied reader*.[110] Recall, too, that whereas there are many specific references in Matthew's story to the "day of judgment," "that day," and such expressions, none of them has any time limitation attached (cf. 7:24–27; 8:11–12). They are all temporally indeterminate.

Moreover, passages such as 24:14 ("as a witness to all the nations, and then the end will come") and 26:13 ("wherever this Gospel is preached in the whole world") imply a long period of mission outreach to the nations. Finally, as I shall discuss later, the words of Jesus at 12:41–42 imply that "this generation" of Jesus' contemporaries will die before the judgment day, for they "will stand up" (ἀναστήσονται) and "will be raised" (ἐγερθήσεται) with long-deceased Gentiles and be accused by them because of their rejection of him who is greater than Jonah and greater than Solomon.[111] I conclude that the implied reader does not find in the story of Matthew's Gospel a near-expectation of the consummation of the age in the life span of the disciples.[112]

THE MISSION OF THE TWELVE TO ISRAEL

The third question is this: What does the implied reader know about the mission of the Twelve to Israel? There are a number of considerations. Probably most important, the implied reader knows that, at 28:16–20, Jesus gives to the Eleven the climactic Great Commission to make disciples of "all the nations" (πάντα τὰ ἔθνη). The importance of this pericope for the present discussion lies in its "undoing" of the limitation of the mission of the Twelve that occurs at 10:5–6 (and which also characterizes Jesus' own mission during the story-time of the Gospel, 15:24). I would agree with those who see Israel as included at 28:19 in "all the nations."[113] Therefore, at 28:19, one can say that the Twelve's mission, formerly limited to the lost sheep of the house of Israel, now embraces all the peoples of the world, "all the nations," including Israel. The limitation of the Twelve's mission to Israel receives a decisive alteration at 28:19. In this view the mission to Israel itself is not brought to an end. It is simply incorporated under the larger mission to all the nations.[114]

After matrixing the two passages, 10:5–6 and 28:19, with 10:23, some interpreters simply stop there. They conclude that, originally, Jesus gave the Twelve a mission that was directed exclusively to Israel and said that they would not finish it until this man would come, that is, until the Parousia. The final pericope of the Gospel's story changes not the termination point, but only the scope of the mission: "I will be with you all the days, until the end of the age" (28:20). Thus, in 10:23, the mission limited to Israel has its terminus ad quem at the coming of this man, that is, at the Parousia. In this view the mission is, by virtue of 28:18–20, expanded to "all the nations," but the terminus remains the same.[115] Under yet another view, the mission to Israel described at 10:23 is regarded as still in force, but the natural sense of "the cities of Israel" is altered more or less violently in order to subsume the mission to Israel under the more universalistic perspective of 28:18–20.[116]

It is significant that 28:18–20 is not the only passage at the disposal of the implied reader that speaks of the mission of the Twelve to Israel. Two other key passages must be included in the discussion. They are the parables of the Wicked Tenants (21:33–44) and the Wedding Feast (22:1–14). In brief, note that in both of those parables, there is a turning away from, and a rejection and punishment of, Israel by God. In the Wicked Tenants, this turning away is described thus: "He will utterly destroy the evil ones and give out the vineyard to other tenants, who will give to him the fruit at their times" (21:41). This speaks unequivocally of the time, after the death of the son (21:39), when Israel as a nation[117] would be rejected by God.

The second parable is even more forceful. In the parable of the Wedding Feast, the rejection and punishment of Israel occurs through the wrath of the king, after those invited to the son's wedding feast not only refuse to come but also abuse the king's servants. "The king became angry and sent his soldiers and destroyed those murderers and burned their city" (22:7). Only after this is the invitation to come to the feast given out to others. The parable of the Wedding Feast, then, portrays the sequence of (1) invitation to Israel, (2) Israel's rejection of the invitation, (3) God's punishment of Israel by destroying "their city," and (4) the subsequent invitation or calling of the Gentiles.

These two parables are also available to the implied reader, who thus understands that God, after the rejection and murder of God's Son by the religious leaders of Israel, will visit judgment and punishment upon the nation and, specifically, upon their city (22:7). In light of these verses, the implied reader knows that the mission to Israel as a nation has a terminus in the time period after the death and resurrection of Jesus but before the consummation of the age. The implied reader knows that the mission of the Twelve to Israel is brought to an end by the destruction of the city and the temple, prophesied by Jesus in Matthew's Gospel.

Again, the third question pertinent to the discussion surrounding 10:23 is this: What does the implied reader know about the mission of the Twelve to Israel? The following two answers apply. First, he or she knows that the Eleven are given a worldwide mission at 28:18–20 that includes Israel under the canopy of "all the nations." Second, he or she knows from 21:43 and (especially) 22:7 that a time does come, after the resurrection of Jesus and before the consummation of the age, when Israel as a nation is punished, while the invitation to eschatological salvation in Jesus continues to be extended to others, namely, to the Gentiles.

JEWISH PERSECUTION OF THE TWELVE

The fourth question is this: Since Jesus clearly predicts Jewish persecution of the Twelve during the course of their mission to Israel (10:17), what passages refer to Jewish persecution of the Twelve in the time after Jesus' resurrection but before the consummation of the age? Two other passages in the Gospel are pertinent. They are 23:34–39 and 24:15–22.

In 23:34–39, Jesus promises to send missionaries[118] ("prophets and wise men and scribes") to rebellious Israel and to its leaders, and he predicts the murderous persecution those emissaries will experience (23:34). Note especially the conceptual parallelism of 23:34, "And you will persecute them from city to city" (καὶ διώξετε ἀπὸ πόλεως εἰς πόλιν), and 10:23a, "When they persecute you in this city, flee to the other" (ὅταν δὲ διώκωσιν ὑμᾶς ἐν τῇ πόλει ταύτῃ, φεύγετε εἰς τὴν ἑτέραν). This persecution will sum up all of the pouring out of righteous blood from the very beginning, the murder of Abel, until the last murder of a prophet recorded in the Scriptures (23:35).

As is the case at 10:23, Jesus' words in 23:34–39 contain a temporal limitation: all these things will come upon "this generation" of Jesus' contemporaries who reject him (23:36).[119] Jerusalem, unwilling to be gathered by Jesus, will likewise refuse to be gathered by those whom Jesus has sent. Jerusalem will find its house left desolate (23:37–38). The persecution of the missionaries sent by Jesus will ultimately result in the destruction of Jerusalem and the ruin of the temple, which constitute the "burning of their city" of which Jesus spoke at 22:7. At 24:2, Jesus baldly predicts such destruction: "Truly I say to you, a stone will certainly not be left upon another here which will not be thrown down."

The second passage that also speaks of Jewish persecutions of the Twelve after the resurrection and before the consummation of the age is 24:15–22. The local, Judean scope of the troubles there described is indicated by the references to "the holy place" (24:15) and "those in Judea" (24:16). Although persecutions are not specifically mentioned in this unit of the ED, they are implicit in the concept of "the abomination that causes desolation" (24:15). The occurrence of the command to "flee!" (φευγέτωσαν, 24:16) is a noteworthy parallel to φεύγετε in 10:23a for two reasons. First, these are the only two times in Matthew's story that Jesus commands his disciples to flee persecutions. Second, there are other times when Jesus speaks of persecutions experienced by his disciples. He does not, however, tell them to flee these persecutions but to accept them (16:24) or to rejoice in them as a sign of blessing (cf. 5:11–12). Thus, the view is strengthened that sees the difficulties encountered by the disciples in 24:15–22 as parallel to 10:23a. Accordingly, the fourth question necessary for the understanding of 10:23 is answered by noting that, like 10:17–23, both 23:34–39 and 24:15–22 speak of Jewish persecution of the Twelve in the time after the resurrection of Jesus and before the consummation of the age.

I now summarize the answers to the first four questions in the discussion of 10:23. First, the implied reader knows that Jesus does not contradict himself in his teaching. Second, 10:23 does not teach a near-expectation of the consummation of the age during the lifetime of the disciples to whom 10:5–23 is so directly addressed. Third, the implied reader also knows that the Twelve will not always be restricted to Israel as far as the scope of the eschatological mission task is concerned. At 28:18–20, the mission task is expanded to include all the nations, with Israel as one of them. The implied reader also knows that Jesus predicts rejection, judgment, and destruction for Israel and its leaders precisely because they will refuse to respond either with appropriate fruit-bearing (the parable of the Wicked Tenants) or by coming to the eschatological celebration given by God for his Son (the parable of the Wedding Feast). Fourth and finally, the implied reader also knows that, following a time of persecuted missionary activity initiated by Jesus (23:34), all of the righteous blood shed throughout the whole of history will come upon the generation of Jesus' contemporaries (23:36). Because it will come upon "this generation," the implied reader is invited to see in the predicted fall of Jerusalem and of the temple an event that will take place during the lifetime of the disciples to whom 10:23 is also spoken.

THE IMPLIED READER AND MATTHEW 10:23: WHAT DO JESUS' WORDS MEAN?

How, then, does this information help to shape the understanding of 10:23? To repeat the fifth question from above, which reading of this passage will be most consistent with what the implied reader knows from other material in the Gospel's story? That is to say, which interpretation dovetails most faithfully with the other things that the implied reader knows and understands about the mission of the Twelve and the eschatological nature of the time of the Gospel's story? A number of questions arise from the wording of 10:23 itself.

First in order is the meaning of the verb "to complete, finish" (τελέω). One view holds that it refers to the act of fleeing through the cities of Israel.[120] This is to be rejected. The command to flee from one city to the next (10:23a) occurs in the context of the command to mission. The urgency enjoined upon the Twelve in their missionary endeavors makes it clear that τελέω refers to missionary activity.[121] It is the preaching of the reign of heaven (and the accompanying miracles, 10:7–8) that will not take place in all the cities of Israel until this man, Jesus, comes. The saying puts a limitation on the task of evangelization.[122] That task will not be completed.

The second question addresses the meaning of the phrase "the cities of Israel." All attempts to extend the meaning to include the Gentiles are far-fetched and can be dismissed without discussion.[123] More reasonable, but still to be rejected, is the view that extends "cities of Israel" to include the Diaspora.[124] In view of Matthew's use of "Israel" (2:6; 20, 21; 8:10; 9:33; 15:24), the natural sense of "Palestinian cities of Israel" is to be preferred.

Next is the referent of the clause "until this man comes." There are two problems to be addressed. One is the precise relationship that "until" (ἕως ἄν) establishes between the independent clause ("you will certainly not finish the cities of Israel") and the dependent clause ("this man comes"). The second problem is the meaning of "this man comes" (ἔλθῃ ὁ υἱὸς τοῦ ἀνθρώπου). First to be addressed will be the precise relationship established by the use of "until" (ἕως).[125]

Does the construction in the dependent clause state a simple termination point of the activity of the main clause? Or does the dependent clause imply a point in time at which the condition of the main clause is reversed? Specifically, does 10:23b in effect state, "You won't finish the cities of Israel"? Or does it allow for the meaning, "You won't finish until the Son of Man comes ... and then you will finish them"?

Matthew employs the conjunction[126] ἕως ("until")[127] twenty-one times in a variety of constructions.[128] Charles Giblin[129] has attempted a categorization and evaluation of the use of ἕως (and other conjunctions) under four headings: (1) with the indicative, in dependence on a positive main clause, meaning "until" (2:9; 13:33); (2) with the indicative, in dependence on a negative main clause, meaning "until" or "before" applied to the main clause (1:25; 24:39); (3) with the subjunctive, in dependence on a positive main clause, meaning "until." According to Giblin, this third category also "regularly" indicates finality or intention (2:13; 10:11; 14:22; 18:30, 34; 22:44). Finally, (4) there is ἕως used with the subjunctive, in dependence on a negative main clause, "with an indication of finality and ful-fillment" (5:18, 26; 16:28; 17:9; 23:39; 24:34). By his categorization, Giblin attempts to connect formal characteristics and translational sense in order to indi-cate which constructions, on the one hand, carry a sense of actual termination and finality, and which constructions, on the other, bear a more open-ended meaning.

Giblin's work is precise and thorough. I would, however, question his schema as too neat; it is not sufficiently sensitive to contextual factors. For instance, examples from the last three of his categories are flexible enough to allow for more than just a sense of finality or termination. Indeed, several of the different constructions with "until" can bear the sense of "when the dependent clause is fulfilled, the effect or action of the main clause will actually be reversed." For instance, in 17:9 (Giblin's category 4, expressing "finality and fulfillment"), Jesus commands the disciples, "Tell the vision to no one until this man has been raised from the dead." What seems likely, however, is that this statement permits (but does not demand) an additional implication, namely, "But, after this man has been raised from the dead, then tell the vision to others." It is possible to under-stand 5:26 similarly. To say, "You will not get out from there until you pay the last penny," carries with it the theoretical possibility of release, namely, "When you pay the last penny, you will be released."[130] From Giblin's category 2, Matt 1:25 has a similar flexibility: "But after she gave birth to a son, he did know her" (cf. 13:55–56). As clear as Giblin's categories are on formal grounds, they do not seem to solve the problem of meaning.

The problem of the relationship that ἕως establishes between the two claus-es of 10:23b can be solved by attending to contextual features. All dependent clauses introduced by "until" indicate a temporal limitation of the action or state in the independent clause. Other factors, such as lexical meaning and contextual meaning, determine whether the notion of "limitation" extends only to "finality, termination," or whether it allows for a time after the "until clause," when the effect or activity of the main clause is reversed or undone.

With regard to 10:23b, I would argue that two elements in the context limit the meaning of the dependent clause, "until this man comes," to a sense of "finality, termination." First, there is the element of haste inherent in 10:23a: "Flee to the next." Simple termination is in view. This explains the need for haste. Second, there is γάρ, the explanatory (or perhaps causal) particle that stands at the head of 10:23b. Jesus' emphatic statement about not completing the cities of Israel explains why the disciples are to hasten on their missionary work, fleeing when opposition and persecution ensue. In simple language, they must hurry on their eschatological mission proclamation in the cities of Israel because of the temporal limitation imposed by the "until" clause. These two factors, and not the construction of 10:23b itself, give a strong sense of termination to the clause "until this man comes." Therefore, the intent of Jesus' statement to the Twelve is that the event described as "the coming of this man" will effectively prevent the completion of the mission activity of the Twelve[131] to all the cities of Israel in Palestine.

I am attempting to understand how, in light of other knowledge, the implied reader will understand 10:23. The final question to be answered concerns the meaning of the expression "this man comes" (ἔλθη ὁ υἱὸς τοῦ ἀνθρώπου). The majority opinion is that this phrase refers to the Parousia of Jesus at the consummation of the age.[132] In this view, although the spatial limitation of the mission to Israel is superseded and expanded at 28:18–20, the temporal limitation of the mission remains the same. Accordingly, "until this man comes" (10:23) means the same as "until the consummation of the age" (28:20).[133] The major problem with this view, however, is that it fails to acknowledge the unique element of flight, haste, and urgency that is connected to the mission to Israel's lost sheep.[134] This element of urgency is lacking at 28:18–20, just as it is also absent at 24:14 ("And this Gospel of the reign will be preached in the whole world as a witness to all the nations, and then the end will come") and at 26:13 ("wherever this Gospel is preached in the whole world, also what this woman did will be spoken as a remembrance of her"). To underscore an earlier conclusion, I reiterate that the implied reader of Matthew's Gospel knows that there is no near-expectation of the consummation of the age in the teaching of Jesus. It will be a long time, even from the time of the implied reader (25:19). But the "coming of this man" in 10:23 is so near that it imposes hasty flight on the Twelve as they carry out their mission to the cities of Israel in the time after the resurrection of Jesus. To what does this "coming of this man" refer?

Note first of all that the phrase is unadorned by features that would unmistakably determine its meaning to be the consummation of the age.[135] This "coming of this man" is simply an event that is in the future for the disciples in the story to whom 10:23 is addressed and yet near enough to cause them haste in their mission to Israel's lost sheep in the period after Jesus' resurrection.

Moreover, one must attend to the way that a "coming"[136] of "Jesus" or "this man" occurs in Matthew's Gospel.[137] It applies often to the present reality of Jesus' eschatological ministry. Thus, John the Baptist predicted judgment at the hands of the "Coming One" (3:11; 11:3). Jesus is already that "Coming One," but his primary task in carrying out end-time preaching, teaching, and miracles is to offer salvation to Israel, especially to preach the Good News to the poor (11:4–6). Jesus repeatedly expresses both the purpose for which, and the manner in which, he, this man, has "come": to fulfill the Law and the Prophets (5:17); to call sinners (9:10–13); to cast a sword upon the earth (10:34–36); in joyful celebration ("eating and drinking," 11:19); to give his life as the ransom for the many (20:28).

With regard to the eschatological nature of the present time of the story, Jesus also responds to the disciples' misinformed question about a future coming of Elijah by declaring, "On the one hand, Elijah *is coming* [ἔρχεται] and will restore all things; on the other hand, I say to you that Elijah already *has come* [ἦλθεν], and they did not know him, but they did to him whatever they wished" (17:11–12). Elijah has already come in John the Baptist. Although the verb "to come" is never unambiguously connected with "the reign of heaven" in reference to the present reality of the story, the narrator has made it abundantly clear that the end-time reign of heaven is a present, albeit hidden, reality in the person of the Son of God. Thus, the implied reader knows that the present ministry of Jesus can be spoken of as the "coming" of this man, as well as the presence of the reign of heaven.

It is clear that the future "*coming* of this man" at times refers to the Parousia of Jesus at the consummation of the age (ἔρχομαι in 16:27; 24:44; 25:31). This point is so obvious as to need no verification. What is not so widely acknowledged is that "comings" of this man (or of God or of the reign of heaven) in the future (with respect to the story-time of the Gospel) may refer to events other than the consummation of the age.

The prime example of this occurs in Jesus' answer to the high priest at his trial (26:64). There his reply is, "You said; but I say to you, from now on you will see that this man is sitting at the right hand of power and is coming on the clouds of heaven." A more detailed exegesis of this important utterance will occur in chapter 5. But sufficient for the present point is this assertion. Although some interpreters divide Jesus' reply into two temporally distinct parts, "the session at the right hand of this man" and "the coming on the clouds of heaven of this man,"[138] the more natural understanding[139] of these words is that the two participles are parallel in meaning. That is, the "coming" of this man refers to a manifestation of his power that is to be experienced "from now on," in the time that begins with the utterance of the words to the high priest.[140] The implied reader knows that such "coming" language in Matthew is patient of a flexible range of meaning.[141]

A second example of a future "coming" of this man that does not refer to the consummation of the age occurs at 16:28: "Truly I say to you that there are some of those standing here who will certainly not taste death until they see that this man is coming with his royal power." Again, more detailed treatment will occur in chapter 4. As before, it should be noted that some will understand the clause "until they see that[142] this man is coming with his royal power"[143] as a reference to the Parousia,[144] and thus as (among other things) a restatement of Jesus' words in the preceding verse, 16:27. Preferable, however, is the view that finds (at least a partial) fulfillment of 16:28 within the story of the Gospel itself, especially in light of the concept of "the reign of this man" that is present in Matthew's Gospel and in 16:27 itself.[145] Thus, many commentators see a partial fulfillment of 16:28 in the transfiguration story[146] that follows immediately,[147] while others point to the resurrection of Jesus[148] or to other less likely fulfillments.[149] In the next chapter, I shall offer my own, more detailed interpretation of the coming of this man in 16:28. At this point, suffice it to say that 16:28 stands as another example in Matthew's story of a "coming" of this man in the "future" of the story-time that does not refer to the Parousia at the consummation of the age.

In addition to the "coming" of the reign of God at 6:10, a third passage offers another possible occurrence of a future divine "coming" that is not the Parousia. The passage is 21:40, within the parable of the Wicked Tenants. Henry Alford notes the wording of 21:40, "Therefore, when the lord of the vineyard comes [ὅταν οὖν ἔλθῃ ὁ κύριος τοῦ ἀμπελῶνος], what will he do to those tenants?" The answer from Jesus' opponents serves as a reference to the destruction of those opponents and, by implication[150] (in context with the more explicit parable of the Wedding Feast) of Jerusalem as well. Alford writes of 21:40:

> We may observe that our Lord here makes ὅταν ἔλθῃ ὁ κύριος *coincide with the destruction of Jerusalem*, which is incontestably the overthrow of the wicked husbandmen. This passage forms therefore an important key to our Lord's prophecies, and a decisive justification for those who, like myself, firmly hold that *the coming of the Lord* is in many places to be identified, primarily, with that overthrow.[151]

Notice that to interpret the parable precisely, 21:40 does not refer to a "coming" of this man, but of God. Moreover, I think that Alford overstates the importance of this verse. But the passage can still stand as evidence to show that the Parousia is not always the reference when a future "coming" of God, the reign of heaven, or of this man is foretold.

The Implied Reader and Matthew 10:23:
Summary and Conclusion

From the passages considered (16:28; 21:40; 26:64) and from the entire context of the Gospel,[152] the implied reader will conclude that "the coming of this man" at 10:23b does not necessarily refer to the Parousia. Further, the implied reader understands (in light of the command to hasty flight in 10:23a) that this "coming of this man" will bring a premature termination to the end-time ministry of the Twelve to the cities of Israel. The implied reader knows as well that Jesus has foretold that judgment, in the form of the destruction of Jerusalem and of its temple, will surely come (21:43; 22:7; 24:2). Finally, the implied reader knows that this judgment, following the persecution of Jesus' emissaries (23:34), has a severe temporal limitation. It will come upon "this generation" of Jesus' contemporaries who oppose and reject him (23:36). Armed with this information, the implied reader will understand "the coming of this man" predicted at 10:23 as a reference to the ruin of Jerusalem and the laying waste of the temple that this same Jesus predicts elsewhere, especially in 23:34–39 and 24:2.[153]

After this lengthy discussion of the implied reader's understanding of 10:23, we return to the missionary discourse, in which the implied reader has learned that the Twelve disciples have been empowered for a ministry that offers eschatological salvation for those who receive them and their message (10:11–13b) and results in end-time judgment for those who do not receive them or their message (10:13c–15). This mission activity, commanded within the temporal boundaries of the Gospel, will extend beyond these boundaries into the time after the resurrection of Jesus. The implied reader has learned this about the disciples' mission. The implied reader has not, however, alongside the disciples, been effectively "included" or fully addressed by this discourse.

That changes at 10:24. At this point, by means of "generalizing" language, predominately in the form of "proverbial speech," Jesus begins to address and include the implied reader as fully as the character of "the disciples."[154] The disciples within the story remain the audience of the discourse (cf. second person address, 10:26, 27, 28, 31, 34). At the same time the implied reader receives, as the discourse moves towards its ending, the words of Jesus as addressed also to him or her. No disciple (including the implied reader) is above the master (10:24). If unbelievers have reviled the householder as satanic, so will they regard the servants of the householder, including the implied reader (10:25). The implied reader, along with the disciples in the story, accepts and believes that his or her own faithful response (or lack of it) to Jesus will determine eschatological faith on the last day (10:32–33).[155]

The last verses of the discourse also fully include and address the implied reader (10:37–42). The implied reader, with every disciple of Jesus, hears and accepts the urgent, exclusive call to discipleship and cross-bearing found in

10:37–39. Because the implied reader stands in the time after Jesus' resurrection, during which the Twelve's mission task to the cities of Israel will continue until the "coming" of this man in judgment over Jerusalem and the temple (10:23), the implied reader, along with the Twelve in the story,[156] also hears and receives the comforting words of 10:40–42.

Jesus' words at 10:40–42 do represent a change in subject matter, away from the call to endurance and discipleship. Whereas 10:24–39 are chiefly strong exhortation, verses 40–42 reveal the ultimate significance[157] and meaning of the end-time mission of the Twelve and of the implied reader who stands in the time period when that mission will be carried out. Here at the end of the discourse, Jesus explicitly refocuses his words on the mission itself.[158] His words function to encourage and uplift the disciples (and the implied reader) and to give perspective to the difficulties that they will certainly face.[159] Jesus identifies himself with those whom he has sent[160] and with their eschatological mission of salvation and judgment. Indeed, Jesus links all his missionary disciples[161] with God who first sent Jesus to bring end-time salvation to his people (1:21). Jesus also pronounces, to disciples and the implied reader, the reality of "eschatological response" to the mission and preaching of the disciples. It is in the receiving of the messengers[162] sent by Jesus to proffer end-time salvation that the inhabitants of the cities of Israel will be saved.

At 11:1, the narrator, by means of the integrating formula of the discourse, directs the implied reader back to the story-line of the Gospel. The implied reader is invited to assume that the disciples do, in fact, engage in the mission regarding which the narrator explicitly says, "These twelve Jesus sent and charged them, by saying..." (10:5).[163] But the focus of the story returns to Jesus himself.

THE RISING OPPOSITION TO JESUS (11:2–16:20)

DOUBTS AND OPPOSITION: THE BAPTIST AND "THIS GENERATION"

Indeed, the story begins its focus on an aspect of Jesus' ministry at which the narrative thus far has merely hinted. With 11:2 and the developments that are introduced,[164] the story of the Gospel presents a significant new development. To this point in the story the theme of "end-time response" to Jesus' ministry of word and deed has worked itself out primarily in positive terms. Some have indeed become disciples and begun to receive the blessings of the reign of heaven (5:3). Some have responded in faith to Jesus' eschatological authority and have determined their end-time salvation. Those who reject Jesus, and correspondingly determine their end-time judgment, have remained largely in the background. Their presence and hostile activity are only presaged by the narrative (9:11, 34) or predicted by Jesus' words (7:21–23).

Now the situation changes. Here in the second half (11:2–16:20)[165] of the second major section of the Gospel, the hostility to Jesus emerges with lethal force (12:14). The plot heats up.[166] Jesus' own words to his opponents become more direct and confrontational; he begins to call them "this generation" (11:16; 12:39, 41, 42, 45; 16:4). The theme of "eschatological response" is increasingly emphasized[167] in light of the growing opposition to Jesus. Those who reject him also are sealing their fate of judgment on the last day.

The introduction into the narration of increased hostility and opposition to Jesus comes via the Baptist's question concerning Jesus' identity as the eschatological Christ: "Are you the Coming One, or shall we look for another?" (11:3).[168] Here the narrator reintroduces for the implied reader the theme of John's insufficient understanding of the nature of the reign of heaven that is (hiddenly) present in the time of the story through the words and deeds of Jesus. John's insufficient understanding emerged at Jesus' baptism. At that time, John protested when Jesus came to be baptized by him. Here the narrator starkly contrasts the true perception of Jesus with John's insufficient view by saying, "But when John heard in prison the deeds of the Christ, he sent..." (11:2). The reliable narrator explicitly reminds the implied reader of something which is already clear to him or her: Jesus is the end-time Christ (1:1, 16, 17, 18). John, however, is genuinely in doubt.[169]

The implied reader knows the reason for John's doubt. John's message regarding the Coming One proclaimed chiefly the future judgment. By contrast, Jesus' eschatological ministry has thus far centered in words and deeds that offer salvation.[170] Jesus' own answer to John's question reiterates the salvific character of his ministry (11:4–5). In words that echo the eschatological salvation described by Isaiah,[171] Jesus responds to John's question by affirming what the implied reader already knows, namely that in Jesus' ministry of word[172] and deed the end-time action of God has entered the present time of the Gospel. He is the Coming One of John's preaching of the reign of heaven. In him, the reign of heaven has broken into history.[173]

The concluding statement in Jesus' reply to John's question is significant: "Blessed is the one who does not stumble because of me" (11:6). The reality cannot be changed. But the reality can be rejected. Jesus underscores the crisis of opportunity that has come upon every character in the story of Matthew's Gospel and that also comes to the implied reader. The generalizing, third person makarism of 11:6 reaches out to the implied reader, reminding and offering the eschatological blessing already enunciated by Jesus in the Beatitudes (5:3–10). Those who are enabled to see and accept Jesus' true identity will be blessed, both in the present time of the story and on the last day. But the alternate possibility of "stumbling" over Jesus also exists for all the characters in the story: John;[174] the crowds (13:57); the disciples (26:31–33); and especially the religious leaders (15:12). Those who stumble will "stumble into ruin."[175] The implied reader, however, in whom the intention of the Gospel's story finds its fulfillment, believes and accepts the deeds of Christ as proof that he is the one in whom "the promises of salvation are being realized."[176]

Despite the fact that the crowds follow Jesus around,[177] they are neither disciples nor yet open enemies of Jesus. To them Jesus now turns and he speaks about the true significance of the Baptist. Proper understanding of the nature of John's end-time ministry will lead to proper understanding of Jesus.[178] The implied reader already knows that the narrator has presented John as both a prophetic and an eschatological figure whose appearance fulfills the word of God found in Scripture.[179]

Jesus' three rhetorical questions (11:7–9) intensify his inquiry into the crowds' understanding of John. It is true that the crowds hold John to be a prophet (21:26). This is surely correct, but insufficient.[180] Jesus pushes beyond that understanding to declare that John is more than a prophet. John has an end-time significance. John fulfills the prophecy that promised the coming of the prophet Elijah before the Day of the Lord. The quotation from Mal 3:1[181] mentions not "Elijah" but the eschatological messenger[182] whose function is to prepare the way for the Christ.[183] Regardless, Jesus' own words in Matt 11:14 ("this one is Elijah, the one who is going to come") connect the two passages in Malachi, 3:1 (already quoted) and 3:23, in which the return of Elijah is promised before the Day of the Lord. The eschatological character of the present time of Jesus' ministry could hardly be stated more vigorously. The one prophesied as the forerunner of the Day of the Lord is John, the forerunner of Jesus. In Jesus' present activity, the implied reader understands a partial, hidden manifestation of the Day of the Lord, that is, the eschatological reign of God.[184]

As great as John is, he is only the forerunner of someone greater. This is the force of Jesus' words in 11:11. Jesus here neither censures nor rejects nor excludes John from the reign of heaven.[185] Rather, the comparison, "but the least person in the reign of heaven is greater than he," exalts the importance of entrance into that end-time reign and its blessings that are already present through Jesus' words and deeds.[186] It is true that severe opposition to that reign of heaven[187] has been taking place since John, whose ministry stands astride the turning of the ages,[188] first began to proclaim its present activity (11:12–13). Not all respond in discipleship and faith. The very reign of heaven itself, in its present manifestation, can be resisted and opposed![189]

Jesus' appeal to the crowds in 11:14 ("If you are willing to receive") and his third person, generalizing imperative in 11:15 ("Let the one who has ears hear") speak both to the crowds and to the implied reader. The eschatological day has dawned. Be willing to accept that John is Elijah foretold. He is now the one who is "going to come" (11:14). The future is now. Jesus' quotation of Malachi implies that the Day of the Lord has, in some sense, arrived. The end-time reign of heaven is hidden, yet truly present. Let the one who has ears to hear hear.

For the most part, Jesus' contemporaries do not respond in discipleship and faith to the dawning of the eschatological day of salvation. The implied reader has gained glimpses of opposition to Jesus, hints from earlier in the story (8:12; 9:34). Yet Jesus' words now reveal that "this generation" (11:16)[190] is already turning away from him, just as they turned away from John's message (3:7–11). All of the generations from Abraham to David the king, from David to the Babylonian deportation, and from that deportation to the Christ have led up to this present time of the story (1:2–17).[191] But now, "this generation" pouts, refuses, resists the offer of end-time salvation that is present in Jesus, the Christ, Son of God. They are like whining children[192] who are displeased with the polar opposites of behavior on the part of those about whom they whine. Whereas John came with an ascetic cast ("you did not dance"), Jesus' ministry has been marked by meals with sinners ("you did not beat your breast in grief"). Nevertheless, this generation rejects them both (11:16–19).

Armed with this fuller understanding[193] of how Jesus' ministry is progressing, the implied reader is not surprised at the terms in which Jesus' denunciations of Galilean unbelief are couched (11:20–24). The implied reader knows that response to Jesus has end-time consequences and implications. In view here at 11:20–24 is the temporally indeterminate judgment day and the terrible fate that awaits the inhabitants of the cities that have refused to repent in response to Jesus' end-time words and deeds. In the harshest possible terms, the Galilean cities are weighed against ancient Gentile cities of legendary wickedness[194] and are found wanting. It will be better in "the day of judgment" for Tyre and Sidon than for Chorazin and Bethsaida. As Jesus' home, where unbelief even seemingly limits the number of deeds of power Jesus does (13:58), Capernaum is singled out.[195] In language that echoes Isaiah's taunt and judgment against Babylon (Isa 14:13–15),[196] Jesus pronounces eschatological judgment against Capernaum. Its fate will be worse than that of Sodom on the day of judgment (Matt 11:24). Present response determines eschatological fate. Rejection of Jesus now means destruction on the last day.

There is a striking mood shift at 11:25–30. The change emphasizes further the contrast between the two responses to Jesus' words and deeds. In prayer to his heavenly Father, Jesus acknowledges the crucial, end-time significance of his own present ministry. The implied reader is privileged to hear this prayer. All things, including and especially divine authority[197] (8:9; 9:6; 21:23) to complete his task, have been given to Jesus by the Father. He, in turn, imparts knowledge of the end-time realities now present[198] in his ministry to those whom he wishes: not to hostile sophisticates,[199] but to babes, his disciples. In stark contrast[200] to the harsh words of judgment uttered against those who reject him (11:20–24), Jesus' "missionary call" of 11:28–30 shows him to be a gentle messenger of God's mercy for those who will have the ears to hear. He will, already in the present time, impart knowledge of the Father[201] and give rest to those who come to him.

In this second half of the second major section of the Gospel, however, neither the primary focus of the narrator nor the attention of the implied reader is
directed to those who come to Jesus. Rather, the focus centers on those who
increasingly oppose Jesus and who, because of that opposition, will receive eschatological judgment. The conflict continues to rise in Matthew 12. Although the
religious leaders do not publicly attack Jesus himself in 12:1–8, they do accuse his
disciples: "Behold, your disciples are doing what it is not lawful to do on the
Sabbath!" (12:2). After the confrontation in the synagogue, the narrator's comment accentuates and underscores the extent to which opposition and hostility to
Jesus has now grown: "But the Pharisees went out and took counsel against him,
so that they might destroy him" (12:14). From this point in the story, the irreconcilable hostility to Jesus will remain.[202]

Indeed, the conflict continues to mount in chapter 12. As the narrator and
Jesus himself never tire of repeating, rejection of Jesus' end-time ministry entails
implications of end-time judgment. After Jesus performs exorcisms, and the
crowds hesitantly[203] speculate on his messianic identity (12:23), the religious
leaders repeat their point of view, already mentioned at 9:34. In their view Jesus
performs exorcisms by means of satanic power (12:24). Jesus' retort shows the
nonsensical nature of the evaluation. Why would Satan oppose Satan (12:25–27)?

The other alternative, of course, is that Jesus' exorcisms are performed by the
Spirit of God[204] and thus are signs of God's in-breaking end-time rule (12:28).[205]
If this is so (and the implied reader knows that it is),[206] then the reign of God has
indeed come upon[207] the opponents of Jesus. The eschatological binding of Satan
is already taking place. In utterly unmistakable terms,[208] Jesus declares the present reality and activity of the end-time reign of God.[209]

It is true that the consummation of the age is not yet. Neither is the time of
the consummation in any way indicated. But the consummation will come. And
those who resist and speak against the Spirit of God operative in the ministry of
Jesus will find no forgiveness on that day (12:31–32). Now that opposition to
himself has reached an irreconcilable level, Jesus uses the harsh words of John the
Baptist to denounce the religious leaders. Their request for a present, validating
indication of Jesus' authority is denied.[210] They will be supplied only one validating indication: Jesus' own death and resurrection, referred to cryptically as the
"sign of Jonah."

But Jesus knows it will not be enough for "this generation" who opposes him
(12:41, 42). At the resurrection on the temporally indeterminate last day,[211] his
opponents will be denounced by Gentiles who repented and responded.[212] The
condemnation of Jesus' opponents will be all the more severe, for something
greater than Jonah or Solomon is present in Jesus himself. The fate of this evil
generation, then, will be seven times worse than it is now (12:43–45).

The final pericope (12:46–50) in this long section of mounting conflict and
opposition between Jesus and "this generation" who opposes him (11:2–12:50)

shows the stark contrast between Jesus' opponents and his disciples. The latter, who, by their obedient allegiance to Jesus, perform the will of Jesus' heavenly Father,[213] are Jesus' true family. Thus, the whole of Matthew 11–12 displays "a pattern of interchange which displays Israel's hard-hearted opposition in dramatic relief."[214] Therefore, as the implied reader comes to the third major discourse in the Gospel, he or she knows more fully than ever the urgent reality of "Let the one who has ears hear." Opposition to Jesus' end-time ministry will certainly bring the full judgment of God down upon all who are not with Jesus. Eager to receive all of the eschatological revelation that Jesus has to offer, the implied reader experiences just that in the parables of Matthew 13.

The Implied Reader and the Parables of Matthew 13

Matthew 13 is not, as in the opinion of some, the major dividing point in the plot of the Gospel of Matthew.[215] It is rather an important reinforcement of the theme of "eschatological response" that has already been building in strength, especially since 11:2. There is a change in focus in chapter 13, as Jesus turns away from the crowds and begins to focus his instruction and teaching more fully on the disciples (13:36).[216] Jesus' parabolic instruction in end-time realities includes the truth that the reign of heaven is an already-present, though hidden, reality that is moving towards the time of its consummation.[217] This is not a new realization for implied readers, for they learned at 11:25–27 that Jesus' ministry to "the babes" includes eschatological revelation. But the emphasis is strong here in the seven parables of chapter 13, especially for the implied reader. By means of these "stories within the story," Jesus will fully include and inform the implied reader, even as he addresses those characters in the story who hear his parables.[218]

The parable of the Sower connects the chapter with the foregoing account of the rising opposition to Jesus.[219] Only one portion of the seed that is sown grows and bears fruit. So also are many in Israel in danger of stumbling over Jesus (13:57). The appeal and warning go out to the crowds (13:2); to the disciples (13:10); and to the implied reader: "Let the one who has ears hear!" (13:9, 43). Revelations concerning end-time realities are present. But the crowds are not receptive. For that reason, Jesus speaks to them in parables, and not directly, as to the disciples (13:10–13). For it is those who respond in discipleship to Jesus' end-time ministry who have already begun to receive end-time blessing and to whom the revelation of eschatological mysteries already at work in the world are given. For long years God's people have waited for such revelations. The eschatological blessing ("Blessed are your eyes ... and your ears...," 13:16) is now bestowed on the disciples of Jesus.[220] The word of the reign of heaven has been sown among them, and they have heard the word and understood it (13:23; cf. 7:24, "hear and do").

After telling the parables of the Mustard Seed and the Leaven (13:31–33), which reinforce the reality of the reign of heaven as a present, though hidden, reality,[221] Jesus leaves the crowds and enters the house. There (13:36), Jesus imparts to his disciples the meaning of the parable of the Wheat and the Tares. The parable presents a picture of the present situation, which will continue until the eschatological gathering and separation.[222] Note that the agents of the eschatological action of harvesting are called "harvesters" and not "workers" (cf. 9:37–38), and they are expressly identified as the angels of this man (13:39, 41). Also, the essential action that takes place at the consummation of the age here described is that of separation, of "gathering out" (συλλέξουσιν ἐκ, 13:41).[223] Also, as the parable includes and addresses the implied reader along with the disciples, he or she has heard the words of the master, "Leave them both to grow together until the harvest" (13:30). For the implied reader, the final eschatological separation "belongs to an undisclosed future."[224]

Most noteworthy of all for the implied reader is the reference in Jesus' explanation of the parable to the "reign" of this man (13:41). Some interpreters deny that there is a distinction between the concepts of "the reign of this man" and "the reign of heaven" in Matthew's Gospel.[225] But the reference to the reign of this man at 13:41 is only the first of three such occurrences in the Gospel. The other references are 16:28 ("Until they see that this man is coming with his royal power") and 20:21 ("Say that these two sons of mine may sit on your right and left in your reign"). I have indicated, and shall support more fully in chapter 4, my understanding that both 16:28 and 20:21 refer to events within the story of the Gospel. That is to say, Jesus' "reign" manifests itself even already within the story-time of the Gospel. The parable of the Wheat and the Tares goes beyond that idea. The one who sows the good seed is this man—already, now. Yet, the field in which the seed, both good and bad, is sown is "the world" (13:38). Both the wheat and the tares are to be allowed to grow together until the consummation of the age. The implied reader knows to combine the future perspective in this parable with the parallel reality that, because of and after his resurrection, Jesus will be enthroned in power, especially with respect to his enemies,[226] even before he fully and finally comes to sit on the throne of his glory (19:28; 25:31). Thus, although it is not valid to equate "the reign of this man" either with the world as a place or with the church as a gathering of people, this reign does extend spatially over all humanity and temporally until the consummation of the age. To speak thus of "the reign of this man" is to speak of the present, hidden aspect of the reign of heaven that will go on exerting its influence and growing in the world (cf. the parables of the Mustard Seed and the Leaven, 13:31–33).[227] The implied reader stands in this time of the reign of the Son of Man.

The parable discourse continues with the second set of "double" parables, the Treasure and the Pearl (13:44–46),[228] and ends with the parable of the Dragnet (13:47–50) and the saying about "the scribe trained for the reign of heaven" (13:52). The Dragnet reinforces the message of the Wheat and the Tares, teaching that only after the net is full is it dragged onto shore, and rotten fish are separated from good fish and burned.[229] The implied reader, after learning all of the end-time revelation contained in the parable discourse, also is included as one "discipled" for the reign of heaven (13:52). He or she understands all of the things that Jesus has taught, especially the relationship between the present, hidden reality of the reign of this man, Jesus, and the future, temporally indeterminate consummation of the age. The implied reader has had ears for hearing (13:9, 43).

JESUS' MINISTRY CONTINUES (13:53–16:20)

The narrator effectively returns the implied reader to the flow of the story with the standard reintegrating formula at 13:53. The implied reader understands that the conflict between the reign of heaven and its violent attackers (11:12), those who refuse to have ears for hearing (11:15; 13:9, 43), will characterize the time of the reign of the Son of Man, from the story of the Gospel itself on until the consummation of the age. That conflict continues to unfold in the events that move the second major section of the Gospel (4:17–16:20) forward.

The implied reader watches as the narrator immediately presents the unbelief of the inhabitants of Jesus' hometown. They show their unbelief by naming Jesus not Son of God, but "the son of the carpenter" (13:55). The theme of conflict receives further expression through the account of the death of the Baptist (14:3–12). Herod had him killed, the one who was Elijah, the forerunner of the Christ. The implied reader will look forward also to the death of Jesus, as the denouement of the story.[230] But because the denouement is not to occur until Jesus' death and resurrection, the narrator recounts the withdrawal of Jesus when Jesus hears that Herod is aware of his fame and thought that Jesus was John raised from the dead.[231] After Jesus withdraws, the crowds continue to follow after him, and he continues his ministry of compassion and healing to them. After the feeding of the five thousand (14:15–21), the disciples witness Jesus' walking on the water. Peter believes but then shows little faith in sinking into the waves. Despite the fear and misunderstanding of the disciples (14:26) and Peter's reaction as a "person of little faith" (14:31), the implied reader sees clearly the growing distinction between the crowds and the religious leaders on the one hand and the disciples on the other hand. For the implied reader witnesses the disciples' confession of Jesus in the boat, "Truly you are the Son of God."[232] Even though he or she knows that this confession is still not fully informed (as the disciples' continuing failings in the Gospel's story make clear), the implied reader knows that this is the declaration par excellence of the identity of the end-time Christ: He is the Son of God (3:17; 17:5; 28:19).

From this confession of the disciples, the story returns to opposition to Jesus. At 15:1–11, a controversy with the Pharisees arises.[233] After the controversy the disciples show themselves to be concerned in some way with the Pharisees' point of view (15:12). Jesus responds by emphasizing that eschatological judgment awaits his opponents. They are trees that his Father in heaven did not plant; they will be uprooted (15:13). In contrast to the disciples, whose eyes have seen the eschatological realities already present in Jesus (13:16), the religious leaders are blind guides (15:14). Still, the disciples continue to show their lack of insight, for they understand (15:15–16) neither the "parable" that Jesus has just told them nor the nature of the controversy with the religious leaders.

Even in the face of this hostility on the part of Israel and especially its leaders, Jesus continues to carry out his mission on behalf of that nation which is in the process of rejecting him. Although he grants the request of the Canaanite woman, he tells her that he was not sent except to the lost sheep, namely, the house of Israel (15:24). Jesus continues to heal the crowds who come to him (15:29–31), although he does not teach them. While the disciples again show a lack of faith in the situation with the crowd of four thousand men (plus women and children), Jesus feeds the multitude before dismissing them (15:32–39).

The contrast between disciples and opponents continues into chapter 16. When religious leaders tempt Jesus by seeking a sign from heaven a second time (cf. 12:38), Jesus, in abbreviated fashion, repeats his earlier promise: no sign will occur to validate his authority and reliability except his resurrection from the dead. This repetition reinforces for the implied reader the obduracy and intransigence of the religious leaders.[234] In addition, this oblique reference to Jesus' death and resurrection emphasizes the time and place when and where Jesus' conflict with the religious leaders will finally be resolved.[235] Again, even though the disciples do not understand the nature of the conflict, they do receive and understand Jesus' explanation of the dangers of "the leaven of the Pharisees and Sadducees" (16:5–12).

The concluding pericope (16:13–20) of the Gospel's second major section contains within itself a number of themes that are important to the implied reader. We will highlight two of them. First, the contrast between the disciples and the general populace ("Who do people say this man is?" 16:13) is present. Peter, who represents the group of the disciples as *primus inter pares*,[236] confesses Jesus, by divine revelation, to be the Christ, the Son of the living God (16:16). This confession, which corresponds to the view of the narrator and of God himself (1:1, 16, 17, 18; 3:17), stands in sharpest contrast to the incorrect and inadequate thoughts about Jesus among "people" in general.

Second, also present is the theme of the disciples as recipients of eschatological revelation. As in 13:10–17, Jesus' words to Peter show that the disciples are the recipients of end-time mysteries. Only by means of this revelation from Jesus' heavenly Father can Peter confess Jesus as the Christ, the Son of the living God (16:17).

In addition, not only have the disciples received such revelation, but they also are empowered to offer it to others. The reference to the "keys" of the reign of heaven probably refers to revelation, spiritual insight, which can open for others the way to life.[237] By means of the end-time revelation concerning Jesus as the

Christ, the Son of the living God, Peter and the other disciples will be able to offer to humanity in the present age realities which have already been determined by God for the age to come.[238] With his account of Jesus' command to tell no one yet of his identity as Christ, Son of the living God (16:20), the narrator brings to a close the second major section of the Gospel (4:17–16:20).

At this point, we do well to summarize under five headings the things the implied reader has learned in this portion of the story. First, the voice of the narrator has continued to instruct the implied reader. Jesus' ongoing end-time ministry to the lost sheep, the house of Israel, has the purpose of saving his people from their sins (1:21). Even after the opposition to Jesus has risen to the point of deadly opposition (12:14), the narrator relates how Jesus continues his ministry to Israel, especially to the crowds.

Second, throughout 4:17–16:20, it has been the voice of Jesus that has granted deeper insight to the implied reader concerning the end-time character both of Jesus' own present ministry and of future events beyond the temporal boundaries of the story of the Gospel. Thus, Jesus' own words have reinforced the eschatological nature of both the events related in the Gospel story (12:28) and the events yet to come within that story (6:10).

Third, Jesus' teaching has also revealed and reinforced the theme of "eschatological response" to Jesus' present ministry; that is to say, present response to Jesus determines one's final eschatological fate. Those who become Jesus' disciples receive already in the present time of the story the end-time blessing of the reign of heaven (5:3). And because of this present response, those who hear and do the words of Jesus now will be received into the consummated reign of heaven and experience its full and final blessing on the last day (7:24–27). Until the coming of that last day, the disciples of Jesus are those who have been entrusted with the revelation of end-time mysteries (11:25–27; 13:10–17; 16:17) and most especially with the knowledge that the eschatological reign of heaven is already at work in a real, yet hidden, manner in the ministry of Jesus, the Son of God.

Present response determines fate on that day. This also is true for the opponents of Jesus and all who reject him. In this second major section of the Gospel, the implied reader has witnessed opposition to Jesus, at which the teaching of Jesus and the narration of the story only first hinted (7:24–27; 8:11–12; 9:34). In the second part of this major section, however, the opposition to Jesus in Israel,[239] described as "this generation" (11:16; 12:39, 41, 42, 45; 16:4) and personified in the religious leaders of the people (9:11, 34; 12:2, 14, 24, 38; 15:1; 16:1) has reached a level of lethal intensity. This present response of opposition to Jesus' end-time ministry will receive a corresponding eschatological result, that of condemnation and judgment.

Fourth, the implied reader has learned that this crisis or opportunity of end-time response to Jesus extends also into his or her own time, beyond the end of the story of the Gospel and before the consummation of the age. Although a more precise location of the implied reader within the time period has yet to be discussed,[240] the implied reader has learned through the Missionary Discourse of chapter 10 that the crisis of end-time response extends into his or her own time as well. The activity of working in the end-time harvest among the lost sheep of Israel (10:5–6) will take the Twelve into the time period after the resurrection of Jesus (10:17–23). Also, the implied reader himself or herself is included in this activity by means of the generalizing speech that dominates the third section of the discourse (10:24–42). The mission to Israel is an urgent one, for it is temporally delimited by the predicted "coming" of this man (10:23; 23:36). However, the implied reader knows that the mission to all the nations, under which the mission to Israel is subsumed at 28:18–20, will continue throughout the period of the reign of this man (13:41) and until the consummation of the age (28:20). As the one in whom the intention of the text finds its fulfillment, the implied reader will readily take upon himself or herself a participation in that end-time mission to all the nations.

Fifth, the implied reader will continue to read the story of Matthew's Gospel. Armed as he or she is by information that has hinted at the fate that awaits Jesus at the hands of his opponents (10:38; 12:38–40; 16:4), the implied reader will continue to anticipate the goal and climax of Jesus' end-time ministry to Israel. It will be in Jerusalem that the conflict between Jesus and his enemies reaches its culmination and denouement. It will be against Jerusalem that Jesus also speaks the word of end-time judgment that will result in the ruin of the city and of the temple. This ruin will be God's judgment for their unwillingness to receive Jesus Christ, the Son of God.

NOTES

[1] The issue of the structure of Matthew's Gospel is, of course, widely discussed and debated. I am following the structure elucidated by Kingsbury in *Structure, Christology, Kingdom*, 1–39, and further refined in his later works. Cf. Bauer, *Structure*; Schnackenburg, *Matthäusevangelium 1,1–16,20*, 41; Sabourin, *L'Évangile*, 47.

[2] Philippe Rolland, "From the Genesis to the End of the World: The Plan of Matthew's Gospel," *BTB* 2 (1972): 159.

[3] Howell, *Inclusive*, 201.

[4] Davies and Allison, *Matthew*, 1:404, write that the speech of Jesus in 4:17 acts "to stand over the entire public ministry of Jesus." Cf. Bruner, *Matthew 1–12*, 120.

[5] Anderson, "Over and Over," 72, writes:

> The implied reader reads each episode in the light of the other, in prospect and retrospect. The similarities between the episodes are important in their own right. They engage the implied reader's memory and at times emphasize an aspect of characterization or an element of the plot, etc. However, the similarities are also important because they cause variations between episodes to stand out in relief. The implied reader must account for the variations.

The combination of the two features of (1) the tension between John and Jesus in chapter 3 and (2) Jesus' verbatim repetition of John's words acts to create a "gap" in the story that requires the implied reader to "solve" the problem of how to fit the pieces together; cf. Leitch, *What Stories Are*, 35.

6   Schweizer, *Good News*, 75, says that although the message is identical, John preaches as forerunner and Jesus as fulfiller. This is certainly true as far as it goes. But the proclamation of both is that the (hidden) reality of the reign of heaven is truly present.

7   Recall the discussion from chapter 2, which demonstrated that the phrase ἤγγικεν ... ἡ βασιλεία τῶν οὐρανῶν not only can, but should be translated, "the reign of heaven has arrived."

8   Marie-Joseph Lagrange, *Évangile selon saint Matthieu* (7th ed.; Paris: J. Gabalda, 1948), 69, says: "l'événement déjà inauguré, puisque Jésus commence l'oeuvre du salut." Pertinent in a more sweeping sense is Kingsbury's comment, *Matthew as Story*, 12: "The single most fundamental character trait ascribed to Jesus is the power to save."

9   Luz, *Matthew 1–7*, 197, argues that "not until and only in 11:12 and 12:28 does the reader learn that [the kingdom] begins already now!" In response, I borrow the words of Bruner, *Matthew 1–12*, 122, although he is not specifically discussing this verse. He writes that the kingdom is "both a place ... and a power.... The kingdom is also an activity in time.... The kingdom is the king at least. The kingdom is wherever Jesus is."

10 One can readily demonstrate the complexity of the concept of "the reign of heaven" in Matthew's Gospel. The reign of heaven is said to "approach" or "be present" (3:2; 4:17; 10:7; 12:28). The reign of heaven can be the subject of preaching (4:23; 9:35; 13:11, 19; 24:14). This reign can be "possessed" or "inherited" (5:3, 10; 19:14; 25:34) or taken away from some who formerly possessed it (21:43). The reign of heaven can be entered (5:20; 7:21; 16:19; 18:3; etc.), and persons can be said to be "in" it (5:19, 19; 8:11, 12; 11:11; 13:43; 18:1, 4; 20:21; 26:29).

Temporally, the reign of heaven also exhibits a flexible point of reference. The reign of heaven applies to Israel's past (21:43; cf. 8:12). Cf. Ned Bernard Stonehouse, *The Witness of Matthew and Mark to Christ* (Grand Rapids: Eerdmans, 1944), 229–31. It is clearly in a real sense present already in Jesus' ministry (12:28). However, disciples are to pray for its ongoing "coming" (6:10), and the final experience of its consummation is reserved for the future (25:34). Note Carson's careful study, "The ΟΜΟΙΟΣ Word-Group as Introduction to Some Matthean Parables," *NTS* 31 (1985): 277–82, in which he discerns the specific time-reference for parables on the basis of the tense of the verb in the introductory formulae.

For discussion of the "complexities" of the concept of the reign of heaven in Matthew's Gospel, see the following: Kingsbury, *Structure, Christology, Kingdom*, 128–60; Meier, *Law and History*, 98–99; Davies and Allison, *Matthew*, 1:390; Lagrange, *Évangile*, clvi–clvii.

11 Hagner, "Apocalyptic," 69, says: "Such is the significance of the appearance of the Messiah in history that only apocalyptic language is adequate to describe his coming and work."

12 John's point of view regarding the reign of heaven is not simply "wrong," for the narrator has already informed the implied reader that John's coming fulfills the prophecy of Isaiah (Matt 3:3; cf. Jesus' words at 11:7–15; 21:23–32).

13 Kingsbury, "Sermon," 137.

14 From the vast literature on the Sermon, note Joachim Jeremias, *The Sermon on the Mount* (London: Athlone, 1961); W. D. Davies, *The Setting of the Sermon on the Mount* (Cambridge: Cambridge University Press, 1964); Hans D. Betz, *Essays on the Sermon on the Mount* (trans. L. L. Welborn; Philadelphia: Fortress, 1985); Georg Strecker, *Die Bergpredigt: ein exegetischer Kommentar* (Göttingen: Vandenhoeck & Ruprecht, 1984); Robert Guelich, *The Sermon on the Mount: A Foundation for Understanding*

(Waco: Word, 1982). For bibliography, see Lorin Crawford, "Bibliography for the Sermon on the Mount," *Southwestern Journal of Theology* 35 (1992): 34–38.

15 As obvious as this point may seem, it is intended as a contrast with the common redaction-critical reading which views the discourses in Matthew as essentially "to" the community of the evangelist. In the story of Matthew's Gospel, Jesus is a "private" narrator, who addresses the character of the disciples (Lanser, *Narrative Act*, 138).

16 Recall the kinds of "generalizing" speech, as outlined in chapter 1: 1) lengthy direct discourse; 2) use of the historic present; 3) reference to events in the time beyond the temporal boundaries of the Gospel's story; 4) "timeless," "impersonal," or "inclusive" expressions, such as (especially conditional) relative clauses, expressions with πᾶς, and the use of rhetorical questions; 5) proverbial speech; 6) story-like speech and story-parables; 7) direct address to the implied reader, which the narrator injects directly (and abruptly) into the story-world.

17 Vorster, "Literary Reflections," 208; Rimmon-Kenan, *Narrative Fiction*, 109–10.

18 The "degrees" to which the implied reader is "included" along with the character of "the disciples" can be described as follows:

   1. When Jesus speaks to "the disciples" of events that are in the future time, beyond the story-world's boundaries, the implied reader, who also stands in that general "time beyond the story," is addressed.

   2. When Jesus speaks in generalizing ways to "the disciples" in the story, the implied reader, who is also a disciple, will understand the words as applying also to himself or herself.

   There is a third category of address, which bypasses "the disciples" (or any other character in the story-world) completely and speaks exclusively to the implied reader. Three times the narrator thus speaks (24:15; 27:8; 28:15).

19 Hahn, "Rede," 113.

20 Note the use of substantized participles at 5:4, 6, 10, and the third person address of "those who are poor" or "meek" or "merciful" or "pure" at 5:3, 5, 7, 8.

21 The Beatitudes are primarily pronouncements of "eschatological blessing," although the element of ethical demand is certainly not absent; cf. Davies and Allison, *Matthew*, 1:440; Carson, "Matthew," 131, Gnilka, *Matthäusevangelium*, 1:122; Robert Mounce, *Matthew* (Peabody, Mass.: Hendrickson, 1985), 37; Guelich, *Sermon*, 66. For the Beatitudes as "entrance requirements," see Strecker, *Der Weg*, 157; Bornkamm, "End-Expectation," 16, and Barth, "Matthew's Understanding," 60.

22 Cf. Davies and Allison, *Matthew*, 1:436–38, for an excellent summary of the relationship of the Matthean beatitudes to Isaiah 61.

23 The implied reader of Matthew's Gospel is a disciple of Jesus (Kingsbury, "Reflections," 456).

24 The future passives in 5:4, 6, 7, 9 imply that the deliverance there described will be God's own action and doing.

25 This is the first of many opportunities to note that, in the story of Matthew's Gospel, when Jesus speaks of the final salvation or judgment, he gives absolutely no indication whether that day is near to, or far away from, the time of the story of the Gospel.

26 I cannot but side with those who take the explicit present tense, "theirs *is*" at 5:3, 10, with all seriousness; cf. Schweizer, *Good News*, 81; Ladd, *Presence*, 202–3. Carson, "Matthew," 132, writes that, whereas the primary sense of the beatitudes is future, "the present tense 'envelope' (vv. 3, 10) should not be written off as insignificant.... Matthew must have meant something when he chose *estin* ('is') instead of *estai* ('will be')."

Those who give a consistently future orientation to all the Beatitudes include Filson, *Matthew*, 77; Beasley-Murray, *Jesus and the Kingdom of God*, 165–66; Luz, *Matthew 1–7*, 235; Pamment, "The Kingdom of Heaven," 213.

The genitive pronouns, "theirs" (5:3, 10), are then taken as genitives of possession; cf. John P. Meier, *Matthew* (Wilmington: Michael Glazier, 1980), 40; Mounce, *Matthew*, 39. Probably the sense is that the *blessings* of the reign of heaven are already, in some real but hidden sense, the property of Jesus' disciples.

27 Hagner, "Apocalyptic," 73.

28 For the Lord's Prayer as completely dominated by future eschatological thinking, see Raymond E. Brown, "The Pater Noster as an Eschatological Prayer," in *New Testament Essays* (Milwaukee: Bruce, 1965), 217–53.

29 Beasley-Murray, *Jesus and the Kingdom of God*, 151: cf. Bruner, *Matthew 1–12*, 243; Brown, "Pater Noster," 237–38; Erich Grässer, *Das Problem der Parusieverzögerung in den synoptischen Evangelien und in der Apostelgeschichte* (Berlin: Verlag Alfred Töpelmann, 1957), 97. See especially Birger Gerhardsson, "The Matthean Version of the Lord's Prayer (Matt 6:9b–13): Some Observations," in vol. 1 of *The New Testament Age: Essays in Honor of Bo Reicke* (ed. William C. Weinrich; Macon, Ga.: Mercer University Press, 1984), 207–20.

30 Caird, *Language*, 29; cf. Brown, "Pater Noster," 229, 231; Davies and Allison, *Matthew*, 1:602; Gnilka, *Matthäusevangelium*, 1:218.

31 Guelich, *Sermon*, 310; Schweizer, *Good News*, 152.

32 Brown, "Pater Noster," 217–18; Beasley-Murray, *Jesus and the Kingdom of God*, 152.

33 Brown, "Pater Noster," 232; Gerhardsson, "Version," 209–11; Guelich, *Sermon*, 289.

34 Carson, "Matthew," 170; cf. also Schweizer, *Good News*, 152; Gnilka, *Matthäusevangelium*, 1:220; Schnackenburg, *Matthäusevangelium 1,1–16,20*, 65; Davies and Allison, *Matthew*, 1:603–4; Mounce, *Matthew*, 56–57.

35 Luz, *Matthew 1–7*, 377–80.

36 Beasley-Murray, *Jesus and the Kingdom of God*, 151.

37 The noun "temptation" occurs in Matthew's Gospel only in the Lord's Prayer (6:13) and in Jesus' words to Peter, James, and John in the garden, "Watch and pray, so that you may not enter into temptation" (26:41).

Also in Matthew's story, the phrase ποιεῖν τὸ θέλημα τοῦ πατρός μου refers to the obedience of the disciples at 7:21; 12:50 (cf. 21:31). However, the prayer that God would cause his will to occur (γενηθήτω τὸ θέλημά σου) is found only and identically in the Lord's Prayer (6:10b) and in the Garden (26:42).

38 Brown, "Pater Noster", 236; Gnilka, *Matthäusevangelium*, 1:221.

39 Davies and Allison, *Matthew*, 1:660, say: "The kingdom, being God's sovereign rule which will reach its climax at the consummation, is already present (in Jesus) and one should make it his first concern to belong to it in the here and now, to come into its sphere of working." Cf. Ladd, *Presence*, 137.

40 Carson, "Matthew," 189, argues that "entrance through the gate into the narrow way of persecution begins *now* but issues in the consummated kingdom at the other end of that way.... The narrow gate is not thereby rendered superfluous; instead, it confirms that even the beginning of this path to life is restrictive. Davies and Allison, *Matthew*, 1:697–98, note this exegesis but reject it.

41 The fruit of prophets is their teaching, by which they can be known as false prophets. For a similar warning against false teaching, note Matt 16:5–12.

[42] In Matthew's Gospel, "to enter into the reign of heaven" (5:20; 7:21; 18:3; 19:23, 24; 23:13), as well as "to enter into life" (18:8, 9; 19:17; cf. also 7:13; 25:21, 23), refers to the final experience of the consummated reign of God at the end of time.

See Gerhard, Delling, "ἡμέρα," *TDNT* 2:951, for contemporary Jewish usage of "day"; cf. Davies and Allison, *Matthew*, 1:714. In Matthew, "that day" occurs at 7:22 and 26:29; "day of judgment" occurs at 10:15; 11:22, 24; 12:36; and "day" occurs at 24:42, all with reference to judgment day.

[43] Carson, "Word-Group," 279; cf. Luz, *Matthew 1–7*, 453; Schweizer, *Good News*, 109–10; Davies and Allison, *Matthew*, 1:720.

[44] Wolthuis, "Experiencing," 269, says: "The division between the disciples of Jesus who carry out his service and those who are not his disciples is taking place now in this life. At the coming of the Son of Man in glory the consequences of this division will be meted out." Cf. Bauer, *Structure*, 119; Carson, "Matthew," 188; Guelich, *Sermon*, 413.

[45] The religious leaders function in the Gospel as "false prophets" (16:5–12). In view of 24:11, 24, however, "false prophets" at 7:15 most likely points beyond the temporal boundaries of Matthew's story.

[46] Note also that there is a conspicuous lack of second person plural address to the character of the disciples in 7:21–28. The distinction between "disciples" and the implied reader is completely removed.

[47] Rimmon-Kenan, *Narrative Fiction*, 92; Kingsbury, *Matthew as Story*, 110.

[48] Meier, *Law and History*, 40.

[49] Kingsbury, "Sermon," 132; Wolthuis, "Experiencing," 167.

[50] Schnackenburg, *Matthäusevangelium 1,1–16,20*, 74, says: "Das Kriterium für das Gute is das Sich-Abmühen, das Frucht-Bringen, das Tun des Willens Gottes bzw. *der Worte Jesu*" (emphasis added).

[51] Rolland, "Genesis," 161, comments on "the dramatic progression" that is effected in Matthew's story by 7:24–27. Along with 9:34, the parable of the Two Builders "is a signal of the drama which is about to unfold."

[52] David Bauer has fully discussed this issue, focusing especially on the way that the concluding formulae act to connect the discourses to the narratives that follow them; cf. Bauer, *Structure*, 129–34.

[53] France, *Evangelist*, 155.

[54] Lanser, *Narrative Act*, 139.

[55] Herbert Weir Smyth, *Greek Grammar* (rev. Gordon M. Messing; Cambridge, Mass.: Harvard University Press, 1956), § 2086, notes:

> With participles of cause or purpose, etc.: ... This particle [ὡς] sets forth the ground of belief on which the agent acts, and denotes the thought, assertion, real or presumed intention, in the mind of the subject of the principal verb or of some other person mentioned prominently in the sentence, without implicating the speaker or writer.

[56] Kingsbury, *Structure, Christology, Kingdom*, xxii.

[57] There is an explicit focus on the response of the crowds at 7:28–29. Implicit, however, is the theme of the rejection of Jesus by Israel's religious leaders, for the crowds specifically contrast Jesus' authoritative teaching and the teaching of their scribes.

[58] For a summary discussion of the structuring options, see Davies and Allison, *Matthew*, 2:1–5.

59 Wilhelm Michaelis, "λέπρα, λεπρός," *TDNT* 4:233. Note that in 11:5 "lepers are being cleansed" is one of the indications that Jesus is, in fact, the Coming One.

60 Stonehouse, *Witness*, 231, cites 8:12 as evidence that the reign of heaven is not a completely new reality but was present in Israel before the coming of Jesus.

61 On this verse as a warning of judgment to Israel, see Marcellus Kik, *Matthew Twenty-Four* (Philadelphia: Presbyterian and Reformed, 1948), 18. Beasley-Murray, *Jesus and the Kingdom of God*, 172, writes: "The shock of this saying is difficult for us to imagine."

62 France, *Evangelist*, 212, notes that in the OT parallels to "gathering from east and west" it is Israel who is gathered back from exile.

63 Again, the implied reader learns of how flexibly end-time language can function. At 8:12, "sons of the reign" means "Israelites who, tragically, don't enter into the end-time banquet with the patriarchs." At 13:38 the same phrase means "the good seed," that is, "the disciples of Jesus"; cf. Carson, "Matthew," 326.

64 Much of the discussion over the import of "Son of Man" has focused upon the historical Jesus. For discussions, see H. E. Tödt, *The Son of Man in the Synoptic Tradition* (London: SCM Press, 1965); Chris C. Caragounis, *The Son of Man: Vision and Interpretation* (Tübingen: J. C. B. Mohr, 1986); R. Bultmann, *Theology of the New Testament* (trans. K. Grobel; New York: Charles Scribner's Sons, 1951), 1:26–32; Seyoon Kim, *The "Son of Man" as the Son of God* (Grand Rapids: Eerdmans, 1985). For a helpful summary, see Beasley-Murray, *Jesus and the Kingdom of God*, 219–30.

65 Cf. Maurice Casey, *The Son of Man: The Interpretation and Influence of Daniel 7* (London: SPCK, 1979); William Horbury, "The Messianic Associations of 'The Son of Man,' " *JTS*, New Series, 36 (1985): 34–55; T. W. Manson, "The Son of Man in Daniel, Enoch, and the Gospels," *BJRL* 32 (1949–50): 171–93; C. F. D. Moule, *The Origin of Christology* (London: Cambridge University Press, 1977), 11–22.

The significance and influence of *1 Enoch* 37–81 (the Similitudes) depends on the date assigned to this section of the composite Enoch literature. Scholars seem reluctant to date the Similitudes in the pre-Christian era; cf. Charlesworth, "Concept," 207, who places their origin at the same time as the origins of Christianity.

66 The champion of this position has been Geza Vermes. See "The 'Son of Man' Debate," *JSNT* 1 (1978): 19–32; *Jesus the Jew: A Historian's Reading of the Gospels* (Philadelphia: Fortress, 1973), 160–91. For the "conversation" among Aramaists, see also Matthew Black, "Jesus and the Son of Man," *JSNT* 1 (1978): 4–18; Joseph A. Fitzmyer, "Another View of the 'Son of Man' Debate," *JSNT* 4 (1979): 58–68.

67 See Horbury, "Messianic Associations."

68 I. Howard Marshall, "Son of Man," in *Dictionary of Jesus and the Gospels* (ed. Joel B. Green, Scot McKnight, and I. Howard Marshall; Downers Grove, Ill.: InterVarsity, 1992), 780; Carson, "Matthew," 212; Allison, *End of the Ages*, 128–29; France, *Evangelist*, 290.

69 "Son of Man" occurs thirty times in Matthew's Gospel: 8:20; 9:6; 10:23; 11:19; 12:8, 32, 40; 13:37, 41; 16:13, 27, 28; 17:9, 12, 22; 19:28; 20:18, 28; 24:27, 30, 37, 39, 44; 25:31; 26:2, 24, 45, 64.

70 Note the pronouns at 4:19; 5:11; 7:24, 26. Note also the first person singular verbs, such as "I say to you," at 5:17, 20, 22, etc.

71 Kingsbury, "Probe," 31–32. For objections and rebuttal, see Hill, "Response," 37–52; Kingsbury, "Rejoinder," 61–81.

Regarding this "prism" on the "the Son of Man" sayings in Matthew, note the following categorization of usage:

     1. Outsiders addressed or referenced: 8:20; 16:13.

     2. Opponents addressed or referenced: 9:6; 11:19; 12:8, 32, 40; 26:64. Included here is also probably 13:37, where the Son of Man, the one who sows the good seed, stands in stark contrast to "the enemy [the devil] who sows the bad seed" (13:39).

     3. Reference either to Jesus' passion or resurrection: 12:40; 16:28 (see the discussion in chapter 4 for support); 17:9, 12, 22; 20:18, 28; 26:2, 24, 45.

     4. Reference to judgment, visited either in history or on the last day: 10:23; 13:41; 16:27; 19:28; 24:27, 30, 37, 39, 44; 25:31; 26:64.

[72] Kingsbury, *Matthew as Story*, 96–103. Persuasive are these four points: 1) "Son of Man" never occurs in a "predication formula," in contrast with other "titles" such as "Son of David" (12:23) or "Son of God" (26:63); 2) no character in the story ever "reacts" to Jesus' use of the phrase; 3) "Son of Man" does not occur in 1:1–4:16, where the narrator is most powerfully identifying "who Jesus is"; and 4) in 16:13–16, to posit a "titular" sense to "Son of Man" would turn Jesus' first question ("Who do people say 'the Son of Man' is?") into nonsense, for Jesus would be answering his own question.

[73] Kingsbury, *Matthew as Story*, 99–100.

[74] This is a good opportunity to restate the conviction that the "implied reader" is not a naive or first-time reader. Indeed, the implied reader is only able to understand the import of Jesus' self-designation ὁ υἱὸς τοῦ ἀνθρώπου after repeated readings of the Gospel's story. The narrator apparently expects this of the implied reader, for the first use of "this man" on Jesus' lips occurs abruptly, with no form of explanation or interpretive key.

[75] William G. Thompson, "Reflections on the Composition of MT 8:1–9:34," *CBQ* 33 (1971): 375; Davies and Allison, *Matthew*, 2:81; Beare, *Matthew*, 218.

[76] Jack D. Kingsbury, "Observations on the 'Miracle Chapters' of Matthew 8–9," *CBQ* 40 (1978): 571; cf. Farmer, "The Kingdom of God," 128.

[77] For an extensive narrative-critical analysis of the religious leaders in Matthew's Gospel, see Powell, "Religious Leaders."

[78] Wolthuis, "Experiencing," 247–48; Powell, "Religious Leaders," 64. Carson, "Matthew," 234, notes the imperfect tense at 9:34 (ἔλεγον). He conjectures that this "may imply that the ferment was constantly in the background." In view of the preliminary and undeveloped nature of the conflict, and of the full-blown Beelzebul controversy in chapter 12, it would be better to give the imperfect an inceptive sense; here, at this point in the story, they only "began to say."

[79] Many note that there is no evidence in the Jewish sources that shows the Messiah to be compared to a bridegroom; cf. Ladd, *Presence*, 210–11. However, since the messianic age was at times compared to a wedding feast (Ladd, *Presence*, 211; Davies and Allison, *Matthew*, 2:110), Jesus' words reveal the presence, through his own ministry, of the messianic age.

[80] Filson, *Matthew*, 120; Carson, "Matthew," 227. Beare, *Matthew*, 229, writes: "This is realized eschatology if it is to be found anywhere!"

[81] A probable reference to Jesus' suffering and death; cf. Beasley-Murray, *Jesus and the Kingdom of God*, 142; Beare, *Matthew*, 229.

[82] Note also the "flexible" usage of the image of the wedding feast by comparing the parables of the wedding feast (22:1–14) and the ten maidens (25:1–13). In the former, the wedding feast for the Son has begun. In the latter, the wedding feast has not begun, because the bridegroom has not yet arrived.

83 Bauer, *Structure*, 90.

84 For a thorough narrative-critical analysis of the Missionary Discourse in Matthew's Gospel, see Dorothy Jean Weaver, *Matthew's Missionary Discourse: A Literary Critical Analysis*, JSNTSup 38 (Sheffield: Sheffield Academic Press, 1990).

85 Cf. Davies and Allison, *Matthew*, 2:147, for the messianic significance of "shepherd" in the first century. For the "shepherd/sheep" motif in Matthew, see John P. Heil, "Ezekiel 34 and the Narrative Strategy of the Shepherd and Sheep Metaphor in Matthew," *CBQ* 55 (1993): 698–708.

86 Cf. Friedrich Hauck, "θερίζω, θερισμός," *TDNT* 3:132–33; Box, *Matthew*, 173; Schweizer, *Good News*, 234. For "harvest" as a time of salvation, see Blaine Charette, "A Harvest for the People? An Interpretation of Matthew 9:37f.," *JSNT* 38 (1990): 29–35; Schnackenburg, *Matthäusevangelium 1,1–16,20*, 90.

87 Carson, "Matthew," 235.

88 In Matthew's story, "workers" are "disciples in the time *before* the consummation of the age"; cf. 10:10; 20:1, 2, 8. Along with 9:37–38, these are the only occurrences of the term in Matthew's Gospel.

89 Those who err and miss the crucial distinction between "workers" and "reapers" include Morna D. Hooker, "The Prohibition of Foreign Missions (Mt 10:5–6)," *ExpTim* 82 (1970–1971): 361–65; Schweizer, *Good News*, 234.

90 This is the second instance of an "abrupt" narrative technique, noted already at 3:12–13. Recall that the technique is that of a prediction or reference to a future event, followed by its immediate fulfillment or occurrence. The purpose for emphasizing the use of this technique by the narrator of Matthew's story is that it will have interpretive significance at 16:28.

91 I take the genitive as epexegetical.

92 Cf. Kingsbury, "Reflections," 452.

93 Hooker, "Prohibition," 363; Beare, *Matthew*, 242; Schnackenburg, *Matthäusevangelium 1,1–16,20*, 91.

94 Recall the demonstration in chapter 2 that this is the best translation for ἤγγικεν ... ἡ βασιλεία τῶν οὐρανῶν at 3:2 and 4:17.

95 Ladd, *Presence*, 256.

96 Filson, *Matthew*, 130; David Garland, *Reading Matthew: A Literary and Theological Commentary on the First Gospel* (New York: Crossroad, 1993), 113–14.

97 Davies and Allison, *Matthew*, 2:176.

98 Weaver, *Missionary Discourse*, 18; Luz, "The Disciples," 120.

99 The only example of "generalizing" language that could more directly address and include the implied reader is 10:22b: "And the one who endures to the end will be saved." By contrast, note the way that the discourse, starting with 10:24, begins, through more "generalized" language, to address the implied reader. Matt 10:24–25 is proverbial in character. Matt 10:26a includes second person address to the disciples in the story, followed by proverbial speech in 10:26b. The repeated commands regarding "fearing" and "not fearing" are linked to timeless realities about the power of human opponents in contrast to the power of God (10:28–29). And so the discourse continues to its end. This shift to more generalized speech is recognized by Charles H. Giblin, "Theological Perspective and Matthew 10:23b," *TS* 29 (1968): 643: "In the third major section (10:24–42) warnings and assurances are more clearly widened to encompass all disciples."

[100] William G. Thompson, "An Historical Perspective in the Gospel of Matthew," *JBL* 93 (1974): 253.

[101] Weaver, *Missionary Discourse*, 94; Beare, *Matthew*, 245.

[102] There is no need, indeed, no demand to take "until the end" at 10:22b as a reference to the consummation of the age. The proverb only takes this meaning when 10:23b is interpreted as a reference to the Parousia. Many, of course, do interpret 10:22b in this way; cf. Gnilka, *Matthäusevangelium*, 1:378; Gundry, *Matthew*, 194–95. Craig Blomberg, *Matthew*, The New American Commentary (Nashville: Broadman, 1992), 175, notes that "to the end" means "for the duration of the hostility however it may end."

[103] For a thorough history of the interpretation of this passage, see Martin Künzi, *Das Näherwartungslogion Matthäus 10,23: Geschichte seinen Auslegung* (Tübingen: J. C. B. Mohr, 1970). For a brief summary and discussion of interpretive options, see Beasley-Murray, *Jesus and the Kingdom of God*, 285–86.

[104] Powell, "Expected," 32–33.

[105] The features that receive the most "flexible" treatment at the hands of interpreters include the phrases "you will certainly not complete," "the cities of Israel," and "until the Son of Man comes." See further in the discussion for examples.

[106] Scot McKnight, "Jesus and the End-Time: Matthew 10:23," in *SBLSP, 1986* (ed. Kent Richards; Atlanta: Scholars Press, 1986), 502, quotes C. F. D. Moule, *The Birth of the New Testament* (3d ed.; London: Adam & Charles Black, 1981), 127–28. Moule, after discussing the options for interpreting the referent of "until the Son of Man comes" in 10:23, concludes, "None of these is easy to believe."

[107] Grässer, *Problem*, 82, views Matt 24:36 ("but concerning that day and hour, no one knows") as a purposeful "renunciation" of the near-expectation in the sayings of Jesus at 10:23; 16:28; 24:34.

[108] For redaction-critical agreement, see Sabourin, *L'Évangile*, 139; Davies and Allison, *Matthew*, 2:192; Strecker, *Der Weg*, 42–44; John McDermott, "Matt 10:23 in Context," *BZ*, New Series, 28 (1984): 232; McKnight, "Jesus and the End-Time," 514.

[109] From a narrative-critical point of view, it is invalid to ask the question using the phrase "limited to the life span of the *implied reader*" for the following reasons. First, it cannot be determined with exact precision where, in the time period between the resurrection and the consummation of the age, the implied reader in fact stands, although this question will be addressed in the treatment of 24:15 in chapter 6 of this book. Second, as has been shown with regard to 10:23, if it is true that the implied reader is being addressed or included, it is also (and more directly) true that the twelve disciples, as characters in the story, are the primary audience of the address. Thus, the saying in 10:23 has to "make sense" to the Twelve first, and the implied reader cannot be "substituted" for the Twelve as audience.

[110] Recall the insight, first enunciated in chapter 1, that story-like speech and story-parables, because they act to create their own "world within the story-world," act to blur the boundaries between implied reader and the characters in the story to whom the speech is addressed, thus more fully addressing the implied reader. Thus, in 24:48, 25:5, and 25:19 Jesus tells the *implied reader* that, also from his or her temporal position between the resurrection of Jesus and the consummation of the age, it will be a long time before the master returns.

[111] I owe this observation to Marcus Borg, "A Temperate Case for a Non-Eschatological Jesus," *Forum* 2 (1986): 91. For the same point, see Werner G. Kümmel, *Promise and Fulfillment: The Eschatological Message of Jesus* (Naperville, Ill.: Alec R. Allenson, 1957), 44.

112 Cf. Sabourin, "You Will Not," 9; Strecker, *Der Weg*, 43; Schnackenburg, *Matthäus-evangelium 1,1–16,20*, 95.

113 On this point, see the discussion below of both 28:19 and 24:9, 14.

114 Some interpreters, who emphasize the change in mission scope at 28:18–20, operate with a logical syllogism as follows:

1. Matt 10:23 says the Twelve will not finish the cities of Israel until the Son of Man comes.

2. Matt 28:18 brings an end to the limitation of the mission to the cities of Israel.

3. Therefore, the "coming of the Son of Man" to which 10:23 refers is the resurrection of Jesus.

Modern examples of this understanding, first put forth by Ephraem the Syrian in the fourth century (Künzi, *Näherwartungslogion Matthäus 10,23*, 23), include (cautiously) Sabourin, *L'Évangile*, 139; Meier, *Matthew*, 111.

The syllogism fails, however, in view of the words of Jesus in Matthew 10 that have led up to 10:23. Therein Jesus describes persecutions and difficulties that point to a time period beyond the story-time of the Gospel (10:17–20), after the resurrection of Jesus. The termination of the mission cannot come before the events that character-ize its ongoing activity!

115 So Kingsbury, "Reflections," 458.

116 Wolthuis, "Experiencing," 315, simply extends the force of 10:23 to include the uni-versal mission given at 28:18–20. Giblin, "Theological Perspective," 658, claims that "cities of Israel" stands for "those to whom Jesus himself has come," and this includes the Gentiles; cf. Schweizer, *Good News*, 244; McDermott, "Matt 10:23 in Context," 235; Gnilka, *Matthäusevangelium*, 1:379.

117 Note well the words of Jesus at 21:43: "On account of this I say to you that the reign of God will be taken from you and given to a *nation* which produces its fruits." Thus, it is not Israel, composed of Israelites, which is rejected. Rather, the nation of Israel loses its salvation-historical primacy as a result of the rejection of Jesus as the Son of God ("Last he sent to them his son," 21:37).

118 Daniel Marguerat, *Le Jugement dans l'Évangile de Matthieu* (Labor et Fides Editeurs, 1981), 363, says that these envoys are, "above all," missionaries.

119 This does not, as Marguerat, *Jugement*, 366, thinks, refer to "Matthew's church."

120 McKnight, "Jesus and the End-Time," 517; Lagrange, *Évangile*, 205.

121 A. L. Moore, *The Parousia in the New Testament* (Leiden: E. J. Brill, 1966), 144.

122 Giblin, "Theological Perspective," 646; Sabourin, "You Will Not," 6; Grässer, *Problem*, 137.

123 Cf. Giblin, "Theological Perspective," 658.

124 Schweizer, *Good News*, 244; McDermott, "Matt 10:23 in Context," 235; Gnilka, *Matthäusevangelium*, 1:379. To be rejected also is the view exemplified by Blom-berg, *Matthew*, 176, who thinks that 10:23b is "a reference to the perpetually incomplete Jewish mission." This view founders on the strong element of "haste" present in 10:23.

125 Giblin, "Theological Perspective," 638, is quite correct in rejecting as "a mistranslation" those English versions that render the conjunction "before." When used as a temporal conjunction, ἕως does not, according to the standard lexica, ever mean "before."

126 The particle also functions as a preposition twenty-five times in Matthew's Gospel.

127 The construction ἕως ὅτου + present indicative at Matt 5:25 means "while."

128 In Matthew, ἕως is used absolutely, with indicatives following, at 2:9 and 24:39. It is used absolutely, with the aorist subjunctive following, at 18:30. (Note the variant reading that includes οὗ, supported strongly by D, W, Θ, families 1 and 13, and most other texts). Also used by Matthew to mean "until" are ἕως οὗ (with aorist indicative, 1:25 and 13:33; with aorist subjunctive, 14:22; 17:9; 18:34; and 26:36) and ἕως ἄν (always with aorist subjunctive, 2:13; 5:18, 26; 10:11, 23; 12:20; 16:28; 22:44; 23:39; 24:34).

129 Giblin, "Theological Perspective," 646–47. Giblin includes in his listing all the instances in the NT.

130 Note that there is a virtually identical meaning at 18:30, 34, two sentences that fall into Giblin's category 3, with positive main clauses. There is no real difference of meaning between "He cast him into prison until he should pay what was owed" (18:30, 34) and "You will not get out of prison until you pay what is owed" (5:26).

131 Since 10:23 in its context shows no signs of being a word of Jesus that bypasses "the disciples," the temporal limitation imposed on the mission of the Twelve to Israel refers to an event that will happen within the lifetime of the Twelve.

132 Beasley-Murray, *Jesus and the Kingdom of God*, 286; McKnight, "Jesus and the End-Time," 520; Davies and Allison, *Matthew*, 2:190; Theodor Zahn, *Das Evangelium des Matthäus* (Leipzig: A. Deichert, 1903), 405; Schniewind, *Evangelium*, 131.

133 Kingsbury, "Reflections," 458.

134 Moore, *Parousia*, 145–46, is certainly wrong in denying a "delimitation" at 10:23. Incredibly, he says that "we conclude that there is *no* necessary delimited expectation here."

135 Contrast this with 16:27, where a future "coming" (μέλλω ἔρχεσθαι) of this man is further described with the words "in the glory of his Father with his angels, and then he will give to each person according to his deed." In similar manner, 25:31 describes the day when this man "comes" (ἔρχομαι) "in his glory and all the angels with him, then he will sit on his glorious throne."

136 For a major form-critical study of "coming" sayings, see Eduardo S. M. Arens, *The ΗΛΘΟΝ-Sayings in the Synoptic Tradition: A Historico-Critical Investigation* (Göttingen: Vandenhoeck & Ruprecht, 1976).

137 Moore, *Parousia*, 145, is in error when he writes that the meaning of "the coming of this man" at 10:23 is "too distinctive to allow for a meaning other than the Parousia."

138 Filson, *Matthew*, 283; Sabourin, *L'Évangile*, 359; Stonehouse, *Witness*, 242. Craig Evans, "In What Sense Blasphemy? Jesus before Caiaphas in Mark 14:61–64," in *SBLSP, 1991* (ed. Eugene H. Lovering Jr.; Atlanta: Scholars Press, 1991), 220–21, argues that Matt 26:64, with the background of God's divine chariot as the throne on which the Son of Man is seated, combines elements of Psalm 110 and Daniel 7. This, he thinks, explains the combination of "sitting" and "coming" at 26:64.

139 The temporal marker in 26:64, "from now on," modifies the main verb, "you will see," and most naturally fully applies to the direct object of the verb, "this man." The two present tense, predicate-position participles express indirect discourse (Stanley E. Porter, *Idioms of the Greek New Testament*, Biblical Languages: Greek 2 (Sheffield: Sheffield Academic Press, 1992), 274; BDF, § 416; W. Goodwin, *A Greek Grammar* (repr., New York: St. Martin's Press, 1987), ¶ 1494.

140 Barnabas Lindars, *Jesus Son of Man: A Fresh Examination of the Son of Man Sayings in the Gospels in the Light of Recent Research* (London: SPCK, 1983), 121, says, "But *from*

now on his status will be visible, and the proof of his power to judge and to save will be available. Thus the resurrection, as proof of the heavenly *session*, guarantees the parousia." Cf. Caird, *Language*, 252; France, *Evangelist*, 315; Giblin, "Theological Perspective," 652; Sabourin, "You Will Not," 11.

[141] One should also note that the "sitting" of this man, Jesus, in Matthew's Gospel also has a diversity of reference. It refers to the Parousia in 19:28 and 25:31. On the other hand, the exalted status of Jesus, in the time after his resurrection and before the Parousia, is also spoken of as his "sitting" (cf. 22:24; 26:64). Finally, I will argue in chapter 4 that in the request of the mother of Zebedee's sons, "Say that these two sons of mine may sit [καθίσωσιν], one on your right and one on your left, in your reign" (20:21), and in Jesus' reply, "But to sit [τὸ δὲ καθίσαι] on my right and on [my] left is not mine to give, but [it is] for those prepared by my Father" (20:23), this "sitting in Jesus' reign" is fulfilled at the crucifixion.

[142] Here also the construction ἴδωσιν τὸν υἱὸν τοῦ ἀνθρώπου ἐρχόμενον is understood as expressing indirect discourse.

[143] Cf. Meier, *Matthew*, 188, for this translation. Similarly, Anton Vögtle, "Das christologische und ekklesiologische Anliegen von Mt. 28,18–20," in *Papers Presented to the Second International Congress on New Testament Studies Held at Christ Church, Oxford, 1961*, vol. 2 of *Studia Evangelica* (ed. F. L. Cross; Berlin: Akademie-Verlag, 1964), 287; Robert G. Bratcher, *A Translator's Guide to the Gospel of Matthew*. Helps for Translators (London: United Bible Societies, 1981), 207; Carson, "Matthew," 381; Zahn, *Evangelium*, 552; Newman and Stine, *Translator's Handbook*, 549; Herman Ridderbos, *The Coming of the Kingdom* (ed. Raymond O. Zorn; trans. H. de Jongste; Philadelphia: Presbyterian and Reformed, 1962), 503. This translation is demanded by the awkwardness of imagining this man coming "in" his own kingdom.

[144] Filson, *Matthew*, 190; Box, *Matthew*, 268; Grässer, *Problem*, 130.

[145] Wolthuis, "Experiencing," 314; Giblin, "Theological Perspectives," 651; Lagrange, *Évangile*, 333.

[146] Frye, "The Jesus of the Gospels," 80–81; Meier, *Matthew*, 190; Kingsbury, *Matthew as Story*, 92; Davies and Allison, *Matthew*, 2:675–76; Schnackenburg, *Matthäusevangelium 16,21–28,20*, 161; Chilton, *God in Strength*, 261.

[147] As I have noted in the discussion of 3:11–13 and 9:38–10:1, the narrator of Matthew's Gospel at times offers immediate, even "abrupt" fulfillments of predictions that take place within the course of the story. The fourth example of this technique occurs at 26:2–3.

[148] Wolthuis, "Experiencing," 315; Stonehouse, *Witness*, 240.

[149] Alford, *Matthew*, 177, and Sabourin, *L'Évangile*, 228, refer the "coming of this man" in 16:28 to the destruction of Jerusalem. Box, *Matthew*, 268, and Guthrie, *Theology*, 798, include Pentecost. This is hardly permissible from a narrative-critical perspective, since the Pentecost account occurs only in a different story, that of Luke-Acts.

[150] Kingsbury, "Husbandmen," 645.

[151] Alford, *Matthew*, 216–17.

[152] After this lengthy discussion of 10:23, it is appropriate to recall that, for narrative criticism, "the implied reader of Matthew's Gospel knows everything that the Gospel expects him or her to know, but does not know anything that the Gospel does not expect him or her to know" (Powell, "Expected," 32).

[153] Cf. Carson, "Matthew," 252; France, *Evangelist*, 315; Donald Hagner, *Matthew 1–13* (Dallas: Word, 1993), 278–80.

[154] Although Weaver, *Missionary Discourse*, 104, agrees in seeing a structural change, with 10:24–42 as "the third section of the discourse," she does so on the basis of content, discerning that 10:24–42 "now shifts the focus of attention back to the initiatives of the disciples." She indeed notes the beginning of "proverbial sayings" at 10:24–25 but does not discern the increased effect this has on the implied reader (105).

[155] Weaver, *Missionary Discourse*, 111.

[156] The Twelve are addressed at 10:42: "The one who receives you, receives me."

[157] The phrase "ultimate significance" is from Weaver, *Missionary Discourse*, 118.

[158] Schweizer, *Good News*, 252.

[159] Carson, "Matthew," 258, says: "The foregoing teaching about what it means to be a disciple of Jesus has its darker side. This final section of the discourse is more encouraging"; cf. Davies and Allison, *Matthew*, 2:224; Beare, *Matthew*, 251.

[160] David R. Catchpole, "The Poor on Earth and the Son of Man in Heaven: A Re-Appraisal of Matthew XXV.31–46," *BJRL* 61 (1978–1979): 358, believes that the Jewish concept of the *shaliach* is behind the identification of Jesus with his disciples.

[161] The parallelism of "the one who receives a prophet ... a righteous person ... one of these little ones" directs the implied reader to regard the three descriptions of "a person received" as parallel in meaning. Cf. Weaver, *Missionary Discourse*, 118, 121; Beare, *Matthew*, 251; Davies and Allison, *Matthew*, 2:227.

[162] Note well, in anticipation of 25:31–46, Hagner, *Matthew 1–13*, 295, who writes that this hospitality "is to accept the message of the disciples and thus the message of Jesus and his person, which is inseparable from the disciples' message"; cf. Alford, *Matthew*, 112; Davies and Allison, *Matthew*, 2:226.

[163] Cf. Kingsbury, *Matthew as Story*, 71; Davies and Allison, *Matthew*, 2:239. Contra, Weaver, *Missionary Discourse*, 126; Luz, "The Disciples," 100.

[164] For a thorough and stimulating study of Matthew 11–12, see Verseput, *Messianic King*.

[165] Kingsbury, "Probe," 12.

[166] Kingsbury, "Probe," 12; "Sermon on the Mount," 132; Beare, *Matthew*, 254; Wolthuis, "Experiencing," 249.

[167] Davies and Allison, *Matthew*, 2:294.

[168] Meier, *Matthew*, 120, notes that "the Coming One" is not known to be a Jewish messianic title, but that "the meaning is obvious enough."

[169] Davies and Allison, *Matthew*, 2:241, comment: "Most of the Fathers convinced themselves that John was inquiring for the sake of his disciples."

[170] Manson, *Sayings of Jesus*, 66; Meier, *Matthew*, 119; Schnackenburg, *Matthäusevangelium 1,1–16,20*, 100; Beare, *Matthew*, 256; A. W. Argyle, *The Gospel according to Matthew* (Cambridge: Cambridge University Press, 1963), 86.

[171] Verseput, *Messianic King*, 69.

[172] Note the ascending order of the "deeds of Christ" in 11:4–5, culminating with "the poor are having good news preached"; cf. Verseput, *Messianic King*, 72; Ladd, *Presence*, 165.

[173] Schnackenburg, *Matthäusevangelium 1,1–16,20*, 100; Verseput, *Messianic King*, 70; Schweizer, *Good News*, 256.

[174] Filson, *Matthew*, 137, overstates the case when he writes that "there is no convincing evidence" in Matthew that John acknowledged the validity of Jesus' answer to him in 11:4–5. There is simply no discussion of the matter at all. One might logically deduce from the positive role that John continues to play in the speech of Jesus (11:7–15;

21:23–27, 28–32) that, in the view of the narrator, John did in fact receive Jesus as the Coming One.

175 Beasley-Murray, *Jesus and the Kingdom of God*, 83.

176 Davies and Allison, *Matthew*, 2:243.

177 Jack D. Kingsbury, "The Verb *AKOLOUTHEIN* as an Index of Matthew's View of His Community," *JBL* 97 (1978): 61.

178 Cf. 21:23–27.

179 Matt 3:3–4; cf. the discussion of John the Baptist in chapter 1.

180 Recall the "dual nature" of John's identity, as discussed in chapter 2, under 3:1–12. John is both a prophetic figure and an eschatological one.

181 I would side with Verseput, *Messianic King*, 84–85, who thinks that use of Exod 23:20 is possible, but inconsequential nonetheless. The effect of the quotation on the implied reader, in light of Jesus' explicit statement about John's *being* Elijah, is to direct the implied reader's attention exclusively to Mal 3:1; cf. Hagner, *Matthew 1–13*, 305. But, for evidence that Exod 23:20 and Mal 3:1 were conjoined in Jewish exegesis, see Davies and Allison, *Matthew*, 2:250.

182 Note well this use of ἄγγελος in an eschatological context to mean "human messenger" and not "angel."

183 The change of pronoun from "me," as in Mal 3:1, to "you" in Matt 11:10, is both intentional and significant, in light of Jesus' identity in Matthew's Gospel as Emmanuel, God with his people (1:23). For this point, see R. T. France, *Jesus and the Old Testament: His Application of Old Testament Passages to Himself and His Mission* (London: Tyndale, 1971), 92; Lagrange, *Évangile*, 220. Alford, *Matthew*, 116, overstates the case.

There is a discussion over whether Jewish eschatological expectation viewed "Elijah" as a forerunner of the Christ or of God himself. Those who believe that Elijah was expected to precede "Christ" include Walter C. Kaiser, "The Promise of the Arrival of Elijah in Malachi and the Gospels," *GTJ* 3 (1982): 221–33; Joachim Jeremias, "Ἠλ(ε)ίας," *TDNT* 2:928–41; Str-B 1:597. For the opposite position, see Morris M. Faierstein, "Why Do the Scribes Say That Elijah Must Come First?" *JBL* 100 (1981): 75–86; Joseph A. Fitzmyer," More about Elijah Coming First," *JBL* 104 (1985): 295–96, agrees with Faierstein.

184 Ladd, *Presence*, 199.

185 Ladd, *Presence*, 201; I. Howard Marshall, *The Gospel of Luke: A Commentary on the Greek Text* (Grand Rapids: Eerdmans, 1978), 293.

186 A possible solution to the problem of the seeming "censure" of John in 11:11 is to take "the least person in the reign" as a reference to entrance into the future, consummated kingdom; cf. Verseput, *Messianic King*, 87.

187 I take both of the independent clauses of 11:12 as expressing opposition to the reign of heaven. This means that I understand βιάζεται as passive voice, with hostile sense, and the βιασταί in a parallel fashion. The narrative context, which is now turning to a description of the opposition to Jesus, guides in this direction. Also important is the naturally negative sense of βιασταί; cf. Beare, *Matthew*, 260; Filson, *Matthew*, 139; Schweizer, *Good News*, 262; Meier, *Matthew*, 122; Allison, *End of the Ages*, 122–24; Strecker, *Der Weg*, 168; France, *Evangelist*, 197; Gottlob Schrenk, "βιάζομαι," *TDNT* 1:611; Hagner, *Matthew 1–13*, 307.

Some take βιάζεται as passive, but with positive force, and the noun βιασταί also in a positive way: "The kingdom of heaven is forcibly seized by its friends. An eager crowd enthusiastically lays hold of it and takes it by storm" (Ladd, *Presence*, 159, 164; cf. Alford, *Matthew*, 117).

Still others understand the verb (seen as middle voice) and the noun as contrasting: "The kingdom of heaven is powerfully breaking out (into the world), and violent men are strongly attacking it" (Beasley-Murray, *Jesus and the Kingdom of God*, 93; Wolthuis, "Experiencing," 310; Carson, "Matthew," 267).

For a survey of the history of interpretation of this verse, see Peter S. Cameron, *Violence and the Kingdom: The Interpretation of Matthew 11:12* (Frankfurt am Main: Peter Lang, 1984).

[188] In 11:12, John is linked to the presence of the reign of heaven, that is to say, "the time of fulfillment"; cf. Allison, *End of the Ages*, 121; Verseput, *Messianic King*, 94; Schweizer, *Good News*, 261–62. However, in 11:13, John is linked to the old order as well, although this should not be maintained to his exclusion from the new; cf. Beare, *Matthew*, 260; Schrenk, *TDNT* 1:610.

[189] Beasley-Murray, *Jesus and the Kingdom of God*, 95, writes about the unexpected fact of opposition to the reign of God: "But to think of the kingdom of God suffering powerful opposition once it had come among men was an extraordinary notion." Cf. Schweizer, *Good News*, 262; Carson, "Matthew," 267; Hagner, *Matthew 1–13*, 307.

[190] The term is a collective one. It includes the religious leaders who opposed Jesus, but is not limited to them, as the reference to "the cities in which his greatest works happened" (11:20) makes clear; cf. Verseput, *Messianic King*, 47–48, 107.

The question of whether "the crowds" are included in "this generation" is a difficult one. Perhaps the best answer is to say that some of them are included. On the one hand, Jesus begins in this second part of the second major division of the story to direct his ministry and teaching more exclusively to his disciples (cf. ch. 13). On the other hand, Jesus continues to minister to the crowds (cf. 14:13–21). Even as late in the story as 21:26, the crowd occupies an ambivalent position with respect to their view of Jesus. The narrator relates that the religious leaders fear the crowd(s), because they hold both John and Jesus to be prophets (21:26, 46). Yet the very fact that the crowds' point of view regarding Jesus is that he is a prophet shows their misunderstanding of him. It is not until 27:20–23 that the crowds side wholeheartedly with the religious leaders by opposing Jesus and clamoring for his crucifixion.

[191] The only times that the Gospel of Matthew uses the term "generation," γενεά, are in the genealogy of 1:2–17 and in Jesus' phrase that describes those who oppose him as "this generation" and variants of that phrase.

[192] Meier, *Matthew*, 123, says that "this generation" stands either for (1) "the children who pipe and wail"; (2) both sides of the wasteful childish debate; or (3) "the moody, finicky children who refused to be moved."

Option 1 is to be preferred. It is the objectionable attitude of the children who are quoted that is being criticized ("We piped, but you didn't dance; we wailed, but you didn't beat your breast in grief"). This interpretation also preserves the temporal sequence of "John's asceticism, then Jesus' celebratory lifestyle." So Bauer, *Structure*, 92; cf. Donald Senior, *The Passion of Jesus in the Gospel of Matthew* (Wilmington: Michael Glazier, 1985), 25; Davies and Allison, *Matthew*, 2:261. For other views, see Verseput, *Messianic King*, 114; Gundry, *Matthew*, 212; Leon Morris, *The Gospel according to Matthew* (Grand Rapids: Eerdmans, 1992), 285.

[193] Jesus' words in 11:16–19 and in 11:20–24 "fill in" a gap of information for the implied reader. There has been no great amount of rejection and opposition to Jesus' ministry to this point in the Gospel. However, Jesus' references to the "deeds of power" done in Chorazin, Bethsaida, and Capernaum, and to the lack of repentance in the face of the deeds of power, inform the implied reader of activities of Jesus heretofore unknown.

194 Schweizer, *Good News*, 267, citing Isa 23; Ezek 26–28; Joel 3:4.

195 Verseput, *Messianic King*, 127.

196 Leopold Sabourin, "Apocalyptic Traits in Matthew's Gospel," *Religious Studies Bulletin* 3 (1983): 23. Oddly, Verseput, *Messianic King*, specifically denies a connection to Isaiah 14.

197 Filson, *Matthew*, 142; Carson, "Matthew," 277; Verseput, *Messianic King*, 141.

198 Davies and Allison, *Matthew*, 2:277; Verseput, *Messianic King*, 137–38.

199 Verseput, *Messianic King*, 137.

200 Verseput, *Messianic King*, 148–52.

201 Schweizer, *Good News*, 271.

202 Kingsbury, "Developing Conflict," 69–70; Witherup, "The Cross of Jesus," 155.

203 The particle μήτι marks the question as expecting a negative answer: "This man isn't the Son of David, is he?"

204 For the association of the Spirit of God and the Messiah, see Verseput, *Messianic King*.

205 For the view that exorcisms would mark the messianic age, see Carson, "Matthew," 290; Meier, *Matthew*, 135; Verseput, *Messianic King*, 230–31; Argyle, *Matthew*, 96.

206 Powell, "Religious Leaders," 84.

207 The possible translation, "the reign of God has come against you," is supported by that meaning for ἐπί + the accusative at 12:26: "Satan is divided against himself." Contextually, the translation "against you" would correspond to the contrast that is rejected by Jesus. His words would in effect say, "My exorcisms are not 'Satan against Satan.' Rather, they are 'Spirit of God against Satan'; indeed, they are 'Spirit of God against *you*.' " These would be harsh words indeed.

208 Matt 12:28, of course, is the one place in the Gospel where virtually all agree that the presence of the reign of God in Jesus' earthly ministry is asserted. Strecker, *Der Weg*, 169, writes: "Sind die Machttaten Jesu als Zeichen der gegenwärtigen Gottesherschaft verstanden.... die Basileia nicht nur zeichenhaft, sondern real gegen-wärtig ist." Also, Ladd, *Presence*, 140; Schweizer, *Good News*, 286; Schnackenburg, *Matthäusevangelium 1,1–16,20*, 111; Kingsbury, "Sermon," 134; Beasley-Murray, *Jesus and the Kingdom of God*, 75.

209 Davies and Allison, *Matthew*, 2:339, are probably correct in supposing that "reign of God" is parallel to "Spirit of God" and antithetical to "reign of Satan" ("his reign," 12:27); cf. Verseput, *Messianic King*, 228.

210 Cf. Olof Linton, "The Demand for a Sign from Heaven (Mk. 8,11–12 and Parallels)," *ST* 19 (1965): 112–29. Linton argues persuasively that the request for a sign is not, as commonly thought, a demand for an "irresistibly convincing" miracle, greater even than the works of power and exorcisms already performed by Jesus. (For this common understanding of the request, see Meier, *Matthew*, 137; Davies and Allison, *Matthew*, 2:353.) Citing both biblical and rabbinic parallels, Linton shows that what is being requested is some testimony of trustworthiness, some ful-filled prediction to demonstrate the reliability of Jesus and his ministry (p. 128); cf. Keith H. Reeves, "The Resurrection Narrative in Matthew: A Literary-Critical Examination," (Ph.D. diss., Union Theological Seminary in Virginia, 1988), 155; Verseput, *Messianic King*, 253.

211 Note the comment of Borg, "A Temperate Case," 91, who sees as "the most natural" reading of 12:41–42 the view that this generation will die and have to be raised, along with the men of Nineveh and the Queen of the South; cf. Kümmel, *Promise and Fulfillment*, 44.

[212] Verseput, *Messianic King*, 266, aptly notes an intensification of the judgment theme found in the "contrast" with Gentiles here at 12:41–42, in comparison with a similar contrast at 11:20–24. In 11:20–24 the Gentiles would have responded had they witnessed Jesus' great deeds of power. In 12:41–42 Jesus presents two examples of Gentiles (the men of Nineveh and the Queen of the South) who actually did respond appropriately to God's opportunity for repentance and change. Verseput writes: "Here, the Gentiles shame Israel by their righteousness."

[213] Verseput, *Messianic King*, 288–93.

[214] Verseput, *Messianic King*, 294–95.

[215] Peter F. Ellis, *Matthew: His Mind and His Message* (Collegeville, Minn.: Liturgical Press, 1974), 60; Wolthuis, "Experiencing," 258.

[216] Bauer, *Structure*, 93. From a redaction-critical perspective, Jack D. Kingsbury, *The Parables of Jesus in Matthew 13* (London: SPCK, 1978), 28, sees 13:1–35 as directed to the "crowds," that is, to those outside of the evangelist's community, whereas 13:36–52 is direct through the "transparent" disciples to the evangelist's own church and its members.

[217] Kingsbury, *Matthew as Story*, 138. Cf. Wolthuis, "Experiencing," 312; Ladd, *Presence*, 222; Carson, "Matthew," 307. Davies and Allison, *Matthew*, 2:389, call this "the consensus of modern scholarship."

[218] For the hermeneutics of parable interpretation, see Craig Blomberg, *Interpreting the Parables* (Downers Grove, Ill.: InterVarsity, 1990), 13–167.

[219] Kingsbury, *Parables*, 35.

[220] Kümmel, *Promise*, 112.

[221] Filson, *Matthew*, 34; Beasley-Murray, *Jesus and the Kingdom of God*, 194.

[222] Davies and Allison, *Matthew*, 2:411; Carson, "Matthew," 316.

[223] This is the primary way that Jesus, in Matthew's Gospel, speaks of the divine action at the judgment, whether it be carried out by angels or by the Son of Man himself: 13:39, 41, 49; 25:31; cf. 7:21–23; 22:9–13; 25:1–13; 25:14–30.

[224] Beasley-Murray, *Jesus and the Kingdom of God*, 199. Verseput, *Messianic King*, 28, contrasts John's view of an *immediate* separation in judgment (3:12) with Jesus' teaching here in 13:30.

[225] Cf. Argyle, *Matthew*, 106; Ladd, *Presence*, 233.

[226] The crucial verses here are 22:44 and 26:64.

[227] Cf. Vögtle, "Anliegen," 289–90 (who thinks that the reign of the Son of Man is this world); Schnackenburg, *Matthäusevangelium 1,1–16,20*, 127; Meier, *Matthew*, 150; Lagrange, *Évangile*, clxi; Beasley-Murray, *Jesus and the Kingdom of God*, 199.

[228] The interpretive consensus understanding of these parables is that the reign of heaven is the valued object, and the human actor in the parables represents the disciples of Jesus. For an alternate understanding, see Jeffrey A. Gibbs, "Parables of Atonement and Assurance: Matthew 13:44–46," *CTQ* 51 (1987): 19–43. Gibbs' study is criticized by Blomberg, *Parables*, 279, as interpreting the parables "too woodenly."

[229] Davies and Allison, *Matthew*, 2:442, note that in a "true to life" story, fish would not normally be burned, but either thrown back or used for fertilizer.

[230] For the parallels between John and Jesus and their respective fates, see Davies and Allison, *Matthew*, 2:476.

[231] There are two ways of understanding the relationship between 14:13, "But when Jesus heard, he withdrew," and the preceding material. Either it refers to Jesus' hear-

ing of the death of John the Baptist, or (with more difficulty) it refers to Jesus' hearing of Herod's attention being drawn also to him and his miraculous activity.

The former understanding reveals 14:13 to be "the only major temporal deformation between story and narrative" in Matthew's Gospel (Howell, *Inclusive*, 96). It is possible, however, to take the participle, "hearing," at 14:13 as a more remote reference to 14:1–2. That is, Jesus withdrew because he heard of Herod's attention being turned toward Jesus. For a defense of this reading, see Cope, "The Death of John"; cf. Tasker, *Matthew*, 141.

232 The implied reader sees progress in the "story" of the disciples, for in the prior stilling of the storm at 8:23–27, the disciples' response was only to ask, "What sort of man is this?" (8:27).

233 The narrator writes in 15:1 that the Pharisees and scribes are "from Jerusalem." This, the first mention of the city of Jerusalem by name since 5:35, anticipates the violent eruption of the confrontation between Jesus and his opponents that will take place during the time of his activity in Jerusalem (21:1–23:39) and especially in Jesus' death and resurrection (26:2–28:20).

234 Anderson, "Over and Over," 80.

235 Anderson, "Over and Over," 80, 84.

236 Jack D. Kingsbury, "The Figure of Peter in Matthew's Gospel as a Theological Problem," *JBL* 98 (1975): 72–73, notes that almost everything that is said about Peter in Matthew's Gospel is elsewhere said of disciples in general.

237 Ladd, *Presence*, 275; Lincoln, "Story for Teachers," 109–10; Schweizer, *Good News*, 342. For a survey of interpretations, see Davies and Allison, *Matthew*, 2:630–33.

238 I take the periphrastic future perfect tenses in 16:19 at face value; cf. Gundry, *Matthew*, 325; Joel Marcus, "The Gates of Hell and the Keys of the Kingdom (Matt 16:18–19)," *CBQ* 50 (1988): 448–49.

239 Recall that there are indications that "the crowds," too, are already acting as "this generation" that is rejecting Jesus; cf. 11:20–24; 13:36; 13:53–58.

240 The difficult question of where the implied reader stands in relation to the predicted event of the ruin of the temple and of Jerusalem will be taken up in the treatment of the ED itself, chapter 6.

4

THE ROAD TO JERUSALEM

At 16:21, the story of Matthew's Gospel begins its third and final major section (16:21–28:20). This third section focuses on the goal and climax of the story, namely, the death and resurrection of Jesus in Jerusalem. Although Jesus' passion as the climax has been implied previously in the story (12:38–40; 10:38; 16:1–4),[1] Jesus now for the first time openly predicts his passion, as the narrator first describes in 16:21. Jesus' movement toward Jerusalem is not especially marked by rising conflict with the religious leaders, for they already are planning to destroy him (12:14). Rather, the story's movement toward Jerusalem is marked by Jesus showing and teaching his disciples about his upcoming death and resurrection. This takes place from 16:21 to 20:34.

It is when Jesus enters the city of Jerusalem (21:1–11) that the conflict with the religious leaders erupts. While he is in Jerusalem (21:1–23:39), Jesus finally turns away from Israel as God's unique chosen people. In Jerusalem, Jesus not only declares the final judgment upon those who reject him. He also, in deed and word, predicts divine punishment within history upon the nation and the capital city, owing to their refusal to accept him as the Christ, the Son of God.[2] This judgment upon the nation and the capital city will take place before "this generation" of Jesus' opponents passes away (23:36). The ED is intimately concerned with the fate of Jerusalem, as predicted by Jesus in the narrative framework to the discourse (24:2). Therefore, the implied reader's understanding of Jesus' relationship with, and words about, Jerusalem after he enters the city are of crucial importance in understanding the content and function of the ED in Matthew.

As the implied reader continues to respond to the narration and the direct discourse of Jesus found in the story, he or she receives additional insight into the end-time character of Jesus' present ministry. By means of Jesus' speech and the narrator's storytelling, the implied reader comes to appreciate the entire passion of Jesus in eschatological terms. That end-time character of the passion of Jesus (Matthew 26–28) will be the special focus of chapter 5 of this book. But this chapter will also devote attention to it as Jesus' own words direct the implied reader.

THE ESCHATOLOGICAL CHARACTER OF JESUS' SUFFERING, DEATH, AND RESURRECTION

The end-time character of the passion of Jesus is reinforced by the form and function of 16:21, the "hinge" verse that introduces the Gospel's third major section. This verse is parallel in form to the statement that introduced the second major section of the story (4:17).[3] It is also parallel in function in that both 4:17 and 16:21 introduce a new major phase in the Gospel's narrative.[4] Thus, the implied reader is invited to see parallelism in the two complementary infinitive clauses that indicate what Jesus, in each case, "began" to do. At 4:17, Jesus "began" to proclaim and to say, "The reign of heaven has arrived." Thus Jesus himself advances what the narrator had already presented, namely, the end-time character of Jesus' entire life and ministry.

Here in 16:21, Jesus "began" explicitly to show his disciples that according to God's plan[5] he must, in Jerusalem, suffer at the hands of the religious leaders[6] and be killed and be raised on the third day. The significance of the parallelism between 4:17 and 16:21 for the implied reader can be baldly stated. The events of Jesus' passion have an eschatological character. The reign of heaven (4:17), present in Jesus' entire life and ministry in a hidden way, will find its climactic expression and fulfillment in Jesus' suffering of many things and in his death and resurrection (16:21). To proclaim the present reign of heaven is to point ineluctably toward Jesus' suffering, death, and resurrection.[7] The narrator portrays this fulfillment of Jesus' end-time life and ministry also in end-time colors, as will be seen most fully in the examination of the passion narrative in chapter 5. Until then, the words of Jesus himself will inform the reader regarding the end-time character of his climactic death and resurrection.

The implied reader knows and accepts the necessity of Jesus' death and resurrection. Still, the disciples, and specifically Peter, do not yet have the reader's perspective. This divine plan for Jesus' ministry is opposed by what is ultimately a satanic alternative through the mouth of Peter: "Mercy to you, Lord! This will certainly not be for you!" (16:22). In the strongest possible terms, Jesus denounces Peter's attempt to deflect him from the obedient path of suffering, death, and resurrection: "Go behind me, Satan!" (16:23). Jesus then reiterates, in generalized speech that includes the implied reader, the theme of "eschatological response" (16:24–27). The cross is not only the way that Jesus must go. It is also the way of anyone who would be his disciple (16:24). *Whoever* (ὃς … ἐάν) loses his or her life in the present time for Jesus' sake is the one who, ultimately, will find his or her life (16:25). The danger in refusing the call to discipleship is an eschatological one. This is so because[8] this man is going to come in his Father's glory with his angels[9] and will administer the end-time judgment to everyone, including the implied reader. As has been the case throughout the Gospel, Jesus does not specify when this end-time judgment will occur. But the prediction from the mouth of Jesus stands.[10]

The certainty of Jesus' prediction about his own role as eschatological judge on the last day (16:27) is underscored by an additional prediction that follows immediately. The translation of 16:28 is as follows: "Truly I say to you that there are some of those standing here who will certainly not taste death until they see that[11] this man is coming with his royal power."[12] At this juncture I will examine how the implied reader of the Gospel will understand the prediction of 16:28, coming as it does on the heels of 16:27.

THE IMPLIED READER AND MATTHEW 16:28: THREE GUIDING QUESTIONS

The interpretation of this verse[13] may be organized around three questions that the text itself suggests. First, what is the relationship between 16:27 and 16:28? Are they parallel in meaning, or do their form and content suggest that they are complementary in meaning? Second, what is the relationship between the emphatic negation, "who will certainly not taste death," and the dependent clause, "until they see that this man is coming"? Third, how will the implied reader, on the basis of all that he or she knows from the story, understand the reference of the clause "that this man is coming with his royal power"?

WHAT IS THE RELATIONSHIP BETWEEN MATTHEW 16:27 AND 16:28?

The first question is the relationship of 16:27 to 16:28. Are they parallel or (in some sense) complementary in meaning? In the view of some, 16:28 simply repeats the prediction of 16:27 and adds a temporal limitation. In this view, 16:28 predicts the Parousia within either the lifetime of the disciples in the story or the community of the evangelist.[14] In contrast to this first view, others believe that 16:28 has a different "horizon" than 16:27, especially since the reference is to the reign of this man.[15] For still others, 16:28 functions on both of these levels, although this third approach is in reality simply another way of viewing 16:28 as a second reference to the Parousia.[16] A comparison of the two sayings will make clear the likelihood that they are, in fact, referring to two different, though related, events.

It can be stated quite simply that Jesus does not utter the same words twice. In 16:27, he speaks of the end-time judgment of this man that will affect every person ("to each one"). In 16:28, Jesus declares that only some of those standing with him in the story will see the predicted event before their death. Second, in 16:27, Jesus describes the judgment day as this man's coming "in his Father's glory with his angels." In 16:28, Jesus predicts the event of this man's "coming with his royal power."[17] Third, the prediction in 16:27 is temporally indeterminate: "For this man is going to come" (μέλλει γὰρ ὁ υἱὸς τοῦ ἀνθρώπου ἔρχεσθαι).[18] Differently, the prediction of 16:28 is temporally delimited in a very specific manner: "There are some of those standing here who will certainly not taste death until...." These two verses are not the same description. They could refer to the same event. But the description is not the same.

Moreover, the prediction in 16:28 is related to that in 16:27 by the solemn phrase "Truly I say to you." In Matthew's story there are six ways in which the amen-statements of Jesus may be said to function with respect to material that immediately precedes them. First, an amen-statement can be explanatory or causal, when γάρ is also present.[19] Second, the amen-statement can introduce a more general truth that supports and enlarges upon what came before, especially when πάλιν is present.[20] Third, an amen-statement also may act as a summary conclusion to the preceding paragraph.[21] Fourth, at times amen-statements of Jesus seem to narrow, specify, or intensify the scope of what was already said.[22] Fifth, amen-statements of Jesus generalize, expound upon, or say even more than the material that immediately precedes the amen-statement.[23] Sixth, in Matthew's Gospel, an amen-statement of Jesus at times simply functions emphatically, underscoring the importance of what is being said. In this last category there is no particular relationship between the amen-statement and the prior material, other than that the amen-statement is an emphatic response of some sort. This "emphatic" function most often occurs when the amen-statement introduces a response of Jesus directly on the heels of the words or actions of another character in the story.[24] In one case, however, a new statement of Jesus is thus introduced (26:21) and, in another, the amen-statement seems to function purely for emphasis (18:13). In each of these cases, the common element is that the amen-introduction shows the reliability of Jesus' word.[25]

Given these six options for the functional relationship of 16:28 to 16:27, how shall we decide their sense? Note that 16:27 explains why whoever wishes to save his life will lose it and whoever loses his life for Jesus' sake will find it. The reason is this: the same Jesus will come on the last day as judge of all. Each one who obediently follows him in the way of the cross will receive the recompense according to his or her work (κατὰ τὴν πρᾶξιν αὐτοῦ, 16:27). Each one who did not deny self, carry the cross, and follow Jesus will receive the recompense for this work. This is so because the one who calls to end-time discipleship in the present is the same one who will render eschatological judgment on the last day.

As if this promise (16:27) were not sufficiently reliable in and of itself, Jesus adds to it an amen-statement. The function of 16:28 would seem to be to verify, authenticate, and underscore the validity of the statement in 16:27, without being a reduplication of its content. Even before the day when this man comes in his Father's glory to repay each according to his or her work, some present with Jesus in the story of Matthew's Gospel will not die until they see that this man is coming with his royal power. The implied reader will regard the event to which 16:28 refers as a different event than that to which 16:27 refers.

WHAT IS THE RELATIONSHIP BETWEEN THE INDEPENDENT AND DEPENDENT CLAUSES OF MATTHEW 16:28?

Thus we come to the second question regarding this saying, namely, the relationship of the clause "there are some of those standing here who will certainly not taste death" to the dependent clause, "until they see [ἕως ἂν ἴδωσιν] that this man is coming with his royal power." We may recall the discussion of "until" clauses in the treatment of 10:23 in chapter 3 and observe that the difficulty is essentially the same. Does the construction in the dependent clause state a simple termination point of the activity of the main clause (cf. 12:20)? Or does the dependent clause imply a point in time at which the action or condition in the main clause is reversed (cf. 2:13; 10:11)?[26] In other words, does 16:28 simply mean "Some of those standing here will never die"? Or does it mean "Some of those standing here will not die until they see that this man is coming with his royal power, and after that, they will die"? As noted in the prior discussion, the construction in and of itself is not conclusive; context must supply the answer. But whereas 10:23 and its linguistic context provided reason to see a pure limitation with no reversal of the main clause, there is no such evidence present in 16:28 or its linguistic context. The question, considered contextually, remains an open one.

WHAT DOES "THAT THIS MAN IS COMING WITH HIS ROYAL POWER" (16:28) MEAN?

So we move to the third question. How will the implied reader, armed with information from the entire story, understand the meaning of the clause "that this man is coming with his royal power" in 16:28? Recall first the discussion above that this event is described differently from the judgment day in 16:27. The likelihood is that the two verses refer to different events. Second, recall from chapter 3 the discussion surrounding the meaning of 10:23. There it was shown that, especially on the basis of 26:64 and 21:40, a future "coming" of this man (or of God, in the case of 21:40) does not always refer in Matthew's story to the last day. Rather, other manifestations of the dynamic "reign" of Jesus, this man, can qualify as examples of his "coming" in the time that is in the future with regard to characters in the story. Third, recall as well that, especially on the basis of the Parousia-delay motif as forcefully exhibited for the implied reader in 24:48; 25:5; and 25:19, it is virtually certain that the implied reader does not find in Matthew's story a near-expectation of the judgment day during the lifetime of the disciples in the story. Yet here in 16:28 the lifetime of some of the disciples in the story is precisely the temporal delimitation that occurs. Therefore, to what event of Jesus' royal power, which will be witnessed by only some of the disciples standing with Jesus in the time of the story at 16:28, does Jesus refer?

The answer I would offer is, with respect to the history of the interpretation of this verse, like the expression "one who draws out of his treasure new things and old things" (13:52). First, I offer the "old things." It seems obvious that, in some sense, the narrator intends for the disciples and the implied reader to find in the account of Jesus' transfiguration a fulfillment of the prediction "Some ... will ... see that this man is coming with his royal power."

Textual features that link the two events include the following: First, only some (Peter, James, and John) of those standing with Jesus in 16:28 are witnesses of the scene on the mountain (17:1). Second, there is a verbal parallelism in the use of "here," ὧδε, that at least one scholar identifies as a link between 16:28 ("some of those who are standing here") and the transfiguration ("Lord, it is good that we are here," 17:4).[27] Third, both the altered appearance of Jesus and the other features of the account are such that they impart to the transfiguration scene a wealth of "eschatological associations" that are consistent with Jesus' reference in 16:28 to this man coming with his royal power.[28] Fourth, the emphatic concluding statement of the account of the transfiguration, in which the narrator says that the three disciples looked up and "saw no one except Jesus himself alone" (εἶδον εἰ μὴ αὐτὸν Ἰησοῦν μόνον, 17:8) corresponds to the prediction in 16:28 that some would see (ἴδωσιν) this man; the transfiguration is fundamentally a seeing of Jesus himself, alone. Thus, there is every likelihood that the narrator, by abruptly placing[29] the transfiguration account after the prediction of 16:28, intends the implied reader to see a vital connection between the two. It is not surprising that this understanding is common in the history of interpretation. It is something "old."[30]

Yet, there are two major objections to finding in the transfiguration the only fulfillment of the prediction of 16:28. The first major objection is substantial, though not insurmountable. It is the observation that Matthew's adverbial comment "after six days" (17:1) hardly seems to comport with Jesus' prediction "some … will certainly not taste death."[31] As I have noted earlier at 3:11–13 and 9:38–10:1 (cf. also 26:2), the narrator of Matthew's Gospel does at times abruptly juxtapose predictions and fulfillments in his story. In light of this technique, it would not be unthinkable to posit that the narrator intends an event that occurs six days later to fulfill the prediction of Jesus at 16:28. But one must admit that "after six days" does not seem to justify the use of a phrase such as "some … will certainly not taste death."

The second objection to finding in the transfiguration the only fulfillment of 16:28 arises from Jesus' words to the three disciples as they descend the mountain: "Tell the vision to no one until this man has been raised from the dead" (17:9). The transfiguration's vision of Jesus' power and glory, his "royal power," cannot be told until after his death and resurrection. The reason is that it cannot be understood apart from his death and resurrection. When the three disciples immediately ask about the scribes' insistence on the coming of eschatological Elijah, Jesus' response reiterates what they should already know,[32] just as the implied reader knows. Yes, there will be an appearance of eschatological Elijah to restore all things. Indeed, the one who, according to Mal 4:5–6, was to prepare for the great and terrible Day of the Lord had already come in the story's world. It has already happened.[33] John the Baptist, dead at the hands of the reign of heaven's enemies, was Elijah. "But I say to you that Elijah already came, and they did not know him, but they did to him whatever they wished. Thus also this man is going to suffer at their hands. Then the disciples understood that he was speaking to them about John the Baptist" (17:12–14).[34] The one who was to announce the Day of the Lord, as prophesied by Malachi, had already come.

As the story later reveals, the disciples' understanding of this eschatological truth, even though explicitly mentioned by the narrator, is short-lived and inadequate. By contrast, the implied reader understands all of the implications of what Jesus is saying. He or she already knows from 11:14 that, because John is Elijah, Jesus' present activity has brought a real, though partial and hidden, manifestation of the eschatological Day of the Lord. Therefore, through Jesus' command to silence (17:9) and the conversation between Jesus and the disciples on the way down from the mountain (17:10–14), the implied reader is directed away from the transfiguration as the only fulfillment of Jesus' prediction of 16:28. It is true that the implied reader is encouraged to associate the predicted "royal power" of Jesus (16:28) with the splendor of the transfiguration vision. But the *words of Jesus himself* that follow the transfiguration direct the implied reader to look elsewhere, namely, to look toward the passion of Jesus, toward this man's rising from the dead (17:9). In what way, or at what point in the passion of Jesus, does the prediction of 16:28 come true?

In this way, something "new" emerges in my presentation of how the implied reader understands the fulfillment of 16:28. For there is another time when only "some" of those standing with Jesus at 16:28 bear witness to a manifestation of Jesus' royal eschatological power. That event is Jesus' agony in the garden (26:36–46). There, "some," indeed the same three that accompanied Jesus when he was transfigured, see that this man is coming with his royal power.

I would argue that the implied reader will understand[35] Jesus' agony in the garden as the true fulfillment of 16:28. Several factors support this position. As indicated above, Jesus' words (17:9, 12) direct the attention of the implied reader (and the three disciples in the story) beyond the transfiguration, toward the passion, which culminates in the resurrection of this man from the dead. Thus, the glory and power of the transfiguration are linked closely to the passion of Jesus.[36]

Moreover, there are at least two obvious parallels between 16:28–17:8 and 26:36–46. Most obviously, it is the same three disciples who accompany Jesus each time (17:1; 26:37).[37] In addition, in each place the narrator says that Jesus "takes along" (παραλαμβάνω) the three disciples.[38]

There are also significant conceptual links between "this man … with his royal power" (16:28) and Jesus' agony in the garden in 26:36–46. Of overarching importance is the fact that the passion narrative as a whole is that portion of the story in which Jesus' kingship and royalty is most fully depicted.[39] Through the frequent use of irony, the narrator shows the implied reader[40] that Jesus' suffering and death reveal him to be the true eschatological King of Israel and the one who, by his suffering and death, fulfills his mission of saving his people from their sins (1:21; 20:28; 26:29).[41] It is preeminently in the account of Jesus' passion, toward which the entire Gospel story has been moving from its earliest stage, that the implied reader sees and acknowledges Jesus as the eschatological, royal, messianic Son of God who is accomplishing the will of his Father.[42]

These comments apply generally to the passion narrative. The royalty of Jesus the Christ is portrayed by means of the events of the passion narrative. Although the disciples and other characters in the story remain uncomprehending concerning the true nature of these events, the implied reader sees and understands.

Narratively, the agony of Jesus in the garden initiates the Gospel's portrayal of the royalty of Jesus, the end-time Christ.[43] The account of Jesus in Gethsemane is the point in the story's plot at which the divinely ordained suffering, death, and resurrection of Jesus (16:21) actually begin. The agony in the garden moves the story from anticipation of the cross to fulfillment of the cross. In the garden, the narrator shows Jesus' obedience to the Father's will in that he finally and irrevocably chooses the way that leads to the cross. There, while the disciples succumb to weariness and sleep,[44] Jesus prevails over the eschatological temptation to turn away from the cross.[45] There, while the disciples stumble so as to deny Jesus (and thus to deny the Father's will), Jesus powerfully[46] exerts his obedient will and fulfills in part the eschatological prayer that he taught to the disciples, "Let your will be done" (6:10; 26:42).[47] There, the implied reader knows, with Peter, James, and John close at hand, Jesus shows the coming of this man with his royal power.[48]

In summarizing the implied reader's understanding of 16:28, we have argued that Jesus' words there underscore and emphasize his statement in 16:27 about the judgment day. Because some (Peter, James, and John) of those standing in Jesus' presence in the time of the story did see[49] that, through his willing submission to the Father's will, this man was coming with his royal power, the implied reader has further validation and verification of Jesus' promise to come as judge of each person. With the disciples in the story, the implied reader accepts the call of Jesus to cross-bearing and self-denial.

In the transfiguration account immediately following (17:1–8), the implied reader is privileged, with the three disciples, to witness for a brief moment the true glory and power of the Son of God whose bringing of the reign of heaven in the time of the story is, at all other times, a "hidden" thing. On the mount, Peter, James, and John literally see the glory that the royal eschatological Christ will manifest for all to see on the last day (16:27; 25:31). But because the words of Jesus (17:9) and the conversation with the disciples (17:10–14) teach otherwise, the implied reader does not attempt to remain on the mountain in search of the end-time glory of the Christ. He or she knows that Christ's glory will be manifest as his end-time ministry of word and deed to Israel continues. Accordingly, the implied reader continues to observe the eschatological events in Matthew's story that now so directly point to Jesus' suffering, death, and resurrection.

JESUS MOVES TOWARD JERUSALEM

Even though Jesus has repeatedly instructed the disciples regarding his upcoming death and resurrection,[50] the disciples do not show that they have understood. As already noted, by their uncomprehending question regarding the coming of Elijah (17:10) they show misunderstanding of the eschatological nature of the present time of the story. In the exorcism story that immediately follows, the disciples' inability to cast out the demon evokes Jesus' rebuke, "O faithless and perverse generation" (17:17). Such speech is elsewhere reserved for the opponents of Jesus.[51] The disciples' faith is not like a mustard seed. If it were, nothing would be impossible for them (17:19–21). Indeed, when Jesus repeats the explicit prediction of his upcoming passion to them, their uncomprehending reaction is to be severely grieved.

The disciples' lack of faith and comprehension shows itself in their relationships with one another. The "Ecclesiological Discourse" (18:1–19:1)[52] portrays the disciples' relationships with one another in end-time categories and points the disciples to the kinds of behavior that are consistent with the gracious reign of heaven, whose blessings they already enjoy in their discipleship with Jesus. Greatness consists not in power, but in childlike humility (18:1–4). Those who show such humility will enter the reign of heaven on the last day. Final punishment awaits those who cause others to stumble. Self-amputation, could it remove the causes of stumbling, would be a better alternative (18:6–9). Seeking the wandering brother or sister (18:12–14) is the performance of the divine will. Confession and absolution are the goal in the life of the church during the period between the resurrection and the last day (18:15–20).[53] Indeed, the gift of forgiveness of sins that already[54] characterizes the life of the disciples in their relationship with God must flow outward and characterize their relationships with one another (cf. 6:12, 14–15). If it does not, eschatological judgment awaits the disciples on the temporally indeterminate last day: "Thus also my Father in heaven will do to you" (18:35).

Even after one becomes a disciple of Jesus, response now determines fate then. As will become clear in the second half of the ED, the reality of the final day of judgment sends forth a ringing summons to faithfulness and obedience on the part of both the disciples and the implied reader, who is also a disciple of Jesus.

After debating hypocritical religious leaders (19:3–9) and blessing the children (19:13–15), Jesus uses the occasion of a conversation with the rich man (19:16–22) to teach again about future entrance into the consummated reign of heaven. As Jesus never tires of repeating in Matthew's story, present response to Jesus determines one's fate on the last day. Yet, for all their familiarity with this teaching, the disciples show a misunderstanding in this matter, as in so many others. They are astonished (ἐξεπλήσσοντο σφόδρα, 19:25) when confronted with the stark reality that it is only through the gracious power of God that anyone can thus finally be saved (19:26).

In spite of their immaturity and incomprehension, Jesus does not reject the Twelve. On the contrary, their present response of discipleship and their status as the designated "sent ones" of Jesus (οἱ δώδεκα ἀπόστολοι, 10:2) to the lost sheep that are the house of Israel (10:5–6) will have glorious consequences for them on the last day, the day of "regeneration."[55] To the cities of Israel the Twelve will urgently go, preaching in the period of time that began with their commissioning in Matthew 10 and that will end prematurely when divine judgment comes upon "this generation" of Jesus' opponents, who will also persecute them (10:23; 23:36). Indeed, on the last day the Twelve will act as judges over all of Israel ("the twelve tribes of Israel," 19:28).[56] They will sit on thrones with this man who will be seated on his glorious throne (19:28).[57] All, including the implied reader (πᾶς ὅστις, 19:29), who sacrifice for the sake of Jesus' name will inherit the riches of eternal life, that is, the blessings of the consummated reign of heaven.[58] That day will bring a reversal of worldly standards and fortunes; many will be first who are last, and last who are first (19:30; cf. 5:4–9).[59]

Caution is necessary, however, lest the disciples (or the implied reader) improperly direct their attention to that time of consummation and blessing and away from the road that leads to the cross. So the teaching of Jesus, as it continues in Matthew 20, counteracts pretensions of "glory" on the part of the disciples. It is true that on the last day, the last will become first in relation to the world. Yet the parable of the Workers in the Vineyard (20:1–16) teaches that on that day there will be no "levels" of greatness among the disciples of Jesus. When the time comes for wages to be paid, all the workers receive the same regardless of the length of their labor. Even the least of the "workers" receives an equal reward. The last will be first and the first will be last (20:16).

It is because they are going up to Jerusalem that Jesus takes the Twelve aside privately on the way and utters his most complete prediction of his upcoming passion. Jesus enunciates his betrayal and condemnation by the religious leaders, his being handed over to the Gentiles for torture and crucifixion, and his being raised on the third day (20:17–19). The story of Jesus, who brings the blessing and crisis of the reign of heaven into the present time of this story and who calls people to the end-time reality of discipleship, is moving towards its goal. The deeds of Christ (11:2) have brought the reality of the reign of heaven into the present throughout the entire story. Now the Christ moves to the city where the final conflict and its resolution will take place.

Even after Jesus' third passion prediction, the disciples do not understand and they show it once again. The mother of the sons of Zebedee, with her sons, comes to Jesus. Her focus is still on the regeneration and the promise of session in glory (19:28). Surprisingly, it is not enough to have the promise of session on a throne with Jesus, this man, and the others of the Twelve (19:28).[60] This mother and her two sons ask for more: "Say that these two sons of mine may sit, one on your right and one on your left, in your reign" (20:21). She and her sons[61] are asking for the two places of eschatological prominence in Jesus' reign. Their unthinking question has reference to the final, consummated reign on the last day.[62]

Their understanding is flawed. Indeed, Jesus says to them, "You do not know what you are asking," and then follows with his own question: "Are you able to drink the cup which I am going to drink?" (20:22). Owing to Jesus' response to James and John, the implied reader knows that the sons of Zebedee are, in fact, not able to drink the cup that Jesus is going to drink. Nevertheless, James and John fully display to Jesus (and to the implied reader) the depth of their misunderstanding. They reply, "We are able" (20:22). Regardless of their folly, their request is denied. It is not for Jesus to give the places on his right and his left. They are for those for whom his Father prepared them (20:23).

When the ten join in the folly of the two (20:24), Jesus teaches them, one last time, about the road that he and they are taking. It is not a road that leads to places of greatness as the world measures greatness. It is a road that leads to greatness as God measures greatness. For in God's point of view, greatness is service. In God's point of view, true primacy means deep servanthood, in imitation of the ministry of this man. His purpose in coming and bringing the reign of heaven is not to be served by others, but to serve others by giving his life as the ransom for the many (20:26–28). The giving of Jesus' life will accomplish the goal appointed for him before his birth. He will save his people from their sins (cf. 1:21).

The implied reader observes this interaction and knows to distance himself or herself from the disciples' way of thinking. The implied reader embraces the call to discipleship and knows that James and John intended to ask for eschatological glory, for the two places of eschatological prominence. But they did not even realize that for which they truly were asking. They did not know that session at Jesus' right and left in his reign would mean drinking the cup he will drink, giving his life as he gave his life. They thought they were asking for preeminent participation in Jesus' reign on the last day. When they asked for greatness, they were asking for the cross.

The implied reader knows, better than the disciples do, that Jesus' reign has already come and that it is still coming. The implied reader knows that the agony in the garden, where Jesus obediently chooses the Father's will, shows this man coming "with his royal power" (ἐν τῇ βασιλείᾳ αὐτοῦ, 16:28). The implied reader knows that the climax of Jesus' end-time ministry of word and deed occurs in Jerusalem, toward which this third major section of the Gospel has been directly and repeatedly pointing.

Therefore, the implied reader knows what the mother of the sons of Zebedee is really asking for her sons. She is asking for the places next to the one who drinks the cup, who gives his life as the ransom for the many, who sits in his royal reign. With deepest irony, the narrator will show that when Pilate questions him

(27:11), the soldiers mock him (27:27–31), and he is crucified, Jesus shows himself to be the end-time King of the Jews.[63]

How does the narrator depict the actual event of Jesus' crucifixion? After crucifying him, the soldiers divide his garments and sit at the foot of the cross, keeping watch there (27:35–36). Then they put the "accusation" over his head: "This is Jesus, the King of the Jews" (27:37). Then two thieves are crucified with him, one on the right and one on the left (27:38). There is the King, "sitting"[64] in his reign as the one who brings end-time salvation by obediently saving his people from their sins. On his right and left[65] are the two for whom the places were prepared.[66] Then, when the account of the crucifixion and death of Jesus is over, after all of the end-time signs (27:45, 51–53) that reveal that the death of Jesus is an eschatological event and a "coming" of the reign of heaven, who is there as witness? "There were many women there, beholding from afar, who followed Jesus from Galilee to serve him. Among them were Mary the Magdalene, and Mary, the mother of James and Joseph, and the mother of the sons of Zebedee" (27:55–56). The implied reader has no way of knowing if the character of the mother of the sons of Zebedee understands that she has seen Jesus, the end-time Christ, in his reign.[67] But the implied reader does know that this, the divinely ordained climactic goal toward which the story of Matthew's Gospel has been moving, is a manifestation of the eschatological reign of Jesus. Here, in truth, Jesus is sitting in his reign (20:21).

As the implied reader observes Jesus and his disciples on the way (20:17) to Jerusalem, he or she knows that Jesus' words to James and John point forward to Jesus' own crucifixion as a manifestation of his present (yet hidden) end-time rule as Christ and King.[68] That crucifixion (and resurrection), thrice predicted by Jesus (16:21; 17:22–23; 20:17–19), will take place owing to two "levels" of causality. The first cause occurs on the purely human level. The deadly hostility of the religious leaders of Israel (cf. 12:14) will, once his conflict with them breaks out openly in the city of Jerusalem, lead them to seek and achieve the death of Jesus. But the second cause for Jesus' death is on the supernatural, divine level. For it is necessary (δεῖ) that Jesus suffer, die, and be raised in Jerusalem (16:21). God has planned it. Thus, Jesus will bring to completion his ministry of eschatological deliverance in the offering of his own life as a ransom payment (20:28) and an atoning sacrifice (26:29).

At the very beginning of the story, God's own messenger had informed the astonished Joseph, and the implied reader as well, that God's purpose in the sending of the Christ was that he should save his people from their sins (1:21). Now, years later, the disciples are not prepared for this. They have not understood the import of Jesus' passion predictions. They still seek after power and greatness, even as the story draws near to the final, open conflict in Jerusalem (20:20–28). The implied reader distances himself or herself from this attitude on the part of Jesus' disciples and notes well the contrast that the narrator offers through the request of the blind men in Jericho (20:29–34). Along with other "marginal persons" in the story, they acclaim Jesus as "Son of David" (20:30, 31)[69] and cry out purely for mercy. Jesus asks them what it is that they wish, just as he had queried the mother of the sons of Zebedee.[70] Their answer to Jesus' question is structurally parallel[71] to that of James and John, but diametrically opposite in content. Through their mother, James and John asked for power and glory (20:21). The two blind men ask only that their eyes might be opened (20:33). To James and John in their "blindness," Jesus' reply was, "You do not know what you are asking" (20:22). To the two blind men, Jesus' reply is to touch their eyes and hence to heal them immediately.

CONFLICT AND REJECTION: JESUS IN JERUSALEM

Jesus draws near (ἐγγίζω, 21:1) to Jerusalem. The implied reader has no particular reason to identify with the disciples' errors. Rather, he or she will observe the rising conflict between Jesus and the city to which he must go and will await the eschatological consequences that will take place because the "city of the great King" (5:35) rejects and crucifies her true, eschatological King.

In the persons of its religious leaders and people, Jerusalem will reject Jesus. Although this rejection does not become full-blown until, in the presence of Pilate, all the people cry down Jesus' blood upon their heads (27:25),[72] Jerusalem's rejection of Jesus is implicit in the account of his entry into the city (21:1–11). As the narrator portrays this event, Jesus enters Jerusalem as one who exercises royal authority.[73] He orders his disciples to bring his mount, and the disciples go and do just as Jesus commands them. This event, the narrator informs the implied reader, is the fulfillment of OT prophecy that foretold the coming of Zion's true King (21:5). Because it is the Word of God that thus interprets Jesus' arrival in Jerusalem, the implied reader knows that no lesser understanding will do.

At first blush the crowds seem to understand. The city seems to be receiving Jesus as the Scripture says they should. They cry out, acclaiming Jesus in royal, messianic terms: "Hosanna to the Son of David." Their words, "Blessed is the Coming One in the name of the Lord" (21:9), recall the end-time endorsement of Jesus by John the Baptist (cf. 3:11; 11:3). But when Jesus enters the city, the implied reader learns that the whole city is shaken, wondering about Jesus' identity.[74] Once before, the implied reader knows, "all Jerusalem" was troubled over the birth of the King of the Jews (2:3).[75]

Is the reaction of Jerusalem a rejection of Jesus' true identity? It is indeed. For the answer that the crowds give to the question of "Who is this?" shows their inadequate understanding of the one who has thus entered the city: "This is the prophet Jesus, the one from Nazareth of Galilee" (21:11). It is true that some interpreters understand this declaration of the crowds to be, in the perspective of Matthew's story, a proper one.[76] Yet data from the story, to which the implied reader has ready access, prohibit this conclusion. Here in the story of Jesus' entry into Jerusalem, the narrator's citation of Scripture (21:5) has already given a proper understanding of Jesus. According to Zech 9:9, he is the King of Zion. At first the crowds themselves have acclaimed Jesus in royal and eschatological terms from the Scriptures. Even though they do not understand or accept the words of Scripture from LXX Ps 117:26 (ET 118:26),[77] these words have told the truth. This is the messianic, end-time Son of David who has entered the city of David.[78]

In addition to the data from the account of Jesus' entry into Jerusalem, one other passage suffices to show the insufficiency of calling Jesus "prophet." The passage is, of course, 16:13–20. There the point of view that holds Jesus to be "Elijah, Jeremiah, or one of the prophets" (16:14) stands as the view that "people" hold toward this man.[79] In stark contrast to this view, the divinely revealed perspective on Jesus' identity is that he is the Christ, the Son of God (16:16–17). This is the perspective accepted by the implied reader. He or she knows that the crowds' naming of Jesus as a "prophet" is an indication that they are rejecting him.[80]

JESUS AS A PROPHET OF JUDGMENT

Yet herein lies a strongly tragic irony, which the implied reader learns to appreciate as he or she observes Jesus' deeds and words in Jerusalem. With respect to the crowds in the city that only receive him as a prophet (21:11, 46), Jesus will speak and act like a prophet: a prophet of judgment. Just as Jesus first adopted the judgment language of John the Baptist (12:34, "brood of vipers!") after his enemies' opposition reached the level of lethal intent (12:14), here in Jerusalem Jesus shows that aspect of the reign of heaven which John most emphasized, namely, that of judgment. Jesus brings the prophetic message of judgment against those who will not accept his true identity.[81]

That message is demonstrated at once through Jesus' expulsion of the merchants from the temple. In this sweepingly comprehensive action,[82] Jesus mounts a frontal assault on the institution that represents the authority and integrity of the religious leaders.[83] In a way that evokes both the judgment prophecy of the Baptist[84] and the judgment prophecy of Mal 3:1,[85] Jesus shows the divine anger against the religious establishment.

To be more specific, Jesus' own words in 21:13, "You are making it a den of robbers," recall the identical phrase from Jer 7:11: "Has this house, which is called by my name, become a den of robbers in your eyes? Behold, I myself have seen it, says the Lord." Thus it becomes clear to the implied reader that Jesus' action is not simply an attempt to reform the temple. It is an action that is symbolic of the temple's destruction.[86] For the Jeremiah passage is embedded in a prophecy concerning the inevitable[87] destruction of the Jerusalem temple and the laying waste of the land of Israel.[88] By his healings in the temple[89] and by the scripturally endorsed acclamations of the children, Jesus is shown to be the true end-time King.

The city of Jerusalem ought to have known and welcomed him. But the people have not, and they will not. Accordingly, Jesus' cursing of the fig tree early the next day underscores for the implied reader the message of the tumult in the temple. Unfruitful Israel will be rejected and punished.[90] The leaders and the crowds have not had "ears to hear" (11:15; 13:9, 43) nor "eyes to see" (13:16) what the disciples, despite their shortcomings, have heard and seen (14:33; 16:16).

Jesus again enters into the temple (21:23). He does not come out until its rejection and denunciation are complete (24:1). During the time in the temple, the confrontations between Jesus and the various groups of religious leaders become agonizingly acute, with Jesus himself directly challenged concerning crucial issues.[91] The conflict with the religious leaders now becomes unrelentingly "the driving force of the story."[92] The implied reader, who so thoroughly understands that present response to Jesus determines eschatological fate on the last day, is riveted on the outworking of this conflict between the religious leaders and Jesus, the Christ, the true King of Israel.

When confronted over the issue of his own authority, Jesus counters with the question of the authority of John the Baptist. Because he was the forerunner of Christ (3:3, 11), the rejection of John's ministry inevitably meant a rejection of Jesus himself. The religious leaders did not "believe" John (21:25; cf. 21:32, 32). John preached the message of judgment to these religious leaders (3:7–10). So it is with Jesus. The leaders refuse to answer Jesus lest they be trapped between their rejection of John and the wrath of the crowd, for the crowd, at least, holds John to be a prophet.[93] To expose the result of the leaders' rejection of John, Jesus tells the parable of the Two Children (21:28–32). The upshot of the religious leaders' present rejection of John's ministry is that, whereas notorious sinners will enter the reign of God because they believed John's message,[94] the religious leaders will not enter it at all.[95]

This sentence of final eschatological doom upon the religious leaders is not new to the implied reader. He or she has heard it from both John (3:7–10) and Jesus (12:31–37). With the parable of the Wicked Tenants (21:33–45), the implied reader learns for the first time the specific cause for the judgment that will fall upon Jerusalem. The judgment will come because this present generation of Jesus' contemporaries, represented especially in the persons of their religious leaders, has refused and rejected Jesus' true identity as the Son of God.[96] The parable of the Wicked Tenants casts this truth in eschatological terms. The crucial events of this "story within the story" occur "when the time of the fruits drew near" (21:34).[97] It will be the very reign of God, formerly the prerogative and privilege of Israel and its leaders, that will be taken away and given to others,[98] to the church.[99] Although there is an indirect reference to the judgment day in the parable,[100] the focus is on the eschatological meaning of the death of God's Son,

the punishment by God of those who killed his Son, and the transfer of the reign
of God to the church as the eschatological people of God.

ISRAEL'S REJECTION OF JESUS AS THE SON OF GOD
AND THE DESTRUCTION OF JERUSALEM
(21:33–46; 22:1–14; 22:41–46)

I should like to emphasize another connection as well. In the parable of the
Wicked Tenants, the implied reader meets, for the first time,[101] Jesus' own self-
designation to the Jewish public as the Son of God. That public, here represented by the persons of their leaders, now rejects Jesus' self-designation. The result
is the predicted destruction of Jerusalem and the nation's loss of salvation-historical primacy.[102] The narrator thus links the Jewish rejection of Jesus' open declaration of himself as Son of God and the destruction of Jerusalem in a relation of
cause and effect. Jerusalem will be destroyed because the city and its leaders reject
Jesus as the Son of God. Remarkably, this connection will be repeated in
Matthew's story no less than four times before the story has ended (22:2–7;
22:41–46; 26:61–64; 27:51–54). Comments will accompany each text. But the
meaning for the implied reader will include the following.

First, in Matthew's story Jesus' identity is preeminently that of the Son of
God. To reject him as God's Son is to reject him indeed.[103]

Second, rejection of God's Son brings certain judgment on the last day
(21:44). But it also results in end-time judgment ("the reign of God will be taken
away from you," 21:43) within the life-span of this generation of Jesus' contemporaries, who spurn his present, end-time reign. The language and concepts of
the parable of the Wicked Tenants are eschatological ("When the time of the
fruits drew near," 21:34; "When the lord of the vineyard comes," 21:40; "On
account of this I say to you that the reign of God will be taken away from you,"
21:43). Still, the parable is not chiefly concerned with judgment day. Rather, the
parable predicts the end-time events connected to Jesus' present ministry in the
generation of his contemporaries. Those events are Jesus' death, his vindication,
his exaltation, the destruction of Jerusalem, and the existence of the church as the
end-time people of God living in the sphere of his rule.[104]

The implied reader learns these things from the parable of the Wicked
Tenants. This "story within the story" draws him or her in so as to instruct. How
could that reader not marvel at the opposition of the religious leaders? For this
is their reaction: "They knew that Jesus was speaking about them, and they were
trying to seize him" (21:45–46). But they feared the crowds, who thought Jesus
was a prophet (21:46). The implied reader who accepts and believes in Jesus as
the Son of God also knows that, with respect to the religious leaders and the
nation of whom they are representatives, the crowds' evaluation of Jesus carries
a bitterly ironic truth. For Jerusalem, Jesus is a prophet—a prophet of judgment.

With the slightest of narrative transitions (22:1), Jesus tells another parable of the reign of heaven that is focused on the way things have now become (ὡμοιώθη, 22:2).[105] For the second time (cf. 21:41) the Jewish rejection of Jesus as the Son of God stands in a relation of cause to the effect of the destruction of Jerusalem as the divine judgment against the nation. The parable of the Wedding Feast (22:1–14) portrays the reign of heaven, now present through Jesus' words and deeds (cf. 9:15).[106] Those who were called but who were not willing[107] to come are the ones who, even as the parable is being spoken, reject and oppose the Son of God. It seems likely that the slaves sent to them, coming as they do after the feast is prepared, represent for the narrator and for Jesus the missionaries sent to Israel during and after the time of the story (10:5; 23:34a), whose persecution and mistreatment by Israel Jesus predicts (10:17–22; 23:34b).[108] The garishly remarkable element of the king's wrathful destruction of the murderers and the burning of their city[109] is the fate of those who refuse to come to the wedding feast of the king's son.

To this point, the parable of the Wedding Feast has run parallel to the meaning of the parable of the Wicked Tenants. But now the former parable moves "farther." The parable of the Wicked Tenants does include the vineyard owner's intention, supplied by the mouth of Jesus' opponents: "He will give the vineyard to other tenants, who will give to him the fruits in their times" (21:41). The parable of the Wedding Feast, however, actually describes what is only implied by the Wicked Tenants, that is, the invitation and response of others who were not originally invited. The narrator and Jesus in the story intend this to be understood as the mission to the Gentiles. Then, unlike the Wicked Tenants, the parable of the Wedding Feast ends on a note of final (though individualized) eschatology when the servants of the king bind the inadequately dressed guest and cast him into the outer darkness,[110] the place of weeping and gnashing of teeth.[111]

For the second time, then, the implied reader learns that divine judgment[112] will fall upon "this generation" of Jesus' opponents, even upon "their city" (22:7), because they have rejected him who is now revealing himself openly as the Son of God.[113] As the controversy between Jesus and the religious leaders continues, the incidents center around key issues of doctrine and practice. In every instance, Jesus shows his superiority over his opponents by besting them, turning the tables on their hypocritical attacks (22:15, 35), and eliciting their grudging and hostile amazement (22:22, 33). The things that properly belong to God are to be God's alone (22:21). Resurrection life on the last day will be radically different than earthly existence (22:30). There certainly will be a resurrection, for God is God of the living (22:32). The greatest commandment is supreme love for both God and the neighbor (22:40). In all the confrontations in 22:15–40, initiated by his opponents, Jesus emerges the victor.

In the last and most important confrontation, Jesus takes the initiative (22:41–44). At stake is the central issue: "What do you think concerning the

Christ? Whose Son is he?" The answer of the religious leaders is that the Christ is David's Son (22:42). This understanding of the leaders was already revealed at 21:15, for there the chief priests and scribes were indignant that Jesus was being acclaimed by the children as "Son of David." So they repeat their understanding of who the end-time Christ is to be.

Jesus directly challenges their understanding as insufficient. For the word of God in Scripture demands a further answer. Divinely inspired, David in Ps 110:1 calls the Christ "Lord," and recounts the words of God to the Christ, promising both the Christ's exaltation ("Sit at my right hand") and the ensuing subjugation of the Christ's enemies under his feet ("until I put your enemies under your feet"). This Christ is more than David's Son. From the entire christological emphasis of the story of Matthew's Gospel,[114] it is clear that the normative understanding of the Christ's identity holds him to be the Son of God.[115]

The leaders neither know this, nor will they confess it. Thus, they show themselves to be the enemies of the Christ, described in the words of Psalm 110. It is as the enemies of Christ that they will be denounced in Matthew 23. When the Christ, David's Lord and the Son of God, is exalted,[116] as the word of God in the psalm promises, then God will act to put his enemies under his feet. Here, then, is the third occurrence of the linking of Jewish rejection of Jesus as the Son of God with the promise of judgment upon "this generation." It is "while" Jesus is exalted (22:44, κάθου ἐκ δεξιῶν μου, ἕως ἂν θῶ τοὺς ἐχθρούς σου ὑποκάτω τῶν ποδῶν σου) that God will put his enemies, the religious leaders (and "this generation" of Israel whom they represent) under his feet. In light of the promised judgment at 21:41 and 22:7, the implied reader knows to apply this to the predicted destruction of Jerusalem that will occur during the time span of the generation of Jesus' contemporaries.[117] Matthew 22:41–46, then, for the third time connects the religious leaders' refusal to acknowledge Jesus as the Son of God with the divine judgment caused by such refusal. As the enemies of the Christ, the Son of God, they will be put under the feet of that same Christ.

MATTHEW 23: JESUS REJECTS HIS ENEMIES

As chapter 23 begins, Jesus turns away from any interactive conversation with the religious leaders. Never again will he debate with them. Because they were not able to answer him a word nor dared any longer to question him (22:46), his relationship with them changes, radically and finally. Now they will be denounced, as is fitting the enemies of the end-time Christ.[118] Although the words of Jesus in chapter 23 are overtly addressed to the crowds[119] and to his disciples (23:1), the discourse turns and addresses the religious leaders at 23:13 ("Woe to you, scribes and Pharisees," 23:13, 15, 23, 25, 27, 29) and the rebellious city of Jerusalem itself in 23:37 ("O Jerusalem, Jerusalem").

Jesus roundly condemns his enemies in the discourse of chapter 23. The religious leaders, in contrast to Jesus himself, burden other people without helping to lift the burden (23:4; cf. 11:28).[120] They love to be regarded as exalted over other Israelites and to be called "rabbi," whereas it is humility that avails on the last day (23:12) and the Christ who is the true teacher (23:5–12). In a series of scathing eschatological "woes"[121] that stand in sharpest contrast to the earlier beatitudes directed to his disciples,[122] Jesus describes, with an ever-increasing intensity, the content of their folly as "hypocrites" (Mt 23:13, 15, 23, 25, 27, 29).[123]

The first pair of woes (23:13, 15) concerns the scribes and Pharisees as those who prevent others from entering the reign of heaven. They themselves will not enter[124] the reign of heaven, nor do they wish to permit to enter those who, in fact, will enter.[125] Indeed, the results of their eager evangelistic efforts are that their proselytes become "son[s] of gehenna" (23:15). Just as the religious leaders will reap a final eschatological condemnation for their rejection of Jesus, so also will those who are drawn to the way that those religious leaders teach.[126]

The second pair of woes (23:16–24) is joined together by a similar content, even as the woes are bracketed by the phrase "blind guides" (23:16, 24). Jesus condemns the tendency towards nit-picking casuistry. This tendency renders one unable to answer the question "What is greater?" (23:19) and leads to the neglect of the matters that are necessary to do: justice and mercy and faithfulness (23:23).

The third pair of woes (23:25–28) is an attack against a focus on "external" things, as opposed to the truly important "internal" matters. Although the scribes and Pharisees appear to human beings[127] to be righteous in outward things, inwardly they are filled with hypocrisy and lawlessness (23:28).

The seventh and last woe concerns the scribes and Pharisees as the "sons" of those who murdered the prophets (23:29–31). The linking of the murdered prophets and Jesus, Son of God, who is enacting the role of prophet of judgment over against his enemies who oppose him, is clear. It is in Jerusalem that Jesus will die, for this is the place that always kills God's messengers (23:37). With an ironic imperative that also functions as a curse (23:32),[128] Jesus orders them to act out their true nature. With the fury first seen in the Baptist's denunciation[129] of the religious leaders ("brood of vipers," 3:7; cf. 12:34), Jesus rhetorically underscores the inevitability[130] of their final doom on the last day (23:33).

JESUS' PRONOUNCEMENT OF JUDGMENT ON JERUSALEM (23:34–39)

Yet, there is more. On the basis of the scribes' and Pharisees' ultimate doom, an additional prophetic oracle of judgment begins.[131] On account of this fact, Jesus, the Son of God,[132] promises to send emissaries whom his opponents will kill, crucify, beat in their synagogues, and persecute from city to city. This will take place in the time after the resurrection of Jesus, beyond the temporal boundaries of the Gospel's narrative (cf. 10:17–23; 22:1–6).[133] The purpose,[134] at least in part,[135] of this sending of emissaries is to bring upon Jesus' opponents the punishment for all the righteous blood of the entire period of human history,[136] which even now is being poured out upon the earth. With solemn authority, Jesus affirms to the representative religious leaders[137] that all these judgments will come upon this generation of those who have rejected and opposed him (23:36). From the final eschatological judgment (23:33), Jesus' words have moved to focus on the judgment of God that, through an event in history[138] that Jesus predicts, will be poured out during the time of "this generation" (23:34–36).

All these things will fall upon the city of Jerusalem, and so Jesus laments (23:37). The city is the one that kills the prophets and stones those who are sent to it. Despite Jesus' longings to care for and save Jerusalem's children, the city, which represents the people of Israel,[139] was not willing.[140]

The time of Jesus' stay in the city is coming to an end; he is about to leave it (24:1). While he has been in the city that rejects him, Jesus has acted and spoken as the prophet of judgment.[141] As they killed the prophets, so will they kill Jesus (21:39) and persecute and kill those whom he will afterwards send to them (22:6; 23:34).

Consequently, the prophetic sentence of judgment[142] is pronounced: "Your house is left[143] to you desolate" (23:38). On the one hand, because Jesus has been in the temple area since 21:23 and will soon dramatically depart from the temple (24:1), the reference to "your house"[144] most naturally refers specifically to the temple.[145] Here Jesus pronounces desolation and destruction (22:7; 24:2) on the temple in Jerusalem, just as Jeremiah had predicted the ruin of the "den of thieves" (Jer 7:11; cf. 21:13). On the other hand, all of obdurate Israel is also in view, because the punishment for all of history's "righteous blood" (23:35) will come upon "this generation" (23:36). The implied reader will understand the judgment that will occur within the time of Jesus' contemporaries to apply to the temple itself, to the city of Jerusalem, and extending even to all of Israel.[146]

Jesus' last public words to Jerusalem and in Jerusalem state the reason for the coming desolation: "For I say to you, from now on you will certainly not see me until you say, 'Blessed is the one who is coming in the name of the Lord' " (23:39). Contrary to the view of some, Jesus does not here refer to an acclamation on the part of Jerusalem at his Parousia, either in faith[147] or in despair.[148] There is no reason to think that the implied reader will understand Jesus' words as a reference to the Parousia at all.[149] Rather, Jesus' words promise that Jerusalem's children will only "see" Jesus again if they acclaim him aright[150] as the one who comes to them in the name of the Lord.[151] This they have not done. Furthermore, the implied reader has no reason to believe that they actually will do so in the future.[152] Jesus' words show the tragic reason for the coming destruction of Jerusalem's house, the temple. Only if Jerusalem acclaims Jesus as the royal Son of God will they "see" Jesus who came to save his people from their sins. This they will not do. Therefore, their house is left to them desolate. Accordingly, Jesus' words in 23:39 are words of judgment, offering no specific prediction of hope.

At the same time, Jesus' final words to Jerusalem in 23:39 recall the first words of Jerusalem to Jesus in 21:9, for both utterances quote Ps 118:26. Although the crowds and the city did not even know the truth of their acclamation when Jesus entered the city, their words were true. Jesus did come as the eschatological King, the Son of David, into the city of Jerusalem. But the city has refused to own him as such for themselves. Jesus' time in Jerusalem, then, was a time when the conflict between Jesus and his opponents broke out into the open. It became a time for Jesus' prophetic condemnation of this city and its leaders who refuse to know him as more than Son of David, even as Son of God. They will be condemned on the last day. Even more, Jesus' time in Jerusalem has resulted in the promise that, within the time of this generation of Jesus' contemporaries, divine judgment will come down upon the temple, the city, and indeed the nation as a whole. The whole of Jesus' time in Jerusalem is thus bracketed and summarized for the implied reader in Jesus' saying at 23:39.

Now the breach is complete. The religious leaders have been denounced as the enemies of the Son of God. From this point on in the story, the city will not again "see" Jesus, who came to gather them together under his divine protection.[153] Tragically, the city has refused to "see" Jesus as the one he truly is: the royal Son of God, who comes in the name of the Lord (21:9; 23:39).

The story has progressed to the narrative framework that introduces the ED (24:1–3). In the portion of the Gospel's third major section that has led up to this discourse (16:21–23:39), the implied reader has received and understood, even more fully than before, the use of end-time language and categories to refer to events in the time of the story, as well as in the time period of the generation of Jesus' contemporaries that extends beyond the story's temporal boundaries. The goal, the climax of the story, will be Jesus' predicted suffering, death, and resurrection (16:21; 17:22–23; 20:17–19). The matrix of events that encompasses the passion narrative in Jerusalem is to be seen as evidence that this man is coming with his royal power (16:28), as he obediently accepts his Father's will to suffer and die (26:36–46). The places of honor as Jesus sits in his end-time reign will not go to James and John, for they do not yet understand the nature of Jesus' reign (20:20–23). Jesus has come to give his life as the ransom for the many (20:28).

Before he reigns in glory on the last day, his royal enthronement will be seen in his crucifixion, with two others seated with him, one on his right and one on his left (27:35–38). This complex of events, Jesus' passion, is the eschatological goal of his ministry that in its entirety has brought the reign of heaven into the time of the story.

Although it is God's plan and purpose that all these things should take place (δεῖ, 16:21), the implied reader knows also that it is through the rising conflict with the religious leaders that the events leading to the cross will unfold. The conflict has broken into the open with Jesus' entry into Jerusalem. In this city, which will acknowledge him only as prophet (21:11, 46) and not as the Son of

God (21:37–38; 22:2, 41–46), Jesus acts and speaks like a prophet of judgment. His opponents not only will suffer the temporally indeterminate final judgment of God (23:33). Even more, God's judgment will also come upon this generation and this city that murdered the prophets of old (23:31), that will murder Jesus himself (16:21), and that will murder the messengers that the risen, exalted Jesus will send to them (23:34–35). Within the time of this generation, the temple and the city will be destroyed (23:36–38). For they did not know the one who came to them in the name of the Lord (23:39).

The ED, along with its narrative framework (24:1–26:2), entirely consists of Jesus' teaching about events that project beyond the temporal boundaries of Matthew's Gospel. The entire content of the ED is predictive in nature. Even its exhortation is predicated on future events. So, in order to understand that teaching as the implied reader of the Gospel would, I will continue, in chapter 5, to examine the eschatological point of view of the remainder of the story in 26:3–28:20. Equipped with all of the insight available to the implied reader, I will be able to demonstrate how the implied reader understands and is affected by the teaching contained in the ED.

NOTES

1 Senior, *Passion*, 18, says: "The death and triumph of Jesus are not an unexpected or arbitrary ending to the Gospel drama but its inner core."

2 Marguerat, *Jugement*, 345, writes that the whole Gospel of Matthew is "a meditation on the fact that God's people killed its Messiah."

3 Bauer, *Structure*, 85, notes (1) the common sequence of "from" + "that time" + "Jesus began" + infinitive, followed by (2) the content of the message (direct discourse in 4:17; an object clause introduced by "that" in 16:21); that (3) each verse is asyndetic, and (4) "began" carries a genuine force, rather than being pleonastic. Cf. Gnilka, *Matthäusevangelium*, 2:81.

4 Even France, *Evangelist*, 152, who earlier objects to this structural division of the Gospel, admits that 4:17 and 16:21 function as "deliberate and important notification by the author that a new phase of the story is here being introduced."

5 Kingsbury, *Matthew as Story*, 77, notes that the use of δεῖ involves God, along with Jesus and the religious leaders, as a principal character in this outworking of the story. See also 26:54, which envisions Jesus' submission to arrest (and certain execution) in terms of the same divine necessity: "How then would the Scriptures [which prophesy] that thus it must happen [οὕτως δεῖ γενέσθαι] be fulfilled?" Cf. also δεῖ at 17:10; 24:6.

6 Gnilka, *Matthäusevangelium*, 2:82, notes that the three groups of "elders, chief priests, and scribes" are never again thus linked together in the Gospel until their appearance at Jesus' crucifixion at 27:41. Schnackenburg, *Matthäusevangelium 16,21–28,20*, 158, notes the single article with which the narrator joins the three groups of religious leaders, thus showing them as one "character" in their opposition to Jesus.

7 Gnilka, *Matthäusevangelium*, 1:99; Schweizer, *Good News*, 345.

8 I take γάρ in 16:27 as causal in force.

9 Lagrange, *Évangile*, 333, notes: "La gloire du Fils de l'homme est celle du Père ... mais les anges sont ses anges." Cf. Gundry, *Matthew*, 340.

[10] In the discussion regarding Jesus' first use of the self-designation "this man" at 8:20, I concurred with the view that the bald phrase itself, in the mouth of Jesus, would not communicate to the implied reader overtones of the night vision of Dan 7:13–14. Here in Matt 16:27, however, the designation "this man" is accompanied by "with his Father's glory," "with his angels," and "he will pay to each one according to his deed." Owing to this overt eschatological language, it cannot be denied that the night vision of Dan 7:13–14 serves as context and backdrop for Jesus' words at Matt 16:27.

[11] For this translation option, I am indebted to my colleague Dr. James Voelz in a conversation on July 8, 1993. For this construction, see BDF, § 416; Porter, *Idioms*, 269; Goodwin, *Grammar*, ¶¶ 1494, 1588; Smyth, *Grammar*, § 2112 b.

[12] For this precise translation of ἐν τῇ βασιλείᾳ αὐτοῦ, see Meier, *Matthew*, 188. Vögtle, "Anliegen," 286–87, justifies his translation of "in his royal power" with reference to 13:41. I would add this: It doesn't make good sense to speak of Jesus coming "in his reign." This is not to deny that Jesus at times speaks of his own relationship to the reign of heaven in spatial terms, as at 26:29; cf. 8:11; 13:43a. But here Jesus speaks of this man "in motion," "coming," and to translate with "in" simply doesn't make sense. Davies and Allison, *Matthew*, 2:677; Bratcher, *Translator's Guide*, 207; Zahn, *Evangelium*, 552; Newman and Stine, *Translator's Handbook*, 549.

[13] For the history of interpretation, see Martin Künzi, *Das Näherwartungslogion Markus 9,1 par.: Geschichte seiner Auslegung* (Tübingen: J. C. B. Mohr, 1977).

[14] Zahn, *Evangelium*, 552; Davies and Allison, *Matthew*, 2:678; Beasley-Murray, *Jesus and the Kingdom of God*, 188; Künzi, *Markus 9,1 par.*, 199–200; Argyle, *Matthew*, 130; Filson, *Matthew*, 190; Grässer, *Problem*, 130.

[15] Wolthuis, "Experiencing," 314; Giblin, "Theological Perspective," 651.

[16] Many link the Parousia and the transfiguration account, calling the latter a "foreshadowing" (Frye, "The Jesus of the Gospels," 81), a "foretaste" (Meier, *Matthew*, 190), an "anticipation" (Davies and Allison, *Matthew*, 2:675–76; Schnackenburg, *Matthäusevangelium 16,21–28,20*, 161; Moore, *Parousia*, 128), or a "prolepsis" (Kingsbury, *Matthew as Story*, 92) of the former. Others connect the Parousia with Jesus' resurrection (Ridderbos, *Coming*, 507; Wolthuis, "Experiencing," 315; Stonehouse, *Witness*, 240), with Pentecost (Box, *Matthew*, 268; Guthrie, *Theology*, 798), or with the destruction of Jerusalem (Alford, *Matthew*, 177; Sabourin, *L'Évangile*, 228).

[17] Wolthuis, "Experiencing," 314; Giblin, "Theological Perspective," 651; and Vögtle, "Anliegen," 287.

[18] Davies and Allison, *Matthew*, 2:675, believe that μέλλω at 16:27 carries a sense of imminence and immediacy. They cite as other examples 2:13; 17:12, 27; 24:6. They do note, however, that the verb does not necessarily possess this component of meaning and offer as evidence 3:7; 11:14; 12:42.

[19] In 5:18, Jesus explains why he has not come to abolish the law (5:17): "For [γάρ] truly I say to you ... not one iota or one hook will pass away from the Law until all things happen." Cf. 10:23; 13:17; 17:20.

[20] At 18:18, after the command for the church to make the unrepentant sinner as an outsider (18:17), Jesus enlarges on the church's authority: "Truly, I say to you, whatever you bind on earth will have been bound in heaven, and whatever you loose on earth will have been loosed in heaven." Cf. 18:19; 19:24.

[21] At 5:26, after the exhortation to be reconciled to one's brother or sister, Jesus summarizes the urgency of his exhortation: "Truly I say to you, you will certainly not go out from there until you pay the last quadrans." Cf. 6:2, 5, 16; 10:15.

22 Matt 10:42; 23:36; 24:34; 26:34.

23 Matt 11:11; 21:21; 24:47; 26:13.

24 At 8:10, Jesus responds to the centurion's acknowledgment of his authority by saying, "Truly I say to you, I have found such faith in no one in Israel!" Cf. 18:3; 19:23, 28; 21:31; 24:2; 25:12, 40, 45.

25 Cf. Heinrich Schlier, "ἀμήν," *TDNT* 1:338.

26 At 5:26, the occurrence of ἕως ἄν + subjunctive in Matthew "theoretically" implies a reversal of the main clause; cf. 17:9; 18:30, 34.

27 Chilton, *God in Strength*, 261.

28 Beasley-Murray, *Jesus and the Kingdom of God*, 188; Davies and Allison, *Matthew*, 2:675–76.

29 Recall that the narrator of Matthew's story has twice before given an "abrupt" fulfill-ment of a prediction, at 3:13 and 10:1.

30 Cf. Künzi, *Markus 9,1 par.*, 9–11, 23–24, 35–36, 41–46, 67; Ladd, *Presence*, 323.

31 Cf. Künzi, *Markus 9,1 par.*, 200; Beasley-Murray, *Jesus and the Kingdom of God*, 188; Argyle, *Matthew*, 130; Carson, "Matthew," 380.

32 The disciples misunderstand the eschatological character of the martyred John, of Jesus' ministry, and the necessity of Jesus' path to the cross (16:22). This tendency for the disciples to ask questions based upon misunderstanding will be important for the interpretation of 24:3.

33 Adolf Schlatter, *Der Evangelist Matthäus: Seine Sprache, seine Zeit, seine Selbständigkeit* (Stuttgart: Calwer Verlag, 1957), 709; Argyle, *Matthew*, 133; Beare, *Matthew*, 366; Filson, *Matthew*, 193; Lagrange, *Évangile*, 337. Others envision yet another future coming of Elijah: Alford, *Matthew*, 180; Willoughby C. Allen, *A Critical and Exegetical Commentary on the Gospel according to S. Matthew* (New York: Charles Scribner's Sons, 1907), 187.

34 Wink, *John the Baptist*, 15, says: "What is expressed is the quite offensive paradox that the heavenly Elijah should be this captive, murdered prophet: a *dead* Elijah."

35 Even though the three disciples are present with Jesus in the garden, they "see" but do not understand. Jesus' words to his disciples in 16:28, accordingly, are somewhat ironic.

36 Cf. Davies and Allison, *Matthew*, 2:706–7, for remarkable parallels in Matthew's depiction of the transfiguration and the execution of Jesus.

37 John Paul Heil, *The Death and Resurrection of Jesus: A Narrative-Critical Reading of Matthew 26–28* (Minneapolis: Fortress, 1991), 43, writes concerning 26:37: "Now that the time has arrived for Jesus' suffering and death preliminary to that heavenly glory [as seen in the transfiguration], he appropriately takes these same three disciples to be close companions and witnesses of his sadness and distress over approaching death."

38 In Matthew's story, 20:17 is the only other instance of Jesus' "taking along" other people with him.

39 Heil, *Death and Resurrection*, 10.

40 Howell, *Inclusive*, 240–42.

41 Kingsbury, *Matthew as Story*, 88.

42 Heil, *Death and Resurrection*, 71.

43 To be rejected in part is Heil's structural analysis of the passion in Matthew's Gospel. Heil, *Death and Resurrection*, 2, places the agony in the garden (26:36–46) as the mid-dle of three parts in the unit that he calls "Jesus accepts death through prayer." But

the first part of Heil's unit, "Jesus predicts abandonment/denial by his disciples" (26:30–35), belongs with prior material in the upper room, rather than under a heading such as "Jesus accepts death through prayer." Neither is the third part of Heil's unit, "Jesus is arrested, betrayed by Judas, and abandoned by his disciples" (26:47–56), part of Jesus' act of acceptance of "the cup."

The agony in the garden (26:36–46) stands alone as the event that actually precipitates the events of Jesus' suffering, death, and resurrection. Note the following elements. First, prior to the agony in the garden, Jesus makes a series of predictions (26:2, 12, 13, 18, 21, 23, 29, 31, 32, 34), all of which (except for 26:29) are fulfilled in the remainder of the Gospel, beginning with the account of Jesus' arrest and the scattering of the disciples. These predictions, however, come to an end in the garden. It is Jesus' acceptance of the Father's will that causes the predictions to begin to come true.

Second, Jesus' words and actions betray a dramatic change within him as well. Prior to the entrance into the garden, neither the words of Jesus nor the narrator's descriptions give any indication of internal distress. This changes dramatically in 26:36–46. Jesus "prays" in the garden, an action attributed to Jesus in Matthew's story only elsewhere at 14:23. Jesus "begins" to be grieved and to be in agony (26:37), and this is reinforced by his words to the three in 26:38, "My soul is grieved until death," and by his action of falling to the ground on his face (26:39).

Third, in the garden Jesus prays, not once, but three times, with a notable progression to his praying. Cf. Heil, *Death and Resurrection*, 47–48; Schweizer, *Good News*, 493. When first he prays, he actually asks from God a different fate ("If it is possible, let this cup pass away from me," 26:39), all the while acknowledging the supremacy of the Father's will. When he prays the second time, a different fate is no longer in view ("If it is not possible for this cup to pass away unless I drink it," 26:42). When he has finished praying, Jesus returns to "the disciples" and declares the arrival of "the hour," which brings to reality the betrayal of this man. The remarkable double occurrence of "has arrived" (ἤγγικεν, 26:45, 46) brings the crucial account of the agony in the garden to its close. At the same time, the twofold occurrence of "has arrived" links the pericope inextricably with the account of Jesus' arrest (cf. 26:47: "And while he was still speaking, Judas"). With Jesus' submission to the Father's will, it has begun. The events that will bring his end-time ministry of word and deed to its climax are now taking place. The present, though hidden, reign of heaven is here, for the implied reader to see.

Finally, the narrator of Matthew's Gospel uses historical presents exceedingly sparsely. Yet the scene in Gethsemane contains eight (and perhaps nine, if the variant reading at 26:43 is read) historical presents, thus imparting to this narrative unit a vividness that is literally unique in all of Matthew's Gospel; cf. Matt 4:1–11, which has five historic presents, the next highest concentration in the Gospel.

44 This question may arise: "If the disciples sleep, how can they be said to fulfill 16:28, which says that some will 'see'?" Note the following explicit data.

1. After taking the three with him apart from the larger group of disciples, Jesus tells them, "My soul is grieved to the point of death. Remain here and pray" (26:38). Thus, he informs them of his anguish and they witness it.

2. Even though Jesus does remove himself from them, it is only a "little distance" (προελθὼν μικρόν, 26:39). It cannot be supposed that the disciples instantly fell asleep the moment Jesus left them!

3. Jesus returns to his sleeping disciples, awakens them, and speaks to them about the need to watch and pray lest they enter into the test (26:40–41). In this way also the disciples are witnesses of the agony.

Yet they do not understand, nor do they watch and pray. They are "witnesses" of Jesus' agony, but "incomprehending witnesses."

45 The noun "temptation" occurs in Matthew's Gospel only in the Lord's Prayer (6:13) and in the account of the agony in the garden (26:41). The reference in both places is to eschatological crisis, indeed, "to God's final struggle with and conquering of the powers of evil, which is now reaching a crescendo with the suffering and death of Jesus" (Heil, *Death and Resurrection*, 47; cf. Meier, *Matthew*, 324; Senior, *Passion*, 82).

46 Nils A. Dahl, "The Passion Narrative in Matthew," in *The Interpretation of Matthew* (ed. Graham Stanton; Philadelphia: Fortress, 1983), 49.

47 Jesus' prayer to the Father in the garden is the same as the one he taught the disciples, γενηθήτω τὸ θέλημά σου ("Let your will be done"). Jesus' prayer is not merely modeling suffering (Strecker, *Der Weg*, 183) or believing prayer (David Stanley, "Matthew's Gethsemane [Mt 26:36–46]," in *Jesus in Gethsemane* [New York: Paulist Press, 1980], 171). Jesus brings to fulfillment the reality for which he commanded his disciples to pray. This eschatological prayer, "Let your will be done," echoes the parallel petition in form and meaning: "Let your reign come."

48 Stanley, "Gethsemane," 180, cogently remarks:

> We have seen that Matthew's Jesus is, throughout this Passion narrative, imbued with power.... "May your will be done" is an explicit quotation of the dominical prayer at Mt 6:10b. It is of paramount importance that Jesus resolve his struggle by manifesting the attitude he had taught his followers to adopt. Thus here the words can only mean, "May you carry out *your will for the realization of your sovereign rule in history through all the concrete circumstances of my death.*" (emphasis added)

49 Note how this understanding of 16:28 matches well with the whole ironic message of Jesus' eschatological royalty that is revealed in the passion narrative. Neither in the passion narrative nor in Gethsemane do the characters involved understand what the implied reader knows.

50 Weaver, *Missionary Discourse*, 140, notes that "prior to Jesus' arrival in Jerusalem there are only three scenes which do not explicitly mention the presence of the disciples (19:1–2, 3–9, 16–22); and in each of these cases the most natural reading of the text leads the implied reader to assume that the disciples are present, even though they are not mentioned."

51 The unusual character of such a singular rebuke addressed to the disciples is granted. It is not, however, unprecedented. On one occasion, Jesus calls his disciples "Hypocrite!" (ὑποκριτά, 7:5), whereas all other uses of the epithet are reserved for the religious leaders of Israel (6:2, 5, 16; 15:7; 22:18; 23:13, 14, 15) or those who are destined to eternal punishment (24:51)!

52 For a major compositional study, see William G. Thompson, *Matthew's Advice to a Divided Community: Mt. 17:2–18:35* (Rome: Biblical Institute, 1970).

53 The implied reader will join the reference in 18:17 to the "church," ἐκκλησία, with the only other occurrence of the term at 16:18: "And upon this rock I will build my church." The future tense in 16:18 most naturally will be understood as a reference to the time after the resurrection, when the disciples have begun the mission to "all the nations" (24:14; 28:19).

54 Note the aorist (and not future) introductory verb, "was likened to," ὡμοιώθη, in 18:23; cf. Beasley-Murray, *Jesus and the Kingdom of God*, 116.

55 For "regeneration" as the equivalent of "the age to come," see Schnackenburg, *Matthäusevangelium 16,21–28,20*, 186.

56 For parallels in Jewish literature to "the faithful" acting as co-judges at the judgment, see Evans, "In What Sense Blasphemy?" 223–24, 229.

57 The correspondence of "twelve" apostles and "twelve" tribes carries to the implied reader some nuance of Jesus' disciples as "true" Israel, in contrast to the empirical Israel that opposed and rejected the Son of God. Cf. Ladd, *Presence*, 251–55.

Rejected is the view of Douglas R. A. Hare and Daniel Harrington, " 'Make Disciples of All the Gentiles' (MT 28:19)," *CBQ* 37 (1975): 365, who see the implication that "Jews will be treated as a special category distinct from the rest of mankind in the eschatological drama." Simply stated, the rest of mankind ("all the nations" of 24:9, 14; 25:32; 28:19) is simply not in view here. For references to "God's people participating in the judgment," see Schweizer, *Good News*, 389, who cites 1 Cor 6:2; Dan 7:22; Wis 3:1, 8.

58 Note the parallel usage of "entering into the reign of heaven" (19:23, 24), "having or entering into or inheriting eternal life" (19:16, 17, 29), and "being saved" (19:25).

59 Meier, *Matthew*, 223.

60 Carson, "Matthew," 431, says that "the link with 19:28 … is unmistakable." Cf. Schnackenburg, *Matthäusevangelium 16,21–28,20*, 190.

61 Although the mother asks the question, Jesus' second person plural reply (20:22) is directed to James and John. In turn, they are the ones who answer him.

62 Carson, "Matthew," 431; Alford, *Matthew*, 204; Argyle, *Matthew*, 153; Filson, *Matthew*, 216.

63 The only times in Matthew's story when Jesus is called "King" are 2:2 (by the Magi, rightly); 21:5 (by the Scriptures, rightly); 25:34, 40 (by Jesus himself, rightly); and 27:11, 29, 37, 42 (all in mockery, but rightly with irony).

64 Cf. Heil, *Death and Resurrection*, 10–11.

65 There are, of course, two Greek words for "left" that occur in Matthew's story: ἀριστερός (6:3) and εὐώνυμος (20:21, 23; 25:33, 41; 27:38). The terms for "right and left" at the crucifixion match the terms of the question in 20:21.

66 Commentators often make the connection between "for whom it has been prepared [ἡτοίμασται] by my Father" (20:23) and "inherit the reign which has been prepared [ἡτοιμασμένην] for you from the foundation of the world" (25:34). The obstacle to this view, of course, is that "right" and "left" mean different things at 20:21 and at 25:31–46. In the former, both right and left are the places of honor. In the latter, right denotes blessing, while left denotes damnation.

Interestingly, a literary dramatist made the same connection that I have made between 20:20–23 and 27:35–38, although I discovered her insight after I developed my own. Sayers, *The Man Born to Be King*, 299, places (in agreement with the Fourth Gospel's passion account) John son of Zebedee at the crucifixion. His words to the dying Jesus are as follows: "Jesus, my lord, I am here—John bar-Zebedee, the friend who loves you. We ran away from you, Master. We refused the cup and the baptism [cf. Mark 10:38], not knowing what we asked, and the places on your right hand and on your left have been given to these two thieves."

67 Reeves, "Resurrection Narrative," 56–57, makes a connection between the presence of the mother of Zebedee's sons in 20:20–23 and at 27:56. He goes no farther, however, than to say that her presence in chapter 20 shows that "she is guilty of the same desire for power as the disciples." For a similar "near miss," see John P. Heil, "The Narrative Structure of Matthew 27:55–28:20," *JBL* 110 (1991): 424.

68 For a thorough study of Jesus' crucifixion in Matthew, see Witherup, "The Cross of Jesus." For comments linking 20:20–28 and the crucifixion, see Witherup,

"The Cross of Jesus," 258–59. I reached my own conclusions regarding the link between 20:20–23 and Jesus' crucifixion independently, long before reading Witherup's fine study.

[69] For other "marginal persons" acclaiming Jesus as "Son of David," see 9:27 (two blind men), 15:22 (the Canaanite woman), and the children in the temple (21:15).

[70] τί θέλεις, 20:21; τί θέλετε ποιήσω ὑμῖν, 20:32.

[71] A ἵνα clause that expresses the content or object of the verb. Cf. Porter, *Idioms*, 238–39.

[72] Kingsbury, *Matthew as Story*, 5.

[73] The authority of Jesus will become the issue in the controversy with the religious leaders at 21:23, 27. Cf. Kingsbury, *Matthew as Story*, 125–26.

[74] The issue of Jesus' "identity" is central to the narration of his time in Jerusalem. The question "Who is this?" (21:10) occurs at the beginning of this time period. When the confrontation between Jesus and the religious leaders in Jerusalem comes to its head, in the final pericope of confrontation (22:41–46), the issue of Jesus' "identity" comes to the fore once again: "Whose son is he [the Christ]?" (22:42). The ultimate answer to the question of Jesus' identity is that, while yes, he is surely the royal Son of David, he is preeminently the Son of God, as Ps 110:1 implies.

[75] Beare, *Matthew*, 415, notes a conceptual parallel between "was troubled" (ἐταράχθη, 2:3) and "was shaken" (ἐσείσθη, 21:10), but he does not develop it. Sabourin, *L'Évangile*, 270, notes the same parallel.

[76] Cf. David E. Garland, *The Intention of Matthew 23* (Leiden: E. J. Brill, 1979), 39; Meier, *Matthew*, 234; Schnackenburg, *Matthäusevangelium 16,21–28,20*, 197; Sabourin, *L'Évangile*, 270; Filson, *Matthew*, 221.

[77] Verseput, *Messianic King*, 25, comments: "Yet the multitudes display absolutely no comprehension of their own words, for they are represented as glibly identifying the object of their acclamation as 'the prophet Jesus, from Nazareth' (21:22)—an appellation glaringly insufficient as far as Matthew is concerned (cf. 16:14)." Other uncomprehending or insincere uses of Scripture occur in the mouths of the chief priests and scribes (2:4–6); Satan (4:6); the scribes (as reported by Jesus' disciples, 17:10); the Pharisees (19:7); and the Sadducees (22:24).

[78] Kingsbury, "Probe," 8–9.

[79] The crowds think that both John and Jesus are prophets (21:10, 26, 46). Yet even that understanding of John is insufficient. Jesus has already taught the crowds that John is a prophet, yes, but something greater than a prophet (11:7–15).

[80] Powell, "Religious Leaders," 85; Kingsbury, *Structure, Christology, Kingdom*, 22; Schweitzer, *Quest*, 340. Contrast the view of Michael Knowles, *Jeremiah in Matthew's Gospel: The Rejected-Prophet Motif in Matthaean Redaction*, JSNTSup 68 (Sheffield: Sheffield Academic Press, 1993), 91, who thinks that the popular opinions about Jesus are "not erroneous alternatives raised only for the sake of rejection, but intimations or approximations of the messiah's true identity as one who suffers."

[81] Marguerat, *Jugement*, 347–48. For a full examination of this theme, see Knowles, *Jeremiah*.

[82] Note that the narrator writes (21:12) that Jesus expelled "all" those who were selling and buying in the temple.

[83] Kingsbury, *Matthew as Story*, 81.

[84] At 3:12, the Baptist had prophesied of the Coming One "whose winnowing fork is in his hand, and he will clean out his threshing floor" (διακαθαριεῖ τὴν ἅλωνα αὐτοῦ). The

implied reader might be expected to know that the temple in Jerusalem was built upon the threshing floor of Ornan (ἐν ἅλῳ Ορνα) the Jebusite (2 Chr 3:1). Also, *Pss. Sol.* 17:30, which speaks of the coming Davidic, messianic King, promises that "he will purge Jerusalem."

85 Carson, "Matthew," 442; Argyle, *Matthew*, 157; Filson, *Matthew*, 222.

86 Cf. Knowles, *Jeremiah*, 174. For the case that this was also the intent of the historical Jesus, see E. P. Sanders, *Jesus and Judaism* (Philadelphia: Fortress, 1985), 61–76. For a rebuttal of Sanders, see Craig Evans, "Jesus' Action in the Temple and Evidence of Corruption in the First-Century Temple," *SBLSP, 1989* (ed. David J. Lull; Atlanta: Scholars Press, 1989), 522–39.

87 Cf. Jer 7:16: "As for you, do not pray for this people, or lift up cry or prayer for them, and do not intercede with me, for I do not hear you" (RSV).

88 Cf. Jer 7:5, 7: "If you truly amend your ways and your doings ... then I will let you dwell in this place, in the land that I gave of old to your fathers for ever" (RSV). Also, Jer 7:34: "And I will make to cease from the cities of Judah and from the streets of Jerusalem the voice of mirth and the voice of gladness, the voice of the bride-groom and the voice of the bride; for the land shall become a waste" (RSV).

89 Schweizer, *Good News*, 408, writes that Jesus' healings in the temple already demon-strate "that the eschaton promised by Isaiah has come; now their [the cripples'] exclu-sion from the Temple community is annulled." Cf. Meier, *Matthew*, 235.

90 David J. Zucker, "Jesus and Jeremiah in the Matthean Tradition," *JES* 27 (1990): 298, asserts a connection between the cursing of the fig tree and Jer 8:13: "When I would gather them, says the LORD, there are no grapes on the vine, nor figs on the fig tree; even the leaves are withered, and what I gave them has passed away from them" (RSV). Cf. France, *Evangelist*, 215; Carson, "Matthew," 445; Knowles, *Jeremiah*, 177.

91 Kingsbury, "Developing Conflict," 71; cf. Kingsbury, *Matthew as Story*, 122–25.

92 Weaver, *Missionary Discourse*, 137.

93 Cf. the discussion of 21:10 above. Even though the crowds thought John was a prophet, it is not the crowds whom Jesus describes as "believing" John (21:32), but rather the tax gatherers and the whores.

94 I take the present indicative, προάγουσιν (21:31) as futuristic, on the basis of Matthew's normal usage of entering "into," εἰς, the reign of heaven as a future possibility and not a present one (5:20; 7:21; 18:3; 19:23, 24). A similar futuristic present is likely at 23:13.

95 Cf. BDF, § 245a.3: "Comparative expressing exclusion."

96 It is possible to write "will be destroyed" because, as Filson, *Matthew*, 229, notes, "The parable offers a last warning, with little hope that they will accept it."

97 Powell, "Religious Leaders," 119.

98 Note the second-century B.C. parallel in *T. Benj.* 9:1–2, in which God is said to remove "the kingdom of the Lord" because of Israel's sin. Str-B 1:175 notes a parallel attributed to a fourth-century A.D. rabbi.

99 Kingsbury, "Husbandmen," 645. Knowles, *Jeremiah*, 114.

100 See Kingsbury, "Husbandmen," 645, with reference to 21:44: "And the one who falls upon this stone will be crushed, but upon whomever it falls, it will crush him."

101 Kingsbury, "Husbandmen," 643.

102 In agreement that the judgment comes upon Israel *as a nation* are France, *Evangelist*, 224; Ladd, *Presence*, 321; Hare and Harrington, "Make Disciples," 359; Pesch, "Eschatologie und Ethik," 226.

[103] Kingsbury, *Matthew as Story*, 20; Powell, "Religious Leaders," 117.

[104] Kingsbury, "Husbandmen," 645.

[105] Carson, "Matthew," 456; Beasley-Murray, *Jesus and the Kingdom of God*, 120.

[106] Beasley-Murray, *Jesus and the Kingdom of God*, 120.

[107] οὐκ ἤθελον ἐλθεῖν, 22:3. Cf. 11:14 ("And if you are willing to receive," εἰ θέλετε δέξασθαι) and 23:37 ("How many times I was willing [ἠθέλησα] to gather together your children, in the way that a hen gathers together her chicks under [her] wings, but you were not willing [οὐκ ἠθελήσατε]").

[108] Cf. Knowles, *Jeremiah*, 116.

[109] Commentators are quick to point out the extent to which this feature doesn't fit into the story of a king hosting a wedding banquet for his son: Caird, *Language*, 164; Schweizer, *Good News*, 418; Meier, *Matthew*, 247; France, *Evangelist*, 224.

[110] There may possibly be a distinction intended by Jesus in the parable of the Wedding Feast between the "slaves" (δοῦλοι, 22:3, 4, 6, 8, 10) and the "servants" (διάκονοι, 22:13). That is, the "slaves" serve the king in the time up until the Parousia, but the "servants" are those responsible for carrying out the separation of the chosen from those who are merely called (22:14). This would correspond to the distinction between "slaves" and "reapers" (θερισταί, 13:24–30, 36–43). See also the use of "workers" (ἐργάται), not "reapers" (θερισταί) at 9:37–38. Cf. Alford, *Matthew*, 221.

[111] The phrasing "there will be weeping and gnashing of teeth" is uniquely Matthean, occurring in exactly the same form at 8:12; 13:42, 50; 22:13; 25:30. At 8:12; 22:13; and 25:30 it is linked with "the outer darkness." In all five instances, the reference is to final eschatological judgment and punishment.

[112] Beare, *Matthew*, 432, 435; Powell, "Religious Leaders," 122.

[113] Garland, *Intention*, 83; Dahl, "Passion Narrative," 50.

[114] Cf. Carson, *Matthew*, 468: "If Messiah is not David's son, *whose son is he?* The solution is given by the prologue to Matthew (chs. 1–2) and by the voice of God himself (3:17; 17:5): Jesus is the Son of God."

[115] Kingsbury, *Matthew as Story*, 82; Argyle, *Matthew*, 170; Powell, "Religious Leaders," 130; Sabourin, *L'Évangile*, 289; Verseput, *Messianic King*, 34; Beare, *Matthew*, 445.

[116] This is the second time (cf. 13:41: "the reign of [this man]") that the exaltation of Jesus is mentioned. Cf. Vögtle, "Anliegen," 290; Beasley-Murray, *Jesus and the Kingdom of God*, 199.

[117] H. J. B. Combrink, "The Macrostructure of the Gospel of Matthew," *Neot* 16 (1982): 14.

[118] It is possible that the "turning point" after 22:41–46 is analogous to the "turning point" of the religious leaders' decision to kill Jesus (12:14). After 12:14, the implied reader knows that the religious leaders' hostility to Jesus is to the death. By starkest contrast, Jesus' willingness (ποσάκις ἠθέλησα ἐπισυναγαγεῖν τὰ τέκνα σου, 23:37) to include even the leaders in the present, eschatological fellowship of his disciples has extended to this late point in the story.

[119] This is the last time in the Gospel of Matthew that Jesus addresses the crowds. The fact that the crowds are persuaded by the chief priests and elders to ask for Barabbas' release (27:20) shows that the crowds reject the appeal of Jesus addressed to them in chapter 23.

[120] Cf. Strecker, *Der Weg*, 173.

[121] See Garland, *Intention*, 72–81, for the development of the "woe-cry" in the OT.

122 Anthony J. Saldarini, "Delegitimation of Leaders in Matthew 23," *CBQ* 54 (1992): 672–73.

123 The English word *hypocrisy* carries an inevitable connotation of "insincerity." For the case that ὑποκριτής in biblical usage (in contrast to classical and Hellenistic literature) does not necessarily carry that nuance of meaning, see Ulrich Wilckens, "ὑποκρίνομαι κτλ.," *TDNT* 8:559–71; Garland, *Intention*, 96–117; Saldarini, "Delegitimation," 673. Robert Smith, "Hypocrite," in *Dictionary of Jesus and the Gospels* (ed. Joel B. Green, Scot McKnight, and I. Howard Marshall), 353, writes, "The English word *fraud* or *imposter* seems to capture the sense of *hypokrites* in Matthew 23 and in most other uses in Jewish-Greek literature and the NT. It is regularly used of teachers and leaders who are inauthentic, *whether consciously or unconsciously*" (emphasis added).

124 I take the present tenses in 23:13 as futuristic tenses. See the discussion of 21:31 above.

125 The choice in 23:13 is where to place the conative force. Does it belong with the present participle, τοὺς εἰσερχομένους, "those who wish to enter," or with the present indicative, ἀφίετε, "you do not wish to permit"? The former might be taken to imply that the scribes and Pharisees are effectively preventing anyone from future entrance into the reign of heaven. Thus, the latter is more likely.

126 Saldarini, "Delegitimation," 674.

127 Recall the irony at 9:13: "For I did not come to call righteous people, but sinners."

128 Garland, *Intention*, 167; Saldarini, "Delegitimation," 675; Filson, *Matthew*, 248; Sabourin, *L'Évangile*, 297.

129 Walter Grundmann, *Das Evangelium nach Matthäus* (Berlin: Evangelische Verlagsanstalt, 1968), 495.

130 Cf. Marguerat, *Jugement*, 360; Garland, *Intention*, 168.

131 Marguerat, *Jugement*, 360, thinks that in 23:34 διὰ τοῦτο echoes the introductory לָכֵן of a prophetic judgment oracle. Cf. Judg 10:13; 2 Kgs 1:6; Amos 4:12.

132 The implied reader knows that it is the Son of God who thus will send messengers to Israel, because it was the vineyard owner's son who was killed (21:37–38), the king's son for whom the wedding feast was given (22:2), and God's Son (and David's Lord, 21:41–46) whom these opponents refused to acknowledge. This merely reinforces the explicit and emphatic portrait in Matthew's Gospel of Jesus' identity as the Son of God.

For the view that a Wisdom Christology underlies Jesus' words at 23:34–39, see Burnett, *Testament*, 31, who is dependent on the work of M. Jack Suggs, *Wisdom, Christology, and Law in Matthew's Gospel* (Cambridge: Harvard University Press, 1970). For a critique of Burnett, see Douglas Hare, review of *The Testament of Jesus-Sophia: A Redaction-Critical Study of the Eschatological Discourse in Matthew*, by Fred W. Burnett, in *JBL* 102 (1983): 644–46. For a critique of Suggs, see Marshall Johnson, "Reflections on a Wisdom Approach to Matthew's Christology," *CBQ* 36 (1974): 35.

133 Cf. Kik, *Matthew Twenty-Four*, 22; Alford, *Matthew*, 232; Schweizer, *Good News*, 436; Sabourin, *L'Évangile*, 297–98; Grundmann, *Evangelium*, 496. Burnett, *Testament*, 51–56, contends that, because Jesus speaks in 23:34 as "pre-existent Sophia," who throughout history has sent the prophets, the time frame of "I am sending" (ἀποστέλλω) in 23:34 refers to the past time in Matthew's story-world. This is far-fetched.

134 It is impossible to avoid the syntax of ἵνα + subjunctive. It expresses purpose; cf. BDF, § 369; Porter, *Idioms*, 232–33; Knowles, *Jeremiah*, 136.

135 The implied reader knows also that the mission to Israel that takes place after the resurrection of Jesus also has the purpose of preaching the reign of heaven and its end-time salvation to the "lost sheep" which are Israel's house (10:6–7).Thus, Schuyler Brown, "The Matthean Apocalypse," *JSNT* 4 (1979): 5, and Douglas R. A.

Hare, *The Theme of Jewish Persecution of Christians in the Gospel according to St. Matthew* (Cambridge: Cambridge University Press, 1967), 88, severely overstate the impact on the implied reader of the purpose clause in 23:35.

[136] Saldarini, "Delegitimation," 677; Garland, *Intention*, 184. The reference to "Zechariah" in 23:35 is a reference to the son of Jehoida (2 Chr 24:20–22); cf. Garland, *Intention*, 182; Grundmann, *Evangelium*, 495; Beare, *Matthew*, 459.

[137] Hare, *Jewish Persecution*, 151–52; Carson, "Matthew," 485; Jan Lambrecht, "The Parousia Discourse: Composition and Content in Mt., XXIV–XXV," in *L'Apocalypse Johannique et L'Apocalyptique dans le Nouveau Testament* (ed. Jan Lambrecht; Leuven: University Press, 1980), 315.

[138] Garland, *Intention*, 179, cites the work of O. H. Steck, *Isarel und das gewaltsame Geschick der Propheten: Untersuchungen zur Überlieferung des Deuteronomischen Geschichtsbildes im Alten Testament, Spät-judentum and Urchristentum*, WMANT 23 (Neukirchen: Neukirchener Verlag, 1967), 289–316, for the conclusion that Israel's guilt over the violent death of the prophets "was used to explain the apparent divine rejection of Israel and the ensuing punishment *in historical events*" (emphasis added).

[139] Note the switch to second person plural address: "you (pl.) were not willing" (23:37); "your (pl.) house is left to you (pl.) desolate" (23:38); and "you (pl.) will not see me until you (pl.) say" (23:39).

[140] Note the correspondence between "you were not willing" at 23:37 and the parable of the Wedding Feast, in which the previously invited guests "were not willing to come" (22:3); cf. Marguerat, *Jugement*, 368.

[141] I here summarize all of the ways that Jesus has appeared as the "prophet of judgment" to those who will only acknowledge him as a "prophet" (21:11, 46):

1. Jesus' entry into the city fulfills the prophetic word (Matt 21:4; Zech 9:9).

2. Jesus' casting people out of the temple is closely connected to Jeremiah's oracle against Israel and the temple ("den of robbers," Matt 21:13; Jer 7:11).

3. The cursing of the fig tree (Matt 21:18–19) is a symbolic action, similar to the prophetic אוֹת.

4. The scribes and Pharisees are truly the "sons" of those who murdered the prophets (23:29–33). As such, they will also murder Jesus and the messengers that he will afterward send (23:34–36).

[142] The theme of God making something "desolate" (ἔρημος and related words) as divine punishment occurs in the LXX with respect to the land (Isa 1:7; 6:11; Jer 4:27; 7:34; Ezek 33:28, 29); the houses of the rich (Isa 5:9); Jerusalem (Jer 51:2); the house of the king of Judah (Jer 22:6); the cities of Judah (Isa 17:9; Jer 9:11; 41:22; 51:2); the nation as a whole (Ezek 5:14). The Pseudepigrapha also uses the image concerning the sanctuary (*T. Levi* 15:1–12; *Sib. Or.* 3:280) and the land (*Sib. Or.* 3:273–279). At times the invasions of foreign nations are specifically the agent of desolation, with respect to the land (Jer 2:15; 12:10, 12) and the sanctuary (1 Macc 1:39) and Jerusalem (1 Macc 3:45). The appearance of desolation is called "the day of the Lord" at Isa 13:9. Its cause in Jer 7:34 is the abominations (τὰ βδελύγματα) set up in the temple (7:30) and the high places of Topheth (7:31).

[143] Bratcher, *Translator's Guide*, 297, thinks that the passive verb "is left" (ἀφίεται) probably refers to God's abandonment of the temple.

[144] Kik, *Matthew Twenty-Four*, 22, observes the change of pronoun from "my house" (i.e., God's house, 21:13) to "your house." That is to say, with Jesus' pronouncement of judgment, the temple is no longer the house of God.

145 Grundmann, *Evangelium*, 496; Beare, *Matthew*, 460; Meier, *Matthew*, 274. To the contrary, Burnett, *Testament*, 124, and Hare, *Jewish Persecution*, 153, claim that the temple is specifically not in view at 23:38. I find this incredible.

146 John F. Hart, "A Chronology of Matthew 24:1–44" (Th.D. diss., Grace Theological Seminary, 1986), 56, 63; Garland, *Intention*, 199; Schweizer, *Good News*, 444; Marguerat, *Jugement*, 369.

147 Beasley-Murray, *Jesus and the Kingdom of God*, 306; Nikolaus Walter, "Tempelzerstörung und synoptische Apokalypse," *ZNW* 57 (1966): 47; Zahn, *Evangelium*, 653.

148 Lambrecht, "Parousia Discourse," 316; Garland, *Intention*, 207; Schlatter, *Evangelist*, 691; Meier, *Matthew*, 275; Marguerat, *Jugement*, 372.

149 Contra Hahn, "Rede," 115; Ernst Haenchen, "Matthäus 23," *ZTK* 48 (1951): 56; Marguerat, *Jugement*, 371. Note that when Jesus later describes the Parousia (25:31–46), no one among either the righteous or the wicked acclaims him as "the one who comes in the name of the Lord."

150 Dale Allison, "Matt. 23:39 = Luke 13:35b as a Conditional Prophecy," *JSNT* 18 (1983): 75–84, is persuasive in rejecting the possibility that those who *oppose* Jesus would ever, even at the Parousia, mouth the words "Blessed is he...." Allison notes that "εὐλογεῖν and εὐλογημένος are not words of fear and trembling, nor are they typically voiced by the ignorant, the condemned, or those in mourning" (p. 75).

151 Allison, "Conditional Prophecy," 75–84, puts forward as his main thesis the view that Matt 23:39 functions like a conditional sentence that could be rephrased thus: "If you say, 'Blessed is the one who comes in the name of the Lord,' you will see me." While not endorsing all of Allison's conclusions, I concur that Matt 23:39 does function like a conditional sentence. The emphatic negative in 23:39 ("You will certainly not see me") would cause the rephrasing of the sentence to be something like this: "*Only* if you say, 'Blessed is the one.' " Indeed, Allison adduces examples from the NT (Matt 5:26; 18:30; Luke 15:59; Acts 23:12; 2 Thess 2:7) and other literature in which the meaning of ἕως "is not simply temporal but properly conditional (close to 'unless')" (pp. 78–79).

152 As Jesus' words in 23:34–36 show, Jerusalem's children and Israel's leaders will in the future persecute the missionaries whom Jesus will send to them.

153 It may be significant that Jesus says in 23:39, "From now on you will not see *me*." He does not say, "You will not see this man," that is, he does not use the self-designation that so often occurs in contexts where Jesus' opponents are in view. It is, in fact, noteworthy that Jesus does not ever refer to himself as "this man" during his time in Jerusalem (21:1–23:39). This fact could conceivably underscore the tragedy of Jesus' time there. He came as "Jesus," who would "save" his people from their sins. But the people were not willing (22:3; 23:37).

By contrast, note Jesus' words to the high priest: "From now on, you will see that this man is sitting...." (26:64). Evidence of the exaltation of this man will be forthcoming to the eyes of the high priest "from now on." But it will not be "Jesus" whom the high priest will "see," but rather "this man," who will judge his enemies.

5

"To the End and Beyond":
The End-Time Character
of Jesus' Suffering, Death,
and Resurrection

The ED in Matthew is unique among the great speeches of Jesus in that it refers exclusively to events that take place beyond the temporal boundaries of the Gospel's story. Before examining the discourse itself it will be helpful to complete the "sweep" of the Gospel's story by examining the narrative of Jesus' passion, resurrection, and post-resurrection appearances. Not only will it be helpful thus to complete the examination of the Gospel's story; it is imperative. For in the concluding portion (26:1–28:20) of the Gospel's third major section (16:21–28:20), the plot of the narrator's eschatological story of Jesus reaches its goal. Predominantly through the voice of the narrator, but also through the words of Jesus and other characters, the climax of Jesus' entire ministry is seen also to be eschatological in nature. In addition, the Gospel's concluding pericope (28:16–20), open-ended as it is, acts to define in the mind of the implied reader the nature of the time interval that will stretch from the resurrection of Jesus to his Parousia.

Specifically, there are four themes[1] that stand out in this concluding portion of the Gospel. First, as has been the case with his entire life, the end and goal of Jesus' ministry are painted in overt, dramatically eschatological colors. Second, the mounting conflict with the religious leaders reaches its resolution with Jesus' atoning death and consequent vindication through resurrection. As the implied reader already knows, the vindication of Jesus as the obedient Son of God will have as its tragic corollary the destruction of Jerusalem as an end-time judgment upon the city and nation that have opposed and rejected Jesus.[2] This corollary, already presented to the implied reader three times in the account of Jesus' activities in the city of Jerusalem,[3] twice comes to explicit expression in the concluding portion of the Gospel's story at 26:64 and 27:51–54. In addition, this theme is implicit in other portions of the narrative. Third, the narration of Jesus' suffering, death, and resurrection shows the implied reader that, in these events that constitute the climax and resolution of the story, Jesus completes the saving ministry that the angel announced to Joseph, namely, through his atoning death Jesus saves his people from their sins (1:21; 26:28; 26:39, 42, 44; 27:46). Fourth and

finally, by means of the story's concluding pericope (28:16–20) the implied reader understands that Jesus' session at his Father's right hand (22:44; 26:64) has
begun and that the whole of the time between Jesus' resurrection and his
Parousia is to be understood as a time of mission. During this time of mission the
disciples of Jesus, beginning with the Eleven, are to go to all the nations and
make disciples.

THE CONCLUDING SECTION OF THE GOSPEL

At 26:1, the narrator's reintegrating formula functions with unique emphasis[4] to
return the implied reader to the plot of the Gospel's story: "And it happened
when Jesus completed *all* these words, he said to his disciples...." The presence of
"all" alerts the implied reader to the cessation of the major speeches of Jesus.
Now the narrator's voice returns as the primary (though not exclusive) mode of
presenting eschatological point of view during the rest of the story.

In the next verse (26:2), Jesus' words forcefully focus the implied reader upon
that complex of events to which the Gospel's story has been overtly pointing since
16:21: "You know that after two days the Passover is happening, and this man is
being delivered up in order to be crucified."

Now the climax and goal of the narrative have drawn near. The implied read-
er, of course, does not need to be told what the goal of the story's plot is, for Jesus
has already thrice predicted the story's denouement (16:21; 17:22–23; 20:17–19).
What the implied reader does need to know is how that goal will work itself out.
There is no existential suspense for the implied reader. There is, however, "nar-
rative suspense," that is, "an interest in recounting how this event took place."[5]
The implied reader now has opportunity to focus on that to which the entire
Gospel has been pointing.[6]

The implied reader does not have to wait to learn more of the "how" of Jesus'
betrayal.[7] In keeping with their unswerving opposition to Jesus, the religious
leaders are immediately[8] portrayed as plotting Jesus' death (26:3–5), followed by
Judas' decision to betray Jesus (26:14–16). These two accounts bracket the story
of Jesus' anointing at Bethany. At Bethany Jesus shows the disciples (and the
implied reader) two truths. First, Jesus is aware that the true effect of his anointing has been for the purpose of preparing him for his burial (26:12). Second, Jesus
knows that this action of the unnamed woman will become part of the proclamation of "this Gospel" (26:13) of his end-time life and ministry wherever that Gospel
is proclaimed in the time of mission after the end of the Gospel's narrative.[9]

In the account of the Last Supper in the upper room, Jesus again speaks of
his upcoming death. He specifically predicts[10] his betrayal by one of the Twelve.
He offers them a meal, which in the time between his death and resurrection and
his Parousia will provide an eschatological foretaste of the final consummated
banquet (26:29).[11] In so doing, Jesus gives the true interpretation and meaning of

his impending death. His "blood," which is poured out for the forgiveness of sins, will establish the covenant foretold in Jer 31:31–34 (Matt 26:28).[12]

By his death, Jesus will complete the eschatological work of saving his people from their sins (1:21; 20:28). After Jesus and his disciples depart for the Mount of Olives and Gethsemane, he utters his final predictions about the general falling away of his disciples, his appearance to them in Galilee, and Peter's apostasy before the crowing of the rooster (26:31–35).

I have argued in chapter 4 that the agony of Jesus in Gethsemane is the final, paradoxical fulfillment of Jesus' prediction of 16:28: "Truly I say to you that there are some of those standing here who will certainly not taste death until they see that this man is coming with his royal power." In terms of the story's plot, it is through Jesus' obedient prayer in the garden that the story actually begins to present its goal, that is, Jesus' suffering, death, and resurrection. The internal prolepses come to an end. The predictions of Jesus are absent from Gethsemane. No longer is the passion something being anticipated. Now, even as the one who betrays Jesus appears, the hour has arrived.[13]

Recall further that the presence of elements from the Lord's Prayer helps to show that Jesus' experience in the garden is a manifestation of the eschatological reign of heaven. Jesus' own prayer reduplicates precisely the eschatological prayer he taught his disciples: "Let your will be done" (26:42; cf. 6:10). In so praying and fully accepting the divine plan, Jesus brings about a fulfillment of the parallel petition of the Prayer, "Let your reign come." Whereas Peter and the sons of Zebedee (present also at the transfiguration) fail the eschatological time of testing (πειρασμός, 26:41; cf. 6:13),[14] Jesus obediently[15] passes through the test in order to accept the eschatological cup that his Father wills him to drink.[16] Informed by all of the narrative's perspectives, the implied reader discerns the paradoxical power of the reign of heaven at work in the willing obedience of Jesus in Gethsemane.[17]

The implied reader observes the outworking of Jesus' willing obedience as the narrative moves toward its goal. On one level, Jesus is arrested as the helpless victim of his opponents' actions. On another level, the implied reader understands through the words of Jesus that God, through Jesus, has complete mastery over the developments that lead to Jesus' trial, condemnation, and death.[18] Receiving Judas' treacherous kiss, Jesus exhorts him to carry out his purpose. Jesus restrains his disciples from defending him with the sword and refrains from invoking the aid of twelve of his Father's legions of angels (26:52–53). To both his disciples and those who have come to arrest him, Jesus asserts that the events now unfolding take place for the purpose of fulfilling the divinely ordained scriptural plan (26:54, 56). The narrator pointedly comments that Peter follows Jesus and his captors from a distance, in order to see "the end," τὸ τέλος (26:58), that is, the resolution of the conflict between Jesus and those religious leaders whose opposition ironically results in Jesus' naming of them as "sinners" (26:45).[19]

JESUS' TRIAL BEFORE THE RELIGIOUS LEADERS

The trial of Jesus before the chief priests and the Sanhedrin centers on the question of Jesus' identity. False witnesses are unable to offer testimony sufficient for the purposes of the religious leaders (26:59–60a). When two others[20] come forward to accuse Jesus, he remains silent. Jesus responds only when, in 26:63, the question of his identity is raised by the high priest in terms that echo the confession of Simon Peter (16:16): "Are you the Christ, the Son of God?" In focusing upon Jesus' identity as the Son of God the high priest is reformulating[21] the claim that Jesus had raised thrice during his time in Jerusalem (21:33–46; 22:1–14; 22:41–46). In each of those three earlier passages, the refusal to acknowledge Jesus as the Son of God resulted in Jesus' prediction of Jerusalem's destruction and the rejection of Israel from its position of salvation-historical primacy. Now the high priest demands an answer of Jesus regarding the same issue of Jesus' identity as the Christ, the Son of God.

Jesus' answer is indirect but affirmative:[22] "You said." Importantly, Jesus' response continues with a prediction regarding the high priest and those with him: "But I say to you, from now on you will see that[23] this man is sitting at the right hand of power and coming on the clouds of heaven" (26:64). Jesus' reply is pregnant with meaning for the implied reader.

As the implied reader knows, the proper answer to the high priest's question is the affirmative one: Jesus is the Son of God. But the high priest asks not with understanding but with hatred and opposition. Jesus' predictive response comes in second person plural form because the high priest is the representative of the whole Sanhedrin; Jesus speaks of a reality that his opponents[24] will see "from now on." Three questions emerge from Jesus' prediction to the high priest. First, what is the sense of "from now on" (ἀπ᾽ ἄρτι)?[25] Second, what is the relationship of the two participles of indirect discourse, "sitting" and "coming," to the expression "from now on"? Third, to what future event or events does Jesus refer when he speaks of what the high priest and the Sanhedrin will see "from now on"?

WHAT DOES "FROM NOW ON" MEAN IN MATTHEW 26:64?

First, I stand with other interpreters in understanding the meaning of "from now on" in 26:64 in its usual sense. That is to say, what Jesus predicts the high priest and the other religious leaders will see is something that will begin from the time of his utterance and extend out from there.[26] The implied reader notes and accepts the stark contrast between the two relationships portrayed by the narration of the scene and the prediction of Jesus. As he speaks, Jesus stands captive, ready to be condemned to certain death by crucifixion. Yet this Jesus solemnly promises an utter reversal of his fortunes and his vindication over the very enemies who are in the process of condemning him to death.[27] To determine more precisely the sense of immediacy inherent in the phrase "from now on," I shall pass to the next question, namely, the relationship between the expression "from now on" and the realities signaled by the two participial phrases of indirect discourse, "sitting at the right hand of power" and "coming on the clouds of heaven."

What Is the Relationship of "From Now On" to the Two Participial Phrases "Sitting..." and "Coming..." in Matthew 26:64?

Commentators understand this relationship in various ways. A seeming majority see two temporally separate realities predicted: (1) the fact of Jesus' session at the right hand of power and (2) the additional event of his return at the Parousia. For those who make this distinction, the expression "from now on" is applied effectively to the first reality only. Thus, Robert Gundry writes:

> First there is a mental seeing of the Son of man sitting at God's right hand, a seeing that will begin immediately as a result of the events described in 27:51b–53 and the report of the guards, related in 28:11–15 (both passages being peculiar to Matthew); then a literal seeing of the Son of man coming on the clouds of heaven, a seeing that awaits the Parousia.[28]

Others are more willing to see a closer temporal connection between the two phrases, seeing "from now on" as referring also to "that this man is ... coming on the clouds of heaven."[29] Still others understand "from now on" as applying to the two participial phrases with equal force. Charles Giblin writes,

> But the connoted judgment by the one now on trial is not viewed as an event placed solely at the end of the end-time; it is "from this moment." ...Thus it is viewed complexively, as being operative within the Passion itself.... This complexive perspective is borne out in subsequent events of the Passion as Matthew describes them, where eschatological events like earthquakes and the resurrection of the dead are anticipated at the moment of Jesus' death (27:50–54).[30]

Even a brief examination of the grammar of 26:64 gives strong support for Giblin's words. The phrase "from now on" can modify either the clause "But I say to you" or the main verb of the clause that reports the content of Jesus' speech, "You will see that." Neither I nor any commentator of whom I am aware opts for the first possibility. Thus, the phrase "from now on" modifies the verb "you will see."[31] Very soon after Jesus utters the words of 26:64, the high priest and the Sanhedrin will see things that are true about this man, namely, that he is sitting at the right hand of power and coming on the clouds of heaven. Those who place a temporal separation between the two participial phrases do so in violation of the sentence's syntax. This answers the question of the temporal relationship between the two participial clauses. They both indicate realities that the high priest and the Sanhedrin will see "from now on."

To What Does the Phrase "Sitting at the Right Hand of Power" in Matthew 26:64 Refer?

Our discussion arrives at the third and most difficult question, namely, to which future event or events does Jesus refer when he speaks of what the high priest and the Sanhedrin will see "from now on"? Note the following observations.

It is to the high priest and the members of the Sanhedrin, characters within the story itself, that Jesus speaks his words. In seeking to understand the referents of Jesus' prediction, the implied reader will search for events or realities that are seen or perceived by those persons or their representatives.[32]

Furthermore, I underscore the phrase "from now on." The implied reader will search for the fulfillment of Jesus' prediction in events or realities that, at the very least, begin to take place very soon after Jesus has uttered his words.[33]

Then, note the first participial phrase: "From now on you will see that this man is sitting at the right hand of power." The implied reader already knows about the session of Jesus at God's[34] right hand. In 22:44, Jesus had quoted Ps 110:1 in full.[35] There the issue was the religious leaders' failure to know and confess that the Christ was not only Son of David but also Son of God. The prophecy of Ps 110:1 applies to Jesus and his relationship to his "enemies" ("until I put your enemies under your feet"). In view of the parables where Jesus reveals that the refusal to acknowledge his divine Sonship will result in the destruction of Jerusalem (21:43; 22:7), the implied reader understands the putting of the Son of God's enemies under his feet at 22:44 as a reference to the destruction of Jerusalem that Jesus predicts at the end of chapter 23 (23:34–39).

Owing to this connection between Jesus' session at God's right hand and the destruction of Jerusalem, it is likely a priori that here at 26:64, where Jesus publicly assents to his true identity as Son of God and is most vigorously rejected with regard to that identity, the implied reader would associate Jesus' words of judgment[36] to the high priest and Sanhedrin with the predicted destruction of Jerusalem. Since the destruction of Jerusalem will come upon "this generation" (23:36), at least some of the religious leaders to whom Jesus speaks the words of 26:64 could be expected to see that terrible event.

One important issue, however, needs specific clarification. The narrator of Matthew's story never indicates that the high priest, the Sanhedrin, or any character in the Gospel literally *sees* Jesus himself sitting as God's Son at God's right hand until the Parousia when all peoples will see that reality (25:31–32). Yet, Jesus says, "*From now on* you will see that this man is sitting at the right hand of power." What Jesus predicts, therefore, is that from now on the high priest and the Sanhedrin will see[37] evidence of what, on the last day, they and all people will see.[38] The religious leaders will see proof, manifestations of the fact that this man, Jesus,[39] is sitting at God's right hand.[40] Although they will not perceive its significance, those who condemn Jesus for acknowledging that he is the Christ and Son of God will see that he is such. When do they see this evidence? There are three likely fulfillments.

First, the chief priests, scribes, and elders are present at Jesus' crucifixion (27:41). Although they mockingly recall Jesus' claim to be the Son of God (27:43), they do not believe it. Yet, along with the centurion and his fellows, the implied reader knows that, when Jesus dies and the apocalyptic signs occur it is truly as *the Son of God* that Jesus has died (27:54). The first sign that occurs after Jesus' death is God's splitting of the curtain of the temple from top to bottom (27:51). As I shall argue below, this sign symbolizes the predicted destruction of the temple and of the city of Jerusalem.[41] At the crucifixion, the implied reader's eyes of faith see Jesus, the Son of God, sitting in his salvific reign.[42] Besides, after Jesus, the Son of God, dies in obedient submission to the will of his Father, the unbelieving eyes of the religious leaders see without comprehending the evidence of this man's session at the right hand of power and of the judgment that he will bring against them and their temple.[43]

Second, the chief priests and the elders gather to hear the report from the guard at the tomb concerning "all the things that had happened" (28:11–12). Even in the face of this evidence, the religious leaders to whom Jesus had spoken the words of 26:64 refuse to repent of their obduracy and believe in Jesus as the Son of God. The implied reader knows, however, that through the testimony of the tomb guard the religious leaders have seen (though not perceived) additional proof of Jesus' session at God's right hand.[44]

Finally, because the destruction of the temple and of Jerusalem has been predicted within the life span of "this generation" (23:34–36), the implied reader will also assume that the religious leaders to whom Jesus spoke the words of 26:64 will be present for the actual event of the temple and city's destruction. They will witness this tragic judgment, which will be evidence that this man, Jesus, whom they rejected as the Son of God, is seated at the right hand of power.[45]

To What Does the Phrase "Coming on the Clouds of Heaven" in Matthew 26:64 Refer?

Now I turn to the understanding of the second participial phrase, "from now on you will see that this man is … coming on the clouds of heaven." Two horizons of interpretation must be considered. The first horizon concerns the meaning of the night vision of Dan 7:13–14 to which Matt 26:64 unmistakably makes reference. The second horizon is the extent to which the meaning of Daniel 7 shapes and informs Jesus' words in their context in the story of Matthew's Gospel.

My presupposition throughout this treatment of Matthew's Gospel has been that Jesus' use of the self-designation "this man" (ὁ υἱὸς τοῦ ἀνθρώπου) was not in itself a reference or allusion to the night vision of Dan 7:13.[46] This is a different matter when "this man" is accompanied by other appellations that have parallels in Daniel 7. Here at Matt 26:64, Jesus is unmistakably alluding to Daniel 7.

The LXX at Dan 7:13 reads as follows: "I kept on looking in the night vision and lo, with[47] the clouds of heaven [one] like a son of man[48] was coming,[49] and he came before the ancient of days and he was presented before him." The use of Jesus' self-designation, "this man," the reference to this man as "coming," and the reference to "clouds of heaven" all combine to show that in some sense Jesus' prediction to the high priest and the Sanhedrin claims that from now on, they will see Jesus himself manifested as the exalted figure in the night vision of Daniel 7. Jesus is here claiming to be *that* "son of man." To what extent does the night vision of Dan 7:13 shape for the implied reader the intent of Jesus' words in Matt 26:64?

It should first be shown that not all of the themes attached to the phrase "[one] like a son of man" in Dan 7:13 correspond to the narrator's portrayal of Jesus before the high priest. Indeed, a number of the Danielic themes are absent from the story-world of Matthew's Gospel. First, in Daniel 7, the overarching contrast is between the power of the different beasts or world empires that is taken away by God's judgment and the power that is in turn given to the one like a son of man.[50] There is a dramatic reversal in authority and in who is exercising it. This is not the case in Matthew's story. Jesus in this Gospel's narrative already teaches with authority (7:29), exercises divine authority in forgiving sins (9:6, 8), possesses and grants authority over unclean spirits (10:1), and holds authority by which he cleanses the temple (21:23–24). Further, all things have already been given to him by his Father in heaven (11:27), and on the basis of his death and resurrection, Jesus restates his possession of authority with a universal and cosmic sphere of influence (28:18). In this regard Jesus, as he stands before Caiaphas, is not like the "[one] like a son of man" of Dan 7:13.

Second, the very identity of the "[one] like a son of man" in Dan 7:13 is a vexing question that focuses in part upon the relationship between the "individual" and "corporate" character of this visionary figure. At the very least, one must conclude on the basis of the angelic interpretation in Dan 7:18, 22, 25, 27 that there is a crucial and primary sense in which the "corporate" dimension of the individual who is seen in the night vision at 7:13 predominates, perhaps to the extent that it is really not an individual at all.[51] By contrast, the narrator of Matthew's story presents the one who speaks to Caiaphas at Matt 26:64 as an individual, a man, Jesus of Nazareth. The presence of "corporate" aspects in the narrator's presentation of Jesus[52] are of secondary importance.

Other examples might be adduced. This much suffices to show that the implied reader is not to apply all of the legitimate meaning in Daniel 7 regarding the coming of one like a son of man to the words of Jesus to the high priest and the Sanhedrin.

Nevertheless, the very use of Dan 7:13 in the words of Jesus in Matt 26:64 indicates that the implied reader should apply some of the meaning in Daniel 7 in understanding Jesus' words. The following observations can be offered.

For one thing, in Dan 7:13 it is important to note that the coming of one like a son of man is a coming to the Ancient of Days, that is, to God. It is to God that this figure comes and is presented with the result that he receives authority, honor, and a reign so that all the peoples, tribes, and tongues might pay reverence to him (Dan 7:14). Here is, indeed, a strong connection with Matt 26:64. This theme of coregency with God[53] is one that has already been expressed by Jesus' words to the high priest "from now on you will see that this man is sitting at the right hand of power." The Danielic theme of "one like a son of man who rules with divine power with God" finds a ready place in the understanding of Jesus' words in 26:64. This aspect of "coming on the clouds to be invested by God" reinforces and repeats what Jesus has already expressed. Both participial phrases in 26:64, then, would convey the prediction that from now on, the high priest and the Sanhedrin will see, yet not perceive, manifestations of the end-time reality that all will see at the consummation of the age, namely Jesus' session at God's right hand.

Another significant feature of the vision of Daniel 7 is that it contrasts the beasts or enemies of God and his people with the one like a son of man whose rule is through God and on behalf of God's people. Although, as we have noted, the setting of Matthew's Gospel as a whole and 26:64 in particular do not present a theme of removal and transfer of authority, still there is a confrontation. On the one side of the confrontation stand the high priest and the Sanhedrin, the religious leaders and representatives of the people of Israel. Their power on the overt level of the narrative is plain. They are gathered for the purpose of putting Jesus to death for blasphemy. They will plan this and succeed at it because Jesus avers, albeit indirectly, that he is the Christ, the Son of God. On the other side of the confrontation stands Jesus, this man, whose own words in 26:64 now cause the implied reader to seek ways of understanding him in this Matthean setting as the "[one] like a son of man" in Dan 7:13.

In both Dan 7:13 and Matt 26:64, the implied reader observes two sides of a confrontation. If Jesus, Son of God, corresponds to the "[one] like a son of man," then the religious leaders of Israel must correspond to the beasts. They are the enemies of God and of God's people. That this theme from Daniel 7 is part of the understanding of the implied reader is supported once again by the first of the participial phrases in 26:64. The allusion to Ps 110:1 ("that this man is sitting at the right hand of power") contains within it this theme of the Christ, the Son of God, sitting at the right hand of power until God puts his enemies under his feet (cf. 22:42). Jesus' further allusion to Dan 7:13 thus serves to underscore and repeat the theme of God's victory over his enemies and his empowerment of his Son, who is here portrayed as the Danielic figure.

On two counts, then, the second participial phrase reinforces realities communicated by the first participial phrase. In the first place, Jesus asserts that, from now on, the high priest and the Sanhedrin will see evidence that he is seated at

God's right hand. That is to say, he is like the Danielic figure in that he has received from God authority and a reign. In the second place, Jesus' words assert that, as Ps 110:1 declares and Dan 7:13 implies, the religious leaders of Israel will, from now on, see evidence that they as God's and Jesus' enemies will be put under Jesus' feet, their authority and power abolished. The irony is not lost on the implied reader. The religious leaders surely will see these events. Yet they will not give up their obdurate unbelief, and consequently, they will not perceive the significance of the events that their own eyes will see.

Since the meaning of the two participial phrases is thus seen to be largely parallel,[54] the implied reader will understand the fulfillment of the second phrase in the same way he or she understands the fulfillment of the first phrase. That is to say, the apocalyptic signs at Jesus' death and resurrection, the testimony to Jesus' resurrection given by the tomb guard, and the predicted destruction of Jerusalem all serve as the events that the religious leaders actually will see from now on. These events show that Jesus is the Christ of Ps 110:1 and the "[one] like a son of man" of Dan 7:13, but only the implied reader will understand this.

To summarize the implied reader's understanding of Jesus' words in 26:64: the contrast could not be drawn more starkly for the implied reader. On one level, Jesus is helpless before the power of the Sanhedrin. His assent to the high priest's question will result in his condemnation, sentencing, and execution. The power of the Son of God's enemies could hardly be greater.

The implied reader, however, is aware of another level of the portrait being presented. Jesus is not powerless. All these things are taking place as God's plan foretold in the Scriptures (26:54, 56) and through Jesus' perfect filial obedience to that plan (26:39, 42, 44). The power of the religious leaders only appears to have the upper hand. They neither perceive the true nature of the events at Jesus' trial nor will they perceive the true character of the events that Jesus' words of 26:64 predict.

Nonetheless, the words of Jesus assert the deeper reality: "But I say to you, from now on you will see that this man is sitting at the right hand of power and coming on the clouds of heaven." From now on the religious leaders of Israel will see manifestations of the eschatological judgment that all will see on the last day (16:27; 25:31–32). For they condemn as worthy of death the end-time Christ and Son of God who stands before them (26:65–66). Ironically, they acclaim him as Christ through their mockery (26:68). They lead him away to Pilate, who alone holds the power of *imperium* (27:1–2).[55]

THE "FIELD OF BLOOD," JESUS' TRIAL BEFORE PILATE, AND THE CROWDS' REJECTION OF JESUS

The narrator now offers the incidents of Judas' remorse, his return of the price paid for Jesus' betrayal, and his suicide (27:3–10). This brief narration is significant in that it offers the first example in our examination of the Gospel of a direct address from the implied author[56] to the implied reader. The comment "Therefore that field has been called[57] a field of blood until today" (27:8) speaks directly to the time of the implied reader where he or she stands with the narrator and the implied author of the Gospel's story. The incident whereby the "field of blood" receives and still possesses its designation at the time of the implied reader is significant enough to justify this kind of "alert" on the part of the implied author. The implied author wants the implied reader to know the significance of the naming of the field. Indeed, the incident in 27:3–10 reinforces for the implied reader two important themes.

The first theme is that of Jesus' wrongful condemnation by the chief priests and elders of the people. Judas remorsefully declares to these religious leaders, "I sinned by betraying innocent blood" (27:4a–b). Their answer is callous and indifferent: "You will see what that is to us" (27:4c).[58] It matters not a whit to the religious leaders that innocent blood has been betrayed. Thus, the enduring name of the field purchased with Judas' blood money reminds the implied reader in his or her own day of the opposition of Israel's religious leaders to the Son of God. Although Judas' despair and suicide prevent him from actually seeing what the betrayal of Jesus' innocent blood means to the chief priests and elders, the implied reader sees,[59] through the events of the passion narrative.

The second significant theme in 27:3–10 is that of the coming destruction of the temple. This theme is present by means of four textual features. The first feature is the phrase "innocent blood." The implied reader will connect Judas' confession with Jesus' words of judgment at 23:35, "So that upon you may come all the righteous blood which is being poured out upon the earth, from righteous Abel's blood until the blood of Zechariah son of Barachiah, whom you murdered between the temple and the altar."[60] The fact that Jesus' blood is "innocent" underscores the judgment promised upon those who shed his blood.[61]

The second feature that emphasizes the coming destruction of the temple is the very action of hurling the blood money into the temple itself.[62] It was the destruction of the temple (ναός) that was part of the testimony against Jesus (26:61) and that will be part of the mockery of Jesus by those who pass by his cross (27:40). It will be the curtain of that same temple that will be torn in proleptic judgment after Jesus dies as the Son of God (27:51). Despite the removal of the defiled money from the temple (27:6–7), the judgment remains.

In the third place, the narrator attributes the OT citation in 27:9 to Jeremiah, owing to Jeremiah's status as "the archetypal prophet of woe who here foreshadows the rejection of Israel for failing to accept Jesus as the Messiah."[63] In the fourth and final place, the address to the implied reader recalls the reason why the "field of blood" continues to have its name to his or her own day. It is because Israel's leaders rejected and condemned the end-time Christ, and it is a reminder of the Christ's judgment on Jerusalem and the temple.[64]

Without pausing, the narrator's presentation of Jesus' trial before Pilate (27:11–26) reinforces for the implied reader the very lessons underscored in both the trial before the Sanhedrin (26:59–66) and in the account of Judas' remorse and suicide (27:3–10). The narrator reveals Pilate's awareness of the religious leaders' motives in handing Jesus over to them. This inside view underscores Jesus' innocence (27:18), which is further emphasized by Pilate's desire to release Jesus (27:22–23). The irony of a helpless and rejected Jesus who is in reality the fulfillment of the taunts his enemies hurl at him is obvious and repeated.[65] The truth of the end-time King of the Jews (2:2), who has come to shepherd his people (2:6), is portrayed for the implied reader to see and believe.

Most powerfully, however, does the narrator repeat the theme of judgment on Jerusalem and on the nation of Israel. Here at last the ambiguity of "the crowds" in Matthew's Gospel is resolved. Throughout the narrative the crowds have been "favorably" disposed to Jesus, while neither espousing the correct understanding of him nor following him as disciples. When the chief priests and elders persuade the crowds to ask for the release of Barabbas and the crucifixion of Jesus (27:20–23), the crowds align themselves with the opponents of Jesus.[66] Pilate's response takes place before the crowd (27:24). He says, "You will see that I am innocent of this blood."[67] His words strongly echo Jesus' words of judgment to the high priest and Sanhedrin, "From now on you will see that this man is sitting at the right hand of power and coming on the clouds of heaven" (26:64).

The tragic[68] response of "all the people" is grammatically ambiguous[69] but semantically unequivocal: "His blood be upon us and upon our children" (27:25). Here the people of Israel's rejection of their Christ and of the reign of heaven that he has brought into the time of the story is complete.[70] Now they as a nation will lose their status as tenant-farmers in the eschatological vineyard-reign (21:41, 43).[71] Now all the people call down upon themselves the judgment[72] that the Christ whom they now have rejected has predicted.[73]

THE DEATH OF JESUS AS
ESCHATOLOGICAL SALVATION AND JUDGMENT

The irony continues unrelentingly, as characters unknowingly acclaim the identity of Jesus as King of the Jews (27:30, 37, 42) and the Son of God (27:40, 43).[74] The theme of the temple's destruction is reiterated (27:39).[75] Despite the point of view of those who mock him, Jesus, by his refusal to save himself, saves others in his dying on the cross (27:42; cf. 26:53–54). The implied reader alone knows that, as the mother of the sons of Zebedee looks on (27:56), the crucified Jesus with thieves on his right and his left is the eschatological King, enthroned and "sitting in [his] reign" (20:20–23).[76] The characters in the story misunderstand Jesus' cry of dereliction; they think he is calling for Elijah so that Elijah might come and save him (27:45–49). The implied reader knows,[77] however, that eschatological Elijah already came and the enemies of heaven's reign did to him what they wished and killed him (17:11–12). So also with the eschatological King himself. Precisely because he is King, he is not saved from death, but he dies (27:50). Thereby he saves his people from their sins (1:21; 20:28; 26:28).[78]

As the entire discussion of this thesis has shown, the implied reader has known from the very first naming of the story's protagonist as "Christ" (1:1) that the eschatological action of the reign of heaven has been present in a hidden manner through the entire life and ministry of Jesus. Now, at the climax and resolution of the story, at the death of Jesus, eschatological signs break forth from God[79] in unprecedented fashion.[80] As the confession of the centurion and his fellows indicates, the signs act as God's confirmation that Jesus is indeed the Son of God.[81]

Furthermore, the signs' character as apocalyptic events[82] underscores the eschatological character of Jesus' death and resurrection. The implied reader knows that here, for both salvation and judgment, is the "presence of the future."[83] All of the signs together show the vindication of Jesus in the presence of his enemies who condemned him ("the chief priests," "scribes," and "elders" of the people, 27:41).

Each of the signs possesses its own specific character. The darkness over the land[84] that precedes the death of Jesus (27:45) calls to mind the eschatological outer darkness in Jesus' teaching at 8:12; 22:13; 25:30. Connotations of judgment[85] and of the Day of the Lord[86] are present through this image. The opening of tombs, resurrection of many of the saints, and their appearance in "the holy city"[87] subsequent to Jesus' own resurrection (27:53–54) show the eschatological character[88] of the salvation that God has effected through Jesus' death and resurrection.[89] The earthquake and splitting of the rocks underscore the end-time character of the events taking place.

Perhaps most significantly for the narrative of the Gospel and the theme of Jesus' vindication in spite of his enemies, the curtain of the temple is torn from top to bottom into two (27:51). The explicit[90] and dominant theme underscored by this event is that of divine judgment upon the temple in the city where both the leaders and all the people rejected Jesus as the Son of God. Four times earlier in the Gospel the rejection of Jesus by Israel and its leaders was presented as the cause for the effect of the destruction of temple and city (21:43, 22:7; 22:44; 26:64). Now, God gives signs after Jesus' death that elicit[91] the climactic confession of Jesus' divine Sonship (27:54), and the first of the signs that occurs after his death is the tearing of the temple curtain. As confessed by the Gentile soldiers, Jesus is truly the Son of God. As predicted by Jesus himself, the city and temple that have rejected his divine Sonship will receive the eschatological judgment appropriate to the enemies of the end-time Christ. This judgment still lies in the future beyond the temporal boundaries of the story of the Gospel. The tearing of the temple curtain, however, acts as a verification from God that what Jesus has predicted will take place during the lifetime of the generation of his contemporaries (10:23; 23:36). Here, along with the other eschatological signs, is the initial fulfillment of Jesus' words to the high priest and Sanhedrin who condemned him (26:64).[92]

Even after witnessing his eschatological death, the religious leaders continue their opposition to Jesus through their plan to seal and guard Jesus' tomb. Ironically, they bear witness to Jesus' prediction of his own resurrection even while naming Jesus a "deceiver" for his words (27:62–66). Their attempt to forestall God's vindication of Jesus as the Son of God fails. Jesus is raised from the dead in eschatological[93] triumph and promise.[94] As at the very beginning of Matthew's Gospel (1:18–25), God's angelic messenger brings the divine point of view to human witnesses: "He is not here, for he has been raised, just as he said" (28:6a–b). In anticipation of the Gospel's final scene, Jesus himself appears to the women to reinforce the angel's bidding that the women command Jesus' disciples to meet him in Galilee. Significantly, Jesus says, "Go, announce to my *brothers*, so that they may depart into Galilee" (28:10). Jesus names as his "brothers"[95] the disciples to whom he will shortly entrust the eschatological Great Commission.

Before relating the final episode, however, the narrator describes one last scene involving the religious leaders of Israel. The significance of this scene for the implied reader is indicated through the second occurrence[96] of direct address from the implied author to the time of the implied reader: "And this word has been spread widely among the Jews until this very day" (28:15).

The implied reader stands at a time when the field purchased with Judas' blood-stained money is still called "field of blood" (27:3–10) and when the lie that Jesus' disciples stole away his body from the tomb is still being circulated among the Jews. Through the continuing false explanation for Jesus' missing body, the implied reader sees the ongoing hostility of the religious leaders to the Son of God. In ironic contrast to the women witnesses and their obedient announcement (ἀπαγγείλατε, 28:10) of the resurrection to Jesus' disciples, some of the soldiers go to the chief priests and announce (ἀπήγγειλαν, 28:11) all the things that had happened. Under the orders and bribery of the chief priests, these soldiers begin to say that Jesus' disciples stole his body from the tomb. This is what they were taught (ἐδιδάχθησαν, 28:15). By contrast, Jesus' brothers, the Eleven, will be making disciples of all the nations by trinitarian Baptism and teaching (διδάσκοντες, 28:20)[97] of all that Jesus has commanded. Thus, the opposition of the religious leaders to Jesus, the Son of God, continues even in the time of the mission to all the nations, yes, to the very day in which the implied reader finds himself or herself.

THE GREAT COMMISSION

The final pericope of the Gospel (28:16–20) presents Jesus for the last time as the disciples hear his words and receive the Great Commission. Two issues that need

discussion are these: 1) the narrator's (and therefore the implied reader's) understanding of Jesus' identity in 28:16–20 and 2) the effect that Jesus' words have on
the implied reader's perspective on the time that stretches out beyond the temporal boundaries of the Gospel until the consummation of the age. I shall address
the christological question first.

My own view of the Christology of this pericope can be summarized as follows: Jesus speaks as the vindicated Son of God who possesses a universal authority and whose end-time reign will extend until the eschatological harvest at the
end of the age (13:41). Answers to two questions underlie my view. To what
extent is 28:18–20 presented as an enthronement scene that is a fulfillment of
Dan 7:13–14? And what is the explicit christological perspective that informs the
scene? I shall examine each of these questions in brief.

A number of commentators speak of Matt 28:16–20 in formal terms as an
"enthronement" scene.[98] Otto Michel discerns in 28:18–20 the presence of themes
characteristic of ancient Near Eastern enthronement texts.[99] He especially stresses
the cosmic dimension of Jesus' authority as expressed through the repeated use of
"all" in 28:18–20.[100] For many scholars, the connections between Matt 28:18–20
and the night vision of Dan 7:13–14 are perfectly clear and obvious.[101]

However others who think that Daniel 7 is the background of Matt 28:18–20
admit that the explicit textual data that would link Matt 28:18–20 to Dan 7:13–14
are scarce.[102] Moreover, both Anton Vögtle[103] and David Bauer[104] have adduced
significant objections to the view that Matt 28:18–20 portrays Jesus as the fulfillment of Dan 7:13–14.

To their observations, I would add only the following. First, the term
"enthronement scene" is a misnomer for Matt 28:18–20. No enthronement takes
place or is described. Rather, 28:18–20 presupposes Jesus' enthronement and vindication over his enemies. The risen Jesus does not say, "All authority is being
given" or "is now being given." He says, "has been given" (ἐδόθη, 28:18).[105] By
contrast, Dan 7:13–14 actually describes an enthronement.

Second, it is also an error to view 28:18–20 as the fulfillment of Jesus' words
in 26:64 and therefore as the description of an enthronement or session at the
right hand of power. The words of Jesus in 26:64 are spoken to the religious leaders who condemn him, none of whom are present on the mountain in Galilee. As
I have argued above, with respect to events within the temporal boundaries of the
story, the implied reader will understand the apocalyptic signs at Jesus' death
(27:51–54) and the testimony of the guards at the tomb (28:11–15) as fulfillments
of Jesus' prediction in 26:64. These events are seen by the religious leaders to
whom Jesus spoke the words of 26:64. I conclude, therefore, that 28:18–20 is not
significantly informed or shaped by Dan 7:13–14, nor is 28:18–20 an enthronement scene that portrays Jesus as the fulfillment of that Danielic night vision.

This brings us to the second christological issue relevant to the implied reader's understanding of 28:16–20, namely, the explicit perspective that informs the

scene. Jesus appears and speaks, not as "this man," but as the Son of God. Note first the contrast between 26:64 and 28:18–20. To the religious leaders, Jesus predicted that they would see "this man," that is, Jesus as he describes himself in relation to his opponents. On the mountain in Galilee, Jesus appears not as "this man," but as the Son of God who speaks to his eleven disciples.[106] The other obvious feature that establishes the view that Jesus speaks as the Son of God in 28:18–20 is the striking Trinitarian language the risen Jesus uses. This formula, occurring only here in all the Gospel, acts at the very least to underscore the unique filial relationship that Jesus has with God, his Father. For it is, with the Holy Spirit, in their singular(!) name that Baptism is to be administered during the time after the Gospel's story ends. Thus, to repeat my understanding of the Christology of 28:18–20, Jesus here speaks as the vindicated Son of God who possesses an all-embracing authority.[107]

The second issue regarding 28:16–20 is the way that this pericope shapes the implied reader's understanding of the time in which he or she now stands, namely, the time period that stretches from the end of the Gospel's story until the consummation of the age. The answer is explicit. The answer is also important for the interpretation of the ED. From this moment at the end of the narrative forward, the time available to Jesus' disciples is the time of mission to all the nations, including for a time the mission to Israel as a nation.[108] The eschatological character of the time of mission to all the nations is established by the ongoing presence[109] of the risen Son of God with his disciples as they go and make disciples of all the nations.

More than that, the mission to all the nations will continue until the consummation of the age, and with an eye to that last day. The implied reader is included in this commission that extends far beyond the life span of the eleven brother-disciples of Jesus; the implied reader becomes a missionary disciple as well.[110] The risen Lord promises his ongoing presence with his disciples, including the implied reader, as they continue in the task of making disciples of all the nations until the consummation of the age. In addition, when the implied reader turns to the understanding of Jesus' ED, he or she knows that, because all of the events therein predicted by Jesus will occur after the end of the Gospel's story, all of 24:4–25:46 must be viewed under the umbrella concept of the mission to make disciples of all the nations.

Let us now summarize the main themes presented to the implied reader in this last portion of the Gospel's story (26:1–28:20). First, as was true for Jesus' (and John's) entire ministry, the narrator has portrayed the climax and resolution of the Gospel as eschatological events whereby the reign of heaven is presently (though hiddenly and paradoxically) at work in the time of the story. The most overt and dramatic strokes were reserved for Jesus' death and resurrection. Second, the conflict with Jesus' opponents has now come to its climax and resolution. Though rejected as such, Jesus is revealed by the narrator as the Son of

God. God has vindicated his Son through the apocalyptic signs surrounding Jesus' death and resurrection and through Jesus' resurrection. Moreover, God will show Jesus' vindication through the predicted destruction of the temple. Third, the implied reader knows that Jesus has completed his mission and accomplished the eschatological salvation for which he came (1:21). He died, thereby offering the ransom for many (20:28), the forgiveness of sins (26:28). Finally, with universal authority the risen Jesus has established the character of the entire time period that stretches from the end of the Gospel's story to the consummation of the age.

This is a time of mission, during which Jesus' disciples, beginning with the Eleven and including also the implied reader, are active in making disciples by means of baptizing and teaching everything Jesus has commanded throughout the course of the Gospel. The concluding pericope of Matthew's Gospel is certainly a fitting conclusion to the narrative. The story is a coherent one that makes sense as well as impacts the understanding and life of its implied reader.[111]

Summary of the Implied Reader's Understandings

Before proceeding to the examination of the ED (24:1–26:2), I offer the following summary. Under four points, I review the most significant perspectives that the implied reader possesses as he or she reads and understands the last of Jesus' great speeches in the Gospel of Matthew.

In the first place, the implied reader knows that there is no true near-expectation of Jesus' Parousia and of the consummation of the age within the lifetime of the disciples who are characters in the story. Further, through Jesus' own words within the ED itself, the implied reader knows that, from his or her own temporal location, it will be "a long time" until the Parousia.[112]

In the second place, the implied reader has observed both the narrator of the Gospel and Jesus himself using eschatological language with a marked flexibility of reference. A significant number of examples have come to light in the examination of the Gospel's story to this point. The following seven examples may be listed.

1. The reality signified by the expression "the reign of heaven" has a flexible temporal dimension that is determined only by context. The reign of heaven is present in the time of the story. There is expectation of a future manifestation of the reign of heaven within history and before the consummation of the age. The reign of heaven also at times refers to the consummation of the age and the judgment day itself.[113] Also, because "the reign of heaven" possesses the dynamic meaning of "God's rule and power, especially as it has come in Jesus," it is an unwarranted assumption that "the reign of heaven has exactly the same reference each time it is used."[114]

2. The second example of "flexible" eschatological language in Matthew's Gospel pertains to the concepts "bridegroom" and "wedding feast." In his present ministry, Jesus is already the eschatological bridegroom who is with his atten-

dants (9:15) and the wedding feast is said to be "ready" (ἕτοιμός, 22:8). Yet the disciples who watch faithfully for Jesus' Parousia throughout the time period after the resurrection are still awaiting the bridegroom's arrival at the feast (25:1–13).

3. "Sons of the reign" can refer both to "Israelites who don't gain entry into the messianic banquet on the last day" (8:12) as well as "the good seed sown by this man" (13:38).[115]

4. The concept of "sitting [καθίζω, κάθημαι] in eschatological glory" refers to three related, though distinct, events. At both 22:44 and 26:64, it refers to Jesus' session at God's right hand, which session will last from the time of his death and resurrection until the Parousia. Both 19:28 and 25:32, however, refer to Jesus, this man, taking his throne and "sitting" at the judgment day. By contrast, I have argued that to sit with Jesus on his right and his left in his reign at 20:23 refers to Jesus' crucifixion (27:35–38).

5. While "the harvest" (ὁ θερισμός) at times refers to the consummation of the age (13:30, 39), it also refers to the eschatological opportunity for mission to Israel's lost sheep in the time of the story (9:37–38).

6. It is noteworthy that, whereas ἄγγελός in Matthew's Gospel normally carries the meaning of "angel,"[116] in a quotation from the OT Scriptures the word refers to John the Baptist as God's eschatological "messenger" (11:10).

7. The last example of "flexible" eschatological language consists of the references to the "coming" (ἔρχομαι) of this man, Jesus, and of the reign of heaven. Frequently both Jesus and the reign of heaven are said already to have "come" into the story of the Gospel.[117] At other times, the future "coming" of Jesus, this man, refers to the Parousia and consummation of the age.[118]

In addition, I have argued that future "comings" of Jesus, this man, refer to events within history and not to the consummation of the age.[119] I have also attempted to demonstrate, in the discussion of 6:10, "Let your reign come," that a future "coming" of the reign of heaven does not refer exclusively to the consummation of the age.[120] Informed by this extensive data from elsewhere in the story, the implied reader knows that end-time language within the ED itself will require careful and nuanced understanding.

In the third place, the implied reader stands in the time period after the resurrection of Jesus and before the consummation of the age. In light of the concluding pericope of the Gospel (28:16–20), the implied reader knows that this entire time period is the time of mission when the disciples of Jesus, beginning with the Eleven, will make disciples of all the nations. This mission to all the nations will include for a time the mission to the nation of Israel. However, the implied reader also knows that the destruction of Jerusalem, which Jesus has repeatedly predicted (10:23; 21:43; 22:9; 22:44; 23:34–39; 26:64) will occur during the lifetime of the generation of the disciples in the Gospel's story. As repeatedly emphasized in the story, this judgment will fall upon the nation precisely because the people have rejected Jesus as the Christ, the Son of God (21:33–46; 22:2–7; 22:41–46; 26:61–64; 27:51–54). It still remains to be discovered, however, whether the implied reader himself or herself still anticipates the destruction of Jerusalem or looks back upon it retrospectively.

In the fourth and final place, we do well to recall how the story has brought the implied reader to the ED itself, namely, through the conflicts in Jerusalem between Jesus and Israel's religious leaders (21:1–23:39). These conflicts reached their climax in Jesus' denunciations in Matthew 23 and his judgment pronounced against "this generation" (23:34–36) and the temple (23:37–39). In the city that will only receive him as a prophet, Jesus has acted and spoken like a prophet of judgment.[121] Like Jeremiah of old, he has enacted and uttered the promised destruction of the temple. Adopting the language of John the Baptist in response to his enemies' opposition,[122] Jesus has at last turned away from Israel's leaders and capital city who neither confessed him as Son of God (22:41–46) nor received him as the one who came in the name of the Lord (23:39).[123]

Informed by all of these awarenesses and perspectives gained from the entire Gospel, the implied reader will experience the ED. In chapter 6, I will demonstrate how the implied reader understands Jesus' words in 24:4–25:46. Further, I shall show the extent to which Jesus' words address the implied reader along with "the disciples." The goal will be to discover both the implied reader's understanding and the effect that the ED will have on him or her.

Notes

1 Obviously, the four themes mentioned here in no way exhaust the themes of the Matthean passion narrative.

2 Frank J. Matera, *Passion Narratives and Gospel Theologies: Interpreting the Synoptics through Their Passion Stories* (New York: Paulist, 1986), 81.

3 Recall the theme of "Jesus' rejection as the Son of God by Israel" as the *cause* for "the destruction of Jerusalem" as presented in the parables of the Wicked Tenants and the Wedding Feast and in the controversy over "whose son is the Christ?"

4 Thus, part of the function of "*all* these words" (26:1) is energetically to restore the implied reader to the flow of the Gospel's story. I encountered a charming example of this kind of forceful narrative technique in reading to my children. During the course of the story in C. S. Lewis' *Prince Caspian: The Return to Narnia* (New York: Scholastic, 1951), 94, the character of Trumpkin the dwarf functions as a narrator within the story for more than fifty-seven pages of text. To facilitate the implied reader's exit from Trumpkin's narration and reentry into the narrator's story, the narrator begins a new chapter thus: " 'And so,' said Trumpkin (for, as you have realised, it was he who had been telling all this story to the four children, sitting on the grass in the ruined hall of Cair Paravel)—'and so....' "

5 Witherup, "The Cross of Jesus," 179; cf. Rimmon-Kenan, *Narrative Fiction*, 49; Leitch, *What Stories Are*, 86.

6 Note the extent to which the story-time of the Gospel decelerates in the passion narrative. Most of two chapters (eleven pages of Greek text) is devoted to a span of less than seventy-two hours.

[7] Various structures for the Passion Narrative have been worked out; cf. Garland, *Reading Matthew*, 246; Matera, *Passion Narratives*, 94–99; Heil, *Death and Resurrection*, 2. For a major study of both the tradition history of the Synoptic passion narratives as well as the interrelationships and theologies of the canonical Gospels' accounts, see Joel B. Green, *The Death of Jesus: Tradition and Interpretation in the Passion Narrative* (Tübingen: J. C. B. Mohr, 1988).

[8] Note this last in the series of four instances of "abrupt" fulfillments presented by the narrator; cf. 3:11–13; 9:36–10:5a; 16:28–17:8.

[9] Heil, *Death and Resurrection*, 27. The content of "this Gospel" is rightly described by Guido Tisera, *Universalism according to the Gospel of Matthew* (Frankfurt am Main: Peter Lang, 1993), 256, as "Jesus' overall activity as presented and handed down in Matt." Cf. Kingsbury, *Structure, Christology, Kingdom*, 128–37.

[10] Ten times in the Passion Narrative prior to the Gethsemane scene Jesus predicts an upcoming event; all of his predictions come to pass. This underscores both Jesus' reliability and the extent to which the unfolding events are under his and, through him, God's control.

[11] Box, *Matthew*, 338. Matera, *Passion Narratives*, 93.

[12] John P. Heil, "The Blood of Jesus in Matthew: A Narrative-Critical Perspective," *Perspectives in Religious Studies* 18 (1991): 119; Matera, *Passion Narratives*, 93.

[13] In chapter 2, I showed that, in view of the parallelism with the phrase "the reign of heaven has arrived" (ἤγγικεν ... ἡ βασιλεία τῶν οὐρανῶν) at 3:2, ἤγγικεν ἡ ὥρα (26:45) and ἤγγικεν ὁ παραδιδούς με (26:46) should be translated as "the hour has arrived" and "the one who is betraying me has arrived." The utterances of Jesus and the arrival of Judas to betray him take place at the same moment. Jesus' hour has arrived. (Cf. Heil, *Death and Resurrection*, 48–49). Schweizer, *Good News*, 494, notes an intentional parallelism between the narrator's use of "has arrived" at 26:45–46 and 3:2; 4:17; and 10:7.

[14] Heil, *Death and Resurrection*, 47–48; Meier, *Matthew*, 324.

[15] The primary relationship of Jesus to his disciples is one of contrast, not of example as Matera, *Passion Narratives*, 95, apparently thinks. The implied reader is rather to acknowledge and marvel at Jesus, the obedient Son of his Father, and to believe in him.

[16] A full discussion of the significance of the "cup" that Jesus is going to drink is outside the scope of this study. But the following comments express my own assessment.

Some understand "this cup" (26:39; "this" at 26:42) as a metaphor for "suffering" or "suffering unto death": France, *Matthew*, 292; Sabourin, *L'Évangile*, 262, 354; Meier, *Matthew*, 228, 324; Alford, *Matthew*, 273–74. In support of this view are Ps 11:6; *Test. Abr.* 1:3; 16:11–12. Note also that "cup" can serve as a positive metaphor; cf. Pss 16:5; 116:13; *Jos. Asen.* 8:5; 15:5; 19:5; 21:21.

In the OT, however, "the cup" is often used as a metaphor for "the wrath and punishment of God" against sin (Ps 75:8; Isa 51:17–23; Jer 25:15, 17, 28; 49:12; 51:7; Lam 4:21; Ezek 23:31–33; Hab 2:16); cf. Paul R. Raabe, "Drinking the Cup of God's Wrath," in *Obadiah* (AB 24D; Garden City: Doubleday, 1996), 206–54.

Commentators who discern "the cup of wrath" metaphor in Jesus' prayer include Blomberg, *Matthew*, 395; Morris, *Matthew*, 668–69; Gundry, *Matthew*, 533.

If the meaning of Jesus' prayer "Let this cup pass from me," and of his acceptance of "this cup," is informed by the OT metaphor of "the cup of God's wrath," then the eschatological meaning of Jesus' prayer in Gethsemane is heightened all the more. In this view the narrator of the story portrays Jesus as the one who, in a substitutionary manner ("for many," ἀντὶ πολλῶν, 20:28), experiences through his suffering and death the eschatological wrath of God.

17 Cf. Schlatter, *Evangelist*, 751: "In nichts anderem hat Mat. die Herrlichkeit des Todes Jesu und seine sieghafte Kraft erkannt als im vollendeten Gehorsam."

18 Matera, *Passion Narratives*, 82, 86; Kingsbury, *Matthew as Story*, 86.

19 Earlier the religious leaders criticized Jesus to his disciples because he was eating with "sinners" (9:10–11; cf. 11:19). Indeed, Jesus himself characterized his purpose by saying, "I did not come to call righteous people, but sinners" (9:13). Now, however, Jesus styles those very religious leaders who reject his purpose and seek his death as "sinners" (26:45). These are the only occurrences of the adjective ἁμαρτωλός in Matthew's Gospel.

20 The implied reader will be uncertain as to how to understand the testimony of the two witnesses who come last (26:60b). These two are not, like the others, called "false witnesses." Further, they attribute to Jesus words that claim the ability both to destroy "the temple of God" (ὁ ναὸς τοῦ θεοῦ) and to build it again in three days (26:61). The implied reader knows of no such utterance of Jesus. It is possible that the implied reader might know of "current messianic expectation" that included "purification, restoration, or even replacement of the temple and its worship" (France, *Evangelist*, 214; cf. Davies and Allison, *Matthew*, 2:598–99). At the very least, this testimony about Jesus alerts the implied reader to the motif of the destruction of the temple; cf. 27:40.

21 Kingsbury, "Husbandmen," 643.

22 David R. Catchpole, "The Answer of Jesus to Caiaphas (MATT. XXVI.64)," *NTS* 17 (1970–1971): 226, persuasively notes that 27:43, "For he said, 'I am the Son of God,'" is evidence that seals the case for understanding Jesus' answer as affirmative. Cf. Matera, *Passion Narratives*, 101.

23 I translate the participles "sitting" and "coming" as expressing indirect discourse; see the discussion of 16:28 above. I gratefully acknowledge my colleague, Dr. James Voelz, from whom I derived this translation.

24 Jesus' expression "From now on, you will see that *this man* is ..." calls to mind again the use of Jesus' self-designation, "this man," in contexts that have reference to his opponents. Note the contrast with 23:39. There, Jesus said, "You will certainly not see *me* again until you say...." Jerusalem will not see "Jesus" as the one who saves his people from their sins until they acknowledge him truly as the one who comes in the name of the Lord. Here at 26:64, the relationship is one of opposition. Thus, Jesus speaks of a time when Jerusalem's leaders, the chief priests, *will* see him. But what they see will be a manifestation of Jesus to his opponents as "this man," who will act as judge over them.

25 Casey, *Son of Man*, 183, argues for reading the adverb ἀπαρτί, "certainly," in place of ἀπ᾽ ἄρτι, "from now on." Against Casey, note that the proposed adverb does not occur in the NT, while Matthew uses "from now on" also at 23:39 and 26:29.

26 France, *Evangelist*, 315, writes that this view "is widely accepted"; cf. Matera, *Passion Narratives*, 101; Caird, *Language*, 252; Stonehouse, *Witness*, 241; Garland, *Reading Matthew*, 253; Allison, *End of the Ages*, 48–49.

Less than satisfactory are attempts, often with no supporting evidence, to weaken significantly the temporal immediacy of the phrase "from now on"; cf. Moore, *Parousia*, 141; Schweizer, *Good News*, 499; Morris, *Matthew*, 684. Beasley-Murray, *Jesus and the Kingdom of God*, 302, notes that "it is true that *arti* is occasionally used in late Greek to mean 'in the near future,' but I have been unable to locate any instance of the phrase *ap᾽ arti* with that meaning."

27 Beasley-Murray, *Jesus and the Kingdom of God*, 297, referring to Mark 14:62.

28 Gundry, *Matthew*, 545. Cf. Lindars, *Jesus Son of Man*, 121; Powell, "Religious Leaders," 205; Stonehouse, *Witness*, 242; Heil, *Death and Resurrection*, 61; Senior, *Passion*, 98–99; Sabourin, *L'Évangile*, 359.

29 Filson, *Matthew*, 283.

30 Giblin, "Theological Perspective," 652.

31 R. C. H. Lenski, *The Interpretation of St. Matthew's Gospel* (Columbus Ohio: Wartburg, 1943), 1064.

32 A redaction critic, of course, is free to understand the words of Jesus in 26:64, "You will see," as referring to someone other than the high priest and the Sanhedrin; cf. Filson, *Matthew*, 332.

33 There remains the question of "how soon?" At 23:39, Jesus says, "You will certainly not see me from now on until you say...." Jesus exits the temple in Jerusalem in the next verse (24:1) and is outside the city two verses after that (24:3). At 26:29, Jesus tells the disciples, "I will certainly not drink from now on of this fruit of the vine until...." In the next verse the meal is over and, after singing a hymn, Jesus and the disciples go out to the Mount of Olives. Based on these examples, "from now on" means "very soon."

34 "Power" is a circumlocution for "God"; cf. Gerhard Maier, *Matthäus-Evangelium*, vol. 2 (Neuhausen-Stuttgart: Hänssler-Verlag, 1983), 406.

35 The allusion here in 26:64 to Psalm 110 is noted by Casey, *Son of Man*, 169; Douglas R. A. Hare, *Matthew* (IBC; Louisville: John Knox, 1993), 308.

36 Remarkably, Jesus' prediction to the high priest and the Sanhedrin is understood by Maier, *Matthäus-Evangelium*, 2:406, in a positive manner, and not as a word of judgment.

37 Even though the religious leaders will see, they will not perceive the significance of the events that they will see. This irony between seeing and perceiving is nowhere more powerfully presented than at the crucifixion of Jesus; cf. 27:40–43.

38 Cf. W. Kümmel, *Promise*, 65; J. E. Fison, *The Christian Hope: The Presence and the Parousia* (London, 1954), 192; Moore, *Parousia*, 105–6; F. Borsch, "Mark xiv. 62 and 1 Enoch lxii. 5," *NTS* 14 (1968): 565.

39 Recall from the parable of the Wheat and the Tares (13:41) that the reign of this man extends from the time of the story of the Gospel throughout history to the consummation of the age.

40 Cf. Lindars, *Jesus Son of Man*, 121: "*At present*, on trial before the Sanhedrin, Jesus cannot be seen to be Messiah, so that his power cannot be demonstrated at this moment. But *from now on*, his status will be visible, and the proof of his power to judge and to save will be available."

41 Filson, *Matthew*, 332.

42 Recall the conclusions derived from 20:20–23 about "sitting with Jesus in his reign."

43 Sabourin, "You Will Not," 11, n. 21, writes: "The eschatological signs which especially in Matthew (cf. 27:45–54) accompany the death of Jesus mark, it would seem, that Jesus' prophecy (Mt. 26:64f) is already being fulfilled, that the messianic era is inaugurated." Cf. Giblin, "Theological Perspective," 652; Caird, *Language*, 252.

44 Gundry, *Matthew*, 545, also lists these first two events as fulfillments of 26:64.

    Commentators often cite the resurrection of Jesus as fulfillment of Jesus' words in 26:64, "You will see that this man is sitting at the right hand of power"; cf. Lindars, *Jesus Son of Man*, 121; Allison, *End of the Ages*, 48–49; Sabourin, *L'Évangile*, 359. Yet strictly speaking, no one sees Jesus' resurrection, not even the implied reader (cf. Carson, "Matthew," 555), and the risen Christ appears only to the women and the Eleven (28:8–10, 16–20).

45 Lenski, *St. Matthew's Gospel*, 1065.

46 Cf. the discussion of 8:20 above.

47 The "Theodotionic" text in Alfred Rahlfs, ed., *Septuaginta* (Stuttgart: Württembergische Bibelanstalt, 1935) reads "with," μετά. The "LXX" text has "on," ἐπί.

48 Both the "Theodotionic" and "LXX" texts in Rahlfs, *Septuaginta*, read the anarthrous form, υἱὸς ἀνθρώπου.

49 In Rahlfs, *Septuaginta*, the "Theodotionic" text reads "was coming," ἐρχόμενος ἦν, whereas the "LXX" text reads the imperfect indicative, ἤρχετο.

50 John E. Goldingay, *Daniel* (WBC; Dallas: Word Books, 1989), 190.

51 Sibley W. Towner, *Daniel* (IBC; Atlanta: John Knox, 1984), 104, senses that perhaps the perspective of "corporate personality" can explain the tension between "individual" and "corporate" in the figure in Daniel 7.

52 For a "corporate" dimension to the Matthean Jesus, note that the citation of Hosea 11:1 at Matt 2:15 brings in part the message that Jesus' coming up out of Egypt symbolizes or recapitulates the coming up out of Egypt of Israel as a whole.

53 Goldingay, *Daniel*, 168.

54 Beasley-Murray, *Jesus and the Kingdom*, 300, who disagrees with this conclusion, cites J. A. T. Robinson, *Jesus and His Coming* (London, 1947), 45, who agrees.

55 For a narrative-critical study of Matthew 27, see Witherup, "The Cross of Jesus."

56 The narrative comments in 27:8 and 28:15, along with the enigmatic "Let the reader understand" of 24:15, address the implied reader of the Gospel in an unmediated fashion and therefore are to be highlighted.

57 For a "perfective" translation of the aorist indicative passive form, see Carson, "Matthew," 566; Ernest De Witt Burton, *Syntax of the Moods and Tenses in New Testament Greek* (3d ed.; repr., Grand Rapids: Kregel, 1976), §§ 18, 52.

58 Scholars seem to be in almost universal agreement in translating the future indicative middle deponent forms of ὁράω at 27:4 (σὺ ὄψῃ) and 27:24 (ὑμεῖς ὄψεσθε) as colloquial imperatival futures: "See to it!" Typically, 27:4, 24 are taken as parallel to Acts 18:15. BDF, § 362, renders the future indicative here at 27:4 with "see to it yourself" and makes reference (though with no specific passages) to Epictetus and Marcus Aurelius; cf. BAGD, 578; Turner, *Syntax*, 86; A. T. Robertson, *A Grammar of the Greek New Testament in the Light of Historical Research* (3d ed.; New York: Hodder & Stoughton, 1919), 874; Porter, *Idioms*, 44.

I offer my alternate translation, however, on the basis of both grammatical and contextual factors. Grammatically, it is permissible to translate the phrase, as indicated in the text above, as a clause of indirect discourse introduced by τί; cf. James A. Brooks and Carlton L. Winbery, *Syntax of New Testament Greek* (Lanham, Md.: University Press of America, 1979), 185–86, citing Mark 5:14; 9:6; Luke 12:5; BDF, § 368; cf. also Rom 8:27. The unusual thing about my translation is that the clause expressing the indirect discourse precedes the main verb. This would indicate a strong emphasis and could also therefore be translated thus: "What is that to us? You will see [what it is to us]."

The parallelism with Jesus' words in 26:64 to these same religious leaders is striking: "From now on *you will see* that this man is sitting at the right hand of power and coming on the clouds of heaven." Judas' words in 27:4a–b acknowledge the perfidy of both the religious leaders and Judas' own deed. They are betraying and condemning innocent blood. But the religious leaders do not care. It means nothing to them, and this they express to Judas: "You will see what that is to us."

By way of rebuttal to the majority opinion on the translation of σὺ ὄψῃ at 27:4, I would offer the following observations. First, the parallelism with Acts 18:15 is close but not exact. In Acts the context does not allow for another translational possibility. Also, the use of αὐτός with the verb is more emphatic than the personal pronoun at 27:4, 24, although the latter are certainly emphatic.

Second, BAGD, 578, seems to offer a specious alternative when listing for ὁράω meaning 2 b, intransitive, "see to, take care." The two are not the same meaning. To "take care" is not the same as to "take care of." On the one hand, "to take care" is roughly equivalent to "watch out, beware, be careful," and this is reflected in Heb 8:5 and Acts 22:26 D TR, the other passages listed in BAGD under 2 b. This is a natural lexical extension of the ordinary meaning of "to see." On the other hand, to "see to, take care of" is roughly equivalent to "do something about" and is a meaning that is much farther removed from the basic meaning of "to see." In this regard, it is interesting to note that Filson, *Matthew*, 285, retains the indicative mood in his translation of both 27:4 and 27:24 but gives a lexical sense that cannot be sustained: "You will answer for that/it."

Third, although future indicatives readily can receive from their contexts an imperatival force, it should not be thought that this is common with the verb ὁράω. The NT writers use the future of this verb thirty-two times, of which only Acts 18:15 is imperatival, and possibly John 1:39. The verb is not commonly used in the imperative mood (five times in Matthew; twelve times overall in the NT). Neither did I discover any imperatival future indicatives of the closely related verb βλέπω in the NT.

Fourth, using the IBYCUS research computer, I examined the LXX, Epictetus, and Marcus Aurelius and found no instances of an imperatival future second person (singular or plural) of ὁράω. In addition, the sense "to see to, to take care of" is not found in LSJ. The closest entry is LSJ, 1245, under "transitive meanings": "2. See to, look out for, provide for." Further, the sense of "see to, take care of" does not occur in G. W. H. Lampe, ed., *A Patristic Greek Lexicon* (Oxford: Clarendon Press, 1961). The closest entry is Lampe, 9668: "3. Regard, attend to, be concerned with."

59 Witherup, "The Cross of Jesus," 193.

60 Garland, *Intention*, 199.

61 The judgment theme is the most prominent one associated here with "Jesus' blood." Also implicitly present, however, is the theme of salvation. Heil, "Blood of Jesus," 121, is correct in pointing to the "field of blood" as a reminder both of the "tragic price" and "the salvific value" of Jesus' innocent blood. No Jewish person will be excluded from the salvation offered through Jesus' death and resurrection.

62 The question of the precise referent of "temple" (ναός) in 27:5 is a difficult one. The issues are summarized briefly in Carson, "Matthew," 566. What is significant is that the narrator uses the same vocable at 26:61; 27:5, 40; and 27:51. Thereby the narrator links the ναός defiled by Judas' blood money and the ναός whose destruction is presaged by the tearing of the curtain.

63 Witherup, "The Cross of Jesus," 194–95; cf. Knowles, *Jeremiah*, 52–81, for a complete discussion of this OT allusion.

[64] The problem of the precise temporal location of the implied reader remains. From 27:8, one can see the ambiguity. Does the implied reader realize the presence of the "field of blood" in his or her own day and *anticipate* the judgment on the temple which is yet to come? Or, to the contrary, does the "field of blood" still bear its name even after the judgment has come upon the temple and the city, and thus *remind* the implied reader that the rejection of the Son of God caused that judgment? Resolution of this ambiguity will emerge from the treatment of 24:15: "Let the reader understand."

[65] Cf. Weaver, "Power and Powerlessness," 462–66; Witherup, "The Cross of Jesus," 196; Heil, *Death and Resurrection*, 71; Senior, *Passion*, 110–11.

[66] Garland, *Reading Matthew*, 258.

[67] It is primarily the parallels between 27:24 in its context and both 27:4 and 26:64 that urge me to this translation. First, in 27:4, Judas shows remorse over betraying "innocent" blood, while here in 27:24, Pilate declares himself "innocent" of "this blood." This term for "innocent" (ἀθῷος) occurs in the NT only in these two passages. Second, the repetition of the future indicatives "you will see" is striking parallelism. Third, the theme of judgment against the religious leaders and the people they represent is present in both 26:64 and 27:24–25.

I understand "I am innocent of this blood" as the object clause of the main verb, "you will see." The normal way to express an object clause after a verb of perception is with a clause headed by ὅτι or with an infinitive clause (BDF, § 397.1). The former construction is especially common in Matthew's Gospel where there are forty-two certain examples of ὅτι object clauses following verbs of perception (2:16, 22; 4:12; 5:17, 21, 23, 27, 33, 38, 43; 6:7, 26, 32; 9:6, 28; 10:34; 15:12, 17; 16:11, 12, 20, 21; 17:13; 19:4; 20:10, 25, 30; 21:45; 22:16, 34; 23:31; 24:32, 33, 43; 25:24; 26:2, 53; 27:3, 18, 24, 63; 28:5), including one in the verse under examination.

It is also true, however, that in every instance listed above, the object clause headed by ὅτι *follows* the verb of perception. The clause "I am innocent of this blood" in 27:24 *precedes* the verb "you will see." A literal translation would follow the order of the clauses: "I am innocent of this blood. You will see [that this is so]." Thus, I understand the clause "I am innocent of this blood" as fronted for emphasis and functioning as the object clause of the verb "you will see." Only one commentator of whom I am aware agrees with my translation. Brown, "Matthean Apocalypse," 19, refers to 27:24 as "Pilate's warning" that "parallels Jesus' warning to the high-priest, *ap' arti opsesthe*."

[68] Cf. Jesus' lament over Jerusalem and its children in 23:37.

[69] One needs to supply a verb, either an imperative ("his blood be upon us") or an indicative ("his blood is upon us").

[70] Matera, *Passion Narratives*, 83; Witherup, "The Cross of Jesus," 197; France, *Evangelist*, 227.

[71] Senior, *Passion*, 117–22.

[72] Timothy B. Cargal, " 'His Blood Be upon Us and upon Our Children': A Matthean Double Entendre?" *NTS* 37 (1991): 109–10, is probably correct in seeing a double entendre in the use of "blood" in the Matthean Passion Narrative. Thus, in the narrator's view, the blood of Jesus can certainly be for individual Jews within the story and, in the time of the mission to all the nations, the blood poured out "for the forgiveness of sins" (26:28). But the main lines of Cargal's presentation are exaggerated and unconvincing, as is the argument of Frederick A. Niedner, "Rereading Matthew on Jerusalem and Judaism," *BTB* 19 (1989): 43–47.

73 Garland, *Reading Matthew*, 258; Heil, "Blood of Jesus," 123.

74 Meier, *Matthew*, 348, says: "The enemies of Jesus see his sufferings as proof that he is not God's Son; Mt sees them as a proof that he is."

75 Witherup, "The Cross of Jesus," 268.

76 For similar (though not identical) readings of Jesus' crucifixion, see Witherup, "The Cross of Jesus," 258–59; Heil, *Death and Resurrection*, 80.

77 Note the stark contrast between the awareness of the characters in the story around Jesus' cross and the awareness of the implied reader:

   1. The characters assume that Elijah had not come yet (27:49). The implied reader knows that Elijah already had come (17:11).

   2. The characters assume that, if Elijah should come, he would come for the purpose of saving Jesus (σώσων) from death. The implied reader knows that the true purpose of "Elijah" was as the forerunner of Jesus, the climax of whose ministry is now unfolding in his suffering and death.

   3. The characters mockingly await an eschatological event, namely, the coming of Elijah foretold (Mal 4:5–6). The implied reader knows that the death of Jesus is an eschatological event.

   Note the excellent comment of Witherup, "The Cross of Jesus," 275: "Their mention of Elijah also points out their continual misunderstanding of Jesus and his ministry. The reader knows that Elijah has *already* come because John the Baptist is Elijah."

78 Reeves, "Resurrection Narrative," 41.

79 The verbs are best understood as the "divine passive," implying God as the agent (cf. Schweizer, *Good News*, 515; Witherup, "The Cross of Jesus," 280; Senior, *Passion*, 141).

80 This is not to say that the death and resurrection of Jesus alone are the "turning of the ages" and the beginning of the reign of heaven; cf. Meier, *Law and History*, 30–35; Heil, *Death and Resurrection*, 85; Senior, *Passion*, 38; Wolthuis, "Experiencing," 274. Rather, the end-time reign of heaven has been present throughout the entire time of Jesus' ministry; cf. Witherup, "The Cross of Jesus," 288. The comment from Senior, *Passion*, 183, is close to the mark: "The epicenter of Jesus' mission and the most penetrating revelation of his identity is his death for the many, and so it is at the moment of Jesus' passion that the turning point of history is most manifest."

81 Garland, *Reading Matthew*, 260; Donald Senior, "The Death of Jesus and the Resurrection of the Holy Ones (Mt. 27:51–53)," *CBQ* 38 (1976): 325.

82 Senior, "Death of Jesus," 314; Meier, *Law and History*, 32; Sabourin, *L'Évangile*, 382.

83 The phrase is, of course, the wonderfully apt title of Ladd's major study, *The Presence of the Future: The Eschatology of Biblical Realism*.

84 Agbanou, *Discours*, 115, thinks that the evangelist intends the scope of the darkness as universal, that is, over the whole earth (ἐπὶ πᾶσαν τὴν γῆν, 27:45). In light of the theme of judgment against Israel as a nation, it is more likely that the sense is "upon the whole land."

85 Interestingly, Matera, *Passion Narratives*, 115, notes a possible allusion to Exod 10:22 and the plague of darkness over Egypt.

86 Witherup, "The Cross of Jesus," 272.

87 Witherup, "The Cross of Jesus," 286, notes cogently regarding the appearance of the resurrected saints in the holy city: "They symbolize the vindication by God of his Son in the very city where he was rejected."

88 Hagner, "Apocalyptic," 62.

89 Witherup, "The Cross of Jesus," 284; Senior, *Passion*, 146.

90 The implicit theme is that of the sufficiency for universal salvation of Jesus' atoning death for the many (26:28). This interpretation is made the dominant theme by some; cf. Argyle, *Matthew*, 216; Sabourin, *L'Évangile*, 382. Carson, "Matthew," 581, makes "fulfillment" the dominant theme. Others set the theme of the temple's destruction or cessation and the universal, sufficient salvation now available through Jesus' death on the same level; cf. Tisera, *Universalism*, 287; Witherup, "The Cross of Jesus," 281.

91 The aorist participle active at 27:54, "seeing," can readily bear a causal sense: "And the centurion and those guarding Jesus with him, *because* they saw the earthquake and the things that had happened...."

92 Sabourin, *L'Évangile*, 384.

93 Allison, *The End of the Ages*, 48.

94 Hagner, "Apocalyptic," 68.

95 This will have significance in the interpretation of the final scene in the ED itself, Matt 25:31–46.

96 Cf. 27:3–10.

97 Heil, *Death and Resurrection*, 106, also notes the contrast here.

98 Bauer, *Structure*, 111, notes the influence of this view.

99 Otto Michel, "The Conclusion of Matthew's Gospel: A Contribution to the History of the Easter Message," in *The Interpretation of Matthew* (ed. Graham Stanton; Philadelphia: Fortress, 1983), 36; cf. Ellis, *Matthew*, 23; Hill, "Response," 50; Lincoln, "A Story for Teachers," 113.

100 Michel, "Conclusion," 39.

101 Cf. Barth, "Matthew's Understanding," 133; France, *Evangelist*, 292, 314–15; Meier, *Law and History*, 36.

102 Cf. Schweizer, *Good News*, 531.

103 Vögtle, "Anliegen," 280–86, notes the following:

1. The earthly Jesus, prior to his resurrection, already possessed "authority." Thus, 28:18 is not a new status for Jesus that is the result of his "enthronement."

2. There is no "transfer" of authority from one kingdom to another; there are no "rivals" for the throne, as are present in Daniel 7.

3. The emphasis in Matthew 28 is on the word of the risen Lord.

4. There are significant connections between the account of the risen Lord (28:18–20) and the relationship of the earthly, pre-resurrection Jesus with his disciples. Thus, there is no "radical" difference between the pre-resurrection and post-resurrection periods.

5. The "enthronement" prophecy of which 28:18–20 is a fulfillment is not Dan 7:13–14, but rather Ps 110:1. That is to say, Vögtle thinks that Matt 28:18–20 fulfills only the first half of Jesus' words to the high priest in 26:64: "From now on, you will see that this man is sitting at the right hand of power."

104 Bauer, *Structure*, 111–12. Bauer adds the following observations to those listed above:

1. Daniel 7 points to world conquest, not world evangelization.

2. The reign of the Danielic figure is eternal, whereas the reign of this man will at the eschaton become the reign of the Father (Matt 13:41–43).

3. Daniel 7 does not include the Gentiles.

4. Most importantly, Jesus is portrayed in Matt 28:18–20 not as "this man," or "Son of Man," but as the Son of God.

[105] If one were to identify the moment of Jesus' enthronement and vindication in the view of the narrator, the best answer would be immediately after his death-resurrection.

[106] Cf. Jack D. Kingsbury, "The Composition and Christology of MATT 28:16–20," *JBL* 93 (1974): 581.

[107] The significance of *"All* authority in heaven and earth has been given to me" (28:18) is linked primarily to the all-encompassing scope of the mission on which Jesus now sends the eleven disciples, in contrast to the limited scope expressed at 10:5–6 and 15:24.

[108] For the defense of "nations" rather than "Gentiles" at 28:19, see John P. Meier, "Nations or Gentiles in Matthew 28:19?" *CBQ* 39 (1977): 94–102; cf. Reeves, "Resurrection Narratives," 137; Burnett, "Prolegomena," 423; Matera, "Plot," 242.

For the position that 28:19 specifically has only the Gentiles in mind, see Hare and Harrington, "Make Disciples," 359; Thompson, "Historical Perspective," 258.

In my view, the expanded mission to all the nations includes the mission to Israel as a nation, but only until the predicted destruction of Jerusalem that Jesus has described as the "coming of this man" (10:23). After that judgment, to be sure, individual Jewish persons are invited to become disciples of Jesus.

[109] Many have aptly noted the inclusion of the narrative that is formed by 1:23, "God with us," and 28:20, "I am with you always"; cf. Burnett, "Prolegomena," 102; Michel, "Conclusion," 35; Bauer, *Structure*, 124–25.

[110] Weaver, *Missionary Discourse*, 152.

[111] Leitch, *What Stories Are*, 117. Lincoln, "A Story for Teachers," 111, writes that 28:16–20 "provides an effective closure for the main elements of the plot and makes a final and decisive impact on the implied readers."

[112] Cf. 24:48; 25:5, 19.

[113] Cf. Carson, "Word-Group," 277–82.

[114] Caird, *Language*, 11.

[115] Carson, "Matthew," 326, calls this double referent of "sons of the reign" a "healthy reminder that images can symbolize different things in different contexts."

[116] Cf. 1:20, 24; 2:13, 19; 4:6, 11; 13:39, 41, 49; 16:27; 18:10; 22:30; 26:53; 28:2, 5.

[117] For "this man" already having come, see 11:19; 20:28. For "Jesus" already having come, see 5:17–20; 8:29; 9:10–13; 10:34–36. For Jesus as "the coming one," see 3:11; 11:2. For "the reign of heaven" already having come, see 3:2; 4:17; 10:2; 12:28. Note also that in the person of John the Baptist eschatological "Elijah" is said already to have "come" (17:10).

[118] Cf.16:27; 24:44; 25:31.

[119] Cf. the discussion above on 10:23; 16:28; and 26:64.

[120] Carson, "Matthew," 253, notes that " 'the coming of the Son of Man' bears in Matthew the same rich semantic field as 'the coming of the kingdom' [cf. 6:10; 12:28]."

[121] For the theme of Jesus as "prophet of judgment," see the discussion of 21:10 above.

[122] "Brood of vipers," 23:33; cf. 3:7; 12:34.

[123] France, *Evangelist*, 156.

6

JERUSALEM AND PAROUSIA: THE IMPLIED READER'S UNDERSTANDING OF THE ESCHATOLOGICAL DISCOURSE

The implied reader's understanding and response to the ED, Matt 24:1–26:2, will emerge from the following procedure. First, I shall examine the narrative framework (24:1–3; 26:1–2) of the ED. The proper understanding of the narrative introduction (24:1–3) is crucial for the interpretation of the discourse that follows. In addition, 24:1–3 relates the ED to Jesus' words in chapter 23 in which he pronounced judgment upon and predicted the desolation of Jerusalem (23:34–39). More briefly, the end of the narrative framework (26:1–2) will receive attention.

Second, owing to what I shall argue is the double question of the disciples in 24:3, I will present the evidence for the overall bipartite structure of the ED, namely, 24:4–35 and 24:36–25:46. As will become evident in my discussion, I regard the first half of the ED as Jesus' response to the disciples' first question in 24:3 and the second half of the ED as Jesus' response to the disciples' second question in 24:3.

Third, after presenting the evidence for the general bipartite structure of the ED, I shall delineate the smaller units and show the features that give structural unity to each subunit.

Fourth, the remainder of chapter 6 will show how the implied reader will understand and respond to each of the subunits of the ED and to the discourse as a whole. In the entire discussion, the awarenesses that have come to the implied reader from elsewhere in the Gospel's story, as summarized immediately prior to this chapter, will help to guide the discussion.

THE NARRATIVE FRAMEWORK OF THE ESCHATOLOGICAL DISCOURSE

The narrative introduction to the ED in Matthew's Gospel is 24:1–3. This assertion betrays my convictions regarding two prior questions. One is the relationship of the ED to Jesus' denunciations of the Jewish religious leaders in chapter 23. That is to say, do the two discourses run together as one (23:1–25:46) or should they be regarded as separate speeches of Jesus? The second question is the unitary nature of 24:1–3 itself. That is to say, do the first three verses of chapter 24 introduce the ED, or is there a major structural break between 24:2 and 24:3, by virtue of which a major caesura or division is established?[1] I shall address each of these important preliminary questions in turn.

MATTHEW 24:1–3 AS A TRANSITION
BETWEEN TWO SEPARATE DISCOURSES

A number of scholars view Matt 23:1–25:46 as a unified discourse with its middle point at 24:1–3. They adduce 13:36 as a parallel, where a change of scene and audience occurs in the middle of a unified discourse of Jesus.[2] Further arguments in favor of the unity of 23:1–25:46 include the observation that Matthew's Gospel normally alternates discourse and narrative rather than placing discourses of Jesus back to back.[3] To these observations, one may reply as follows. First, the analogy to the change of scene at 13:36 is inexact and does not constitute sufficient reason to perceive a similarly structured discourse in 23:1–25:46.[4] The change of scene in 24:1–3 is significant enough to identify 24:4–25:46 as a separate major discourse that follows closely upon the "minor" discourse of 23:1–39.[5] Second, Jesus' speech in 23:1–39 concludes emphatically with the amen-statement of 23:39. Indeed, the time period of "Jesus in Jerusalem" is bracketed by the citation of Ps 118:26, spoken first by the uncomprehending crowds at Matt 21:9 and then in lament by Jesus at 23:39. With Jesus' words that are addressed directly to Jerusalem in 23:37–39, the discourse that denounces the religious leaders of Israel is completed.

To identify 24:1–3 as part of the narrative framework for a separate discourse, however, is not to say that the ED is unrelated to Jesus' speech in chapter 23. Jesus' words in 23:38 regarding Jerusalem's "house" being left desolate refer[6] to the temple and its buildings. Thus, when the disciples approach Jesus in 24:1 to show him the structures of the temple, the implied reader knows that this is related somehow[7] to Jesus' earlier words about the temple. Indeed, Jesus reiterates and specifies the earlier prediction of 23:38 with his words of 24:2: "Not even a stone upon a stone will be left here which will not be torn down." Then, when in 24:3 the disciples continue their interaction with Jesus (even though the physical setting has changed once again), their first question regarding "these things" refers naturally to the events that would constitute the temple's destruction, in view at both 23:38 and 24:2.

Accordingly, although 24:1–3 continues the theme of judgment and of Jerusalem's destruction from the end of chapter 23,[8] the most important way that 24:1–3 functions is as the narrative framework to the ED. Jesus no longer speaks to or denounces his opponents. He exits and begins[9] to travel away from the temple. He leaves the city. In all of this only the disciples hear 24:2. Only the disciples approach him in 24:3 with the double question that is the reason for Jesus' long speech in 24:4–25:46.

MATTHEW 24:1–3 AS A UNIFIED NARRATIVE INTRODUCTION TO THE ESCHATOLOGICAL DISCOURSE

The second issue regarding 24:1–3 is the question of its unity. That is to say, is there a break or division between 24:2 and 24:3 that strongly joins 24:1–2 to the theme of Jerusalem's destruction, while 24:3 is joined to the ED itself and does not continue the theme of Jerusalem's destruction? This is the view of Fred Burnett, who argues for and then repeatedly asserts the presence of a caesura between 24:2 and 24:3.[10] Burnett's arguments for the caesura at 24:2, which are of sweeping importance for his entire thesis,[11] include the following. First, Burnett notes that Matthean redactional activity, to wit, the removal of Mark 12:41–44, has created a closer connection between Matt 24:1–2 and the discourse in 23:1–39.[12] Second, Burnett perceives in 24:3 a shift from a "public" audience (24:2) to a "private" audience (24:3).[13] Third, Burnett asserts that themes for the great discourses in Matthew are introduced in the preceding narrative sections. Accordingly, "judgment upon Israel," emphasized in 19:3–22:46, is completed by the discourse and framework of 23:1–24:2.[14] Fourth, Burnett interprets Jesus' departure from the temple in 24:1 as the fulfillment of the judgment predicted in 23:38, and Jesus' words in 24:2 as the "consummation" of that judgment.[15] These are Burnett's arguments to show a major break that separates 23:1–24:2 from the ED, which he envisions as being introduced by 24:3.

In response, the following points can be made. For my purposes, the first argument has no validity. That is to say, however valid for redaction criticism the observation may be that Matthew has omitted Markan material, such an observation is really no observation of the Matthean narrative at all.

Second, Burnett is incorrect in seeing at 24:3 a shift from a "public" to a "private" audience. The "audience" in Matthew 23, beginning from the second person plural address at 23:13 and continuing to 23:39,[16] has been the religious leadership of Israel, even to the point of personifying "Jerusalem" and addressing the unwilling city directly (23:37–39). Thus, the real "shift" in audience occurs when Jesus begins to speak to his disciples in 24:1. Significantly, it is the disciples once again in 24:3 who privately[17] approach Jesus to ask their double question. Thus, 24:1–3 is bound together by the disciples' approach of Jesus. In response, Jesus speaks to the disciples in 24:2 and then continues to speak to them throughout the ED.

Third, even if it is granted that in Matthew's Gospel the narrative sections introduce themes which find their culmination in the following discourses of Jesus, Burnett has begged the question of when the theme of "judgment on Israel" ends. Clearly "judgment on Israel" is in view in 23:1–39. But I am among many who will argue that the theme of "judgment on Israel," and specifically judgment in the form of the destruction of Jerusalem, continues well into

Matthew 24. This is no argument in support of a caesura between 24:2 and 24:3. It is only an assertion that there is one.

Fourth, as mentioned above, Burnett leans heavily on a doubtful Wisdom Christology in interpreting Jesus' physical departure from the temple and from Jerusalem. Moreover, in light of the importance in Matthew's Gospel of the future destruction of the city of Jerusalem (not to mention the tearing of the temple veil in 27:51–54), even Burnett is forced to speak of Jesus' departure from the temple as only a "beginning" of the judgment of God against Israel. As will be evident below in the comments on 24:1–3, a better way of describing the relationship between 23:38 and Jesus' departure from the temple in 24:1 is that the latter event "symbolizes" the fulfillment of Jesus' prediction in 23:38.

With this in mind, I conclude that there is no major caesura or division between 24:2 and 24:3. On the contrary, 24:1–3 as a unity functions as the narrative introduction for the ED, even as it acts as a transition from the earlier discourse of 23:1–39. In brief, I also note that the concluding narrative framework for the ED is 26:1–2, which acts to reintegrate the implied reader into the flow of the narrative. The presence of "all," πᾶς, at 26:1 signals the end of the major discourses of Jesus. I now turn to a closer examination of 24:1–3 and especially to the double question of the disciples and the bipartite structure of the ED as a whole.

THE DOUBLE QUESTION OF THE DISCIPLES (24:3) AND THE BIPARTITE STRUCTURE OF THE ESCHATOLOGICAL DISCOURSE

The narrative introduction to the ED relates the disciples' repeated approach of Jesus, once to show him the buildings of the temple (24:1) and once to question him (24:3). In response to their first approach, Jesus emphatically and unambiguously predicts the demolition of the buildings[18] that the disciples have pointed out: "You see all these things, don't you? Truly I say to you, not even a stone upon a stone will be left here which will not be torn down" (24:2). After this pronouncement and Jesus' progress to the Mount of Olives the disciples again approach Jesus, this time with questioning. The full discussion of the disciples' questions in 24:3 will occur below. For the moment, however, note that the disciples ask two questions at 24:3, as indicated by the use of two interrogatives: "When [πότε] will these things be, and [τί] what will be the sign of your coming and of the consummation of the age?"[19]

In light of this fact, the implied reader might reasonably expect Jesus to give a twofold answer. The full demonstration that this is the case necessarily involves the extensive treatment and interpretation of the various smaller units of the ED. But in support of a basic bipartite structure for the discourse, 24:4–35 and

24:36–25:46,[20] that corresponds to the twofold question for which it is the response, consider the following data.

There are significant themes present in one major section of the ED and absent from the other major section. For example, 24:4–35 contains repeated statements regarding "warnings" and "signs." The whole section is about "observing" things. Thus, 24:4–14 tells of the things that will normally and necessarily happen before the end; false christs, deceptions, wars and various upheavals, hatred and persecutions for the disciples, apostasies, false prophets, and the heralding of the Gospel of the reign of heaven to all the nations. Further, 24:15–22 is marked by the same theme, beginning as it does with "Therefore, when you see." Persecutions, flight during winter or on Sabbath, shortened days of persecution dominate these verses. In 24:23–28, there are the repeated warnings about false christs and false prophets, in view of which Jesus says, "See, I have told you beforehand" (24:25). In 24:29–31, eschatological and cosmic signs are related. All of these things for which the disciples are to look as "signs" and "warnings" are summarized in the parable of the fig tree (24:32–33): when you see the leaves, you know summer is near. All these things are the signs that the event about which Jesus is speaking is near, within the life span of the generation of those who oppose him (24:34).

In stark contrast, the theme of "warnings and signs" is utterly absent from 24:36–25:46. Indeed, the very opposite theme is present, that of the sudden and unpredictable time of the Parousia of Jesus on the last day. After the declaration that not even the Son of God himself knows "that day and hour" (24:36), the comparisons are with the days of Noah (24:37–39); the sudden removal of one of a pair of working persons (24:40–41);[21] a thief breaking into a house unexpectedly (24:43–44); a master who returns when his servant doesn't expect (24:45–51); the unexpected arrival of a bridegroom (25:1–13); and the long-delayed return of a master who went on a journey (25:14–30). For those who do not break the discourse between 24:35 and 24:36, the opposing themes of "warnings and signs" and "sudden, unexpected event" pose a serious problem.[22] For those, like myself, who do break the discourse between 24:35 and 24:36, the "tension" dissolves.[23]

Related to this first contrast in themes is a second contrast. In the first part of the ED, the danger of being "deceived" is very real. This is why both "signs" and explanations are given. The verb "deceive" occurs at 24:4, 5, 11, 24, and two subunits contain warnings about the dangers of false christs and false prophets (24:4–8 and 24:23–28). Jesus' opening words to the disciples in this first part of the ED are, in fact, "Watch, lest anyone deceive you!" (24:4).

By contrast, 24:36–25:46 contains no theme of the danger of deception. The danger in the second part of the ED is rather the lack of readiness. No one is deceived about the Parousia when it happens, just as no one could mistake the flood or a thief breaking in or the return of a master who both rewards and punishes. The danger is that some might not be ready.

Furthermore, the two parts of the ED are different in this regard. Although 24:4–35 contains imperatives for the disciples, chiefly the imperative not to be deceived, it cannot be said to be paraenetic in character.[24] By contrast, the themes of "vigilance," "faithfulness," and "judgment and reward" in 24:36–25:46 create, as the second part of the ED addresses both the disciples and the implied reader, a strong paraenetic message.[25]

On a smaller level of data, note that there are patterns of word usage that also support the division of the ED into two parts, 24:4–35 and 24:36–25:46. In the first part, noted already is the use of "deceive," πλανάω, at 24:4, 5, 11, 24. Also noteworthy is the repetition of "when you see," ὅταν ἴδητε, at 24:15, 33. "All these things," πάντα ταῦτα, occurs at 24:8, 33, 34. Further, "those days," ἐκεῖναι αἱ ἡμέραι/αἱ ἡμέραι ἐκεῖναι, occurs at 24:19, 22, 29. None of these words or phrases occur in 24:36–25:46.

In the second part of the ED, most noteworthy is the repeated use of "lord,"[26] which is absent from 24:4–35. Also, the singular nouns "day" (ἡμέρα, 24:36, 38, 42, 50; 25:13) and "hour" (ὥρα, 24:36, 44, 50; 25:13) and the verb "watch" (γρηγορέω, 24:42, 43; 25:13) occur only in the second major section of the ED. A further contrast relates to the use of verbs of "knowing." On the one hand, in the first half of the ED Jesus indicates that the presence of "warning signs" will enable the disciples to know (γινώσκω) that "summer/it is near" (24:32–33). On the other hand, Jesus asserts repeatedly in the second part of the ED that the disciples and the implied reader do *not* know (24:39, 43, 50 with γιν-ώσκω; 24:36, 42, 43; 25:13 with οἶδα).[27]

If it is true (as the above data suggest) that the ED has a bipartite structure, one might expect some indications of a literary hinge at the break between 24:35 and 24:36. Such a hinge does, in fact, exist. Jesus' words in 24:35 are an affirming oath, assigning permanent validity to the words that Jesus has just uttered.[28] Then, significantly, Jesus' words in 24:36 reveal the "turning of the hinge" into the second part of the ED by beginning with "but concerning" (περὶ δέ). Virtually none of the commentators has picked up on the structural function of these words.[29] The following data are significant.

In Matthew's Gospel, the preposition περί is used with the genitive case twenty times. It is used at the beginning of a sentence only three times: 6:28; 22:31; and 24:36. At 6:28, the combination καὶ περί occurs in Jesus' words: "And concerning clothing, why do you worry?" The force of "and concerning" there might be termed "resumptive." At 6:25, Jesus mentions the twin physical concerns of "food" and "clothing." Then, in 6:26–27, "food" has been in view. By way of "reaching back" and resuming the discussion of "clothing," Jesus says, "And concerning clothing, why do you worry? Observe how the lilies of the field grow." The function of καὶ περί in 6:28 is to reach back a short distance in order to resume discussion of a topic already mentioned.[30]

At 22:31, this resumptive function is strengthened in that not καί but δέ is linked with the preposition περί: "but concerning." Matt 22:23–33 relates Jesus' confrontation with the Sadducees over the issue of the resurrection of the dead. The narrator has showed that the resurrection of the dead is the real "question" through the comment at 22:23, "On that day Sadducees approached him, because they say there is no resurrection, and they asked him, saying...." Their overt question, of course, concerns the case of a woman who had seven husbands. The real question is this: "Is there a resurrection of the dead at all?" Note well that, after he deals with their overt hypothetical question (22:29–30), Jesus in 22:31 "reaches back" to the real question in 22:24–28 by saying, "But concerning [περί δέ] the resurrection of the dead, have you not read...?" The expression "but concerning" reaches back to the beginning of the pericope and addresses the unspoken but fundamental question around which the confrontation with the Sadducees revolved.

These two examples from Matthew's Gospel suggest that περί δέ, heading the opening sentence of the second major section of the ED, reaches back to the beginning of the discourse and brings into focus the disciples' second question concerning the Parousia and consummation of the age. The other examples of περί δέ + the genitive in the NT lend considerable support to this view. Of the twelve NT instances of this construction outside of Matthew's Gospel, Mark 12:36 is parallel to Matt 22:31 and Mark 13:32 is parallel to Matt 24:36. While John 16:11 does not begin a sentence, the nine other examples do stand at the head of a new proposition.[31] In each instance, there is a "reaching back" function, in which the sentence that begins "but concerning" introduces a new topic for discussion. The most dramatic example of this is 1 Cor 7:1, which "reaches back" all the way to a letter which the Corinthians had written to Paul in order to "resume" a subject from that letter!

The most illuminating example for our purposes, however, is 1 Thess 5:1, which stands as a striking parallel to Matt 24:36. In 1 Thess 4:13–18, Paul addresses the concerns of the believers regarding their fellow Christians who had died before the Parousia of Jesus. He ends that unit of material with 4:18: "Therefore, comfort one another with these words."

Because the confusion of the Thessalonians concerning the resurrection of the dead is also connected to the question of "when," Paul seizes the implicit issue and makes it explicit by means of περί δέ: "But concerning the times and appointed hours, brothers and sisters, you have no need...." The striking thing, of course, is that the question of the sudden and unexpected timing of the Parousia is precisely the issue that comes into view in the ED, beginning at Matt 24:36! In 1 Thess 5:1, the effect of "but concerning" is to reach back and bring into focus a question that has been heretofore present only in the background.

Thus the use of περί δέ + the genitive elsewhere in the NT supports my understanding of 24:36. Jesus' words in 24:36, "But concerning that day and hour no one knows" are precisely the hinge that one would expect to find when the ED moves from its first major part to its second major part. Accordingly, the further examination of the ED will build on the conclusion that the first major part of the discourse ends at 24:35 and the second major part begins at 24:36. These two parts correspond to the two questions the disciples ask in 24:3.

THE SUBUNITS OF THE ESCHATOLOGICAL DISCOURSE

I now shall delineate briefly the subunits of each major section of the ED. Following the narrative introduction which culminates in the disciples' double question (24:1–3), the first major section of the discourse (24:4–35) may be divided into five subunits: 24:4–14; 24:15–22; 24:23–28; 24:29–31; 24:32–35. The first subunit, 24:4–14, warns the disciples not to think that the tumultuous events of history, nature, and their own experience are signs of the end. These things are to be regarded as only the beginning of eschatological birth pangs (24:8). Before the end will come, the Gospel of the reign of heaven will have been preached to all the nations. Then the end will come (24:14).[32]

The second subunit, 24:15–22, draws the inference regarding the proper course of action to be followed when the disciples see "the abomination of desolation" (24:15). They are to flee from Judea. Jesus' words give specific instructions for that flight, as well as the admonition to pray for favorable conditions in which to flee. The subunit concludes with the assurance that, for the sake of the elect who are fleeing, the tribulation associated with the appearance of the abomination of desolation will be of a limited duration.[33]

The third subunit, 24:23–28, returns to the theme of "beware of false christs and prophets" that occurred in 24:4–14. Because the disciples are being thus forewarned, this inference follows: "Therefore, do not go out; do not believe [it]." The reason for the inference is that the Parousia of Jesus will be as unmistakable as the lightning flash that stretches from horizon to horizon. Note that this third subunit explicitly mentions the Parousia so that the disciples might not be deceived by the advent of false christs and false prophets.[34] To borrow the phrase from 24:6, the purpose of this parenthetical subunit[35] is to reiterate the message that "the end is not yet."[36]

The fourth subunit, 24:29–31, describes events of cosmic and eschatological significance. To anticipate my full discussion of these verses, I shall argue that in 24:29–31 Jesus utilizes eschatological language in a way that parallels the OT prophets. His purpose is to describe the events of end-time judgment that God will bring upon the nation of Israel through the destruction of Jerusalem, and to underscore the ensuing mission to all the nations.[37] The sequence of events in 24:29–31 parallels the salvation-historical sequence found in the parables of the Wicked Tenants (21:33–46) and the Wedding Feast (22:1–13), namely (1) judgment upon the nation of Israel whose leaders and crowds rejected Jesus as Christ and Son of God, followed by (2) the turning of invitation and outreach to the Gentiles. The subunit is bound together chiefly by its unique use of extravagant eschatological language.

The fifth and final subunit in the first major part of the ED is 24:32–35. This subunit emphasizes the necessity of rightly perceiving "all these things" that Jesus has predicted in order to discern the nearness of the events before they occur. Jesus applies a solemn and specific temporal limitation at 24:34: "Truly I say to you that this generation will certainly not pass away until all these things take place." With these words, Jesus has answered the first of the disciples' questions in 24:3: "*When* will these things be?" Finally, 24:35 acts as an oath to verify and validate the predictions that Jesus has just made in the first major part of the ED.[38]

The second major part of the ED consists of the hinge verse, 24:36, followed by six subunits: 24:37–42; 24:43–44; 24:45–51; 25:1–13; 25:14–30; 25:31–46. I have already examined the character of 24:36 as the hinge verse of the ED. The first subunit, 24:37–42, begins the remarkable thematic emphasis upon the unknowability of the time of Jesus' Parousia. A comparison with the unknowability of the time of the Noachic deluge emphasizes the character of the Parousia as sudden and unexpected. The "concurrent" use of τότε [39] links the "sudden division" assertions in 24:40–41. The subunit ends with an inference with which two other subunits in the second major section of the ED also conclude: "Therefore, watch!" (24:42).[40] The ground for the inference is also given: "because you do not know the day your Lord is coming."

The second subunit is 24:43–44. Though proverbial in form, there is an implied story-parable about an unwary householder and a thief who breaks in. As with the preceding subunit, 24:43–44 ends with an inference and its ground: "Therefore also you be ready, for this man is coming at an hour which you do not reckon."

The third subunit is 24:45–51. Though not strictly a story-parable, it is story-like speech. The two-part structure of this subunit describes a servant who is either wise and faithful or wicked. The subunit ends with Jesus' characteristic description of the place of final eschatological judgment (cf. 8:12; 13:42, 50; 22:13; 25:30). This third subunit also concerns itself with the sudden and unknowable time of the Parousia. In addition, however, for the first time in the second part of the ED the theme of "faithfulness" is introduced.

The fourth subunit is 25:1–13, the parable of the Ten Maidens. This story-parable is a discrete subunit of material. In contrast with the preceding subunit where the wicked slave reckoned on his master returning later than he actually did, the reverse is the case in 25:1–13. The foolish maidens reckon on less of a delay than is the case. Many have noted that the inference and ground given in 25:13, "Watch, therefore, for you know neither the day nor the hour," fit poorly with the parable itself. In the parable, both the wise and the foolish maidens fall asleep. Neither is falling asleep the cause for the separation of the two groups. It is certainly appropriate to understand "watch" in 25:13 to mean "prepare and be ready even if the coming of the Lord is delayed."[41] In addition, 25:13 acts as an inclusio with 24:36, with which it shares a similar expression about not knowing the day or hour. Through the first four subunits of the second major part of the ED, Jesus' words have emphasized the theme of the suddenness and unknowability of the Parousia. That theme drops out after the parable of the Ten Maidens.

The fifth subunit is the story-parable of the Talents, 25:14–30. In this discrete subunit the theme of "faithfulness," introduced in passing in 24:45–51, receives full expression, while the theme of "suddenness" is absent.

The sixth subunit (25:31–46) is the account of the judgment scene at the Parousia of this man, Jesus. It stands apart[42] from the other subunits of the second part of the ED on several counts. Foremost, it is not a story-parable or story-like speech, as has been the case since 24:45–51.[43] Nor does it concern itself with life lived before the Parousia and in preparation for it. Rather, it describes the Parousia itself and the ensuing judgment. Life lived before the Parousia in 25:31–46 is already over and serves as the criterion for carrying out the judgment. The account of the sheep and the goats brings the ED in Matthew's Gospel to a close.

This, then, is the structure of the ED. The narrative introduction is 24:1–3. There are two major sections of the ED proper (24:4–35 and 24:36–25:46) that correspond to the double question asked by the disciples in 24:3. The first major part consists of five subunits (24:4–14; 24:15–22; 24:23–28; 24:29–31; 24:32–35). The hinge verse, 24:36, begins the second major part of the ED. This second major part consists of six subunits, five of which deal with vigilance and preparation for the Parousia (24:37–42; 24:43–44; 24:45–51; 25:1–13; 25:14–30) and one of which is a description of the Parousia and the ensuing judgment itself at the consummation of the age (25:31–46). Last comes the narrative conclusion, 26:1–2. Guided by this structure, I will examine each of the units in pursuit of the goal upon which this entire study has been focused, namely, to read as the implied reader would read. Special attention will be placed on the ways that the implied reader is addressed and the effect that Jesus' words have on the implied reader.

POINT OF VIEW IN MATTHEW 24:1–3

In the discussion above, I have already analyzed the narrative introduction of the ED in terms of both its unitary character and its function to mark the ED as a discourse separate from 23:1–39. Three significant questions remain to be answered regarding the implied reader's understanding of 24:1–3: Who are the disciples and what is their relation to the implied reader? What is the significance of Jesus' departure from the temple (24:1)? What is the disciples' point of view, as revealed in 24:1–3 and from other data within the story? That is to say, do the disciples in the story understand and question Jesus intelligently, or do they misunderstand and therefore question Jesus foolishly?

THE DISCIPLES, JESUS' DEPARTURE FROM THE TEMPLE, AND THE IMPLIED READER

According to a narrative-critical understanding of 24:1–3, the answer to the first question is simple and straightforward. The disciples, mentioned in 24:1 and 24:3, are the "figure of the disciples within the story of Matthew's Gospel." They are not the implied reader. Even though the answer is simple for narrative-critical analysis, it is important to state the answer at the onset. The examination of the ED in Matthew's Gospel has been dominated for many years by redaction criticism. One of the supposed truisms of redaction-critical scholarship has been the principle of "transparency," that is, the view that the "disciples" in Matthew's Gospel are, above all, a representation of the community of the redactor.[44]

By contrast, narrative-critical analysis always maintains the distinction between the characters within Matthew's Gospel and the implied reader, who stands outside of the story and reads it retrospectively. As such, the implied reader has the freedom, according to the point of view established by the reliable narrator and the characters within the story who are aligned with the narrator, either "to draw near" or "to distance" himself or herself from any given character(s) as signaled by the implied author or narrator.[45] This methodological point does not require elaboration. But in light of the influence of redaction-critical studies and of the different purpose of this present study, the reminder is a salutary one.

The second question regarding 24:3 seeks the meaning of Jesus' departure from the temple. Matt 24:1a reads: "And Jesus went out from the temple and began to journey." In light of the prediction of 23:38, what is the significance of Jesus' immediate departure from the temple? As noted above in the discussion of 24:1, to say that Jesus' immediate physical departure brings to "completion" or "fulfillment" his prediction in 23:38 severely overstates the case. Also rejected was the related view that there is a dramatic caesura or division between 24:2 and 24:3. If Jesus' departure in 24:1 and his second prediction of the temple's destruction in 24:2 "completes" or "fulfills" the prophecy of 23:38, then the disciples' question in 24:3 (and the ensuing answer in the ED) has nothing directly to do with the temple and its destruction.

Rather than naming Jesus' departure from the temple in 24:1 a "completion" or "fulfillment," or even a "concrete realization"[46] of 23:38, the best way to describe Jesus' action is to say that it "symbolizes" the destruction of the temple and of the city. This destruction still lies in the future beyond the temporal boundaries of the story. The future destruction of Jerusalem is of immense importance in the story-world of the Gospel. It will show Jesus' vindication over his enemies (22:41–46; 26:64). It will come only after Jesus sends missionaries to Israel, whom Israel will reject (23:34–36). This destruction of Jerusalem is predicted in the parables of the Wicked Tenants (21:33–46) and the Wedding Feast (22:1–14) and is presaged by the tearing of the temple veil (27:51). It is the "flip side" of Jesus' true identity as the Son of God, for it is precisely because Jesus' opponents in Israel refuse to believe that he is the Son of God that their city and temple will be destroyed.[47] Thus, in light of the narrative importance of the actual destruction of the temple, it is best to say that Jesus' departure from the temple in 24:1 "symbolizes" the desolation of the temple and its destruction.[48]

WHAT IS THE POINT OF VIEW OF THE DISCIPLES' QUESTIONS (24:3)?

The third question regarding the narrative introduction to the ED is the most crucial one. What is the point of view of the disciples? Does their point of view, as revealed through both 24:1–3 and other data within the story, align with that of Jesus and the narrator? Or does the disciples' point of view diverge from that of Jesus and the narrator and thus invite the implied reader to distance himself or herself from it? I shall examine in brief the disciples' approach to Jesus in 24:1b and then deal more extensively with the disciples' approach and questions to Jesus in 24:3.

Fred Burnett argues that the narrator's use of language in 24:1b indicates that the disciples' approach to Jesus indicates a full and appropriate understanding both of Jesus' own personal significance as Sophia, or the Wisdom of God, on the one hand, and of Jesus' words in 23:1–39 and especially 23:38 on the other hand. Noting how "approach" (προσέρχομαι) can function in Hellenistic literature, in the LXX, and in Matthew's Gospel, Burnett concludes: "In 24:1 the disciples reverently approach Jesus because they understand that he is the Wisdom of God whose presence is about to leave Israel."[49] The data are not as convincing as Burnett seems to think. Most significantly, the disciples' propensity for misunderstanding in Matthew's Gospel and their repeated need for Jesus' instruction[50] leads the implied reader to know that in 24:1 the disciples have not understood Jesus' prediction in 23:38.[51]

The view that the disciples' action in 24:1 indicates that they have not understood Jesus' prediction of 23:38 is supported by Jesus' own words in 24:2: "You see all of these things, don't you? Truly I say to you, not even a stone upon a stone will be left here which will not be torn down." With these words, Jesus removes any ambiguity from the prediction of 23:38. The disciples' misunderstanding about the fate of the temple is eradicated. All these buildings[52] will be destroyed. Jesus' words in 24:2 remove the disciples' misunderstanding about the fate of the temple.

Yet, the point of view of the disciples remains inadequate, as their questions to Jesus in 24:3 now reveal. After Jesus has taken his seat on the Mount of Olives,[53] the disciples approach him privately and ask their double question (24:3): "Tell us, when will these things be, and what will be that which shows[54] your Parousia and the consummation of the age?" A number of features are of significance to the implied reader.

First, the disciples ask when "these things" will be, that is, the predicted destruction of the temple and the surrounding buildings.[55] Then, their second question is this: "What will be that which shows your Parousia and the consummation of the age?" This second question presents the implied reader with a challenge. The sense of what the disciples say is clear enough,[56] although the term "Parousia" is certainly unexpected.[57] The challenge to the implied reader arises because it is the disciples and not Jesus who have explicitly joined together the consummation of the age and the destruction of Jerusalem that Jesus has predicted.[58] The point of view that thus juxtaposes the two events is perhaps not unknown to the implied reader, given the cultural background when the Gospel of Matthew was written.[59] But how does the implied reader evaluate the point of view revealed through the disciples' questions? Is the implied reader to regard the disciples' double question as well-formulated or mistaken? We need to consider the following factors.

THE DISCIPLES' POINT OF VIEW (24:3)
AND THE IMPLIED READER

First, it bears repeating that for a narrative-critical understanding of 24:3 one cannot posit a priori an agreement between the disciples' point of view and that of the narrator or Jesus.[60] Stated positively, the implied reader aligns himself or herself only with the norming point of view of the narrator of the Gospel and of Jesus. Accordingly, the implied reader is free to agree or disagree with the point of view of the disciples.

Second, there are two kinds of data to aid the implied reader in evaluating the disciples' questions. One kind of data emerges from the Gospel's overall portrayal of the disciples, specifically as they approach Jesus and ask questions that do or do not align with the Gospel's norming point of view. The other kind of data (as obvious as it may seem) is Jesus' response to the disciples' questions (beginning with 24:4–14). As I shall now show, both kinds of data indicate that the implied reader will not align himself or herself with the disciples' point of view in 24:3.

In discussing 24:1, I argued (see the extensive data in the pertinent notes) that when the disciples "approach" Jesus in Matthew's Gospel they almost always reveal their inadequate or even sinful point of view.[61] A similar conclusion emerges when one examines the times that the disciples "question" or initiate conversation with Jesus. There are three occasions when the disciples simply request instruction or explanation and they receive no rebuke from Jesus (13:10, 36; 26:17). But at least[62] seventeen times in Matthew's Gospel the disciples' words or questions show a general failure to understand,[63] a misunderstanding of the nature of discipleship,[64] or a failure or weakness of faith.[65] Moreover, the disciples never show by their questions that they have grasped or understood Jesus and the significance of his words or deeds. There is always something that is deficient in their point of view.[66]

In general terms, then, the "track record" of the disciples in Matthew's story signals the implied reader to distance himself or herself from the eschatological point of view reflected in the disciples' double question of 24:3. Even more significantly, notice that on two occasions the disciples' evidence a misunderstanding regarding the relationship between the final eschatological day and Jesus' present end-time ministry. The two occasions are 20:20–23 and 17:9–13. As I argued in chapter 4, the fundamental misunderstanding of the mother of Zebedee's sons and the sons themselves relates to their request through their mother to sit on Jesus' right and left hand in his reign (ἐν τῇ βασιλείᾳ σου, 20:21). They think they are asking for the places of highest honor when they sit with Jesus and judge the twelve tribes of Israel (19:28). What they are really asking for are places next to Jesus when he is enthroned on the cross as the true King of the Jews (27:33–38).

The second example of "eschatological misunderstanding" occurs at 17:9–13, as Jesus and the three disciples come down from the mountain where he was transfigured. This incident is all the more important as a parallel to 24:3 because it involves the disciples' misunderstanding about the timing of eschatological events. After Jesus commands them not to speak about his transfiguration until after his death and resurrection (17:9), the disciples ask about the scribes' teaching on the coming of Elijah. Jesus' reply switches from quotation in the future tense to assertion in the aorist indicative: "That Elijah come first is necessary, and he will restore all things; but I say to you that Elijah already came, and they did not know him but they did to him whatever they wished. Thus also this man is about to suffer by their hands" (17:11–12). Despite Jesus' explicit teaching to the crowds[67] about John as Elijah in 11:7–14, the disciples have misunderstood eschatological realities and eschatological timing. They evidence the same sort of misunderstanding in their double question at 24:3.

Clearly, the data from the Gospel's portrayal of the disciples point in one direction: the implied reader has every reason to distance himself or herself from the point of view that is reflected in the disciples' double question at 24:3.[68] Simply put, this is so because the disciples in Matthew's Gospel consistently "get it wrong," both in general and specifically with respect to eschatological realities.[69]

The second category of data to consider in determining the implied reader's evaluation of the disciples' point of view in 24:3 is the actual answer that Jesus begins to give to their double question. Without treating the first subunit of the ED in detail just yet, I note only the following.

The first words out of Jesus' mouth in 24:4 are "Watch, lest anyone deceive you." After describing tumultuous and critical events which the disciples themselves will witness (24:5–6a),[70] Jesus repeats his warning: "Watch, lest you be troubled, for [these things] must happen, but the end is not yet" (24:6). Then Jesus describes additional upheavals among nations and in nature (24:7) that are qualified by these words: "But all these things are the beginning of birth pangs"

(24:8). Jesus describes both persecutions that will happen to the disciples ("they will deliver you," 24:9) as well as other tumults within the church and without that extend out into the time of the implied reader.[71] He then concludes the first subunit of the ED: "And this Gospel of the reign will be preached in the whole world for a witness to all the nations and then the end will come" (24:14).

The basic thrust of the first subunit of the ED is to give this message: upheavals, tumults, false christs and false prophets are not signs of the Parousia and consummation of the age.[72] Jesus' first words to the disciples, in response to their double question, are "Don't be deceived." The disciples have erred in the way they have joined together "these things" Jesus has predicted (23:38; 24:2) with the Parousia and the consummation of the age.[73]

I shall summarize the implied reader's understanding of 24:1–3. Both the record of the disciples' mistaken point of view throughout the story and Jesus' opening response alert the implied reader to reject the disciples' joining together of the predicted ruin of the temple and the consummation of the age. In addition, the bipartite structure of the ED (24:4–35 and 24:36–25:46) supports this evaluation of the disciples' questions. As I shall show, the two major sections of the ED answer in turn the disciples' two questions. Recall the demonstration that the hinge verse ("But concerning that day and hour," 24:36) functions to reach back to the second question of the disciples. As the implied reader begins to experience and understand the ED, he or she knows to align himself or herself not with the disciples' point of view but with the point of view that Jesus will reveal through his answer[74] to the disciples' question. As I proceed to the interpretation of the various subunits of the ED, I shall attend especially both to the way the implied reader will understand the future predictions that Jesus is making as well as to the extent to which Jesus' words address the implied reader.

MATTHEW 24:4–14

As Jesus begins to speak to the disciples, his first purpose is to warn them about being deceived as to when the consummation will come.[75] After the command to "keep on watching" (βλέπετε) in order to avoid being deceived, Jesus gives the reason (γάρ) in 24:5. Many will come, claiming to be the Christ[76] who has returned. By implication, these imposters will claim to announce the consummation. Along with such false claimants, there will be wars and rumors of wars (24:6a).[77] Let the disciples go on not being troubled by such things. They are necessary under the divine guidance of history[78] but the end is not yet (24:6). They are not the "announcement" of the end.[79] Once again, the reason (γάρ) is given. International upheaval, famines, and earthquakes will typify life in the world[80] where the disciples live in the time after the resurrection of Jesus and before the consummation. All these things to which Jesus has just alluded, however, are only a beginning of the eschatological birth pangs.[81] Here Jesus marks out the entire time after his resurrection as eschatological in nature. But the disciples must not think that the difficulties and tumults[82] mark the consummation of the age. They are only[83] a beginning.

The words of Jesus that follow (24:9–14) predict both persecution of the disciples and apostasy on the part of many. Along with[84] the troubles already described, the disciples will face persecution, death, and hatred from all the nations to whom they have been sent with the task of making disciples (24:9). The time period after Jesus' resurrection and before the consummation will see apostasy on the part of many disciples,[85] hatreds, false prophets, lawlessness, and lovelessness (24:10–12).[86] The setting for these troubles extends far beyond the boundaries of Judea,[87] encompassing "all the nations" (24:9, 14). In spite of all the tumults and troubles that mark the time of mission, anyone[88] who ultimately[89] endures by remaining true in faith and love[90] will himself or herself be saved.[91]

None of the troubles that Jesus' words have portrayed in 24:5–13 are "that which shows" his Parousia and the consummation of the age (24:3). None of the troubles described are to deceive the disciples into thinking that Christ has returned. The end is not yet. These things are only the beginning of the birth pangs. The one thing that could be called a "sign" of the end is not a "temporal" sign at all (24:14). The heralding of this Gospel of the reign of heaven will have been taking place among all the nations from the very beginning of the post-resurrection period (cf. 28:19).

The entire period will be the time of making disciples among all the nations. When that heralding will have taken place in the whole world as a witness[92] to all the nations, then the end, the consummation of the age,[93] will come. And only then[94] the end will come. The impression is that the time of mission will be a lengthy one,[95] long enough for the mission to spread to the whole world.[96]

Jesus' words in this first subunit of the ED both warn his disciples against the danger of eschatological deception and temporally separate the destruction of the temple and the consummation of the age. This question now needs to be asked: To what extent is the implied reader addressed by these words of Jesus? Does the implied reader merely "overhear" them as he or she reads the ED, or does Jesus also address the implied reader here in 24:4–14?

Indeed, the implied reader only "overhears" the words of Jesus in 24:4–8. These words, which so strongly warn "the disciples" (24:1, 3) against thinking that tumults and troubles are signs of the nearness of the consummation of the age, inform the implied reader as he or she "overhears" them. The implied reader learns not to confuse the things "which must happen" with "the end" (24:6). Further, the events here predicted take place beyond the temporal boundaries of the Gospel's story, in the time in which the implied reader also stands. But he or she is not "addressed" or "included" by Jesus' words, for there are no rhetorically "inclusive" features in 24:4–8.

That situation changes in 24:9–14. The words of 24:9 are still addressed to "the disciples."[97] By contrast, second person address is completely absent from 24:10–14. Devices that address the implied reader in 24:10–14 include the repeated use of "many" with the future indicative (24:10, 11, 12); the impersonal expression of third person plural indicatives, "they will do such and such" (24:10, 11); and the proverbial expression with the substantized participle in 24:13. Most noteworthy is the future indicative passive voice in 24:14, "will be heralded." The implied reader knows that at the beginning of the time of mission, Jesus commands the Eleven (28:16) to "make disciples" (28:19). But now it is not just the Eleven, "the disciples," who will be heralding this Gospel of the reign until the end. The implied reader himself or herself will also participate in that heralding and will witness the kinds of events described by Jesus in 24:10–12. Accordingly, the implied reader is forewarned that as he or she participates in the mission of Jesus' disciples there will be difficulties and trials. The implied reader accepts once again that the time from Jesus' resurrection to his Parousia is the time of mission (cf. 28:18–20). The words of 24:13 are words of encouragement for the implied reader. The one who ultimately endures will be saved.

The first subunit of the ED, then, addresses both the disciples and the implied reader. Matt 24:4–14 affords a framework and perspective on the entire time of mission, so that the disciples and the implied reader might not be confused regarding the relationship between troubles and tumults within history and the time of the consummation of the age. On the basis of that perspective, then, the ED continues with the second subunit, 24:15–22. Jesus' words draw an inference from the perspective given in 24:4–14: "Therefore...."

MATTHEW 24:15–22

The focus in 24:15–22 narrows, leaving the worldwide focus of 24:4–14 and returning to a first-century Judean context. Because[98] troubles and persecutions are not going to be indications that the Parousia necessarily is near, Jesus instructs the disciples regarding an unprecedented time of trouble during their lifetime in which they will participate. The entire instruction to the disciples[99] in 24:15–22 is summed up in the imperative found in 24:16: "Flee!"

Before examining the smaller elements of 24:15–22, the character and scope of the trouble therein described should be noted. In positive terms, it is a tribulation that is limited geographically to the region of Jerusalem and Judea. In negative terms, it is not a universal tribulation such as was thought would accompany the consummation of the age.

The following five points relate to this. First, the limited geographical character of the troubles is indicated by 24:16: "Let those who are in Judea[100] flee to the mountains." Second, "standing in the holy place" is, as I shall indicate, most naturally a reference to the temple in Jerusalem.[101] Third, the prohibitions against entering the house or coming in from the field (24:17–18) imply that by not hesitating in flight, persons in those days could make the difference between saving their lives and losing them. By contrast, the women who are physically hampered in flight by being pregnant or by carrying a nursing child are the target of Jesus' compassionate "Woe!" (24:19).[102] Thus hampered, they might lose their lives in the tribulation. Fourth, a local flight is more difficult during the rainy winter season and made more dangerous if carried out on a Sabbath (24:20).[103] Such a trouble as this must be understood as limited in its scope and power, despite the hyperbolic language[104] of 24:21: "For there will be a great tribulation such has not been from the beginning of the world until now nor certainly will be." Indeed, the last clause of 24:21, "nor certainly will be," implies that in fact there will be other tribulations after the one here being described. This further shows the local and limited character of the troubles.[105] Fifth, common sense notes that the very command to flee this tribulation indicates that it is not cosmic and worldwide, as accompanying the consummation of the age. If it were, it would do no good to flee.

We return to the more detailed examination of Jesus' words to "the disciples" in 24:15–22. This subunit begins, "Therefore, when you see that[106] the abomination of desolation that was spoken through Daniel the prophet is standing in the holy place...." The phrase "the abomination of desolation" (τὸ βδέλυγμα τῆς ἐρημώσεως) is, as Jesus' words indicate, from Daniel, where it occurs with minor variations[107] in Greek at Dan 9:27; 11:31; and 12:11. In its OT context, the phrase refers to the defiling of the temple altar of burnt offering by the Syrian overlords, as 1 Macc 1:54 makes clear.[108]

The exact sense of the genitive construction is impossible to know with certainty. Perhaps an active sense is best, "the abomination that causes desolation."[109] Whatever the precise sense, the combination of this phrase in Matt 24:15 with the abomination's presence in the Jerusalem temple[110] underscores the character of this event as producing a "spiritually loathsome"[111] defilement and destruction.[112] Further, the mention of "the holy place" alerts the disciples that Jesus' words are now focused on their first question of 24:3: "When will these things [i.e., the temple's destruction that you have just predicted in 24:2] be?" Whatever the specific reference of the event depicted in 24:15 might be,[113] the disciples know that Jesus is now instructing them with regard to the judgment upon the city and the authorities that have rejected Jesus and that will reject and persecute those whom he sends to them in the time after his resurrection (10:5–23; 23:34–36; 28:18–20).

When the disciples see these things, they are to flee.[114] Jesus' words in 24:16 first refer generally to the people who are to flee to the mountains, "those in Judea." Jesus then specifies[115] the command to flee in ways that show the urgency of such flight. The one who is on the roof should not come down into the house (24:17). The one who is in the field should not take the time to get the cloak he had left elsewhere (24:18). Those days[116] of tribulation, marked by the appearance of the abomination of desolation, will require efforts at flight that will place in danger women who are pregnant or nursing children. Poor weather and flight on the Sabbath would hinder the necessary journey away from Jerusalem's locale. When the disciples who are listening to Jesus' words see[117] the need for this flight, they are to pray that it might not happen in winter or on a Sabbath (24:21).

The savagery of the tribulation of those days is described in 24:21–22. Although the tribulation in view is still that which will take place in Judea,[118] the hyperbolic language underscores the distress that will take place in those days.[119] As noted above, Jesus' words in 24:21 ("nor certainly will be," οὐδ' οὐ μὴ γένηται) indicate that this is not the last tribulation that the world will ever experience. It is not a tribulation that precedes the consummation of the age.[120] Even as Jesus describes the terror, his words also comfort the disciples. Without the merciful divine shortening[121] of those days of tribulation,[122] no human being would escape alive (24:22a).[123] The time period of tribulation will be shortened, however, for the sake of the smaller number of the elect[124] within the general populace in Judea in those days (24:22).

The subunit 24:15–22, then, informs the disciples about events that will lead up to the ruin of the temple about which the disciples asked in 24:3.[125] When the disciples see the abomination of desolation, they and all other disciples in Judea are to flee to the mountains, for an unprecedented tribulation will come upon that region.

The question arises, how does the implied reader relate to the words of Jesus in 24:15? More specifically, when does the implied reader stand in relation to those events that will take place beyond the temporal boundaries of the story? This is a question that has vexed interpreters. The specific language and rhetoric of the subunit suggest an answer.

First, even as Jesus' words address the character of "the disciples" within the story-world of the Gospel, the implied author's direct address to the implied reader at 24:15 shows the importance of Jesus' words for the implied reader: "Let the reader understand" (ὁ ἀναγινώσκων νοείτω, 24:15).[126] What is not clear on the basis of this statement alone is the precise temporal relationship of the implied reader to the events that Jesus predicts in 24:15–22.[127]

The statement "Let the reader understand" does create an extremely high degree of contact between the implied author and the implied reader.[128] Other features of this subunit combine with "Let the reader understand" to answer the question of the temporal position of the implied reader. Inclusive devices in 24:16–22 show that Jesus' words address the implied reader along with "the disciples." Crucial are the repeated use of substantized participles ("those in Judea," "the one upon the roof," "the one in the field," "those who are pregnant," "those who are nursing") and the inclusive use of "all flesh" in 24:22. The verbs that accompany these inclusive devices are imperatives (24:16, 17, 18), exclamations

(24:19), and future indicatives (24:22). The strong impression is that, just as "the disciples" are being commanded to flee when they see that the abomination of desolation is standing in the holy place, so also is the implied reader being commanded to flee when he or she witnesses the same event.

The author dramatically focuses the implied reader on what Jesus is now saying: "Let the reader understand!" Then, the words of Jesus give both specific commands and information to the implied reader. In sum, the rhetoric of 24:15–22 reveals the specific temporal position of the implied reader in the period between Jesus' resurrection and Parousia. The implied reader stands in the time either immediately before or during the events described in 24:15–22.[129]

MATTHEW 24:23–28

The next subunit, 24:23–28, comprises a parenthetical return to the theme of "beware of false christs and prophets" that was first presented in 24:4–14. Jesus speaks to the disciples,[130] warning them once again[131] that in the context of the troubles that he has predicted they should not be deceived.

The subunit exhibits a striking parallelism. The statements in 24:23–24 and 24:26–27 closely mirror each other. Both 24:23 and 24:26 are present general conditional sentences. Further, direct discourse, introduced by "behold" (ἰδού), occurs in each protasis. In each of the apodoses, prohibitions using μή and the second person plural aorist imperative active occur. Each of the conditional sentences (24:23 and 24:26) is also followed by a proposition (24:24 and 24:27) introduced by "for" (γάρ), which gives the ground or explanation why the imperatives in the apodoses are to be heeded. Thus, 24:23–24 and 24:26–27 are tightly parallel to one another. This tight parallelism also draws attention to the words "Behold, I have spoken beforehand to you" (24:25), situated as they are between the two parallel structures. Further, it is clear that the proverb of 24:28 is the conclusion to the subunit.

When false christs and prophets arise to announce the return of Christ in the troubled days described in 24:15–22,[132] the disciples should not believe their claims. They are to distinguish the trouble of those days from the time of the Parousia itself.[133] Even in the face of miraculous feats of power (σημεῖα μεγάλα καὶ τέρατα, 24:24) by the false christs and false prophets the disciples should know that the Parousia is not being announced. The elect who witness these events[134] will not[135] be deceived because Jesus tells the disciples beforehand (24:25). In contrast to the false christs and prophets who act as if the Parousia were in need of public announcement ("Behold, he is in the desert ... behold, [he is] in the inner rooms," 24:26),[136] the Parousia of Jesus, this man, will carry its own universally effective self-manifestation. It will be as obvious and self-revelatory as the lightning that flashes across the entire sky.[137] The grim proverb[138] with which the subunit concludes underscores this point in a striking[139] way.

When eagles are seen circling, the observer knows they have spotted a corpse below. Jesus' Parousia will be "as evident as birds of prey coming to a carcass."[140]

In this way, 24:23–28 reinforces for "the disciples" the warning given already in 24:5, 11. The presence of messianic pretenders is to be expected.[141] Such persons are not a sign of the Parousia. Rather, the Parousia needs no announcement. The disciples must not be deceived during the Judean tribulation that will accompany the desolation of the temple (24:15) and ultimately result in its destruction (24:2–3). They are not to think that these troubles signal the arrival of this man and the consummation of the age.[142] This much is for "the disciples." Is it also for the implied reader?

It is indeed. As was shown above, Jesus' words in 24:15–22 addressed the implied reader fully along with "the disciples." It is not surprising, then, to observe features in 23:23–28 that show that these words also address the implied reader. Two devices in 24:23–28 address the implied reader. The first is the words of 24:25: "Behold, I have spoken beforehand to you." The second is the proverbial character of 24:28. The latter feature will be discussed first.

Because 24:28 is a proverb, its general "applicability" involves also the implied reader. It is informative and didactic. It is as true in the time of the implied reader as in the time of "the disciples": "Wherever the corpse might be, there the eagles will be gathered." The self-revelatory character of the Parousia is made known to the implied reader. This much is clear.

More significant are Jesus' words in 24:25. The use of "behold" (ἰδού) may have the effect of focusing the attention of the implied reader on these words.[143] It is, however, the very sense of the words "I have spoken beforehand to you" (προείρηκα ὑμῖν) that includes the implied reader. These words of Jesus, spoken within the time of the story, only accomplish their purpose in the time after the temporal boundaries of the story. The perfect indicative active verb (προείρηκα) focuses on the ongoing result of the words having been spoken. They stand as spoken. The function of the words is to warn and guide "in the future," that is, during the troubled days when the abomination of desolation has appeared and the terrible tribulation is taking place in Judea. In other words, the saying has its proper function in the time of the implied reader of the ED.[144] Along with the disciples, the implied reader is reminded that Jesus has warned him or her in advance not to believe the claims of the false christs and prophets. The implied reader, standing in the time either immediately before or during the events described in 24:15–22, will not be deceived into thinking that the time of the Parousia has come. He or she will know that the Parousia will manifest itself, just as when lightning flashes from the east unto the west, in a manner requiring no announcement.

MATTHEW 24:29–31

The next subunit is 24:29–31. Here Jesus describes the events that will immediately (εὐθέως) follow the tribulation that has been described in 24:15–22. The disciples are not addressed directly nor instructed to do anything. Jesus' words are informing them. As will also become evident, Jesus' choice of language interprets the events to which he is referring.

Owing to the way that Jesus' words in 24:15–22 and 24:23–28 have also addressed the implied reader, one concludes that 24:29–31 addresses and informs the implied reader along with the disciples. There are only third person singular and plural verbs in this subunit. Accordingly, the extravagant language of 24:29–31 functions to inform both the disciples and implied reader concerning events of earthshaking and universal significance that will take place immediately after the tribulation of those days.

My interpretation of 24:29–31 will examine each verse in turn. I shall begin with the implied reader's understanding of 24:29. First, I shall indicate the meaning of "immediately after the tribulation of those days." Second, I shall illumine the OT background and use of the theophanic and eschatological language that Jesus echoes in 24:29. I shall present examples to show that the Hebrew prophets at times employed the extravagant language of theophany and eschatology to refer to events within history. Third, I shall argue that the implied reader of Matthew's Gospel will understand 24:29 as figurative language that refers, not to the consummation of the age, but to the complex of events that will culminate in the destruction of Jerusalem and its temple.

THE INTERPRETATION OF MATTHEW 24:29:
"IMMEDIATELY AFTER THE TRIBULATION OF THOSE DAYS"

The implied reader will understand "those days" in 24:29 as a reference to the events described in 24:15–22. This is indicated by presence of the phrase "those days" once in 24:19 (ἐκεῖναι αἱ ἡμέραι) and twice in 24:22 (αἱ ἡμέραι ἐκεῖναι).[145] This is the terrible Judean persecution, the duration of which God will shorten for the sake of the elect in Judea and the likes of which will not be seen again after it has occurred. After the parenthetical warning not to be deceived at the appearances of false christs (24:23–28), Jesus' words in 24:29 return to "those days."

Jesus goes on to say, "And *immediately* [εὐθέως] after the tribulation of those days...." The thirteen occurrences of this adverb in Matthew's Gospel[146] all demand or support the normal sense of "immediately"[147] rather than a more vague translation such as "very soon."[148] The implied reader will expect that the events subsequently described will happen immediately after the graciously shortened tribulation in Judea.

The remainder of 24:29 is a "combination of biblical recollections of features of the Day of the Lord."[149] Jesus' words echo the words of the Hebrew prophets.[150] Jesus speaks like the Hebrew prophets when they at times utilized the theophanic language of "cosmic distress" to describe the coming of God with power.[151] That is to say, the words of Jesus at 24:29 refer to a powerful manifestation of God's power and reign within history, just as similar language in the OT[152] at times refers to such divine self-manifestations within history. In short, the specific reference of 24:29 and indeed the entire subunit 24:29–31 relates to the complex of events that surrounds the destruction of the temple that Jesus has predicted in 24:2. In order to support this understanding of 24:29, I offer the following argument in two parts. First, I shall show that the Hebrew prophets did use the language of "cosmic distress" to refer to events within the course of history. Second, I shall show that this perspective is present in Matthew's Gospel and specifically in the context of 24:29.

THE INTERPRETATION OF MATTHEW 24:29: THE LANGUAGE OF THEOPHANY AND ESCHATOLOGY IN THE HEBREW PROPHETS

The language of "cosmic distress" such as occurs in Matt 24:29 is what Beasley-Murray identifies as one of the two chief characteristics of the OT language of theophany. He writes, with reference to Judg 5:4–5 and Ps 68:7–8: "A comparison of these passages discloses that two ideas are expressed in them: the *coming forth of the Lord*, and the *reactions of nature at his coming*. This twofold structure is basic to the theophany of action; it is expressed in a variety of ways and is assumed in passages in which only one of the pair is mentioned."[153] In the historical context of Israel's faith, the remarkable element in OT theophany texts is the prominent emphasis upon "the concept of a deity going forth to the aid of men," a concept that is largely absent from the descriptions of theophany in the literature of Israel's neighbors.[154]

Closely related to the language of theophany is the OT concept of "the Day of Yahweh."[155] Although the origins of this concept in Israel are untraceable, its relation to theophanic language is observable in the dual conception of God's action on the one hand and the reactions in the realm of nature on the other hand:

> The first time we meet it [the concept of the Day of Yahweh], it does not have the simple form of an early stage in evolution. It is already a complicated construct. A particular complication is the expectation of natural catastrophes and judgments on the Gentiles on the one hand, and of salvation for Israel on the other. The new thing contributed by the writing prophets is the radical transformation of this hope into a message of judgment.[156]

The expressions of theophany in the OT are often retrospective. They describe God's self-manifestation as past events: "LORD, when thou didst go forth from Seir, when thou didst march from the region of Edom, the earth trembled and the heavens dropped, yea, the clouds dropped water" (Judg 5:4 RSV). By contrast, the Day of Yahweh is almost always a future event, a time when Yahweh will act in judgment, salvation, or both: "Woe to you who desire the day of the LORD! Why would you have the day of the LORD? It is darkness, and not light" (Amos 5:18 RSV). Further, prophetic use of the Day of Yahweh at times anticipates a final day of God's decisive intervention in history and in the fortunes of God's people.[157]

Yet God's theophanic self-manifestation and the coming of God's "Day" are also firmly rooted in the events of human history. Often in the OT, the decisive fact in the language of theophany is the fact of God's coming and not literal reactions of nature to that coming. Bealsey-Murray cites Ps 18:6–15 and comments:

> The Psalmist was not seriously claiming that after his prayer a storm took place, followed by an earthquake and volcanic eruption that shook the mountains and raised the sea bed. His intention was to declare that when the Lord came for his deliverance he came with power and glory, and creation was subject to its master.[158]

Beasley-Murray continues:

> The decisive element in the theophany descriptions of the Old Testament, accordingly, is the concept of the coming of God; the descriptions of accompanying phenomena in the natural order are to be viewed as parabolic. The "parables" are not unimportant—they point to the irresistible might of the Lord in his coming, for the resources of the creation are his, and nothing in creation can resist his will—but the supremely important matter is that God *comes* into the world, now in the present and (in the teaching of the prophets) in the future, and in his coming he reveals himself.[159]

It may be debated whether or not "parabolic" is the best way to describe the feature of theophanic language that Beasley-Murray has identified. What is crucial is that theophany and Day of Yahweh texts often use their typically extravagant language to refer to events within the realm of history.[160] That is to say, in these texts the descriptions of distress within the realm of nature or of the larger cosmos figuratively communicate a theological truth without intending a literal referent or fulfillment of the language that describes such upheaval and catastrophe. Perhaps the most common context in which the prophets used such language was in announcing the judgment of God against a particular nation.[161] Israel's faith was that its God was the Lord of history and that he did come in history to rule and judge the nations.[162]

We will examine four representative texts that illustrate this prophetic use of theophanic and eschatological language. First, however, brief attention should be given this question: If it is true that the language of natural and cosmic distress could refer either to God's final and decisive intervention in human affairs or to manifestations of God's sovereignty within the course of nations, how is this to be explained? By what reasoning, in other words, could *a* day of Yahweh's action in history be described in language redolent of theophany and of *the* Day of Yahweh? The words of Beasley-Murray offer a reasonable explanation:

> It is due to the OT view of the day(s) of the Lord as theophanies for judgment and deliverance, when Yahweh steps forth in his power, and nature

goes into confusion and dread before his presence. The theophanies of history, such as the exodus and the victory over Sisera (Judges 5:4–5), become the pattern for the Lord's anticipated action in the future, as may be seen in the classic theophany description of Habakkuk 3. Lesser "days" anticipate the great "day," and the context must make clear when the latter is in view.[163]

Elsewhere the same author also comments:

If it is the case, as is increasingly recognized, that the unique element in Israel's eschatology is its relation to history ... then one can understand that the prophets saw *all* the future as subject to the Lord, and so could speak of impending judgments on contemporary nations in terms of the Day of the Lord in the same way they would speak of the event that will bring history to its climax. This is particularly applicable to Isaiah and Jeremiah in their prophecies, but not alone to them.... Accordingly, Von Rad laid down the following principle: *whenever and wherever great political complications were to be seen on the horizon, especially when hostile armies approached, a prophet could speak of the coming Day of Yahweh.*[164]

I concur with the view expressed by Beasley-Murray. For the faith of Israel, Yahweh was Lord over all of history. He had intervened in the history of his servant, Israel. Because God would intervene finally, other divine interventions could be described with language appropriate also to the decisive event of the Day of Yahweh, however the individual writer might envision that decisive day. Language about *a* day of Yahweh derives its meaning from the promised coming of *the* Day of Yahweh.

The proof of this position is in the OT texts themselves. There are more than a few texts that scholars offer as examples of "parabolic" or "figurative" use of theophanic/eschatological language.[165] We now turn to four texts to illustrate this use of language.

Ps 18:1–19 is a dramatic example of the figurative use of theophanic language. In this psalm, David is in distress and he writes: "In my distress I called upon the LORD; to my God I cried for help. From his temple he heard my voice, and my cry to him reached his ears" (Ps 18:6 RSV). The next nine verses (18:7–15) are linked to 18:6 by a *waw* consecutive. They relate extravagant descriptions of the coming forth of God, including dramatic and disastrous convulsions of the creation:

Then the earth reeled and rocked;
    the foundations also of the mountains trembled
    and quaked, because he was angry.
Smoke went up from his nostrils,
    and devouring fire from his mouth;
    glowing coals flamed forth from him.
He bowed the heavens, and came down;
    thick darkness was under his feet.

He rode on a cherub, and flew;
    he came swiftly upon the wings of the wind.
He made darkness his covering around him,
    his canopy thick clouds dark with water.
Out of the brightness before him
      there broke through his clouds
      hailstones and coals of fire.
The LORD also thundered in the heavens,
    and the Most High uttered his voice,
    hailstones and coals of fire.
And he sent out his arrows, and scattered them;
    he flashed forth lightnings, and routed them.
Then the channels of the sea were seen,
    and the foundations of the world were laid bare,
at thy rebuke, O LORD,
    at the blast of the breath of thy nostrils.
He reached from on high, he took me,
    he drew me out of many waters.
He delivered me from my strong enemy,
    and from those who hated me;
    for they were too mighty for me. (Ps 18:7–17 RSV)

As noted above, the psalmist intends no literal fulfillment of these words. For him they mean that the Lord acted to deliver him.[166]

A second significant example of the figurative use of theophanic or eschatological language occurs at Jer 4:23–28. The context describes the destruction of Jerusalem by "besiegers ... from a distant land" (4:16 RSV), characterized as "horseman and archer" (4:29 RSV). Jer 4:23–28 begins with words that recall the chaos of Gen 1:2: "I looked on the earth, and lo, it was waste and void."[167] It continues by describing scenes of natural disaster and cosmic distress: "For this the earth shall mourn, and the heavens above be black" (Jer 4:28 RSV). Yet the events in view are not, in fact, the decisive intervention of Yahweh that brings destruction to the created order. The prophet speaks of God's judgment upon Judah and adorns the description of that judgment with the most dramatic language available to him.[168]

A third example of such figurative use of language occurs at Ezek 32:7–8. The context for this passage, Ezek 32:1–16, is a lament over Egypt. It describes God's certain judgment of that nation, portraying Egypt mythologically as "a marine monster."[169] After the prophet portrays the fate of the monster, 32:7–8 continues: "When I blot you out, I will cover the heavens, and make their stars dark; I will cover the sun with a cloud, and the moon shall not give its light. All the bright lights of heaven will I make dark over you, and put darkness upon your land, says the Lord GOD" (RSV).

Such expressions "evoke the grim motif of the day of Yahweh."[170] In context, however, the language of Ezek 32:7–8 shows itself as figurative. The prophet describes a day of Yahweh against Egypt in terms appropriate to *the* Day of Yahweh as regards the entire cosmos.[171] Note that the prophetic passages in which theophanic or eschatological language functions figuratively most often speak of God's judgment against a sinful nation, whether one of the Gentile lands as in Ezekiel 32 or Yahweh's own apostate people as in Jeremiah 4.

The fourth OT text is the most important one. As noted above,[172] Jesus' words in Matt 24:29 strongly echo the language of Isa 13:10. Although commentators variously subdivide the units of material in this section of Isaiah, it is agreed that Isaiah 13 in its present form and literary setting is an oracle against the nation of Babylon, whatever the historical setting might be.[173] Isa 13:6–13 uses the language of theophany, cosmic distress, and ruin. As was true of the three previous examples, note the remarkable juxtaposition of historical, "ordinary" language and "Day of Yahweh" language. It is revealing to cite the passage in full.

The oracle concerning Babylon which Isaiah the son of Amoz saw.
On a bare hill raise a signal,
  cry aloud to them;
wave the hand for them to enter
  the gates of the nobles.
I myself have commanded my consecrated ones,
  have summoned my mighty men to execute my anger,
  my proudly exulting ones.
Hark, a tumult on the mountains
  as of a great multitude!
Hark, an uproar of kingdoms,
  of nations gathering together!
The LORD of hosts is mustering
  a host for battle.
They come from a distant land,
  from the end of the heavens,
the LORD and the weapons of his indignation,
  to destroy the whole earth.
Wail, for the day of the LORD is near;
  as destruction from the Almighty it will come!
Therefore all hands will be feeble,
  and every man's heart will melt,
  and they will be dismayed.
Pangs and agony will seize them;
  they will be in anguish like a woman in travail.
They will look aghast at one another;
  their faces will be aflame.

Behold, the day of the LORD comes,
    cruel, with wrath and fierce anger,
to make the earth a desolation
    and to destroy its sinners from it.
For the stars of the heavens and their constellations
    will not give their light;
the sun will be dark at its rising
    and the moon will not shed its light.
I will punish the world for its evil,
    and the wicked for their iniquity;
I will put an end to the pride of the arrogant,
    and lay low the haughtiness of the ruthless.
I will make men more rare than fine gold,
    and mankind than the gold of Ophir.
Therefore I will make the heavens tremble,
    and the earth will be shaken out of its place,
at the wrath of the LORD of hosts
    in the day of his fierce anger.
And like a hunted gazelle,
    or like sheep with none to gather them,
every man will turn to his own people,
    and every man will flee to his own land.
Whoever is found will be thrust through,
    and whoever is caught will fall by the sword.
Their infants will be dashed in pieces
    before their eyes;
their houses will be plundered
    and their wives ravished.
Behold, I am stirring up the Medes against them,
    who have no regard for silver
    and do not delight in gold.
Their bows will slaughter the young men;
    they will have no mercy on the fruit of the womb;
    their eyes will not pity children.
And Babylon, the glory of kingdoms,
    the splendor and pride of the Chaldeans,
will be like Sodom and Gomorrah
    when God overthrew them. (Isa 13:1–19 RSV)

Commentators variously describe the relationship in this oracle between the "earthly, historical language" and the "Day of Yahweh" language. The two are "remarkably intermingled,"[174] "blended,"[175] or "seen as if they are one day, one visitation of God."[176] What is most important for our purposes, however, is the understanding that the historical reference of Isaiah 13, including 13:6–13, is to an event within history, namely, the destruction of Babylon.[177] The language is that which can also apply to the final divine judgment and salvation that also had its place in the prophetic mind. Indeed, it is only in light of the final Day of Yahweh that such extravagant language can refer to historical acts of Yahweh's judgment. But Isa 13:6–13 uses theophanic, eschatological language to refer to an act of divine judgment upon an earthly nation within the course of history.[178]

This examination of the use of the language of "cosmic distress" in OT texts has shown that, at times, those writers used theophanic or eschatological language to refer to events within history, and especially to divine judgments upon nations. The task that remains is to show that such use of language is, in fact, also present at Matt 24:29 and that the implied reader will so understand Jesus' words.

I shall proceed to argue that the implied reader will, indeed, understand Jesus' words at 24:29 as a figurative reference to the predicted destruction of Jerusalem. There are five supports.

First and most obviously, the implied reader will understand Jesus' words in 24:29 as "figurative" language that refers to an event within history because he or she knows that is the way that Isa 13:10 and similar passages function. The implied reader of Matthew's story is able to recognize both scriptural citations and subtle allusions to the OT.[179] The allusions in Matt 24:29 to Isa 13:10 and passages like it are not excessively subtle. Accordingly, the implied reader will know both Isa 13:10 and its context, in which the language of "cosmic distress" describes the overthrow of the Babylonian Empire. The implied reader will thus be able to reason, "If such language is utilized in this manner by Isaiah, then Jesus is using it in a similar manner." [180]

Second, the implied reader will read the eschatological language of Matt 24:29 and apply it to the destruction of Jerusalem because the entire story of Matthew's Gospel has created a world in which the eschatological reign of heaven is already present in the time of the story in a powerful, hidden, and (at times) paradoxical manner. Both the narrator's and Jesus' own words have taught the implied reader that present events, beginning with the origin of Jesus and his birth into the world, are eschatological in nature. The birth of a child in Bethlehem, who narrowly escapes death at the hands of powerful foes, is the coming of the royal eschatological Christ into the world (1:1, 16, 17, 18; 2:1–6). John the Baptist, who was arrested and summarily executed by the powerful forces of evil (14:1–12), was in reality eschatological Elijah, the harbinger of the great and terrible Day of Yahweh (11:14; 17:9–13; cf. Mal 3:1). According to the eschatological point of view of the narrator of this story, the agony, crucifixion, and resurrection of Jesus show that this man is coming with his royal power (16:28) as he sits in his reign (20:20–23) and ushers in the beginning of the resurrection of the dead (27:52–53; 28:1–7). The implied reader has learned to view historical events within the story-world in eschatological terms.

The third point flows from the second, yet is more specific. It may be granted that the extravagance of the language of cosmic distress in 24:29 is unparalleled in the Gospel of Matthew.[181] Yet the implied reader has been taught that eschatological language can refer both to the end of history as well as to events within the course of history. The reign of heaven will come in the future and be entered only then (7:21–22; 25:34); yet the reign of heaven is already present (3:2; 4:17; 10:7; 12:28) and the poor in spirit possess it (5:3). The bridegroom is long-delaying and the feast has not yet begun (25:1–13); yet Jesus the bridegroom is present (9:15) and the wedding feast is ready (22:8). This man, Jesus, will "come" with the angels and judge all people at the consummation of the age (16:27; 25:31); yet the "coming" of this man will also take place when Jesus' eschatological death and its accompanying signs occur, as well as when Jerusalem is destroyed (10:23; 26:64). The implied reader knows, in other words, that eschatological language from Jesus will not always refer to the consummation of the age. Thus, it is the particularities of 24:29 in context that will enable the implied reader to understand Jesus' words aright.

The fourth support for the view that 24:29 refers to the divine judgment upon and overthrow of Jerusalem is precisely that of the near context. I have argued in this chapter that to this point in the ED Jesus' words have functioned as follows:

1. Don't be deceived! Do not juxtapose the destruction of Jerusalem and the Parousia. Tumults do not indicate the nearness of the Parousia, for this Gospel must be preached to all nations (24:4–14).

2. Therefore, flee Jerusalem and Judea when you see the abomination of desolation! Both the disciples and the implied reader must flee the terrible Judean persecution, praying for fortunate circumstances in their flight. Yet God will mercifully shorten those days of persecution for the sake of his elect who are in Judea (24:15–22).

3. Again, don't be deceived! Don't believe those who say in those days that the Christ has come. For Christ's Parousia will need no one to testify to its occurrence (24:23–28).

The ED is focused upon the terrible Judean persecution that will arise when the disciples and the implied reader see that the abomination of desolation is standing in the holy place, the Jerusalem temple. Jesus has portrayed that Judean tribulation in eschatological terms (24:15). On the heels of Jesus' prediction of the temple's destruction (24:2), the disciples asked, "When will these things be?" The implied reader has not aligned himself or herself with the point of view by which the disciples juxtaposed the ruin of the temple and the Parousia. Rather, he or she knows that Jesus' words to this point in the discourse are answering the disciples' first question. The ruin of the temple is in view in the context that has preceded 24:29. When Jesus has mentioned "the end" (24:6, 14) or "the

Parousia" (24:27), he has had the sole purpose of distinguishing it from the events to which he is referring. Thus, when 24:29 begins, "But immediately after the tribulation of those days," the implied reader will know that Jesus' language of cosmic distress is functioning as it does in the prophets' words which Jesus so closely echoes. If such language could describe the realities when Babylon (Isa 13:10) or Egypt (Ezek 32:7–8) fell under God's judgment, how much more could it apply to the tragedy of Jerusalem's ruin.[182] The heavenly powers will be shaken[183] because God's judgment will come down into history upon the city and nation[184] that would not receive Jesus as eschatological Christ and Son of God.[185]

Fifth and finally, the wider narrative context of the ED lends further support to this understanding of Jesus' words in 24:29. Of significance for the implied reader is the theme of "Jesus as prophet of judgment." Recall from the discussion in chapter 4 that in the city that knows him only as "a prophet" (21:11, 46), Jesus speaks and acts as a prophet of judgment. He models judgment against the temple by "cleansing" it (21:12) and evokes Jeremiah's prophecy of the temple's destruction with the expression "den of robbers" (21:13, quoting Jer 7:11). Jesus curses the fig tree, showing that unfruitful Israel will be rejected and punished by God.[186] In his controversies with the religious leaders, Jesus announces that they will not enter the reign of heaven, whereas tax collectors and sinners will (21:31). God's judgment against Jerusalem comes to explicit expression in the parables of the Wicked Tenants (21:33–46) and the Wedding Feast (22:1–14). Jesus' words in Matthew 23 proclaim the harshest of judgments against this city, whose children are the "sons" of those who murdered the prophets (23:29–31). For such as these, the implied reader knows that Jesus speaks indeed as a prophet of judgment.

It is entirely consonant with the larger context of 24:29 to understand Jesus' words as parallel to the prophetic judgments of the OT in language use and effect.[187] Jesus' words in 24:29 have the effect of teaching both the disciples and the implied reader that immediately after the shortened, terrible tumult surrounding the appearance of the abomination of desolation in the Jerusalem temple, the cosmos and its powers will be shaken as divine judgment comes down upon the temple and city.[188]

Jesus' words continue in 24:30–31. My own translation of these verses will serve to introduce the understandings for which I will argue:

> [30]And at that time, that which shows this man who is in heaven will appear, and at that time all the tribes of the land will mourn and they will see that this man is coming on the clouds of heaven with power and great glory. [31]And he with a great trumpet sound will send his messengers and they will gather his elect from the four winds—from the corners of heaven until their corners.

As is evident, a number of important interpretive decisions are reflected in my translation of 24:30–31. I shall now defend them each in turn, beginning with the interpretation of 24:30.

THE INTERPRETATION OF MATTHEW 24:30:
TRANSLATION AND MEANING

Matt 24:30 consists of three independent clauses in Greek: καὶ τότε φανήσε-
ται τὸ σημεῖον τοῦ υἱοῦ τοῦ ἀνθρώπου ἐν οὐρανῷ (24:30a); καὶ τότε κόψονται
πᾶσαι αἱ φυλαὶ τῆς γῆς (24:30b); καὶ ὄψονται τὸν υἱὸν τοῦ ἀνθρώπου ἐρχόμενον
ἐπὶ τῶν νεφελῶν τοῦ οὐρανοῦ μετὰ δυνάμεως καὶ δόξης πολλῆς (24:30c). Before
examining the translation and meaning of each clause in its turn, one small point
calls for clarification. The translation of τότε as "at that time" reflects the coincident sense of this common Matthean connective.[189] The events described in the
subunit 24:30 are of a piece, a complex unity.

Regarding the independent clauses of 24:30, in the first place I have translated the genitive in 24:30a, "the sign of this man," as an objective genitive, "that
which shows this man."[190] It is a sign that reveals this man that will appear. In the
second place, I understand the prepositional phrase "in heaven" (ἐν οὐρανῷ)
adjectivally rather than adverbially. It modifies "this man" rather than the main
verb "will appear." This is, however, not the natural grammatical understanding.
Accordingly, I shall attempt to justify this translation.

It must be admitted that the anarthrous ἐν phrase in 24:30a is more easily
taken as adverbial. Also, the narrator of the Gospel knows full well how to express
unambiguously an arthrous adjectival prepositional phrase with ἐν after an
arthrous noun.[191] Adverbial prepositional phrases with ἐν occur in Matthew's
Gospel in various combinations, including the precise order of sentence parts
that stands in 24:30: verb + arthrous noun + adverbial ἐν phrase.[192] It is also true
that in the NT anarthrous prepositional phrases function adjectivally after both
anarthrous and arthrous nouns. Turner notes a "considerable" number of NT
examples in which the article is omitted from an adjectival prepositional
phrase.[193] In Matthew's Gospel there are several examples. Thus, the order of
verb + arthrous noun + anarthrous adjectival ἐν phrase occurs three times in
sequence at 23:6–7: "And they love the place of honor in the banquets and the
best seats in the synagogues and the greetings in the marketplaces."[194] There are
other examples with slightly different sequences in Matthew's Gospel.[195]

With specific reference to Jesus' arthrous self-designation,[196] "this man"
occurs in a sentence with an adverbial prepositional phrase at five places.[197] At
one other passage, the prepositional phrase may very well be adjectival: "But so
that you may know that this man on the earth has authority to forgive sins...."[198]
The very fact that, in Matthew's Gospel, "this man" (ὁ υἱὸς τοῦ ἀνθρώπου) always
has both of the definite articles prevents any clarifying contrast between prepositional phrases with the arthrous and the anarthrous forms of the expression
"this man." On purely grammatical and stylistic grounds, then, it is possible
(though not the easier rendering) to take "in heaven" in 24:30 adjectivally and to
translate, "then will appear[199] that which shows this man who is in heaven."[200]

According to this translation, then, Jesus' words predict an event, a sign that will show this man, Jesus, in heaven.

If the translation "this man in heaven" is granted as grammatically possible, then one can note two passages in Matthew that offer conceptual parallels to the idea of "this man in heaven." The parallel concept is that of the session of Jesus, this man, at God's right hand.

The first and more important passage is Jesus' answer to the high priest at his trial (26:64).[201] There Jesus promises his enemies, "But I say to you, from now on you will see that this man is sitting at the right hand of power and coming on the clouds of heaven." In chapter 5, I argued that the fulfillment of Jesus' words in 26:64 includes the apocalyptic signs at his death (27:51–54); the testimony of the guards who fled the tomb at Jesus' resurrection (28:11–15); and the predicted destruction of Jerusalem. Although no one in the narrative of the Gospel ever actually sees that Jesus is sitting at God's right hand, his opponents from now on will see these proofs that Jesus is indeed in heaven, at God's right hand.

So it is also at 24:30. The sign that shows "this man in heaven" will appear. That sign will be the destruction of Jerusalem, for in that event the implied reader perceives[202] the truth that God has vindicated Jesus over his enemies, the religious leaders of Israel.

The second conceptual parallel occurs at 22:44. In this final public debate and controversy in Jerusalem with his enemies, Jesus applies the words of Psalm 110 to himself: "The Lord said to my Lord, sit at my right hand until I put your enemies as a footstool under your feet." As noted in chapter 4, when Jesus, the Christ, is exalted by God as Psalm 110 promises, God will act to put under his feet those who refuse to acknowledge him as Son of God. It is "while" Jesus is exalted (κάθου ἐκ δεξιῶν μου, ἕως ἂν θῶ τοὺς ἐχθρούς σου ὑποκάτω τῶν ποδῶν σου, 22:44) that God will put Jesus' enemies, the religious leaders (and "this generation" [24:34] of Israel whom they represent) under his feet. In light of the judgment on Jerusalem disclosed in the parables of the Wicked Tenants (21:41) and the Wedding Feast (22:7), the implied reader knows that the words of Psalm 110 in Matt 22:44 refer to the predicted destruction of Jerusalem. At 22:44, the judgment on Jesus' enemies will happen while he is seated at God's right hand.

As was true of the parallel at 26:64, Jesus' words in 24:30a express the same truth as 22:44. The complex of events around the destruction of the temple and Jerusalem will be the sign of this man in heaven. It will show that Jesus is exalted on high.

I turn now to the understanding of 24:30b. Jesus predicts "and at that time all the tribes of the land will mourn" (καὶ τότε κόψονται πᾶσαι αἱ φυλαὶ τῆς γῆς). Jesus' words are an allusion to Zech 12:10–14. The prophet's words record Yahweh's promise to pour out on the inhabitants of Jerusalem "a spirit of compassion and supplication, so that, when they look on him whom they have pierced, they shall mourn for him, as one mourns for an only child." As Carson rightly notes, every attempt to determine the extent to which Matt 24:30b continues the contextual meaning of Zech 12:10–14 involves changing at least a part of the meaning in Zechariah's prophecy.[203] The task is to determine, on the basis of evidence within the story of Matthew, how the implied reader will understand these words of Jesus. Who is mourning, and what sort of mourning is it?

The only other occurrence of "the tribes" (αἱ φυλαί) in Matthew is at 19:28, where it refers to the people of Israel.[204] Also, the noun γῆ in Matthew's Gospel has various referents, including the meaning "land."[205] Accordingly, the translation "tribes of the land" is, purely on lexical and stylistic grounds, a valid option.

In addition, the context supports the translation "tribes of the land." In 24:15–22, the local tribulation in Judea is in view. After the parenthetical warning against those who will claim that such tumult shows that the Parousia is near (24:23–28), Jesus' words in 24:29 continue, "Immediately after the tribulation of those days." In light of the proper understanding of 24:29, the implied reader knows that 24:29–30b asserts that, immediately after the days of Judean tumult and persecution, God will manifest himself in theophany (24:29), and the appearing of "that which shows this man in heaven" (24:30a) will cause "all the tribes of the land" to mourn.[206]

Moreover, owing to the strong theme of judgment in the immediate context, I concur with the view that the "mourning" of 24:30b is not, as in Zechariah 12, the "mourning" of repentance.[207] Rather, Jesus' words tell of the tribes of the land mourning in response to the destructive judgment that God will pour out upon the city of Jerusalem and its temple. The judgment will show "this man in heaven," that is, that Jesus is the vindicated Son of God who sits at God's right hand until God puts his enemies under his feet (Matt 26:64; 22:44).

The third proposition, 24:30c, alludes strongly to Dan 7:13. Recall the interpretation in chapter 5 of Jesus' answer to the high priest (26:64). In 26:64 Jesus says, "From now on you will see that this man is sitting at the right hand of power and coming on the clouds of heaven" (ἐρχόμενον ἐπὶ τῶν νεφελῶν τοῦ οὐρανοῦ). Here in 24:30 Jesus says, "and they will see that this man is coming upon the clouds of heaven with power and great glory" (ἐρχόμενον ἐπὶ τῶν νεφελῶν τοῦ οὐρανοῦ μετὰ δυνάμεως καὶ δόξης πολλῆς). The strong presumption on the part of the implied reader is that Jesus is speaking of the same perception, the same "seeing" in each verse.

Four features support this presumption. First, in each case it is those who oppose Jesus who will see, the religious leaders on the one hand and the tribes of the land who mourn in the face of judgment on the other. Second, only in these two places in Matthew's Gospel does Jesus allude to Dan 7:13 with the explicit mention of the "cloud rider" motif. Third, the explicit motif of "power" at "the coming of this man" is present only in these two texts in Matthew's Gospel. Fourth, note that in both 26:64 and 24:30c, the allusion to Dan 7:13 is linked to the concept of Jesus, this man, seated at the right hand of God. In 26:64, it is expressed in a way that parallels the allusion to Dan 7:13: "From now on you will

see that 1) this man is sitting at the right hand of power and 2) coming on the
clouds of heaven." Here in 24:30, Jesus' words speak first of "that which will show
this man in heaven," before going on to promise that "they will see that this man
is coming on the clouds of heaven with power and great glory." These four features show that the implied reader will know that the meaning of 24:30c is parallel to the meaning of 26:64.

At this juncture, it will be helpful to review. As I attempted to show in the
discussion of 26:64 in chapter 5, the implied reader takes seriously Jesus' words
"from now on" (ἀπ᾽ ἄρτι). Accordingly, the implied reader knows of three ways
that Jesus' words to the religious leaders in 26:64 will be fulfilled: (1) through the
eschatological signs that accompany Jesus' death and resurrection (27:51–54); (2)
through the testimony to Jesus' resurrection that the tomb guard gives to the religious leaders (28:11–15); and (3) through the predicted destruction of Jerusalem
that lies beyond the temporal boundaries of the story (10:23; 21:41; 22:7; 23:34–
36). The implied reader understands that these events are the things that reveal
that Jesus is seated at the right hand of power. Moreover, the figure like "a son of
man" in Dan 7:13–14 comes to the Ancient of Days and receives power and
authority so as to save the saints of the Most High and judge the enemies of God.
In like manner, the three "from now on" fulfillments of Matt 26:64 show that
Jesus has received authority from God (28:18) and that his enemies are being put
under his feet (22:41–44). In sum, the implied reader knows of three fulfillments
of Jesus' words in 26:64. Two of them take place within the story's narration. One
of them, the destruction of the temple and of the city, takes place in the time
beyond the conclusion of the Gospel.

Jesus' words of 24:30c, however, refer entirely to events that will take place
beyond the temporal boundaries of the story. Accordingly, the implied reader will
know that Jesus' words in 24:30c refer to the destruction of Jerusalem that lies in
the same time period in which will occur all that Jesus has predicted thus far in
the ED. Just as the two participial clauses in 26:64 ("sitting at the right hand" and
"coming on the clouds of heaven") are parallel in meaning, 24:30a ("then will
appear that which shows this man in heaven") and 24:30c ("they will see that this
man is coming on the clouds of heaven") are also parallel. As was the case with the
language of cosmic distress in 24:29, Jesus' eschatological language in 24:30 is
referring to events that will occur within history. Indeed, as our examination of the
following subunit (24:32–35) will demonstrate, the events of 24:30 will occur within the lifetime of Jesus' opponents who are so consistently referred to in Matthew's
Gospel as "this generation" (24:34; cf. 11:16; 12:39, 41, 42, 45; 16:4; 23:36).

THE INTERPRETATION OF MATTHEW 24:31:
TRANSLATION AND MEANING

Jesus' words in 24:31 complete this subunit. The implied reader will understand 24:31 as follows. Following the eschatological judgment upon Jerusalem,

which is also the earthly manifestation of "this man in heaven," Jesus[208] will send out his messengers to carry out the eschatological[209] mission task of gathering the elect from the farthest reaches of the world. In order to support this understanding, I offer the following arguments.

The sequence of "judgment on Jerusalem followed by mission to the Gentiles" is precisely that which occurs in the parables of the Wicked Tenants and the Wedding Feast. After the vineyard has been taken away, it is given to other tenant-farmers who will pay to the master the fruits of the vineyard (21:41). After the wrathful king has sent his soldiers to destroy the ungrateful guests who refused the invitation to the wedding feast for his son and to burn their city, then the king sends his slaves into the street crossings to call others to the feast (22:7–9). The judgment upon Israel as a nation through the destruction of the temple and the city of Jerusalem is followed by the mission to the Gentiles in its fullest expression.[210]

In addition, the activity of the "messengers" (οἱ ἄγγελοι) in 24:31 shows that they are to be understood as human messengers and not as angels.[211] These ἄγγελοι are sent and "they will gather his elect [ἐπισυνάξουσιν τοὺς ἐκλεκτοὺς αὐτοῦ] from the four winds—from the corners of heaven until their corners." The scope of the activity is the widest possible, extending throughout the entire world.[212] The activity itself is "gathering." In support of the view that this "gathering" is the mission activity during the period between Jesus' resurrection and Parousia and not the angelic activity at the Parousia itself, one can note the following.

First, the verb ἐπισυνάγω occurs only three times in Matthew, here at 24:31 and also at 23:37. At 23:37, Jesus twice uses it to refer to his longing to gather Jerusalem's inhabitants to himself as disciples: "How often I longed to gather your children in the manner that a hen gathers her chicks under her wings and you were not willing." There the verb refers to Jesus' desire to gather the lost sheep of the house of Israel (10:6; 15:24). The use of "gather" in 24:31, if understood as referring to the mission to the Gentiles, thus provides a contrast with 23:37 that fits well into Matthew's schema of the turning of the mission to the Gentiles. Jerusalem's children were not willing to be gathered either by Jesus or by the missionaries he will send to them (23:34). His messengers accordingly will turn to gather the elect from among all the nations.

Second, in Matthew's Gospel divine or angelic activity on the judgment day with regard to human beings always includes the concept of "separating," even when a "gathering" on the last day also occurs. Thus, the Baptist says that the Coming One will cleanse his threshing floor, that is, separate out wheat and chaff. Then "he will gather his wheat into the barn, but the chaff he will burn with unquenchable fire" (3:12). Jesus himself consistently portrays the last day as the day when those who are saved and those who are not will be separated (7:21–23; 11:21–24; 12:41–42; 13:48–50; 24:40; 25:1–13; 25:14–30; 25:31–46).

Furthermore, in Matthew's Gospel Jesus always describes the activity of angels on the last day as either a "separating" or as a "gathering and separating" but never only as "gathering." Thus, in the explanation to the parable of the Wheat and the Tares, Jesus says that the angels will "separate out [συλλέξουσιν] of his reign all stumbling blocks and those who do lawlessness" (13:41). In the explanation of the parable of the Dragnet, Jesus says that "the angels will come and separate [ἀφοριοῦσιν] the evil from the midst of the righteous" (13:49). In 25:31–32, when this man comes with all his angels "all the nations will be gathered before him, and he will separate [ἀφορίσει] them from one another." It is evident that the essential image in speaking of the last day is that of "separation," not "gathering."[213]

By contrast, in Matthew's Gospel the motif of "gathering" refers to the period of mission that precedes the last day. The verb συνάγω in the parable of the Dragnet describes the time period during which both evil and righteous are collected into the net before the net is dragged up onto shore: "Again, the reign of heaven is like a dragnet cast into the sea, and they gather [συναγαγούσῃ] from every kind [of fish]. When it became full [ἐπληρώθη], they dragged it onto the shore and sat down and separated" (13:47–48a). The sequence is time of mission (gather until it is full) followed by separation and the judgment ("they ... sat down and separated").

The same scheme occurs in the parable of the Wedding Feast. There Jesus describes the mission to the Gentiles this way: "And those slaves went out into the roads, and they gathered [συνήγαγον] all whom they found, both evil and good, and the wedding was filled [ἐπλήσθη] with those who were reclining" (22:10). Once again, the sequence is time of mission (gather until it is full) followed by separation and the judgment (22:10–14). These two parables, then, describe the period of the mission to the Gentiles as the time of "gathering."

In addition to the concept of "mission to the Gentiles as the time of gathering," the parable of the Wedding Feast contains the further specification that some who are gathered are the "elect." The parable concludes with the only use of the term "elect" outside the ED itself: "For many are called, but few are elect" (22:14). Note that the elect are already gathered into the wedding feast before the final judgment, that is, before the casting out of the man without a wedding robe. The other occurrences of the "elect" are at 24:22, 24. There it is the elect in Judea who are in view, owing to the local Judean character of the "tribulation of those days" (24:29). By contrast with the situation in Judea, immediately after that tribulation (24:29), God's judgment will come upon the city of Jerusalem and all the tribes of the land will mourn over that judgment (24:29–30). Then Jesus will send out his messengers[214] to gather his elect from the farthest corners of the world (24:31).[215]

I now summarize the implied reader's understanding of 24:29–31. Immediately after the terrible Judean tribulation described in 24:15–22, the judgment against Jerusalem will show itself as a theophanic, eschatological event (24:29). As Jesus predicts, Jerusalem will be destroyed. This will show that Jesus, this man, is in heaven at the right hand of God and that he is the exalted figure of Dan 7:13–14. He will not only come as judge on the last day, but he also will visit divine judgment upon Jerusalem in history. All the tribes of the land will mourn at this judgment. Jesus will send out his messengers to the farthest reaches of the earth, and they will gather together his elect ones.[216]

MATTHEW 24:32–35

The subunit 24:32–35 concludes the first half of the ED. Jesus' words address both the disciples in the story and the implied reader. The address to the disciples in the narrative is evident from the four second person plural verbs ("learn"; "you know"; "you see"; "you know") and the two second person plural pronouns (note the emphatic "so also, *you*," 24:33). The use of a proverbial comparison from nature shows that the implied reader is addressed. Moreover, the fact that ever since 24:15 Jesus' words have addressed the implied reader along with the disciples in the story indicates that 24:32–35 speaks also to him or her. Thus, 24:32–35 is information that also applies to the situation of the implied reader.

The subunit begins with a comparison from the natural patterns of fig trees (24:32–33). Tender branches and sprouting leaves are signs that show the nearness of summer. The comparison to be drawn is clear. When the implied reader sees "all these things," he or she will know that "it" is near, at the door (24:33). Interpretive questions surround the understanding of "it"[217] and "all these things." Before examining them, however, I underscore the fact that the point of the comparison in 24:32–33 is that warning signs enable one to know in advance when an event is about to happen. As obvious as this may seem, it needs to be stated. This subunit continues the theme of "warnings signs" that has characterized the entire first half of the ED.[218]

Just as tender branches and sprouting leaves show that summer[219] is near, so will the sight of "all these things" (πάντα ταῦτα) show that "it" is near. The implied reader logically will note that Jesus' words differentiate between "all these things" and the event ("it") that they anticipate. Accordingly, George Ladd correctly notes in 24:33 a distinction between anticipatory signs and the event that those signs anticipate.[220] Jesus' words in 24:33, then, make a distinction between the terrible tribulation in Judea (24:15–22)[221] and the theophanic and eschatological destruction of Jerusalem as described in 24:29–31. Both the disciples and the implied reader are instructed to "discern the times," and to know when "it" is near.

As is obvious from the above discussion, I regard the "it" of 24:33 as the destruction of Jerusalem and the subsequent fullness of the Gentile mission. The implied reader is to discern the nearness of this crucial event in the outworking of the eschatological ministry of Jesus, the Christ and the Son of God.

Then, in 24:34 Jesus unmistakably answers the disciples' first question about the predicted destruction of Jerusalem, "When will these things be?" (24:3). The temporal question receives a direct reply: "Truly I say to you that this generation will certainly not pass away until all these things take place."[222] Two questions require answers at 24:34. First, what is the meaning of the phrase "this generation" (ἡ γενεὰ αὕτη)? Second, what is the specific referent of the phrase "all these things" (πάντα ταῦτα)?

Matthew's Gospel answers the first question unequivocally. In 24:34 the phrase "this generation" carries the meaning that it almost always[223] carries in Matthew's Gospel, namely, the generation of Jesus' contemporaries who have opposed and hated him.[224] Thus, Jesus is here stating plainly that "all these things" will take place during the lifetime of his opponents and therefore of the disciples who are hearing the ED from within the story of the Gospel. We may proceed, then, to the next question, namely, the referent in 24:34 of "all these things."

As noted above, Jesus' words in 24:33 distinguish between the tumultuous events of the tribulation in Judea ("all these things" = 24:15–22) and the eschatological judgment upon Jerusalem ("it" = 24:29–31), the nearness of which is shown by the events in Judea. Does "all these things" in 24:34 have precisely the same referent as the identical phrase in 24:33? Or does "all these things" in 24:34 include the theophanic and eschatological destruction of the temple and the city?

Many commentators believe that the referent of "all these things" in 24:34 is the same as that in 24:33.[225] Others, however, see a shift in the meaning of "all these things" in 24:33 and 24:34 so that the phrase in the latter verse refers to everything of which Jesus has spoken, including the complex of events in 24:29–31.[226] This latter position commends itself on two counts.

First, the implied reader already knows that the events of 24:29–31 will take place "immediately" (24:29) after the terrible tribulation described in 24:15–22. Thus, when in 24:33 Jesus says, "You know that it [24:29–31] is near [to 24:15–22]," he means "immediately."[227] Now, it is certain that Jesus' words in 24:34 aver that the terrible distress of 24:15–22 will take place before his contemporaries pass away. It is not possible, therefore, to think that Jesus is excluding from the lifetime of his contemporaries the events of 24:29–31 that will happen "immediately" after the events of 24:15–22. Purely on the grounds of "immediately" (24:29) and "near" (24:33), it is likely that "all these things" in 24:34 include the events of 24:29–31.

A second support comes from the close parallelism between Jesus' words in 24:34 and his words in 23:36. At 23:36, Jesus tells what will happen after he sends missionaries to Israel in the time beyond the end of the Gospel's story. Israel will persecute those emissaries so that all of history's righteous blood might come upon the opponents of Jesus (23:34–35). They are the "sons" of those who murdered the prophets (23:31). They will kill Jesus and mistreat his emissaries. In 23:36 Jesus says, "Truly I say to you, all these things will come upon this generation." As 23:37–39 shows, "all these things" in 23:36 refers to the judgment and destruction of Jerusalem and its temple.

Note the close parallelism between 23:36 and 24:34:

Matthew 23:36	Matthew 24:34
ἀμὴν λέγω ὑμῖν	ἀμὴν λέγω ὑμῖν
ἐπὶ τὴν γενεὰν ταύτην	ἡ γενεὰ αὕτη
ταῦτα πάντα	πάντα ταῦτα
ἥξει	ἕως ἂν ... γένηται

Given the striking parallelism between 23:36 and 24:34, it is likely that "all these things" in each verse refers to the same thing. This parallel, joined to the strong sense of nearness provided by "immediately" (24:29) and "near" (24:33), shows that "all these things" in 24:34 includes the destruction of Jerusalem and the fullness of the mission to the Gentiles (24:29–31). Accordingly, Jesus' words in 24:34 solemnly promise that the Judean distress (24:15–22) and the theophanic, eschatological judgment on Jerusalem and the ensuing fullness of the mission to the Gentiles (24:29–31) will take place within the lifetime of "this generation." With these words, then, Jesus gives the unequivocal answer to the disciples' first question of 24:3, "When will these things be?"

Not one stone of the temple buildings will be left upon another. It will happen before the generation of Jesus' contemporaries passes away. In addition, owing to the way that Jesus' words have addressed the implied reader along with the figure of the disciples beginning with 24:15, the implied reader learns that the temple will be destroyed within his or her own lifetime as well.

Jesus affirms the enduring validity of all that he has said (24:35).[228] His words are more sure than the heaven and the earth. These words complete the first major section of the ED and the answer to the disciples' first question. Along with the disciples, the implied reader has been instructed not to think that the troubles and tumults of human history are signs that the end is near, for the Gospel must first be heralded to all the nations (24:4–14). Accordingly, when the uniquely terrible persecutions in Judea are inaugurated through the appearance of the abomination of desolation, the implied reader and other disciples in Judea are without hesitation to flee for their lives (24:15–22). During the tribulation of those days, those who claim to announce the Parousia should not be believed, for the Parousia will attest its own presence (24:23–28).

Immediately after that tribulation, the cosmos will tremble (24:29) as God's judgment on Jerusalem, at which the tribes of the land will mourn (24:30b), enters history and shows this man's reign in heaven (24:30a) as the one who has received authority from the Ancient of Days (24:30c). Then Jesus will send his messengers to gather his elect ones from the farthest reaches of the earth (24:31). The implied reader and the disciples are to read the signs, just as one reads the signs of approaching summer (24:32). They will know when the judgment on

Jerusalem is near (24:33). It will all happen before the generation of those who opposed Jesus passes away (24:34). There is no doubt in the mind of the implied reader, for Jesus' words are more certain than the cosmos itself (24:35).

MATTHEW 24:36: THE HINGE VERSE OF THE ESCHATOLOGICAL DISCOURSE

The second major section of the ED begins with the hinge verse, 24:36. Earlier in this chapter I demonstrated the rhetorical effect of "but concerning" (περὶ δέ). Jesus' words "But concerning that day and hour" reach back to the disciples' second question in the narrative introduction to the ED (24:3). In the first major section of the ED, Jesus has answered the first question of the disciples regarding the timing of the destruction of Jerusalem. Now Jesus focuses on the second question in 24:3, "What will be that which shows[229] your Parousia and the consummation of the age?" As the full discussion of the second major section of the ED shall show, Jesus' answer to their second question is this: "There will be no sign that shows my Parousia and the consummation of the age. Your only response until that day is to watch and to be faithful."

Jesus asserts, in 24:36, that no one except the Father knows "that day and hour."[230] In Matthew's Gospel, the singular "day" regularly refers to the last day.[231] The combination "day and hour" in 24:36 also acts as the front end of an inclusio for that part of the ED's second major section that presents the theme of the Parousia's "unknowability." The other end of the inclusio occurs at 25:13: "Watch, therefore, because you do not know the day or the hour." The dominant theme in the four subunits within the inclusio (24:37–42; 24:43–44; 24:45–51; 25:1–13) is the sudden and unknowable time of the Parousia. Accordingly, the dominant exhortation in this portion of the ED is the call to "Watch!" (24:42; cf. 24:44; 25:13).

Many commentators assert that the combination "day and hour" in 24:36 means "the exact day" or "the exact time" of the Parousia.[232] This assertion[233] is attractive because it eases the tension that many detect between 24:29, 33, 34 on the one hand and 24:36 on the other hand.[234] The sequence of 1) "immediately after the tribulation of those days" (24:29), 2) "so also you, when you see all these things, you know that it is near" (24:33), and 3) "this generation will not pass away until all these things happen" (24:34) combines to show the nearness of the events described in 24:4–31. Moreover, 24:33 reveals that "advance warnings" will enable the disciples and the implied reader to know the approaching time of the fulfillment of Jesus' predictions. Jesus' words establish a terminus ad quem for the events in 24:4–31, to wit, the lifetime of "this generation" (24:34).

In marked contrast, Jesus' words of 24:36 assert the unknowability of the time of "that day and hour." Commentators seek refuge in the view that 24:36 only asserts the unknowability of the precise time of "that day and hour." It is commonly stated that Jesus' words in 24:36 act somehow[235] to diminish, soften, or "detemporalize" Jesus' words in 24:29, 33, 34.[236] These terms are, of course, only euphemistic ways of saying that Jesus' words in 24:36 contradict his words in 24:33–34.

The contradiction disappears with the interpretation of the first major section of the ED for which I have argued above. Jesus' words in 24:29–31 do not predict "that day and hour" of the Parousia and the consummation of the age at all. Rather, Jesus speaks for the first time[237] about "that day and hour" of the Parousia at 24:36. In contrast to the events of 24:29–31 that will occur within the lifetime of "this generation" (24:34) and with anticipatory warning signs (24:32–33), no one except the Father knows the time of the Parousia and the consummation of the age.[238]

No one knows—not the angels nor the Son nor the disciples nor the implied reader. Jesus' words in the second major section of the ED exhort the disciples to the proper attitudes and behaviors with respect to the unknowable Parousia. The implied reader receives the words of Jesus for himself or herself as well. The consistent use of proverbial and parabolic speech in the second major section of the ED shows that the implied reader is addressed. From this point in the ED onward, the implied reader is side by side with the disciples, receiving the teaching and responding to the exhortation of Jesus.

MATTHEW 24:37–42

The subunit 24:37–42 gives the reason or explanation[239] as to why no one will know the time of the Parousia. In this one respect that day will be like the day when the Noachic flood came upon the unsuspecting world.[240] The point of comparison is not the wickedness of the generation of the flood.[241] Rather, the comparison is with the unexpected arrival of the flood, unheralded by any advance signs or warnings. Jesus' words in 24:38–39 show that in the[242] days before the flood, people of that generation went about their business as usual,[243] ignorant of the coming catastrophe because there were no warning signs that would show the nearness of the flood.[244] Thus also it will be with the Parousia of this man (24:39). At that time there will be a sudden division of humanity, even to the point of separating persons who are working side by side (24:40–41).[245]

Jesus' next words (24:42) draw the hortatory inference from this information as well as provide its ground: "Therefore, watch, because you do not know the day when your Lord is coming." This lesson recurs twice in the discourse that follows.[246] The lesson is valid for the disciples and for the implied reader, for no one throughout the entire time period from Jesus' resurrection to his Parousia will know the timing of the consummation of the age. The first subunit in the second major section of the ED concludes with 24:42.[247]

MATTHEW 24:43–44

The next subunit, 24:43–44, continues the theme of the sudden and unexpected time of the Parousia. In addition, Jesus' words also add a striking dimension to the teaching. The contrary to fact conditional sentence (24:43) implies a brief narrative. A householder went to sleep without knowing that a thief was going to break in. Since he didn't know the time when the thief was breaking in, the householder's home was ransacked and the householder suffered loss. Jesus again emphasizes the unexpected time of the Parousia in 24:44: "On account of this also you be ready, because this man is coming at a time when you do not expect." The dominant theme and exhortation in this part of the ED is "be ready!"

An additional, shocking dimension of this subunit consists in the comparison between the Parousia of Jesus, this man, and the act of a thief at night[248] breaking into a householder's[249] dwelling. Jesus likens himself at his Parousia to a thief. If the disciples or the implied reader are not "ready" when their Lord comes, then Jesus' coming will be destructive for them. His Parousia will be no more welcome than an act of violent burglary. By means of this shocking analogy,[250] Jesus' words highlight the importance of being "ready." What it means to be "ready" will be revealed in the subunits that follow, especially in the comparison of the slave-supervisor (24:45–51) and the parable of the Talents (25:14–30).

MATTHEW 24:45–51

The story-like comparison of the slave-supervisor[251] continues the address to the implied reader along with the disciples. The subunit's opening rhetorical question draws the implied reader in and invites him or her to participate[252] in the implied narratives:[253] "Who, then, is the faithful and wise slave...?" On the one hand, the faithful and wise disciple will, in the time between Jesus' resurrection and Parousia, act like the first slave. Such a disciple will show readiness through the loving relationships[254] with his or her fellows.[255] "Readiness" for the Parousia does not mean "knowing the time," for no one will know. Rather, "readiness" means "wise and faithful service to others."[256] The disciple, including the implied reader, who is thus found when the master comes will receive the eschatological blessing of the Lord.[257]

The forcefulness of the rhetorical question in 24:45 reveals that the implied reader will respond to Jesus' words in 24:45–51 and act as the faithful and wise slave. He or she will react thus: "Who is the faithful and wise slave? I am one such slave." The subunit also describes the terrible fate of any slave who does not thus respond in loving care for his or her fellow slaves. In this regard, the subunit continues the theme of "division of persons" at the Parousia of Jesus. It is necessary to note that this warning is directed at the disciples and the implied reader. Thus, believers in Jesus, the Son of God, will take this warning to heart. The "division" will apply to those who are among the visible fellowship of Jesus' disciples.

The description of the behavior and the fate of the wicked slave (24:48–51) gives expression to the theme of the delay of the Parousia. On the one hand, the behavior of the faithful and wise slave reveals the character of true "readiness," namely, faithful service to one's fellows. On the other hand, the behavior of the wicked slave reveals the error of those who do not reckon with the unknowable time of the Parousia. The wicked slave is correct in saying, "My master is delaying." The implied reader knows that there will be a delay in the Parousia of Jesus.[258] The wicked slave abuses the period of delay, however, and mistreats the fellows who were entrusted to his care.

Yet the master does not delay forever. He returns suddenly at a day and time the slave does not expect. Such an unfaithful and wicked slave receives the terrible punishment[259] allotted to the hypocrites.[260] So it will be for any who do not recognize the character of the time during which the Parousia delays, and live accordingly.

Matt 24:45–51 teaches the implied reader what it means to "watch" (24:42) and to "be ready" (24:44). It consists in caring for one's fellow disciples. The opening rhetorical question in 24:45 invites the implied reader to live as a faithful and wise disciple of Jesus during the delay between the resurrection of Jesus and the consummation of the age. Finally, the fate of the one who reckoned wrongly with the period of the delay warns the implied reader not to err in this way and to suffer a similar fate on the last day.

MATTHEW 25:1–13

The next subunit is the parable of the Ten Maidens. Jesus' words continue to address both the disciples and the implied reader. After the introductory formula (25:1a), the parable describes the two groups of maidens and their actions in going out to meet the bridegroom (25:1b–5). Here the distinction between "wise" and "foolish" is explained on the basis (γάρ, 25:3) of the extra oil that only five brought with them. Owing to the delay of the bridegroom,[261] all the maidens became drowsy and began to sleep.[262]

The drama of the parable takes its decisive turn at 25:6 with the cry at the arrival of the bridegroom.[263] This event precipitates the following developments in the parable and reveals the importance of possessing enough oil to keep the lamps burning. Because the time to light the path of the bridegroom has come, the five foolish maidens have no choice but to try to procure additional oil for themselves (25:8–9). While they are gone the bridegroom comes and enters the feast with the wise maidens, who are now for the first time designated as "ready" (25:10). When the foolish maidens return, they find themselves excluded from the feast and unacknowledged by the bridegroom (25:11–12). The parable's concluding application is 25:13: "Therefore watch, because you know neither the day nor the hour."

Scholarly discussions of the parable of the Ten Maidens have often focused on the extent to which the details of the parable correspond to the customs surrounding a first-century Palestinian wedding feast.[264] For my purposes, this discussion is irrelevant because it relates to the question of the extent to which the parables in Matthew reflect actual parables told by the historical Jesus.[265]

A pertinent feature of the scholarly discussion is the question of the central thrust or message of the parable. Scholars have offered a number of suggestions.[266] Rather than seeking one central point, however, it is more helpful to note the several themes that the parable of the Ten Maidens has in common with its context in the ED.[267] For one thing, this parable continues the theme of the unexpected and unknowable time of the Parousia (25:6, 13). The sudden cry that announces the arrival of the bridegroom is the dramatic turning point of the parable. In addition, the theme of "readiness" as "wisdom," present in the description of the slave-supervisor (24:45–51), also occurs. The five maidens who are repeatedly termed "wise" (φρόνιμοι, 25:2, 4, 8, 9) are also labeled "ready" (ἕτοιμοι, 25:10) when they enter into the wedding feast. Finally, the motif of the Parousia's delay is present through the only other occurrence of the verb "to delay" in Matthew's Gospel: "And because the bridegroom kept delaying" (χρονίζοντος δὲ τοῦ νυμφίου, 25:5; cf. 24:48).

Accordingly, the parable repeats prominent themes of the ED while also possessing its own unique features. The implied reader knows that this parable that begins "Then[268] the reign of heaven will be likened to ten maidens" pertains to the future consummation of the reign of heaven.[269] The Christ who already in the present time of the story brings the reality of the wedding feast (9:15; 22:1–14) will also come as bridegroom on the last day and bring the fullness of the feast. Yet there will be a delay of the Parousia. In light of that delay, the implied reader must be prepared for "the long haul."[270]

The theme of "division among those who claim to be Jesus' disciples" that was present in 24:45–51 is also present here. The five maidens who are ready when the bridegroom returns are termed "wise" because, unlike the foolish maidens, they brought oil in vessels along with their lamps (25:3–4).[271] Unlike the preceding subunit, 24:45–51, there is no explicit theme of "faithfulness" in the parable of the Ten Maidens, and it is not possible to assign a specific interpretation to the symbol of "oil."[272] The primary impact of this parable on the implied reader is the exhortation to remain ready in the face of an extended delay of the Parousia. Such readiness is an individual matter, for no one can be ready for another. The Parousia will be sudden. In the middle of the night the cry happens, and those who are ready go out to meet the bridegroom.[273] Those wise ones who are ready will enter the consummated eschatological wedding banquet. Those foolish ones who are not ready will be shut out, despite their protestations of a relationship with the bridegroom.[274]

The closing imperative in 25:13 seems, at first glance, ill-suited to the parable's message: "Watch, therefore, because you do not know the day nor the hour." Part of the parable's story is the fact that none of the maidens "watched," but rather all fell asleep during the long wait for the bridegroom.[275] The solution to this apparent problem is found earlier in the ED where it is clear that "watch" (γρηγορέω, 24:42) is equivalent to "be ready" (γίνομαι ἕτοιμος, 24:44).[276] Armed with this understanding, the implied reader receives the exhortation to avoid the fate of those who will be excluded on the last day and to be ready for the Parousia.

The closing imperative in 25:13 also connects with 24:36 as the second half of the inclusio marked by the combination of "day" and "hour."[277] Matt 24:36–25:13 is that portion of the second major section of the ED that emphasizes the Parousia's sudden and unknowable timing. This motif has been a dominant one throughout this portion of the discourse. With the completion of the inclusion at 25:13, this theme of "suddenness" drops out of the ED.[278]

MATTHEW 25:14–30

The parable of the Talents is joined to the material that precedes it by "for" (γάρ, 25:14). The parable offers itself as a comparison to the day and hour of the Parousia.[279] The parable exhibits striking features of parallelism and contrast that focus and underscore its message.

The parable's structure may be described as follows. The first scene (25:14–15) relates the master's act of entrusting large sums[280] of his apparently vast wealth to three of his slaves.[281] The first scene is bracketed by the repetition of the verb "to go on a journey" in 25:14 ("a man who was going on a journey") and 25:15 ("and he went away on a journey").

The second scene (25:16–18) describes the actions of the three slaves. The first two slaves act in strikingly parallel fashion.[282] The behavior of the third slave is a stark contrast.[283]

The transition to the lengthy final scene is provided by 25:19: "And after a long time the master of those slaves comes and settles account with them."[284] The threefold final scene (25:20–30) shows the master settling accounts with each of the slaves. The master's interaction with the first two slaves exhibits a remarkable parallelism[285] that creates a dramatic contrast with the master's interaction with the third slave.[286] On the one hand, the faithfulness of the first two slaves is highlighted by the profit they gained and by the commendation and invitation of their master. On the other hand, both the third slave's own words[287] and the master's condemnation[288] reveal the slave's wickedness. The extraordinary punishment meted out to the third slave (25:28–30) offers the strongest possible contrast with the blessed invitation to the first two slaves to enter into the joy of their master.[289]

The parable of the Talents (25:14–30) emphatically presents the theme of "faithfulness in the time until[290] the Parousia." In this regard it stands in some contrast with the earlier subunits in the second major section of the ED, although the theme of "faithfulness" is also a part of the comparison of the slave-supervisor (24:45–51).[291]

The parable of the Talents continues the theme of "division among those who claim to be Jesus' disciples," which was present in 24:45–51 and 25:1–13. In fact, the parable of the Talents presents this theme more vigorously than any other unit that has preceded it. The stark contrast between the first two slaves and the third slave portrays with powerful artistry the truth that, along with all humanity (24:37–39), the visible fellowship of Jesus' disciples will, at the Parousia, be divided into two groups. In the period of time between Jesus' resurrection and Parousia, the implied reader will remain faithful with respect to the truths and responsibilities that have been given with the knowledge that Jesus, this man, is the eschatological Christ and the Son of God.[292] Sternly warned by the fate of the third slave in the parable and encouraged by the master's gift to the first two slaves,[293] the implied reader will work with and use the things that have been entrusted to him or her by the Master.[294]

What will such "work" entail? The parable of the Talents gives no direct answer. The implied reader knows, however, that faithful "work" will certainly include, as taught in 24:45–51, the loving of the fellow disciple.[295] In addition, the implied reader has learned from the Gospel that other activities, including the activity of mission, will characterize the life of the faithful disciples of Jesus (24:14; 28:19–20).

MATTHEW 25:31–46

We arrive, then, at the final subunit of the ED. The entire second major section of the ED to this point (24:36–25:30) has exhibited a strong paraenetic character. Three themes have dominated. First, the command to "watch" or "be ready" has been a significant part of the first four subunits in this second major part of the ED (24:37–42; 24:43–44; 24:45–51; 25:1–13). Second, the motif of "faithfulness" appeared in 24:45–51 and was, to the exclusion of the theme of "be ready," the dominant motif in 25:14–30. Third, the theme of "division of persons" has run through each of the five subunits that precede the final pericope, 25:31–46. In 24:37–42, Jesus' words exhorted the disciples to watch and be ready, for all humanity will be separated just as it was on the day when the flood came. In the four subunits that have followed, the division of persons has specifically affected the group of those who claim to be Jesus' disciples. In all of this material, Jesus' words have taken the shape of comparison (24:37–39), implied narrative (24:43–44), story-like speech (24:45–51), and story-parable (25:1–13; 25:14–30). In all of this, the implied reader has stood alongside the disciples. Jesus' words have addressed the implied reader as well as the disciples on the Mount of Olives. The emphasis has been upon life until the Parousia. The Parousia has been the backdrop. The focus of attention has been life until the end.

The account of the sheep and the goats is the culminating and climactic sub-unit of the entire ED in Matthew.[296] With 25:31–46, however, Jesus' words change with regard to theme, genre, and intended effect. Matt 25:31–46 does possess, of course, obvious affinities with the subunits that have preceded it. The theme of "division of persons" returns, although I shall argue that 25:31–46 concerns itself with the division of all humanity (as in 24:37–42) and not only with the division of the visible company of Jesus' disciples (as in 24:43–25:30). Obviously, 25:31–46 deals with the Parousia of Jesus, although it does so in a way that stands out from the earlier materials.

Unlike the preceding material, however, 25:31–46 places the Parousia itself at center stage while the manner that life is lived until then forms the back-drop.[297] Further, Jesus' words in 25:31–46 are not parabolic. Rather, this subunit is a direct description of the judgment scene with only minor parabolic fea-tures.[298] Most important, I shall argue that the intended effect of this unit upon the disciples and the implied reader is not paraenetic, but rather encouraging and validating. The ED ends, not with words of challenge for the disciples and the implied reader, but with words of comfort.

In claiming that 25:31–46 functions as encouragement rather than paraenet-ic warning, I have placed myself in line with one of two general interpretive posi-tions. Daniel Marguerat has labeled the two general positions "restrictive-para-cletic" and "universal-paraenetic."[299] Within each of these general positions, there are a large number of differently nuanced understandings.[300] To present the implied reader's understanding of 25:31–46 I shall follow the lead of Sherman Gray who identifies the two most important interpretive questions:

> The two problem areas in the interpretation of the pericope continue to be the identity of πάντα τὰ ἔθνη in v 32 and ἐνὶ τούτων (τῶν ἀδελφῶν μου) τῶν ἐλαχίστων in vv 40, 45. What is the make-up of "all the nations"? Is it to be understood in its Jewish sense of all who are not Jewish, or in its Christian sense of all who are not Christian, or in its widest possible sense of all human beings? Who are the "least of my brothers"? Are they the disciples, or all Christians, or Jews, or any human being who is in need?[301]

Accordingly, I shall first comment upon the structure and basic features of 25:31–46. Next, I shall offer and support my conclusions regarding the precise identity of "all the nations" (25:32). Finally, I shall show how the implied reader will understand the referent of the "brothers" of Jesus (25:40, 45). Following the treatment of this important subunit, I shall show how it functions for the implied reader as the concluding subunit of the ED in Matthew's Gospel.

The Structure of Matthew 25:31–46

The structure of 25:31–46 may be described as follows. The first scene is 25:31–33. This describes the Parousia of Jesus and his subsequent separation of all the nations into two groups. Here is the consummation of the age (24:3; 28:20). Jesus' words portray himself on that day in colors that reflect a glory that approaches that of the Father himself.[302] He comes with the angels (cf. 16:27) and with glory. He sits on the throne of judgment (cf. 19:28). He separates[303] all the nations, placing individual people[304] on his right for blessing and his left for condemnation.[305]

Then,[306] the second scene (25:34–40) relates the dialogue between the King and those who have been placed on his right hand. The royal Son of God[307] names those on his right "you who are blessed of my Father" and invites them to inherit the blessings of the consummated reign of heaven (25:34).[308] The King's words then give the reason why those on the right are invited to inherit. Six acts of kindness were done to the King himself (25:35–36).[309] In reply the righteous ask when it was that they performed such acts of kindness and hospitality for the King.[310] The acts themselves are emphasized as the righteous repeat them back to the King (25:37–39).

The King's emphatic answer to the righteous reveals the true nature of the acts done by the righteous (25:40). The acts of kindness and hospitality actually were done for the brothers of the King, even the least of them.[311] But the King indicates the group of his "brothers" and identifies himself with them dramatically and unreservedly, and in this way the deeds were done for him. Matt 25:40 stands as the climax and crucial key to the conversation between the King and those who are righteous at the judgment.[312]

The next scene (25:41–45) is closely parallel, as Jesus' words relate the conversation between the King and those he rejects. The parallelism with the previous scene highlights the stark contrast between the two groups at the judgment. The King names those on his left "you accursed ones"[313] and sends them away into the eternal fire[314] that God prepared for the devil and his angels.[315] The King explicitly states the reason for their rejection (25:41–43). His words to the cursed ones parallel, in slightly abbreviated fashion, his words to the righteous. The parallel with the dialogue with the righteous continues with the highly abbreviated question of the cursed ones: "When did we not minister to you?" (25:44). The scene concludes with the climactic (also slightly abbreviated) response of the King: "Truly I say to you inasmuch as you did not do for one of the least of these,[316] you neither did for me." The key to understanding the fate of the cursed ones is their failure to show kindness and hospitality to the "brothers" of Jesus, even the least of them.

The subunit concludes (25:46) with Jesus' words that contrast the departures of the two groups who have comprised all the nations. The cursed ones depart into eternal fire, but the righteous go into eternal life (25:46). There are two crucial questions for the interpretation of this subunit: 1) Who are all the nations? 2) Who are the "brothers" of Jesus? I shall examine each question in turn, seeking the implied reader's understanding on the basis of insight available from the entire story of the Gospel.

THE MEANING OF "ALL THE NATIONS" (25:32)

How, then, will the implied reader assign meaning to "all the nations" (πάν-τα τὰ ἔθνη, 25:32) who are gathered before Jesus, this man, when he comes at his Parousia?[317] The literary context affords a clear and simple answer. Two issues are important. First, what does the phrase "all the nations" signify elsewhere in the Gospel of Matthew? Second, to whom are the words of 25:31–46 spoken and what is the temporal position occupied by those addressees?

The phrase πάντα τὰ ἔθνη occurs four times in Matthew's Gospel (24:9, 14; 25:32; 28:19). It will be well to consider the occurrences in "chronological" order, that is, with respect to the order in story-time (or beyond it) to which each usage refers. First in order is the use of "all the nations" in the concluding pericope of the Gospel (28:19). There, Jesus on the mountain commands the Eleven to "make disciples of all the nations." As noted in chapter 5, the implied reader is also included in this mission. He or she stands in the time beyond the temporal boundaries of the story between Jesus' resurrection and the consummation of the age. The risen Son of God promises his own presence with the Eleven and the implied reader as they carry out the mission entrusted to them: "I am with you all the days" (28:20).

Accordingly, the meaning of "all the nations" at 28:18–20 may be expressed as "all the people of the world to whom will be directed the missionary baptizing and teaching of the things Jesus has commanded." The teaching that will be proclaimed everywhere in the world will be the Gospel of the reign of heaven (cf. 26:13). Jesus' words in 28:18–20 establish the entire time period between his resurrection and Parousia as the time of mission, and "all the nations" are those toward whom the missionary preaching will be directed.

The meaning of "all the nations" at 24:9, 14 is precisely the same as it is at 28:19. At 24:4–14 Jesus warns the disciples not to confuse the tumults of history in the future with the consummation of the age. The troubles of history will only be the beginning of the birth pangs (24:8). The one "event" that must occur, however, before the end is the heralding of the Gospel of the reign of heaven to all the nations (24:14). Then the end will come. As was the case in 28:18–20, "all the nations" in 24:14 are "all people in the world to whom will be directed the missionary preaching of the Gospel of the reign of heaven." In addition, the reference in 24:9 to "all the nations" bears the same meaning. Jesus says, "Then they will deliver you into tribulation and they will kill you and you will be hated by all the nations on account of my name." The disciples can expect persecution as they engage in their mission. Jesus' words in 24:9 emphasize that even though the Gospel of the reign of heaven will be heralded to all the nations before the consummation of the age (24:14), not everyone will receive that message.[318] Many will persecute and hate the disciples precisely because they engage in mission. In other words, *many will reject both the message and the messengers themselves and seek to do them harm*.[319] Yet, herald the message they will, and the implied reader will participate in the mission.

At 25:31–46 the consummation of the age has come.[320] The meaning of "all the nations" at 28:18–20; 24:9; and 24:14 is clear to the implied reader. It is also clear that when Jesus describes the Parousia, at which time all the nations will be gathered before him (25:32), those who are gathered will be all the peoples of the world among whom the missionary heralding of the Gospel has taken place.

This understanding of "all the nations" is supported by the answer to the second pertinent question, namely, who are the addressees of 25:31–46 and what is their temporal location? In the first place, the addressees are the disciples on the Mount of Olives. They stand with Jesus in the time of the story before the mission to all the nations has begun. Jesus' words invite them to look across the period of time until the Parousia and to see all the nations from that perspective. From the disciples' temporal location, no one among "all the nations" is a disciple, for the Eleven have not yet been sent on the mission to them.[321] Rather, "all the nations" are the ones to whom the mission *will* go, beginning with the concluding pericope of the Gospel (28:18–20).[322]

In the second place, Jesus' words in 25:31–46 also address the implied reader. As I argued in the discussion of 24:15–22, the implied reader stands immediately before or during the events described in 24:15–22. The implied reader stands prior to the time when God's judgment will come upon Jerusalem and the temple. To be sure, the mission to "all the nations" has begun in the time between the Gospel's ending and the temporal location of the implied reader. Yet that mission has not yet taken place in its fullest expression, for its fullest expression will occur only after the judgment comes upon Jerusalem.[323] Accordingly, Jesus' words in 25:32 speak to the implied reader and direct his or her attention to the mission that will continue from his or her own temporal position until the end. It is still true for the implied reader, in large measure, that "all the nations" are those to whom the Gospel of the reign of heaven will be heralded in the future. With respect to both the disciples on the Mount of Olives and the implied reader, "all the nations" are the peoples of the world to whom the Gospel of the reign of heaven will be preached before the end will come.[324] The arrival of the end in 25:31–46 signals the fact that the mission task that began in 28:18–20 has been carried to completion.

WHO ARE THE "BROTHERS" OF JESUS (25:40, 45)?

We now turn to the second important interpretive question in the understanding of 25:31–46: Who are the "brothers" of Jesus? With even the least member of what group[325] does Jesus, the eschatological King, identify himself at 25:40, 45?

The metaphorical use[326] of the term "brother" in Matthew's Gospel supports the view that the "brothers" of Jesus are disciples of Jesus. In the Sermon on the Mount, Jesus speaks about his disciples' relationships with their brothers. They should not speak angrily or act in a judgmental way toward such (5:22, 23, 24; 7:3, 4, 5). Further, in the "Ecclesiological Discourse" the fellow disciple again is termed "brother" (18:15, 21, 35). Finally, in his denunciations of the religious leaders in chapter 23, Jesus teaches the disciples that no one among them is to be called "rabbi," for they have one teacher and they are all "brothers" (23:8).

All of these references orient the disciples of Jesus to one another as "brothers." In two places, however, Jesus himself names his disciples, "my brothers." The first reference is of a somewhat general nature. In 12:46–50, Jesus' biological family seeks an audience with him. When told that his mother and brothers were seeking to speak with him, Jesus "answered and said to the one speaking to him, 'Who is my mother and who are my brothers?' And he stretched out his hand over his disciples and said, 'Behold! My mother and my brothers! For whoever does the will of my Father who is in heaven is himself my brother and sister and mother' " (12:48–50). The narrator's comment specifies that the disciples of Jesus are his "family." They are his mother, sister, brother. These words reinforce the view that Jesus' "brothers" in 25:40, 45 refer to disciples of Jesus.[327]

The second time that Jesus calls his disciples "my brothers," however, specifies the meaning of "brother" in a way that dovetails perfectly into the interpretation of 25:31–46. In 28:8–10, the risen Jesus meets the women as they obediently leave the tomb after the angel's command to tell Jesus' *disciples* (μαθηταί, 28:7) that he is risen and that he will see them in Galilee. Jesus' words in 28:10 repeat, with one remarkable alteration, the angel's command to the women. Jesus says, "Go, announce [it] to my *brothers* [ἀδελφοῖς], that they may depart into Galilee, and there they will see me." As 28:16 indicates, the group whom Jesus names "my brothers" (28:10) are "the eleven disciples." It is to these, his brothers, that Jesus entrusts the mission to all the nations. Beginning at 28:18–20, the Eleven, Jesus' brothers, carry out this commission. In this capacity they are the missionaries, sent by Jesus. In their missionary enterprise, Jesus himself will accompany them: "I am with you always, even to the consummation of the age" (28:20).

This consistent use of the term "brother" and the crucial alignment of Jesus' "brothers" and the command to mission (28:10, 18–20) signal the implied reader that the "brothers" of Jesus in 25:40, 45 are his disciples whom he has sent as missionary heralds to all the nations.

Moreover, the implied reader will also distinguish in 25:31–46 between the "brothers" of Jesus and "all the nations" to whom they have gone during the time of mission. The "brothers" of Jesus have been the heralds of the Gospel of the reign of heaven; all the nations have been those to whom that message has been heralded.

Through the use of the near demonstrative pronoun "these,"[328] Jesus himself distinguishes between his "brothers" and "all the nations." When Jesus speaks to the righteous in 25:40, he explains that their response to even the least of "these," his brothers, determines their eschatological blessing (25:40). Jesus' words to the wicked also indicate that their response to even the least of "these" (25:45) determines their eschatological condemnation. Jesus directs the attention of both the righteous and the wicked to "these" brothers of his who are standing with him at the judgment.[329]

This understanding[330] of the "brothers" of Jesus in 25:40, 45 corresponds exactly with the understanding of "all the nations" as those to whom the Gospel of the reign of heaven has been heralded in the time between Jesus' resurrection and Parousia. But there remain two questions regarding this interpretation[331] of 25:31–46. First, there is no explicit mention in 25:31–46 that Jesus' "brothers" actually were missionaries whose Gospel was received by the "sheep" among all the nations. Along these lines, can it be shown that the deeds of kindness and hospitality that are the basis for the judgment (25:35–36, 42–43) indicate a reception of missionary preaching? Such an interpretation contends that the group with whom Jesus at his Parousia so thoroughly identifies himself consists of the missionaries, beginning with the Eleven, sent to herald the Gospel of the reign of heaven. This elicits a second question. Does Jesus elsewhere in the Gospel specifically identify himself with his missionary disciples?

Affirmative answers to both questions come from the most significant possible location, namely, Jesus' Missionary Discourse. In the first place, Jesus' words to the Twelve in 10:9–15 reveal that those who receive their message will manifest that reception through hospitality and care for their physical needs. When the Twelve are sent out on their missionary journey they are to take no provisions along for their own support (10:9–10a). The reason that Jesus gives is that "the worker is worthy of his food" (10:10b). During their missionary endeavor there will be houses and persons who are "worthy," that is, they will both receive the message of the Twelve and offer to them their loving care and hospitality (10:11).[332]

In stark contrast, there will be those who neither receive the missionary Twelve nor hear their words (10:14). In fact, such persons also will mistreat, arrest, and beat the Twelve (10:17). Jesus' words in Matthew 10 show the connection between the message and the messenger who bears it. "We need not doubt that welcoming a disciple into one's home is practically the same as one's becoming a disciple."[333] Informed by this significant theme regarding the Twelve's missionary outreach to Israel, the implied reader's understanding of 25:31–46 is solidified. The implied reader realizes that those who receive the message of Jesus' "brothers" in the time between Jesus' resurrection and Parousia will also show deeds of kindness and hospitality to the missionaries whose message they have received.

The implied reader also knows that the missionary disciples of Jesus, including the implied reader himself or herself, will find themselves in situations of dire need. Jesus' words in the ED have predicted such things (24:9). Thus, Jesus' "brothers" will find themselves hungry, thirsty, alone as strangers, naked, sick, and in prison.[334] As the parallel theme in Matthew 10 shows, Jesus teaches in 25:40 that those from among all the nations who have received the Gospel of the reign of heaven will also have shown care and provided for the needs of even the least of Jesus' brothers.[335] By contrast those who did not receive and care for the messengers will have shown thereby their rejection of the message that the missionary disciples proclaimed.

Finally, the missionary discourse also reveals that Jesus does in fact identify himself with the Twelve (and the implied reader) in their role as missionaries. Jesus' words in 10:40 announce that "the one who receives you receives me, and the one who receives me receives the one who sent me." Note that it is in receiving the persons of the missionary disciples that the person of Jesus is also received.[336]

Jesus' words in 10:9–15 show that this reception will include both the receiving of their words and caring for their physical needs. Jesus underscores this point in 10:42: "And whoever gives only a cup of cold water to one of these little ones in the name of a disciple, truly I tell you, he will certainly not lose his reward." Here is the parallel with the deeds of kindness and hospitality shown to the brothers of Jesus. Those who have done such deeds do not, in fact, lose their reward at the Parousia.[337] In 10:9–15 and in 25:31–46 the deeds are done for the missionary disciples of Jesus.[338] In both passages Jesus identifies himself with the missionaries whom he sends.[339]

WHAT EFFECT DOES MATTHEW 25:31–46 HAVE ON THE IMPLIED READER?

I would further emphasize that 10:40–42 and 25:31–46 are parallel in the effect that each subunit has on the disciples and the implied reader. Jesus' words at 10:40–42 conclude the Missionary Discourse and function for the disciples and the implied reader as encouragement and validation for their mission. Earlier, Jesus' words in 10:24–39 offered a warning exhortation and a stern call to faithfulness. By contrast, Jesus' words in 10:40–42 underscore the significance and lasting importance of the mission on which they are being sent. These are words of comfort to the disciples and the implied reader.[340]

The final subunit of the ED (25:31–46) has a similar effect upon the disciples and the implied reader. After the paraenetic subunits that warn the disciples and the implied reader and exhort them to faithful watching and readiness for the Parousia (24:37–25:30), Jesus' words in the final unit of the ED comfort and encourage the disciples and the implied reader in the task of missionary preaching to all the nations.[341] The encouragement is a strong one. They are Jesus' brothers. Their task is truly worthy, for Jesus will judge all the nations on the basis of the response to their eschatological proclamation of the Gospel of the reign of heaven.[342]

MATTHEW 26:1–2

The narrative conclusion of the ED (26:1–2) functions in a twofold manner. First, the words move the story forward and return the implied reader to the narrative level of the Gospel. The addition of "all" to the discourse conclusion formula shows the implied reader that there will be no more major teaching of Jesus in the Gospel: "And it happened when Jesus completed all these words he said to his disciples, 'You know that the Passover is happening after two days and this man is being handed over in order to be crucified' " (26:1–2). The implied reader is reintegrated into the narrator's story.

Second, the narrative conclusion focuses the attention of the implied reader upon the "how" of the story's resolution of conflict and upon the story's final conclusion. The ED has informed the implied reader concerning events beyond the story's time, proper attitudes until the Parousia, and the Parousia itself. It only remains for the implied reader to observe "how" the conflict between Jesus and his opponents is resolved and to observe the events that result in Jesus' vindication through his death and resurrection.[343] The implied reader knows what will take place in the time period after Jesus entrusts the command to mission to the Eleven. It only remains for the story to arrive at its concluding scene (28:16–20).[344]

THE EFFECT OF THE ED ON THE IMPLIED READER

How might we summarize the effect of the entire ED upon the implied reader? Four points will suffice. First, Jesus' words keep the implied reader from misinterpreting the tumults and difficulties of history and the appearance of those who claim to announce the Parousia of Christ. None of these things necessarily show the nearness of the consummation of the age. The implied reader knows that the entire time until the Parousia is the time of mission. When the Gospel has been heralded to all the nations then the end will come (24:4–14).

Second, Jesus' words enable the implied reader to understand and respond to the terrible Judean tribulation and the destruction of Jerusalem and its temple that follows immediately after that tribulation (24:15–31). The implied reader will flee that terrible persecution (24:15–22). Further, he or she will know that the destruction of Jerusalem is a divine judgment upon the nation that rejected the Son of God. This judgment will be a sign that Jesus, the Christ, is seated at the right hand of God in heaven (24:29–30; cf. 22:41–46; 23:36; 26:64). After those terrible events, the mission to the Gentile nations will continue in its fullest expression (29:31; cf. 21:43; 22:7–8).

Third, Jesus' words exhort the implied reader to watchful and faithful living until the Parousia occurs. The implied reader can never know the time of the Parousia (24:36). All humanity, including the visible company who claim discipleship with Jesus, will be divided on the last day. Accordingly, the implied reader will remain watchful (24:37–25:13) and faithfully will live in love toward fellow disciples, serving Jesus with all that has been entrusted to him or her (24:45–51; 25:14–30).

Finally, Jesus' words empower the implied reader for participation in the mission of heralding the Gospel of the reign of heaven to all the nations. Throughout the Gospel's story the implied reader learned the theme of "eschatological response to Jesus." Jesus' life and ministry has, in a hidden way, brought the eschatological reign of heaven into the time of the story. Accordingly, the response one makes to Jesus determines one's fate on the last day. The response of discipleship brings both the present possession of the blessings of the reign of heaven (5:3, 10) and entrance into the consummation of that reign on the last day (5:4–9). The response of opposition and rejection brings both judgment within history (23:36; 24:34; 26:64) and final exclusion from the consummated reign of heaven on that last day (7:21–23).

The opportunity and crisis of "eschatological response to Jesus" will continue during the time of mission. Response to the mission of which the implied reader is part determines one's fate on the last day. Jesus identifies himself with his missionary disciples. Those who receive them also receive Jesus. Those who reject them also reject Jesus. He is with his disciples and the implied reader always, until the consummation of the age. Thus empowered with the importance and significance of worldwide mission, the implied reader heralds the eschatological Gospel of the reign of heaven in Jesus until the consummation of the age.

NOTES

[1] The existence of a caesura between 24:2 and 24:3 is one of the mainstays of the argument of Burnett, *Testament*.

[2] Combrink, "Macrostructure," 11; Beare, *Matthew*, 445; Garland, *Intention*, 29.

[3] Garland, *Intention*, 29; Ellis, *Matthew*, 78.

[4] In chapter 13 the disciples are part of the group to whom the parables of 13:3–35 have been spoken, and they have already received "private instruction" (13:10). Further, the change of scene is, physically speaking, only the move into a house.

By contrast, the change of scene at 24:1–3 is quite dramatic and consists of 1) Jesus' departure from the temple (24:1) and 2) Jesus' sitting on Olivet outside the city (24:3). Further, Jesus addresses the religious leaders and the city beginning at 23:13, resulting in a strong change of address when he begins to speak to the disciples in 24:2 and following.

[5] Cf. Gnilka, *Matthäusevangelium*, 2:309; Sabourin, *L'Évangile*, 292.

[6] Grundmann, *Evangelium*, 496; Beare, *Matthew*, 460; Meier, *Matthew*, 274. To the contrary, Burnett, *Testament*, 124, and Hare, *Jewish Persecution*, 153, claim that the temple is specifically not in view at 23:38. I find this incredible.

[7] The most natural conclusion is that the disciples have not comprehended the import of 23:38, and that their lack of comprehension evokes from Jesus the more specific

and explicit prediction regarding the temple's destruction (24:2). Cf. Carson, "Matthew," 496.

8   Bruner, *Matthew 13-28*, 842, notes the common theme of "judgment" in 23:1–39 and 24:4–25:46.

9   I take the imperfect indicative ἐπορεύετο, 24:1, in an inceptive sense.

10 Burnett, *Testament*. Scholars who agree with Burnett in finding a division between 24:2 and 24:3 include Pesch, "Eschatologie und Ethik," 227; Walter, "Tempelzer-störung," 47; Hart, "Chronology," 67.

11 Cf. Burnett, *Testament*, 198.

12 Burnett, *Testament*, 21; cf. Tisera, *Universalism*, 243.

13 Burnett, *Testament*, 22; cf. Violaine Monsarrat, "Matthieu 24–25: du Temple aux démunis," *FoiVie* 76 (1977): 70.

14 Burnett, *Testament*, 22–23.

15 Burnett, *Testament*, 23, claims that "Jesus fulfills 23:38 when he definitively leaves the temple ('your house') in 24:1; and ... Jesus consummates the judgment when he prophetically announces the temple's physical destruction in 24:2."

    It might fairly be said that Burnett's own comments regarding the relationship of 24:1–2 to 23:38 are inconsistent. On the one hand, he writes that "Jesus' departure from the temple in 24:1 culminates the theme of Jesus' rejection of Israel" (118). On the other hand, Burnett also writes: "From our perspective, therefore, it appears that Matthew sees the judgment of God *beginning* [*sic*] in Jesus' departure from the temple" (128).

16 Burnett, *Testament*, 22, has been led astray by reading only 23:1. After 23:13 Jesus never again speaks to the crowds and the disciples in the chapter.

17 The phrase κατ᾽ ἰδίαν occurs in Matthew's Gospel at 14:13, 23; 17:1, 19; 20:17; 24:3.

18 Admittedly, the neuter plural accusative "all these things" (ταῦτα πάντα, 24:2) is unexpected, if the feminine plural "buildings" (αἱ οἰκοδομαί, 24:1) is the antecedent. The answer may lie in the tendency for the neuter demonstrative to "take up a substantive idea not expressed by a preceding neuter word" (Smyth, *Grammar*, § 1253; cf. Robertson, *Grammar*, 704–5; Carson, "Matthew," 496; Lagrange, *Évangile*, 457).

19 Those who agree in seeing two questions include Thompson, "Historical Perspect-ive," 244; Bruner, *Matthew 13-28*, 844; Newman and Stine, *Translator's Handbook*, 753; Zahn, *Evangelium*, 653; Sabourin, *L'Évangile*, 302; Hahn, "Rede," 118.

    Burnett, *Testament*, 208, discerns one question by taking the καί as epexegetical. Lambrecht, "Parousia Discourse," 318, calls this view "far fetched and uncorrect." Ellis, *Matthew*, 87, in discerning three questions, has overlooked (1) the one interrog-ative particle governing the rest of the verse and (2) the feminine singular genitive definite article τῆς, governing both παρουσίας and συντελείας. Cf. H. E. Dana and Julius R. Mantey, *A Manual Grammar of the Greek New Testament* (New York: Macmillan, 1955), 147, for "Granville Sharp's Rule," in which the second noun "denotes a further description" of the first noun.

20 Cf. Beare, *Matthew*, 446–47; Carson, "Matthew," 496; Kingsbury, *Matthew as Story*, 112; Lambrecht, "Parousia Discourse," 312–13; Sherman Gray, *The Least of My Brothers, Matthew 25:31–46: A History of Interpretation* (SBLDS 114; Atlanta: Scholars Press, 1989), 7; P. J. Maartens, "The Structuring Principles in Mt. 24 and 25 and the Interpretation of the Text," *Neot* 16 (1982): 98–99. Those who break the two-part structure between 24:31 and 24:32 include Burnett, *Testament*, 195–96; Allen, *Matthew*, 252; Brown, "Matthean Apocalypse," 4; Zahn, *Evangelium*, 654; A. C.

Cotter, "The Eschatological Discourse," *CBQ* 1 (1939): 205. Those who break the two-part structure between 24:36 and 24:37 include Agbanou, *Discours*, 40–43; Marguerat, *Jugement*, 521–22; Meier, *Matthew*, 276–77.

[21] In the first half of the discourse, "the one who is in the field" (24:18) is warned not to turn back to get his cloak. In the second half of the discourse, there will be no warning for the two people in the field (24:40).

[22] Admitting the problem are Bruner, *Matthew 13-28*, 883, and Hagner, "Apocalyptic," 66.

[23] Kik, *Matthew Twenty-Four*, 104.

[24] Agbanou, *Discours*, 67, asserts that 24:4–8 "clearly" ("nettement") has a paraenetic character. It is somewhat difficult to see what he means.

[25] Bruner, *Matthew 13-28*, 880, who does not divide the ED between 24:35 and 24:36, comments that at 24:37, "we are now embarked on that part of Jesus' great sermon that all scholars see as the 'paraenetic' or ethical part and that extends in Matthew to the end of chap 25."

[26] Matt 24:42, 45, 46, 48, 50; 25:11, 18, 19, 20, 21, 22, 23, 24, 26, 37, 44.

[27] Bruner, *Matthew 13-28*, 880.

[28] Sabourin, *L'Évangile*, 316; Kik, *Matthew Twenty-Four*, 98.

[29] Only Hart, "Chronology," 228–29, notices a significance to "but concerning" at 24:36. He says that it "marks a new section of thought."

By contrast, Agbanou, *Discours*, 38, in rejecting a major structural break between 24:35 and 24:36, claims that δέ is not a strong enough particle. But he fails to notice the significance of the combination περὶ δέ.

[30] Of thirteen NT instances of "and concerning," only Matt 6:28 and Titus 3:8 begin a sentence or independent clause. The latter instance has less a resumptive than a continuative force: "The saying is faithful, and concerning these things I want you to be established."

[31] Acts 21:25; 1 Cor 7:1, 25; 8:1; 12:1; 16:1, 12; 1 Thess 4:9; 5:1.

[32] This subunit is bound together by the following features:

1. The repeated descriptions of difficulties, tumults, and persecutions; cf. D. B. Knox, "The Five Comings of Jesus: Matthew 24 and 25," *RTR* 34 (1975): 45.

2. The connection of 24:6, "But the end is not yet," with 24:14, "Then the end will come"; cf. Ingo Broer, "Das Gericht des Menschensohnes über die Völker: Auslegung von Mt 25,31–46," *BibLeb* 11 (1970): 210.

3. The double warnings "Watch, lest you be deceived/troubled" (24:4, 6) and the double reference to "all the nations" (24:9, 14); cf. Lambrecht, "Parousia Discourse," 320; Agbanou, *Discours*, 69.

4. The presence of "therefore, when" at 24:15 indicates that a new subunit has begun; cf. Agbanou, *Discours*, 83; Broer, "Gericht," 210.

Both Maartens, "Structuring," 100, and Thompson, "Historical Perspective," 245, offer elaborate structural analyses of 24:4–14. In each case, the analysis is perhaps a bit too complex to be completely convincing or very helpful.

[33] The subunit is bound together by the following:

1. The use of substantized attributive position participles ("those in Judea," 24:16; "the one on the roof," 24:17; "the one in the field," 24:18; "those who are pregnant" and "those who are nursing," 24:19)

2. The triple reference to "those days" (24:19, 22)

3. The double reference to "flight" (24:16, "flee!" and 24:20, "your flight")

34 France, *Jesus and the Old Testament*, 232.

35 Many commentators note the nature of 24:23–28 as an "aside" or parenthetical comment that interrupts the flow of the ED between 24:22 and 24:29; cf. Filson, *Matthew*, 255–56; George C. Fuller, "The Structure of the Olivet Discourse" (Th.D. diss., Westminster Theological Seminary, 1964), 233; Schweizer, *Good News*, 453; Agbanou, *Discours*, 93; Burnett, *Testament*, 257.

36 The subunit is bound together by the following features:

1. The parallelism of two present general conditional sentences (24:23, 26). The two conditional sentences are also parallel in that the protases both use the main verb "to say," followed by the particle, "behold." Both apodoses contain the admonition "do not believe."

2. The parallelism of two sentences that begin with "for," γάρ (24:24, 27), each of which explains or gives the ground for the present general condition that preceded.

3. Each of the γάρ-sentences is followed by a short utterance. In the first case (24:25), Jesus draws specific attention to his words as prediction. In the second case (24:28), a proverb culminates the subunit.

4. The recurrence of "those days" and "tribulation" in 24:29 indicates that the thought progression, interrupted after 24:22 (where "those days" occurs twice) by the aside of 24:23–28, now resumes; cf. Bratcher, *Translator's Guide*, 306.

37 I am profoundly indebted to the work of R. T. France. His seminal discussion dealt with Mark 13 (*Jesus and the Old Testament*, 227–39). Though not agreeing with all the particulars of France's treatment of Matthew's ED, my indebtedness to his work is very great.

38 The subunit is bound together by the following features:

1. The structure of the "parable" or comparison from nature of the fig tree (24:32), and the resulting comparative clause, "so also" (24:33).

2. The repetition of "all these things" links the "parable" (24:32–33) with the amen-statement (24:34).

3. The repetition of the verb "pass away" links the oath in 24:35 with the amen-statement of 24:34.

39 BAGD, 823, "at that time."

40 Following the parallels at 24:44, "Therefore [διὰ τοῦτο] you also be ready," and 25:13, "Therefore, [οὖν] watch," 24:42 is best understood as a concluding statement; cf. Beare, *Matthew*, 475 and Schnackenburg, *Matthäusevangelium 16,21–28,20*, 240–41.

41 Filson, *Matthew*, 264; cf. Carson, "Matthew," 514; Schniewind, *Evangelium*, 248; Sabourin, *L'Évangile*, 325.

42 Some make 25:31–46 a separate major division in itself; cf. Agbanou, *Discours*, 40–43; Beare, *Matthew*, 446–47; Kingsbury, *Matthew as Story*, 112; Marguerat, *Jugement*, 521–22.

43 Richard C. Oudersluys, "The Parable of the Sheep and Goats (Matthew 25:31–46): Eschatology and Mission, Then and Now," *RefR* 26 (1973): 153; Cope, "The Death of John," 33. Gnilka, *Matthäusevangelium*, 2:367, calls the pericope a "Gerichtsdialog," while Grundmann, *Evangelium*, 525, labels it an "Offenbarungsrede."

44 Cf. Burnett, *Testament*, 132; Hart, "Chronology," 114; Agbanou, *Discours*, 57; Schnackenburg, *Matthäusevangelium*, *16,21–28,20*, 231; Gundry, *Matthew*, 474.

45 Kingsbury, "Reflections," 457–58.

46 Marguerat, *Jugement*, 373.

47 Cf. 21:43; 22:7; 22:41–46; 26:64.

48 Cf. Hare, *Jewish Persecution*, 154; Kik, *Matthew Twenty-Four*, 24. Still acceptable
    would be Lambrecht, "Parousia Discourse," 317, who calls Jesus' departure "a first
    step" in the judgment on the temple. It is possible that the narrator intends an allu-
    sion to the glory of the Lord departing from Zion/the temple in Ezek 10:18–19 and
    11:22–23 (Garland, *Jewish Persecution*, 203; France, *Evangelist*, 216; and Ellis,
    Matthew, 87).

49 Burnett, *Testament*, 143–45, notes that (1) "to approach" has cultic overtones in
    Hellenistic literature; (2) in the LXX "to approach" sometimes describes the "approach"
    to God; (3) three times in Matthew those who "approach" Jesus address him as "Lord"
    (8:25; 17:14–15; 18:21); and (4) the "disciples" in Matthew even in his lifetime have a
    "post-Easter understanding" of him and "thus approach him with veneration."

    But that a common term such as προσέρχομαι at times possesses in certain contexts
    "cultic overtones" does not demonstrate that the word automatically carries those over-
    tones with it wherever it goes. This is a case of "false assumptions about technical
    meaning" (Donald A. Carson, *Exegetical Fallacies* [Grand Rapids: Baker, 1984], 45).

    Besides 24:1, 3, the disciples "approach" Jesus nine times in Matthew's Gospel "neu-
    trally" (5:1; 26:17), "lacking understanding" (13:10, 36; 14:15; 15:12), "indifferent to
    another's need" (15:23), "without faith" (17:19), and "arrogantly" (18:1). Note the
    similar "approach" of Peter (18:21) and the mother of Zebedee's sons (20:20). All of
    this undermines Burnett's insistence on a specific and positive meaning to "approach"
    in 24:1, 3.

50 Cf. Luz, "The Disciples," 102–3.

51 Cf. Carson, "Matthew," 496.

52 As indicated above, in note 18, there is a grammatical difficulty in that "buildings" in
    24:1 is a feminine noun, whereas the pronoun "these" in 24:2 is neuter. Burnett,
    Testament, 155–57, resolves the difficulty by taking οὐ βλέπετε in a metaphorical sense,
    that is, "to not understand." He cites Matt 13:13 as a parallel. He then finds it easier to
    think that "these things" in 24:2 refers perhaps as far back as the words of Jesus begin-
    ning in 23:34 and denotes judgment against Israel. Again, Burnett's case founders on
    the use of words in their contexts. While Matt 13:13 does use βλέπω "metaphorically,"
    it is also used "literally" in the same verse, and the *context* demands the sense of "under-
    stand." The context in 24:2 does not demand such an understanding; cf. Carson,
    "Matthew," 496. The grammatical difficulty of the neuter pronoun "these things" is not
    insurmountable; cf. Smyth, *Grammar*, § 1253; Robertson, *Grammar*, 704–5.

53 Kingsbury, *Matthew as Story*, 30, cites 4:8–10; 5:1–2; 14:23; 15:29–31; 17:5; 24:3;
    28:16 as evidence that "the mountain" is the scene of "end-time acts." Note also
    Davies and Allison, *Matthew*, 1:422–23, who give an impressive number of parallels
    from literature that is contemporary with Matthew's Gospel in support of "moun-
    tains" as places of "revelation."

    However, it should be noted that Jesus' significant eschatological acts of salvation for
    the most part do *not* take place upon a mountain, and only one discourse occurs in
    that setting (24:3). It may not be too pedestrian to note with other scholars that, in
    order for Jesus to reach Bethany (26:6), he had to pass over the Mount of Olives; cf.
    Beasley-Murray, *Jesus and the Future*, 208; Schlatter, *Evangelist*, 695; C. E. B.
    Cranfield, "St. Mark 13," *SJT* 6 (1953): 194; Fuller, "Structure," 64.

54 As is apparent, I take the genitives "of your Parousia" and "of the consummation"
    as objective; cf. Newman and Stine, *Translator's Handbook*, 754; Bratcher,
    Translator's Guide, 299.

55 Agbanou, *Discours*, 52, is correct in denying the possibility that "these things" in 24:3 refers to what is about to be spoken; cf. Schnackenburg, *Matthäusevangelium 16,21–28,20*, 231; Brown, "Matthean Apocalypse," 7; Zahn, *Evangelium*, 653.

56 The two genitives are governed by one definite article and thus refer in general to the same reality, namely, "the eschatological consummation"; cf. Ladd, *Presence*, 311. The implied reader understands what "the consummation of the age" is, since Jesus himself uses the expression in 13:39, 40, 49 and 28:20. A. Feuillet, "Le Sens du Mot Parousie dans L'Évangile de Matthieu: Comparaison entre Matth.xxiv et Jac.v, 1–11," in *The Background of the New Testament and Its Eschatology* (ed. W. D. Davies and D. Daube; Cambridge: Cambridge University Press, 1956), 270, attempts unsuccessfully to prove that "the consummation of the age" does not refer to the final judgment day.

57 The term "Parousia" is used in Matthew's Gospel only in the ED (24:3, 27, 37, 39). The implied reader is expected to understand its meaning. Albrecht Oepke, "παρουσία, πάρειμι," *TDNT* 5:859–60, points out that παρουσία is used of the visit of a ruler or of one of the gods . The term also occurs in the NT in noneschatological contexts (1 Cor 16:17; 2 Cor 7:6, 7; 10:10; Phil 1:26; 2:12). It refers to the second coming of Christ at 1 Cor 15:23; 1 Thess 2:19; 3:13; 4:15; 5:23; 2 Thess 2:1, 8; 2 Pet 1:16; 3:4; 1 John 2:28.

58 Beare, "Synoptic Apocalypse," 124; Ingo Broer, "Redaktionsgeschichtliche Aspekte von MT. 24:1–28," *NovT* 35 (1993): 212–13; Alford, *Matthew*, 235; Carson, "Matthew," 495.

59 For an excellent discussion of the wide spectrum of Jewish opinion regarding the destruction of Jerusalem and the end of the world, see Anitra B. Kolenkow, "The Fall of the Temple and the Coming of the End: The Spectrum and Process of Apocalyptic Argument in 2 Baruch and Other Authors," *SBLSP, 1982* (ed. Kent Richards; Chico, Calif.: Scholars Press, 1982), 243–50.

60 Contra Thompson, "Historical Perspective," 245; Agbanou, *Discours*, 49, 57; Beare, "Synoptic Apocalypse," 124–25.

61 I am not asserting that the term "approach" means something like "approach with misunderstanding." It is the case, however, that the implied reader has noted the many times that the disciples "approach" Jesus only to show their misunderstanding. If the disciples have "gotten it wrong" so frequently, it is inherently likely that they are "getting it wrong" once again.

62 The disciples do not "initiate" the conversation with Jesus in every one of these examples. In all of them, however, their comment or question does come at a "break" in the scene, if not explicitly at the beginning of it.

63 Matt 15:12, 15; 16:7; 17:4; 17:10.

64 Matt 8:21; 15:23; 16:22; 18:1, 21; 20:20.

65 Matt 8:25; 14:15; 14:28; 15:33; 17:19.

66 Even when the disciples confess Jesus as the Son of God, the narrator makes it clear that their faith is still as yet immature or inadequate (14:33 and 15:12; 16:16 and 16:22–23; cf. 28:17).

67 It is possible that the disciples' ignorance about John as Elijah is due to the fact that, as I have argued earlier, Jesus actually sends them out on their mission to Israel (10:5) and they are not present when Jesus teaches the crowds at 11:7.

68 In passing, note that Timothy J. Geddert, *Watchwords: Mark 13 in Markan Eschatology* (JSNTSup 26; Sheffield : Sheffield Academic Press, 1989), 21, asserts that in the Markan ED, "we have no assurance that [the disciples'] agenda [in Mark 13:1–14] is endorsed by either the Markan Jesus or by the author."

69 Cf. Kik, *Matthew Twenty-Four*, 26.

[70] Note the second person plural address in 24:6.

[71] Note that the second person address ends after 24:9.

[72] As is evident, I understand "the end" (τὸ τέλος) in 24:6 and 24:14 to mean "the consummation of the age." This view will be discussed and defended in the interpretation of 24:4–14 below.

[73] Cf. Alford, *Matthew*, 235; Carson, "Matthew," 495.

[74] Cf. Lambrecht, "Parousia Discourse," 312. Owing to his interpretation of 24:4–31, Burnett, "Prolegomena," 100, asserts that, despite the expectation of the implied reader, Jesus does not in fact ever directly answer the temporal question, "When?"

[75] Burnett, *Testament*, 277, rightly comments that 24:4–8 are held together by two basic thoughts: 1) don't be deceived, and 2) the end is not yet.

[76] This is probably the sense of "many will come in my name"; cf. Davies and Allison, *Matthew*, 1:715–16.

[77] In the background of the "tumult" language in the ED lies the variegated and varied concept of the "messianic woes"; cf. Allison, *End of the Ages*, 5–25. For examples of this concept in Jewish literature, cf. *1 Enoch* 80; 91:5; 99:3; *4 Ezra* 5:1; 6:11; 13:21; *2 Baruch* 25:1; 26–27.

[78] Behind δεῖ is the assumption of divine providence and control; cf. Bratcher, *Translator's Guide*, 299; Burnett, *Testament*, 230; Schnackenburg, *Matthäusevangelium 16,21–28,20*, 232.

[79] Thompson, "Historical Perspective," 246; Bruner, *Matthew 13-28*, 847.

[80] The general geographical scope of the events alluded to in 24:7 is indicated by κατὰ τόπους. There are no markers that these events are envisioned as happening only in Judea, nor that the disciples themselves will actually experience all of them; cf. Thompson, "Historical Perspective," 246; Alford, *Matthew*, 237.

[81] The use of "birth pang" (ὠδίν) often refers to distress in a non-eschatological sense; cf. Exod 15:14; Deut 2:25; Ps 48:6; Jer 50:43; Sir 48:19. It also, however, along with the cognate verb "to labor" (ὠδίνω) refers to eschatological distress: Isa 21:3; 26:17; 1 Thess 5:3; Rom 8:22; Rev 12:2; *1 En.* 62:4; *4 Ezra* 4:22. Significantly, the word-group also refers to the reaction to God's wrath and judgment against nations in history; Isa 13:8; Jer 4:31; Mic 4:9, 10; Hab 3:10.

[82] Some find an element of "hope" implicit in the use of "birth pangs"; cf. Schlatter, *Evangelist*, 699; Kik, *Matthew Twenty-Four*, 36; Cranfield, "St. Mark 13," 290; Grundmann, *Evangelium*, 503; Bruner, *Matthew 13-28*, 848; Beare, *Matthew*, 465; Fuller, "Structure," 105. The idea seems far-fetched. The background literature does not, to my knowledge, develop or express such a concept.

[83] The majority of interpreters take the sense of Jesus' words in 24:8 as "*only* the beginning"; cf. Knox, "Five Comings," 45; David L. Turner, "The Structure and Sequence of Matthew 24:1–41: Interaction with Evangelical Treatments," *Grace Theological Journal* 10 (1989): 7; Fuller, "Structure," 160; Zahn, *Evangelium*, 654; Schnackenburg, *Matthäusevangelium 16,21–28,20*, 232; Sabourin, *L'Evangile*, 302. Thompson, "Historical Perspective," 246, paraphrases: "Merely the first stage."

[84] Matt 24:9 begins with "then," τότε. Hart, "Chronology," 102, argues on the basis of Matthew's use of this word for a strong "sequential" sense at 24:9: "then, next in time." Cf. Thompson, "Historical Perspective," 246; Gnilka, *Matthäusevangelium*, 2:314.

It seems unlikely that Jesus' words are laying out a strict sequence and that only after the upheavals and tumults of 24:4–8 will the disciples "then" experience betrayal and

persecutions. It is easier to take τότε at 24:9 as "coincident," "at that time"; cf.
Bratcher, *Translator's Guide*, 300; Alford, *Matthew*, 237; Carson, "Matthew," 498.

85 Cf. Tisera, *Universalism*, 251–53.

86 Cf. David Wenham, "A Note on Matthew 24:10–12," *TynBul* 31 (1980): 156–57;
Thompson, "Historical Perspective," 247; Grundmann, *Evangelium*, 504.

87 Hare, *Jewish Persecution*, 163; Hart, "Chronology," 104.

88 Note the generalizing force of the substantized participle, ὁ ὑπομείνας (24:13).

89 The phrase "to the end" (εἰς τέλος) in 24:13 is not a reference to "the end" (τὸ τέλος)
as in 24:6, 14. It is not a question of surviving troubles so as to remain alive at the
consummation of the age, for Jesus has already told the disciples that they will be
killed (24:9). Rather, "to the end" in 24:13 means "to the limit" or "to the uttermost."
Cf. Fuller, "Structure," 146; Sabourin, *L'Évangile*, 304; Lagrange, *Évangile*, 461;
Broer, "Aspekte," 227; Tisera, *Universalism*, 254.

90 Broer, "Aspekte," 227; Barth, "Matthew's Understanding," 61; Brown, "Matthean
Apocalypse," 9; Agbanou, *Discours*, 73; Thompson, "Historical Perspective," 247.

91 Agbanou, *Discours*, 70, nicely notes the contrast of "the one who endures" with
"many will stumble" in 24:10.

92 The force of "as a witness" is positive in the sense of "with a view toward becoming
Jesus' disciples"; cf. Bratcher, *Translators' Guide*, 301; Tisera, *Universalism*, 258–60. It
can also be said to be "neutral" in the sense that there is no guarantee that the
nations will respond positively to the Gospel; cf. Carson, "Matthew," 499; Agbanou,
Discours, 80; Zahn, *Evangelium*, 655.

93 Some argue that "end" in 24:14 refers to the ruin of Jerusalem; cf. Kik, *Matthew
Twenty-Four*, 38; Lagrange, *Évangile*, 461. In light of the obvious connections
between 24:14 and 28:19–20, however, it is certain that "the end" at both 24:6 and
24:14 refers to the consummation of the age; cf. Hahn, "Rede," 118; Bratcher,
Translator's Guide, 301; Sabourin, *L'Évangile*, 306.

94 Thompson, "Historical Perspective," 247.

95 Matt 24:14 does not demand a lengthy period of time. It certainly allows for one,
however, and could be said to imply it. Cf. Zahn, *Evangelium*, 663.

96 Filson, *Matthew*, 254, says that both "inhabited earth" and "all the nations" in 24:14
emphasize the "universal scope of the mission." Beare, *Matthew*, 466, writes that the
Parousia "will not occur until the whole world has been evangelized." Cf. Gnilka,
Matthäusevangelium, 2:319. Note the parallel in 26:13, where the Gospel is heralded
in "the whole *world*" (ὅλος ὁ κόσμος).

97 Note the second person plural pronouns and second person plural address.

98 Logically, if 24:15 begins an inference ("therefore") on the basis of 24:4–14, then it is
also true that 24:4–14 serves as the "ground" or "cause" for 24:15. Accordingly, it is
appropriate to write "because."

99 The remarkable manner in which the implied reader is also addressed by 24:15–22
will be indicated below. But it is imperative to note that "the disciples" are also
addressed, as shown by the second person plural verbs "you see" (24:15) and "[you]
pray" (24:20), as well as by the phrase "your flight" (24:20). Thus, Graham N.
Stanton, " 'Pray That Your Flight May Not Be in Winter or on a Sabbath'
(Matthew 24.20)," *JSNT* 37 (1989): 23–24, errs when he argues that "fleeing from
persecution" here reflects a theme that is not addressed to the disciples, but to the
implied reader alone.

[100] Bruner, *Matthew 13-28*, 859–61, wants both to have and to eat his exegetical cake. For him, "Judea" is both "Judea" and "wherever Christians are." The command to "flee" means both "flee" and "realize the urgency of your life in this world."

[101] Agbanou, *Discours*, 83.

[102] Bruner, *Matthew 13-28*, 861, writes: "This woe is not imprecatory; it is compassionate."

[103] See Stanton, "Pray That Your Flight," 18–20, for six interpretations of why flight on the Sabbath is a problem. It is difficult to find any of them convincing, and the point is not an important one.

[104] Sabourin, *L'Évangile*, 309. Scholars have noted similar phrasing at Dan 12:1: "That is a day of tribulation, which sort did not happen from when they were until that day." Cf. Agbanou, *Discours*, 90; Beasley-Murray, *Jesus and the Kingdom of God*, 330 (regarding Mark 13:19–20). Note parallel language at Exod 9:18, 24; 11:6; Joel 2:2. Allen, *Matthew*, 256, notes a partial parallel at *T. Mos.* 8:1.

[105] Cf. Bruner, *Matthew 13-28*, 862; Bratcher, *Translator's Guide*, 303; Carson, "Matthew," 501.

[106] For participle of indirect discourse, see BDF, § 416; Porter, *Idioms*, 269; Goodwin, *Grammar*, ¶¶ 1494, 1588; Smyth, *Grammar*, § 2112 b.

[107] The variations refer to the presence or absence of the definite article with either or both of the nouns. The Hebrew phrase in Dan 9:27 reads, "the wing of the detested things causing horror" (כְּנַף שִׁקּוּצִים מְשֹׁמֵם); in Dan 11:31, it is the arthrous singular form, "thing," while in Dan 12:11, it is arthrous singular and the modifying participle is the alternate Po'el form, which is identical to the Qal form.

[108] "And on the fifteenth day of Chislev, the one hundred forty-fifth year, he set up an abomination of desolation [βδέλυγμα ἐρημώσεως] upon the altar, and in the cities of Judah surrounding they set up high places." Cf. 2 Macc 8:17, where Judas Maccabee exhorts his troops to keep before their eyes "the outrage which had been lawlessly completed by them in the holy place" (τὴν ἀνόμως εἰς τὸν ἅγιον τόπον συντετελεσμένην ὑπ' αὐτῶν ὕβριν). Note here the presence of the phrase "in the holy place."

[109] So Beasley-Murray, *Jesus and the Kingdom of God*, 328; Hart, "Chronology," 127.

[110] It is quite certain that the Jerusalem temple is the referent of "the holy place." Hart, "Chronology," 131, notes the following evidence: 1) Jesus alludes to the book of Daniel, where the temple is in view. 2) 2 Macc 8:17 specifically calls the temple "the holy place." 3) The parallel in Mark 13:14 refers to the temple. 4) The absence of the definite article after ἐν in Matt 24:15 does not necessarily make the noun indefinite, "a holy place." Cf. Schlatter, *Evangelist*, 704; Grundmann, *Evangelium*, 506; Alford, *Matthew*, 239; Allen, *Matthew*, 256; Schweizer, *Good News*, 452; Lagrange, *Évangile*, 462.

Those who reject any reference to the Jerusalem temple include Hare, *Jewish Persecution*, 163; Burnett, *Testament*, 331; Beare, "Synoptic Apocalypse," 128; Gnilka, *Matthäusevangelium*, 2:322; Walter, "Tempelzerstörung," 48.

[111] Agbanou, *Discours*, 86; Werner Foerster, "βδελύσσομαι κτλ.," *TDNT* 1:599; Zahn, *Evangelium*, 657; Schlatter, *Evangelist*, 702.

[112] It is probably correct to see the concept of "defilement," rather than "destruction" as the primary sense of "abomination of desolation"; cf. Burnett, *Testament*, 304; Fuller, "Structure," 160; Zahn, *Evangelium*, 656. At the same time, both the phrase "abomination of desolation" and the Matthean context ensure that the destruction of the temple is also in view.

113 For a thorough treatment, see Desmond Ford, *The Abomination of Desolation in Biblical Eschatology* (Washington, D.C.: University Press of America, 1979). There is no evidence given within the Gospel of Matthew as to what specific event, in the time period after the resurrection of Jesus, might be the precise fulfillment of Jesus' words in 24:15. Commentators have, of course, often looked back on the historical events of the first century and tried to identify a fulfillment; cf. Bo Reicke, *The New Testament Era: The World of the Bible from 500 B.C. to A.D. 100* (trans. David E. Green; Philadelphia: Fortress, 1968), 256–60. *Jewish War*, 6.93–110, shows that Josephus wanted his readers to regard the Zealot infighting and bloodshed within the temple precincts as a polluting and defiling of the temple. Cf. Alford, *Matthew*, 239; Agbanou, *Discours*, 87; Lagrange, *Évangile*, 462.

114 Cf. 10:23a ("But when they persecute you in this city, flee to the next"). These two verses are also the only uses of φεύγω in the plural imperative in Matthew's Gospel. By contrast, note 5:10–12 and 16:24, where Jesus predicts persecution for his disciples but does not command them to flee.

115 This is the effect of the switch from the plural substantive participle in 24:16 to the singular participles in 24:17–18.

116 Note how the phrase "those days" (24:19, 22) acts both to define the subunit of 24:15–22, as well as to show the parenthetical nature of 24:23–28, "sandwiched" between 24:15–22 and 24:29–31. The events of 24:15–22 are taking place in "those days." The events portrayed in 24:29–31 take place "immediately after the tribulation of those days."

117 Note that the second person plural address prominently returns in 24:20.

118 Beasley-Murray, *Jesus and the Kingdom of God*, 330.

119 For an interesting parallel usage in the OT, compare 2 Kgs 18:5 with 2 Kgs 23:25.

120 Cf. Bruner, *Matthew 13-28*, 862; Bratcher, *Translator's Guide*, 303; Carson, "Matthew," 501. Without assigning an historical fulfillment, one can note in passing the similar language of Josephus, *Jewish War*, 6.429, regarding the slaughter of Jerusalem's inhabitants in and around the temple after it had been set afire: "The victims thus outnumbered those of any previous visitation [φθόρα, 'destruction'], human or divine."

121 I take the passive verb "were shortened" as a divine passive.

122 Beasley-Murray, *Jesus and the Future*, 419, is correct when he writes, with reference to Mark 13:20, that "the motif of the shortening of the days has analogies within the apocalyptic literature of Judaism, but no real parallels." Passages from noncanonical literature cited as parallels turn out to be of no value; cf. the passages cited by Agbanou, *Discours*, 90 (*2 Bar.* 20:1; 83:1; *1 En.* 80:2; *3 Bar.* 9:7). One can note in passing that Albert-Marie Denis, *Concordance Grecque des Pseudepigraphes d'Ancien Testament* (Louvain-la-Neuve: Universite Catholique de Louvain, Institut Orientaliste, 1987) gives only one occurrence of the Greek verb "to shorten" (κολοβόω). At *3 Bar.* 9:7 the verb helps to explain why the moon is sometimes large in the sky and sometimes small.

123 This is the sense of "no flesh would be saved" (οὐκ ἂν ἐσώθη πᾶσα σάρξ) in 24:22. The phrase "all flesh" occurs only here in Matthew's Gospel. It could certainly mean "all humankind," and is so understood by Hart, "Chronology," 157–61; Carson, "Matthew," 502. Yet, as parallels in other NT documents show, it can also mean "no one," with the context supplying the scope: Mark 13:20; Luke 3:6; Acts 2:17; Rom 3:20; 1 Cor 1:29; 15:39; Gal 2:16; 1 Pet 1:24. Those who agree that "all flesh" here in Matt 24:22 means "none of the people present in those days of local tribulation" include Meier, *Matthew*, 284; Broer, "Aspekte," 230.

In Matthew, the verb σῴζω has a "spiritual" sense at 1:21; 10:22; 19:25; 24:13. It means "to rescue from physical danger" at 8:25; 14:30; 27:40–42. It means "to heal physically" at 9:21–22. It means "to preserve, keep" at 16:25.

In light of the local Judean character of the tribulation that has been described since 24:15, the meaning of "no flesh would be saved" is "no one would escape with his or her life intact," for as Broer, "Aspekte," 230, notes, why else would fleeing for one's life help?

[124] The term "elect" occurs elsewhere in Matthew only at 22:14 and 24:24, 31. In 22:14, the "elect" are the smaller subset of the larger number of persons who are "called" to the wedding feast depicted in the parable. The larger number remains together until the king enters and casts out the (presumably representative) man without a wedding garment. Then and only then does it become evident that whereas many are "called," few are "elect."

This provides a useful parallel for 24:22. That "the elect" are a smaller subset of a larger number is shown by the contrast between "the elect" and "all flesh." For the sake of "the elect," other lives also will be spared by God's shortening of those days of tribulation. Once again, there is no compelling reason to think that the scope of the tribulation has changed from 24:21 to 24:22.

[125] Cf. Lambrecht, "Parousia Discourse," 321–22.

[126] David Daube, "The Abomination of Desolation," in *The New Testament and Rabbinic Judaism* (London: Athlone, 1956), 422–24, notes (with reference to Mark 13:14) the grammatical possibility that "let the reader understand" is actually the apodosis of the sentence for which the protasis is "when you see that the abomination of desolation is standing in the holy place." He rightly rejects this view, however, noting especially the difficulty of accounting for "then" in Mark 13:15 and Matt 24:16.

Those who do accept the view that Daube has rejected understand "the reader" in 24:15 to be the reader of Daniel, not the reader of Matthew's Gospel; cf. Carson, "Matthew," 500; Fuller, "Structure," 152; Bratcher, *Translator's Guide*, 302.

[127] The answers vary. Scholars think that the implied reader (or the community of the evangelist) views the events of this subunit as either past or present (Howell, *Inclusive*, 105); as primarily current or present (Maartens, "Structuring," 103; Agbanou, *Discours*, 88); as past (Powell, "Expected," 40); or as future (Burnett, *Testament*, 301, 306; Broer, "Aspekte," 229).

[128] Lanser, *Narrative Act*, 174.

[129] Here is the answer to the question posed but not answered by Jesus' words in 10:17–23 and by the narrator's address to the implied reader in 27:8 and 28:15.

[130] Note the second person plural pronouns at 24:23, 25, 26 as well as the second person plural imperatives at 24:23, 26.

[131] The most natural way of reading the warnings against false christs and prophets in 24:23–28 is as a repetition of the warning in 24:5, 11. Some interpreters, however, assign Jesus' words in 24:23–28 to the period just prior to the consummation of the age, in contrast to Jesus' words in 24:5, 11; cf. Lagrange, *Évangile*, 464; Zahn, *Evangelium*, 658.

[132] Burnett, *Testament*, 257. Note that "then" (τότε) in 24:23 conveys coincident time, "at that time," that is, during the troubled days described in 24:15–22; cf. Hart, "Chronology," 168; Agbanou, *Discours*, 94.

[133] France, *Jesus and the Old Testament*, 230, says: "In any case, the whole point of Mt. 24:27 is to *differentiate* the Parousia from the events of A.D. 70 as described in the previous verses."

[134] Both here and in 24:22, "the elect" refers to "the elect in Judea."

[135] Carson, "Matthew," 503, comments on 24:24 piously but also pertinently: "*Ei dunaton* ('if that were possible') no more calls in question the security of the elect ... than it calls in question the inevitability of Jesus' cup (26:39)."

[136] Some commentators refer to the idea that Messiah's coming would be with hiddenness; cf. Agbanou, *Discours*, 101; Grundmann, *Evangelium*, 507.

[137] This is the point of comparison in the ὥσπερ ... οὕτως structure of 24:27; cf. Bruner, *Matthew 13-28*, 867; Agbanou, *Discours*, 96; Schnackenburg, *Matthäusevangelium*, 16,21–28,20, 236; Meier, *Matthew*, 286; Kik, *Matthew Twenty-Four*, 66; Schlatter, *Evangelist*, 709.

[138] Zahn, *Evangelium*, 659, remarks rightly that 24:28 is a proverb and is not in need of specific "interpretation." Cf. Lagrange, *Évangile*, 466; Schlatter, *Evangelist*, 709.

For attempts to interpret the saying more as a parable, cf. Maartens, "Structuring," 103; Hahn, "Rede," 119; Kik, *Matthew Twenty-Four*, 67–68; Brown, "Matthean Apocalypse," 12.

[139] Schniewind, *Evangelium*, 242, thinks that the image is both striking and horrible.

[140] Burnett, *Testament*, 265; Hart, "Chronology," 177; Alford, *Matthew*, 241.

[141] Commentators debate whether the first-century history of Palestine that led up to the first Jewish War and the destruction of the temple in A.D. 70 actually witnessed the appearance of false christs; cf. Beasley-Murray, *Jesus and the Kingdom of God*, 324; Brown, "Matthean Apocalypse," 8; Reicke, *New Testament Era*, 130–31; Maartens, "Structuring," 103; Schlatter, *Evangelist*, 708; Bruner, *Matthew 13-28*, 846; Hart, "Chronology," 98. For a careful discussion of this issue, see Powell, "Expected," 39–40.

[142] Cf. Mounce, *Matthew*, 225; Filson, *Matthew*, 255–56; France, *Jesus and the Old Testament*, 232.

[143] This effect of "Behold!" is argued strongly by Reeves, "Resurrection Narrative," 96.

[144] Agbanou, *Discours*, 95; cf. Grundmann, *Evangelium*, 507.

[145] Bratcher, *A Translator's Guide*, 306; Lagrange, *Évangile*, 466.

[146] Matt 4:20, 22; 8:3; 13:5; 14:22, 31; 20:34; 21:2; 24:29; 25:15; 26:49, 74; 27:48.

[147] Cf. Turner, "Structure," 18; Grundmann, *Evangelium*, 508; Lagrange, *Évangile*, 466; Guthrie, *Theology*, 795.

[148] Bruner, *Matthew 13-28*, 868 offers the paraphrase "very soon after" without offering any grammatical or linguistic rationale; cf. Fuller, "Olivet Discourse," 161.

[149] Beasley-Murray, *Jesus and the Kingdom of God*, 331; Schlatter, *Evangelist*, 710; Hart, "Chronology," 12.

[150] Note that in Matthew's Gospel, neither the narrator nor Jesus quotes from the intertestamental or so-called "pseudepigraphical" writings of early Judaism. It is noteworthy that Powell, "Expected," 43–47, discusses the implied reader's knowledge of texts other than the Hebrew Scriptures. In this discussion, Powell never suggests that the implied reader knows the apocalyptic or pseudepigraphical writings. For an unsuccessful attempt to show the First Evangelist's knowledge and use of Jewish apocalyptic writings and especially 1 Enoch, see John W. Granger, "Matthew's Use of Apocalyptic" (Th.D. diss., New Orleans Baptist Theological Seminary, 1990), 122–37.

[151] Cf. Gnilka, *Matthäusevangelium*, 2:238–39; Casey, *Son of Man*, 174.

[152] The wording of Matt 24:29 echoes closely the LXX of Isa 13:10, which reads as follows: **οἱ γὰρ ἀστέρες τοῦ οὐρανοῦ** καὶ ὁ Ὠρίων καὶ πᾶς ὁ κόσμος τοῦ οὐρανοῦ τὸ

φῶς οὐ δώσουσιν καὶ **σκοτισθήσεται** τοῦ ἡλίου ἀνατέλλοντος **καὶ ἡ σελήνη οὐ δώ-σει** τὸ φῶς **αὐτῆς** (common elements in bold). Note also these concepts that are common in the contexts of both Isa 13:10 and Matt 24:29: "inhabited earth" (Isa 13:5, 9; Matt 24:14); "birth pangs" (Isa 13:8; Matt 24:8); "desolate" (Isa 13:9; Matt 23:38); and the idea that the judgment will happen quickly (Isa 13:21; Matt 24:34). Other words and phrases in 24:29 can be found in passages such as Isa 34:4; Ezek 32:7; Joel 2:10.

[153] Beasley-Murray, *Jesus and the Kingdom of God*, 5–6; cf. Theodore Hiebert, "Theophany in the OT," *ABD* 6:505–11.

[154] Beasley-Murray, *Jesus and the Kingdom of God*, 9–10.

[155] Beasley-Murray, *Jesus and the Kingdom of God*, 43.

[156] Gerhard von Rad, "ἡμέρα," *TDNT* 2:945.

[157] Gerhard Delling, "ἡμέρα," *TDNT* 2:948.

[158] Beasley-Murray, *Jesus and the Kingdom of God*, 6.

[159] Beasley-Murray, *Jesus and the Kingdom of God*, 10.

[160] Delling, *TDNT* 2:948; Ladd, *Presence*, 62, 74; Caird, *Language*, 219; Kenneth J. Cathcart, "Day of Yahweh," *ABD* 2:85.

[161] Caird, *Language*, 113.

[162] Beasley-Murray, *Jesus and the Kingdom of God*, 11, writes this about the "Day *of* the Lord":

> Clearly the genitive in this case must be subjective; it denotes a day on which the Lord *acts*, bringing disaster on the subjects of his wrath. This is an important datum, for it indicates that the Day of the Lord is an occasion 1) that involves God acting in the historical sphere, 2) that entails judgment for those for whom the day comes, and 3) that occurs at such time as is determined by the Lord (*not necessarily at the end of history*). (emphasis added)

This paragraph is significant in that it is a change from Beasley-Murray's earlier understanding of "the Day of Yahweh"; cf. his earlier (1954) work *Jesus and the Future*, 170.

[163] Beasley-Murray, *Jesus and the Last Days*, 248.

[164] Beasley-Murray, *Jesus and the Kingdom of God*, 13; emphasis original.

[165] I culled this brief list from various sources: Ps 18:6–15; Isa 13:9–11; 14:12–15; 34:1–5, 11; Jer 4:23–26; Lam 1:21; Ezek 28:13–16; 32:7; 34:12; Joel 2:10; 4:15; Amos 8:9; Mic 1:2–6; Zephaniah 1.

[166] Beasley-Murray, *Jesus and the Kingdom of God*, 10. Derek Kidner, *Psalms 1–72* (Downers Grove, Ill.: Inter-Varsity, 1973), 92, writes that the psalmist "sees his perils and deliverance as no less crucial and miraculous than those of Moses' day, to be described in the same tremendous terms, since God Himself 'reached from on high' ([Ps 18:]16) to save him."

Those who see Psalm 18 as a reflection of the royal cultus also acknowledge the use of "figurative" language. Carroll Stuhlmueller, *Psalms 1* (Wilmington, Del.: Michael Glazier, 1983), 130, writes: "Even if God acts through human instruments like a king, still the overall scenario remains supra-natural and cannot be adequately communicated simply by retelling the surface details of history ... we find ourselves in the midst of a type of literature, technically called mythological." Cf. Artur Weiser, *The Psalms: A Commentary* (London: SCM Press, 1962), 189–90.

[167] William L. Holladay, *Jeremiah I: A Commentary of the Book of the Prophet Jeremiah, Chapters 1–25* (Philadelphia: Fortress, 1986), 164. Caird, *Language*, 113, notes that the Hebrew phrase "waste and void" is used in the Scriptures only at Jer 4:23 and Gen 1:2.

168 Peter C. Craigie, Page H. Kelley, and Joel F. Drinkard Jr., *Jeremiah 1–25* (Waco, Tex.: Word, 1991), 82; cf. John Bright, *Jeremiah* (Garden City, N.Y.: Doubleday, 1965), 34.

169 Peter Craigie, *Ezekiel* (Philadelphia: Westminster, 1983), 227.

170 Leslie Allen, *Ezekiel 20–48* (Dallas: Word, 1990), 131, who refers also to Ezek 30:3, 18 and Joel 2:2, 10.

171 Walther Eichrodt, *Ezekiel: A Commentary* (London: SCM Press, 1970), 433; cf. Craigie, *Ezekiel*, 227.

172 See note 152.

173 For opposing views, see Seth Erlandsson, *The Burden of Babylon: A Study of Isaiah 13,2–14,23* (Lund: Gleerup, 1970) and Bernard Gosse, *Isaïe 13,1–14,23 dans la tradition littéraire du livre d'Isaïe et dans la tradition des oracles contre les nations* (Freiburg: Universitätsverlag, 1988).

174 Otto Kaiser, *Isaiah 13–39: A Commentary* (London: SCM Press, 1974), 6.

175 H. C. Leupold, *Exposition of Isaiah*, vol.1 (Grand Rapids: Baker, 1968), 244–45.

176 Ladd, *Presence*, 67.

177 Kaiser, *Isaiah 13–39*, 21; S. H. Widyapranawa, *The Lord Is Savior: Faith in National Crisis. A Commentary on the Book of Isaiah 1–39* (Grand Rapids: Eerdmans, 1990), 82; John D. W. Watts, *Isaiah 1–33* (Waco, Tex.: Word, 1985), 200; Knox, "Five Comings," 50; Beare, *Matthew*, 471; Beasley-Murray, *Jesus and the Kingdom of God*, 12; France, *Jesus and the Old Testament*, 233; Caird, *Language*, 113.

178 It should be clear at this point that I am not here advocating the view that is sometimes called "prophetic perspective." According to Beasley-Murray, *Jesus and the Future*, 131, this hermeneutical device was first applied to Mark 13 by J. Bengel, whose words Beasley-Murray quotes as follows: "A prophecy resembles a landscape painting, which marks distinctly the houses, paths, and bridges in the foreground, but brings together, into a narrow space, the distant valleys and mountains, though they are really far apart. Thus should they who study a prophecy look on the future to which the prophecy refers." For an excellent description of "prophetic perspective" by one who adheres to this view, see Ladd, *Presence*, 65–68.

179 Powell, "Expected," 42.

180 The implied reader of Matthew's Gospel will regard the oracle of Isaiah 13 as genuine to the prophet, Isaiah of Jerusalem; cf. Powell, "Expected," 42.

181 Matt 27:45, of course, speaks of darkness over the whole land while Jesus hangs on the cross. This actual darkness-event (for the narrator relates it as something that literally took place within the world of the story) does serve as a sort of parallel to the interpretation of 24:29 that I am advancing. The death and resurrection of Jesus are eschatological. Just as there will be a literal fulfillment of the language of "cosmic" distress at the consummation of the age, so already with the death of Jesus there is an echo, a manifestation. The darkness at Jesus' death shows the present, yet unconsummated, reign of heaven already in the time of the story.

182 Cf. France, *Jesus and the Old Testament*, 239. There is a notable parallel to this understanding of Matt 24:29 at 2 *Bar.* 10:12. In a lament over the fall of Jerusalem the writer agonizes: "And you, sun, keep the light of your rays within you, and you, moon, extinguish the multitude of your light. For why should the light rise again, where the light of Zion is darkened?" Both before this verse and after it, the writer of 2 *Baruch* calls upon the world of nature and all the courses of humanity to cease their proper function and to join in lamentation over Zion.

[183] Agbanou, *Discours*, 106, is probably correct in seeing the fourth phrase of 24:29, "and the power of the heavens will be shaken," as a summary of the first three phrases of the verse.

[184] Those who agree that Jesus' words in 24:29 have reference to the ruin of the temple and city include France, *Jesus and the Old Testament*, 239; M. Stuart, "Observations on Matthew 24:29–31, and the Parallel Passages in Mark and Luke, with Remarks on the Double Sense of Scripture," *Bibliotheca Sacra and American Biblical Repository* 9 (1852): 336, 339; Knox, "Five Comings," 46; Brown, "Matthean Apocalypse," 13; Garland, *Reading Matthew*, 238. Conceding the possibility of this interpretation are Casey, *Son of Man*, 174; Allen, *Matthew*, 258; Sabourin, *L'Évangile*, 311; Guthrie, *Theology*, 793; David Wenham, " 'This Generation Will Not Pass...': A Study of Jesus' Future Expectation in Mark 13," in *Christ the Lord: Studies in Christology Presented to Donald Guthrie* (ed. Harold H. Rowdon; Downers Grove, Ill.: InterVarsity, 1982), 138.

[185] In our current climate, such language sounds harsh, even anti-Semitic. Yet under investigation is the point of view of an ancient document, the Gospel of Matthew. Marguerat, *Jugement*, 374, is correct in saying that the theme of God's judgment of Israel is a part of Matthew's Gospel that should not be softened.

[186] Zucker, "Jesus and Jeremiah," 295, asserts a connection between the cursing of the fig tree and Jer 8:13: "When I would gather them, says the Lord, there are no grapes on the vine, nor figs on the fig tree; even the leaves are withered, and what I gave them has passed away from them." Cf. France, *Evangelist*, 215; Carson, "Matthew," 445; Knowles, *Jeremiah*, 177.

[187] For a similar understanding of Acts 2:16–21, see F. F. Bruce, *The Acts of the Apostles: The Greek Text with Introduction and Commentary* (3d rev. ed.; Grand Rapids: Eerdmans, 1990), 69.

[188] Note, of course, the close parallels in the parables of the Wicked Tenants ("When the master of the vineyard comes ... he will utterly destroy those wicked ones," 21:40–41) and the Wedding Feast ("And the king was enraged and sent his soldiers and destroyed those murderers and burned their city," 22:7).

[189] BAGD, 823.

[190] Recall that I understood the genitive at 24:3, "the sign of your Parousia," as an objective genitive. Although in my view the two verses are referring to two different things, I take them both as objective genitives.

Some take the genitive as epexegetical, "the sign which is this man"; cf. Pesch, "Eschatologie und Ethik," 229, 234; Lambrecht, "Parousia Discourse," 324; Brown, "Matthean Apocalypse," 13; Knox, "Five Comings," 51; Grundmann, *Evangelium*, 508; Schniewind, *Evangelium*, 243; Bruner, *Matthew 13-28*, 870; Meier, *Matthew*, 287.

A number of scholars follow the view of T. Francis Glasson, "The Ensign of the Son of Man (MATT. XXIV.30)," *JTS* 15 (1964): 299–300. Glasson argues that the σημεῖον means "ensign" or "standard," owing to the LXX translation of כֵּס with σημεῖον; cf. Beasley-Murray, *Jesus and the Future*, 259–60; Carson, "Matthew," 505; Margaret Pamment, "The Son of Man in the First Gospel," *New Testament Studies* 29 (1983): 125. Against the view of Glasson is the comment of Agbanou, *Discours*, 112, who notes that σημεῖον never has the meaning of "standard, ensign" in the NT, and that the word would then have completely different meanings in 24:3 and 24:30.

[191] Cf. 2:16; 6:23; 7:3 (thrice). Adjectival ἐν clauses also occur after πάντες at 5:15, and fourteen times in the patterned phrase "the Father who is in heaven(s)" (5:16, 45; 6:1, 6, 18; 7:1, 21; 10:32, 33; 12:50; 16:17; 18:10, 14, 19).

[192] Matt 2:2; 14:6; 21:8, 41; 24:14; 24:45; 25:31; 26:23. Other adverbial constructions include these:

1. Verb + proper noun + ἐν phrase (8:11; 13:34; 14:10)

2. Verb + anarthrous noun + ἐν phrase (12:36; 13:21, 24; 25:4; 27:29)

3. Arthrous noun + ἐν phrase + verb (1:23)

4. Proper noun + ἐν phrase + verb (6:29; 22:43)

5. Anarthrous noun + ἐν phrase + verb (8:10; 11:8; 22:16)

6. Arthrous noun + [elided copula] + ἐν phrase (3:12; 7:4)

7. Copula + arthrous noun + ἐν phrase (6:4)

8. Copula + proper noun + ἐν phrase (10:15; 12:40)

9. Genitive absolute + ἐν phrase (26:6)

[193] Turner, *Syntax*, 221–22; cf. BDF, §§ 272; 269.2.

[194] Contextually, it makes much better sense to understand these three ἐν phrase adjectivally, rather than adverbially, that is, "they love in the banquets the places of honor."

[195] Note the following:

1. Verb + arthrous noun + adjectival anarthrous ἐν phrase (2:19)

2. Verb + anarthrous noun + adjectival anarthrous ἐν phrase (6:20; 19:21)

3. Verb + πᾶς + anarthrous noun + adjectival anarthrous ἐν phrase (28:18)

4. Arthrous noun + adjectival anarthrous ἐν phrase + verb (12:5; 18:10)

5. Anarthrous noun + adjectival anarthrous ἐν phrase + copula (22:30)

[196] In Matthew's Gospel, Jesus' self-designation is always ὁ υἱὸς τοῦ ἀνθρώπου.

[197] Matt 12:40 (ἐν); 16:27 (ἐν); 17:9 (ἐκ); 19:28 (ἐπί); 25:31 (ἐν).

[198] Several commentators note an ambiguity in the stress afforded by the phrase ἐπὶ τῆς γῆς, although none of these commentators plainly prefer an adjectival sense; cf. Davies and Allison, *Matthew*, 2:93; Morris, *Matthew*, 217.

[199] The verb φαίνω, "shine, give light, be bright," appears in Matthew's Gospel only in the passive voice, with the meaning of "shine, flash" (24:27) and "appear, become visible, appear as something" (1:20; 2:7, 13, 19; 6:5, 16, 18; 9:33; 13:26; 23:27, 28; 24:30).

It is used in 24:27 as a way of comparing the suddenness of the Parousia: "For just as the lightning comes out from the east and flashes unto the west, so will the Parousia of this man be." The mere use of the same verb in 24:27 and 24:30 does not, however, support the view that the Parousia is in view in 24:30. The meaning in 24:27 is drawn directly from the comparison with lightning, and the sense is "flash." In 24:30, the sign that reveals this man in heaven is not said to "flash," but merely to "appear, become visible."

[200] There is a variant reading at 24:30. In place of τοῦ υἱοῦ τοῦ ἀνθρώπου ἐν οὐρανῷ at 24:30a Codex Bezae reads τοῦ υἱοῦ τοῦ ἀνθρώπου τοῦ ἐν οὐρανοῖς. Bezae thus explicitly reads the prepositional phrase adjectivally.

In an unpublished manuscript of April 18, 1993, Rev. Jeffrey Kloha argues that Bezae has preserved the original reading. The results of Kloha's investigation of the scribal tendencies of Bezae include the following:

1. Matt 24:30 is one of five places where Bezae reads the definite article before a prepositional phrase when NA[26] does not do so; the other examples are Mark 3:8; Luke 21:26; John 14:10; Acts 17:17.

2. Of these five cases, only in Matt 24:30 would the meaning of the verse be altered by making the prepositional phrase adjectival rather than adverbial.

3. Bezae does not show a tendency to add the definite article against the manuscript tradition. Rather, thirteen times Bezae does not have the definite article with a prepositional phrase where NA[26] does (Matt 6:6; 21:11; 24:38; Mark 5:27; 13:25; Luke 2:39; 6:41, 42; John 4:11; Acts 10:23; 15:5; 17:19). I also have noted within the text of the ED itself that whereas once Bezae adds a definite article against NA[26] (24:3), once Bezae changes the article to another word (24:17), and thrice Bezae omits the definite article altogether (24:9, 31, 38).

4. The variant reading involves three features: 1) the definite article, 2) the changing of the noun "heaven" from singular to plural, and 3) the resulting change of the prepositional phrase from an adverbial to an adjectival meaning. Accordingly, Kloha argues that the variant reading is an intentional one that shows scribal purpose to alter the meaning of the text.

5. A parallel in *Did.* 16:6 supports the reading of NA[26]. It cannot be conclusively shown, however, that the *Didache* reading is literarily dependent on Matt 24:30.

6. The reading of NA[26], however, is more likely to be a harmonization to the near context since the words of Jesus both in 24:27 and 24:29 have referred to events in the sky.

In conclusion, Kloha cites James Royse, "Scribal Habits in Early Greek New Testament Papyri" (Ph.D. diss., Graduate Theological Union, 1981), 593–615. Royse has demonstrated that in the earliest period of transmission, textual omission occurred far more frequently than additions to the text. Kloha himself remarks: "For the NA (26) reading, the strongest evidence is that provided by the Didache.... The internal evidence, however, favors the reading found in Bezae. The reading of NA (26) appears to be a harmonization to context" (p. 9). Kloha concludes that Bezae has preserved the original reading by retaining the definite article.

[201] As I shall note in the treatment of 24:30c below, 24:64 is strikingly parallel to 24:30. Each verse contains three concepts: 1) the idea of this man in heaven or seated at the right hand of power; 2) the coming of "this man *on the clouds*"; and 3) the presence of the enemies of this man (who "mourn" in 24:30b and who are present before him in 24:64).

[202] As was also true at 26:64, there is "irony" in Jesus' words at 24:30. "All the tribes of the land" will "see" the events that signal Jesus' vindication as God's Son and his session at God's right hand. But they will not "perceive" the significance of the events that they "see." This "perception" is given to the implied reader of the Gospel.

[203] Carson, "Matthew," 505. He notes that in Zechariah, the following are certain:

1. The people who are mourning are "the tribes of Israel in the land."

2. The mourning "is that of repentance."

Carson then mentions two basic positions. First is that of Kik and France, who see Matt 24:30 as retaining the sense of number 1 above, but abandoning number 2 so that the "mourning" of which Jesus speaks is wailing in the face of judgment. Second is that of "most scholars," including Carson himself, who accept change in both components of meaning. In this view, the people who, at 24:30b, are wailing in the face of judgment are not the tribes of Israel in the land but "all the peoples of the earth." Further, the mourning occurs in the face of judgment and is not Zechariah's mourning of "repentance."

There are some who think that the "mourning" in Matt 24:30 is that of repentance; Hart, "Chronology," 196; Brown, "Matthean Apocalypse," 13; Knox, "Five Comings," 51.

[204] The noun occurs thirty-one times in the NT, with twenty-one of them found in Revelation. Outside of Revelation, the noun always refers to a "tribe" of Israel or, in the plural, to the "tribes" of Israel (Matt 19:28; Luke 2:26; 22:30; Acts 13:21; Rom 11:1; Phil 3:5; Heb 7:13, 14; Jas 1:1). Jas 1:1 might be disputed, although it is likely that the reference to the "tribes" of the diaspora refers to the *Jewish* Christians to whom the epistle is written.

A "tribe" of Israel is in view at Rev 5:5; 7:4, 5, 6, 7, 8; 21:12. Elsewhere, "tribe" occurs in a string of nouns describing the peoples of the earth (Rev 5:9; 7:9; 11:9; 13:7; 14:6). At Rev 1:7, the seer alludes to Zech 12:10–14, while including the phrase "every one who pierced him." In this last passage, "all the tribes of the earth" is the correct rendering.

[205] 1. The noun with a genitive modifier refers to the land of Judah (2:6); Israel (2:20, 21); Zebulun and Naphtali (4:15); Sodom and Gomorrah (10:15); and Sodom (11:24).

2. The noun is linked with the far demonstrative pronoun and means "region" at 9:26, 31.

3. The noun may mean either "land" or "earth" at 5:5; 10:34.

4. When linked with "heaven," the noun means "earth" at 5:18, 35; 6:10, 19; 11:25; 24:35; 28:18.

5. It has the wide sense of "earth" at 5:13; 9:6; 12:40, 42; 16:19; 17:25; 18:18, 19; 23:9, 35.

6. It means "ground" at 10:29; 15:35; 25:18, 25; 27:51.

7. It means "soil" at 13:5, 8, 23.

8. It means "land" as opposed to "water" at 14:24, 34.

9. In an important passage, the noun means "land" at 27:45, rather than "earth, world." The narrator states that darkness covered the whole land, the region when Jesus was being crucified, not the entire world; cf. France, *Jesus and the Old Testament*, 237; Gundry, *Matthew*, 572–73 (with caution); Morris, *Matthew*, 720; Meier, *Matthew*, 349. Agbanou, *Discours*, 115, and Lenski, *St. Matthew's Gospel*, 1116, both take the noun at 27:45 to mean "world."

[206] Hart, "Chronology," 197.

[207] Cf. Burnett, *Testament*, 347; Manson, *Sayings of Jesus*, 242; Pesch, "Eschatologie und Ethik," 234; Lambrecht, "Parousia Discourse," 324; Argyle, *Matthew*, 185.

[208] "Jesus" or "this man" is the only subject that can be supplied for the verb "he will send." Casey, *Son of Man*, 171, supposes that "God" might be the subject, but this would have to be supplied from somewhere outside the context.

[209] The "trumpet" is a piece of symbolism that occurs in varying biblical and extrabiblical contexts; cf. Allen, *Matthew*, 259. Note the symbol's eschatological use at 1 Cor 15:52; 1 Thess 4:16; Rev 1:10; 4:1; 8:2, 6, 13; 9:14.

I would concur with Beare, "Synoptic Apocalypse," 130, who writes that in 24:31 the trumpet is "merely an incidental borrowing from the general stock" of imagery. Cf. Burnett, *Testament*, 360.

[210] Recall tension within Matthew's Gospel regarding the timing of the Gentile mission. On the one hand, 21:43 and 22:7 give the following sequence: 1) rejection of God's Son; 2) judgment on those who rejected him; and 3) mission to the Gentiles. On the other hand, the actual plot of the Gospel gives this sequence: 1) rejection of God's Son; 2) vindication of God's Son; 3) mission to all nations, both Jews and Gentiles; and 4) later judgment upon the nation of Israel.

[211] Carson, "Matthew," 506, notes the close parallelism between 13:41 and 24:31 and writes: "Only with considerable difficulty can v. 31 be interpreted as referring to Christian missions." Cf. Lagrange, *Évangile*, 468.

[212] Bruner, *Matthew 13-28*, 873; Bratcher, *Translator's Guide*, 307; Beasley-Murray, *Jesus and the Kingdom of God*, 332.

[213] Others have noted the same contrast that I am here identifying, though interpreting it differently; cf. Schniewind, *Evangelium*, 243; Fuller, "Structure of Olivet Discourse," 264; Agbanou, *Discours*, 116.

[214] One further support for the sense of "messengers" at 24:31 is the fact that in Matt 11:10 Jesus calls John the Baptist "my messenger" (ὁ ἄγγελός μου) when he cites Mal 3:1. Here is one clear instance of an eschatological human messenger being designated as an ἄγγελος.

[215] As is evident from the discussion, the parable of the Wedding Feast (22:1–14) provides important parallels to Jesus' words in 24:30–31. The parable of the Wedding Feast also connects 23:37 and 24:31. According to 23:37, it was the attitude "But you were not willing" (οὐκ ἠθελήσατε) that prevented Jesus from gathering (ἐπισυνάγω) Jerusalem's children. In the Wedding Feast, it is the same attitude that prevents the guests first invited from attending: "But they were not willing to come" (καὶ οὐκ ἤθελον ἐλθεῖν, 22:3). Consequently, the messengers are sent out to gather those who are willing. In addition, the scope of the mission that is portrayed in the Wedding Feast ("Go into the street crossings and call into the feast as many as you find") parallels Jesus' words in 24:31, "from the four winds, from the corners of heaven until their corners."

[216] Brown, "Matthean Apocalypse," 13; Knox, "Five Comings," 52; France, *Matthew*, 343–45. Garland, *Reading Matthew*, 239, writes: "The destruction of Jerusalem is therefore seen as a turning point in the mission of the church."

[217] The Greek, of course, contains no pronoun that necessitates the translation "he is near"; cf. Allen, *Matthew*, 259; Argyle, *Matthew*, 185.

[218] Some interpreters who "break" the ED between 24:31 and 24:32 attempt to show that 24:32–35 properly connects to the material that follows (24:36–25:46). In order to do this, they ignore the obvious sense of the comparison in 24:32–33. Thus, Grundmann, *Evangelium*, 509, groups 24:32–44 together under the heading "The Parousia is sudden and unforeseeable." But the whole point of 24:32–33 is to show that, whatever the referent of "it" and "all these things" may be, "it" is in fact "foreseeable"!

[219] There is no particular nuance of meaning to the term "summer." Those who attempt to draw a connection between "summer" (θέρος) and the eschatological "harvest" (θερισμός) are mistaken; cf. Agbanou, *Discours*, 113; Sabourin, *L'Évangile*, 315; Bruner, *Matthew 13-28*, 875. It is of some significance, of course, that the narrator chose not to include a nature comparison that did employ the eschatological symbol of "the harvest."

[220] Ladd, *Presence*, 321; Zahn, *Evangelium*, 661–62.

[221] Wenham, "This Generation," 130, notes the parallelism between 24:15, "When you see [ὅταν οὖν ἴδητε] the abomination of desolation," and 24:33, "when you see [ὅταν ἴδητε] all these things." This lends support to the view that "all these things" in 24:33 refers to the events of 24:15–22 that lead up to the events of 24:29–31.

[222] Curiously, Beare, *Matthew*, 472–73, agrees that Jesus' words in 24:34 do directly answer the question "When will these things be?" (24:3). He then goes on to comment that Matthew's community already knew that Jesus' answer had proved itself to be wrong.

[223] The one exception is 17:17, where Jesus calls the disciples "faithless and perverse generation." Even here, however, "the disciples" are Jesus' contemporaries.

224 Matt 11:16; 12:39, 41, 42, 45; 16:4; 23:36. Those who agree that "this generation" is a reference to Jesus' own contemporaries include Beare, *Matthew*, 472–73; Beasley-Murray, *Jesus and the Kingdom of God*, 334; Turner, "Structure," 22; Zahn, *Evangelium*, 662; Künzi, *Markus 9,1 par.*, 244; Newman and Stine, *Translator's Handbook*, 774.

Others, against the lexical evidence, claim that ἡ γενεά at 24:34 means "race" or "nation" or "type of person"; cf. Hart, "Chronology," 58; Sabourin, *L'Évangile*, 316–17; Ridderbos, *Coming*, 502; Schweizer, *Good News*, 458. Alford, *Matthew*, 244, claims that in Jer 8:3; Matt 17:17; 23:36; Luke 16:8; 17:25; Acts 2:40; Phil 2:15 ἡ γενεά is equivalent to τὸ γένος. None of these examples is convincing. Evald Lövestam, "The ἡ γενεὰ αὕτη Eschatology in Mk. 13,30 pars" in *L'Apocalypse Johannique et L'Apocalyptique dans le Nouveau Testament* (ed. J. Lambrecht; Leuven: University Press, 1980), 403–13, successfully shows that the "character" of "this generation" as a concept is negative both outside and within Matthew's Gospel. Yet he fails to show that the temporal component of meaning is ever absent.

225 Maartens, "Structuring," 105; Fuller, "Olivet Discourse," 162; Cranfield, "St. Mark 13," 291; Carson, "Matthew," 507; Zahn, *Evangelium*, 662; Bratcher, *Translator's Guide*, 308.

226 Agbanou, *Discours*, 107; Argyle, *Matthew*, 185; Filson, *Matthew*, 257; Stuart, "Observations," 454–55; Beasley-Murray, *Jesus and the Kingdom of God*, 334.

227 The uses of εὐθέως in Matthew's Gospel occur at 4:20, 22; 8:3; 13:5; 14:22, 31; 20:34; 21:2; 24:29; 25:15; 26:49, 74; 27:48. With the exception of 13:5, which means "quickly" in agricultural terms, every other use of "immediately" really does mean just that: immediately!

228 Sabourin, *L'Évangile*, 316.

229 As noted above, I understand "the sign of your Parousia and of the consummation" as an objective genitive.

230 On reading "neither the son," cf. Bruce M. Metzger, *A Textual Commentary on the Greek New Testament* (London: United Bible Societies, 1971), 62; Bratcher, *Translator's Handbook*, 309; Carson, "Matthew," 508.

231 Note "that day" (7:22; 26:29); "day of judgment" (10:15; 11:22, 24; 12:36); and "day" (24:42).

232 Cf. Vorster, "Literary Reflections," 216; Albrecht Oepke, "παρουσία, πάρειμι," *TDNT* 5:867; Brown, "Matthean Apocalypse," 16; Alford, *Matthew*, 245; Filson, *Matthew*, 258; Box, *Matthew*, 32; Sabourin, *L'Évangile*, 317; Allison, *End of the Ages*, 113; Gnilka, *Matthäusevangelium*, 2:336; Ridderbos, *Coming*, 514.

233 Only Schlatter, *Evangelist*, 713, cites verbal parallels to the phrase "day and hour." His references are Josephus, *Jewish War*, 2.457; *Antiquities*, 16.200. The second parallel is not apt; first parallel is quite close.

234 Agbanou, *Discours*, 118; Bruner, *Matthew 13-28*, 879.

235 Cranfield, "St. Mark 13," 288, writes: "The fact that Mark apparently sees no inconsistency in including in one discourse vv. 7, 29, and 32 is surely significant." Agbanou, *Discours*, 118, concludes that since the tradition reports Matt 24:36 right after 24:34, there must be no contradiction between them.

236 Howell, *Inclusive*, 107, says that 24:36 "detemporalizes" 24:34; cf. Meier, *Matthew*, 289; Sabourin, *L'Évangile*, 318; Cranfield, "St. Mark 13," 288; Agbanou, *Discours*, 107.

237 It is true, of course, that "the end" (24:6, 14) and "the Parousia" (24:27) have been mentioned in the first major section of the ED. These references occurred, however, only for the purpose of distinguishing the end and consummation from the tumults and tribulations that Jesus predicts.

[238] Cf. France, *Evangelist*, 216.

[239] Curiously, Hildegard Gollinger, " 'Ihr wißt nicht, an welchem Tag euer Herr kommt': Auslegung von Mt. 24,37–51," *BibLeb* 11 (1970): 239, and Agbanou, *Discours*, 124, claim that the γάρ with which 24:37 begins does not establish a particular connection with 24:36.

[240] Note that the comparison is imprecise. Jesus' words begin by asserting a comparison between "the *days* of Noah" and the Parousia of this man (24:37). As the comparison is drawn out in 24:38, however, it becomes clear that the comparison specifically links the Parousia with "the *day* Noah entered into the ark" (24:38).

[241] Cf. Grundmann, *Evangelium*, 511; Beare, *Matthew*, 474; Schweizer, *Good News*, 459; Zahn, *Evangelium*, 665.

Lövestam, "ἡ γενεὰ αὕτη," 104, incorrectly assumes that the sinfulness of the flood generation is part of the comparison in Jesus' words in 24:37.

[242] NA[26] places the word "those" in brackets. The reading should be omitted on two counts. First, the important witnesses that include "those" are B, D, it, sa. Those that omit it include ℵ, L, W, Θ, and families 1 and 13. Thus, the manuscript evidence is fairly evenly divided. In addition, it is more likely that "those" in 24:38 is an assimilation to the same phrase in 24:22, 23, 29. Accordingly, I omit the reading.

[243] Agbanou, *Discours*, 125, aptly comments that the four present participles (τρώγοντες, πίνοντες, γαμοῦντες, γαμίζοντες) that are linked with "were" (ἦσαν) express habitual behavior, in contrast to the aorists, "Noah entered" and "the flood came." Cf. Bratcher, *Translator's Guide*, 309; Newman and Stine, *Translator's Handbook*, 777.

[244] Owing to the majority understanding that 24:29–31 describes the Parousia, many interpreters detect a puzzling contradiction between the lack of warning signs in 24:37–39 and the dominant theme of warning signs that was present in the first major section of the ED (24:4–31). Bruner, *Matthew 13-28*, 881, is honest enough to write concerning 24:37–42: "Yet we must admit this incalculability, not-knowing, or normalcy paragraph is in an almost unbearable tension with the preceding Sermon of Signs.... There were things you could *see* earlier in the sermon; now in this part there seems to be only total *surprise*." Solutions offered in response to this tension include the following:

1. The majority seem to think that the warning signs of 24:4–31 are implicit in 24:37–39. The contrast is simply between the pagan world that ignores or misunderstands the signs and Jesus' disciples who read them aright; cf. Schlatter, *Evangelist*, 715; Argyle, *Matthew*, 186; Carson, "Matthew," 509. Bruner, *Matthew 13-28*, 881, writes: "This is instructive. The Great Tribulation occurs *while superficially all seems well*. To the unobservant, it's party time."

2. Similarly, Agbanou, *Discours*, 130, thinks that the problem is that the reason why the Parousia will be unexpected as in 24:37–39 is that people will not want to know the nature of "that day."

3. Others argue that there were, in fact, warning signs before the flood came in the days of Noah; cf. Zahn, *Evangelium*, 665; Sabourin, *L'Évangile*, 320.

4. Lagrange, *Évangile*, 471, says that there will be signs before the Parousia, but they are not mentioned in 24:37–39 because they will be very brief.

5. Hart, "Chronology," 247, concludes that the seeming contradiction between "warning signs" in 24:4–31 and "business as usual" in 24:37–39 illustrates the need to perceive the pretribulational rapture of the church.

Once again, the interpretation I have offered for 24:29–31 simply removes the difficulty. There will be signs by which the disciples and the implied reader may know the approach and nearness of the judgment on Jerusalem and the temple. By contrast, 24:37–42 speaks of the Parousia, in advance of which no signs will be given.

[245] Beare, *Matthew*, 474, is correct in noting the ambiguity of "taken" and "left" in 24:40–41. He is also correct in asserting that it doesn't really matter which "fate" is regarded as positive or negative. Matthew's style, however, would support the view that the one who is "taken" is the one who is "saved" at the Parousia. In Matthew παραλαμβάνω means "receive, accept" at 1:20, 24 and means "take along with" at 2:13, 14, 20, 21; 4:5, 8; 12:45; 17:1; 18:16; 20:17; 26:37; 27:27. Thus, it is more likely that "the one taken" is the one who is saved at the Parousia; cf. Schnackenburg, *Matthäusevangelium 16,21–28,20*, 241; Meier, *Matthew*, 291. Mounce, *Matthew*, 229, errs when he opines that "taken away" in 24:39 (αἴρω) shows that "taken" in 24:40–41 (παραλαμβάνω) signifies judgment, for different verbs are used.

[246] Matt 24:43; 25:13.

[247] The pattern at 25:13 shows that it is more likely that 24:42 acts as a conclusion to 24:37–41 than as the opening statement of a subunit 24:42–44 (as indicated by the paragraph break given in NA[26]). Gollinger, "Ihr wißt nicht," 242–43, thinks that 24:42 is transitional between the two subunits. Beare, *Matthew*, 475, and Schnackenburg, *Matthäusevangelium 16,21–28,20*, 240–41, both regard 24:42 as a conclusion to 24:37–42.

[248] Evald Lövestam, "Spiritual Wakefulness in the Synoptic Gospels," in *Spiritual Wakefulness in the New Testament* (Lund: CWK Gleerup, 1963), 85–89, thinks that the motif of the present evil age as the age of "darkness" is in the background of 24:43–44. Sabourin, *L'Évangile*, 321, notes the existence of this motif as well but says in commonsense fashion that the thief in 24:43–44 breaks in at night because that is when most thefts take place. Since there is only an implicit narrative in 24:43–44, I would agree with Sabourin in refusing to assign significance to the mention of "at night."

[249] Agbanou, *Discours*, 131, is correct in noting that one would normally expect the "householder" (ὁ οἰκοδεσπότης, 24:43) to be a reference to God, not a disciple of Jesus; cf. Matt 10:25; 13:27; 20:1, 11; 21:33 (but note 13:52). Lövestam, "Wakefulness," 98, documents the discomfort that this comparison caused the early church.

[250] Schniewind, *Evangelium*, 245, says the comparison is offensive, and therefore stronger for it; cf. Caird, *Language*, 153–155.

[251] The term is from Beare, *Matthew*, 476.

[252] Bruner, *Matthew 13-28*, 888; Alford, *Matthew*, 247; Agbanou, *Discours*, 134; Marguerat, *Jugement*, 531.

[253] Note that, formally, 24:45–51 is not a past-time narrative. Rather, the two contrasting "narratives" of the faithful, wise slave and the wicked slave are implicit.

[254] Being "wise" (φρόνιμος) is found in other eschatological contexts in Matthew's story; cf. 7:24; 10:16; 25:2, 4, 8, 9. It comprises not purely "intellectual" wisdom, but rather a practical insight into the will of God. Cf. Schniewind, *Evangelium*, 246.

[255] That the sense of "household" (οἰκετεία) in 24:45 is "fellow slaves" is made clear by the increase of responsibility in 24:47, "over all his possessions" (τὰ ὑπάρχοντα).

[256] Some believe that this parable primarily (or only) addresses the leadership of the Matthean community; cf. Beare, *Matthew*, 476; Zahn, *Evangelium*, 666; Mounce, *Matthew*, 229; Bruner, *Matthew 13-28*, 889; Meier, *Matthew*, 293.

[257] The use of "blessed" (μακάριος) in Matthew's Gospel is closely connected to the eschatological point of view; cf. 5:3–10; 11:6; 13:16; 16:17.

[258] Owing to the repetition of the theme of "delay" in 24:48; 25:5; and 25:19, it is certain that this feature of 24:45–51 is significant for the implied reader; cf. Maartens,

"Structuring," 107; Grundmann, *Evangelium*, 513; Argyle, *Matthew*, 187; Beare, *Matthew*, 478.

Some, however, insist that the theme of "delay" is only an unimportant feature of the three subunits; cf. Lambrecht, "Parousia Discourse," 329; Brown, "Matthean Apocalypse," 15; Agbanou, *Discours*, 141.

[259] For "weeping and gnashing of teeth," cf. 8:12; 13:42, 50; 22:13; 25:30.

[260] Most commentators understand "he will cut him to pieces" (διχοτομήσει, 24:51) figuratively, although there are no known parallels to this usage; cf. Sabourin, *L'Évangile*, 322; Bratcher, *Translator's Guide*, 313.

[261] I translate the genitive absolute in 25:5 causally.

[262] In translating the imperfect with an inceptive force, I am following the suggestion of Dean O. Wenthe, "The Parable of the Ten Bridesmaids (Matthew 25:1–13)," *Springfielder* 40 (1976): 10; cf. Grundmann, *Evangelium*, 518.

[263] Scholars note the odd perfect tense at 25:6, "a cry has happened" (γέγονεν). Moule, *Idiom Book*, lists this as an example of an "aoristic" perfect; cf. Carson, "Matthew," 513; James Hope Moulton, *Prolegomena*, vol. 1 of *A Grammar of New Testament Greek* by James Hope Moulton, Wilbert Francis Howard, and Nigel Turner (3d ed.; Edinburgh: T & T Clark, 1908), 145–46.

[264] Those who think that the parable's details are incongruous with Palestinian custom include Manson, *Sayings of Jesus*, 243; J. Massingberd Ford, "The Parable of the Foolish Scholars," *NovT* 9 (1967): 107; Grässer, *Problem*, 120; Karl Paul Donfried, "The Allegory of the Ten Virgins (MATT 25:1–13) as a Summary of Matthean Theology," *JBL* 93 (1974): 417. Others maintain that the depiction of the wedding and its customs corresponds to first-century realities; cf. A. W. Argyle, "Wedding Customs at the Time of Jesus," *ExpTim* 86 (1974–1975): 214.

The best position seems to be the agnostic one, namely, that not enough is known about first-century Palestinian wedding customs to evaluate the "peculiarity" of the parable's account; cf. Beare, *Matthew*, 480; Zahn, *Evangelium*, 668; Sabourin, *L'Évangile*, 324; Lövestam, "Wakefulness," 110.

[265] Cf. the section "General Features of a Narrative-Critical Approach" in chapter 1.

A further assumption underlying the debate over the extent to which Matthean parables reflect the teaching of the historical Jesus concerns the very nature of a parable. Those who assume that parables are "true to life" stories will be very concerned with whether Jesus' parables in Matthew conform to "normal" daily existence in first-century Palestine; cf. Joachim Jeremias, *The Parables of Jesus* (2d rev. ed.; New York: Charles Scribner's Sons, 1972). Others maintain (rightly, in my opinion) that even the parables of the historical Jesus were characterized by unlikely or extravagant features and were not simply "true to life" stories; cf. Norman A. Huffman, "Atypical Features in the Parables of Jesus," *JBL* 97 (1978): 207–20; Caird, *Language*, 162.

[266] For some, the central message of the parable is the exhortation "Prepare for the Parousia!" Cf. Wenthe, "Parable," 14; Beare, *Matthew*, 482; Zahn, *Evangelium*, 670. Others see the "delay of the Parousia" as the central motif; cf. J. M. Sherriff, "Matthew 25:1–13: A Summary of Matthean Eschatology?" in *Papers on the Gospels: Sixth International Congress on Biblical Studies, Oxford, 3–7 April 1978*, vol. 2 of *Studia Biblica 1978* (ed. E. A. Livingstone; Sheffield: JSOT Press, 1980), 304; Grundmann, *Evangelium*, 515; Carson, "Matthew," 512. Still others see the theme of "perseverance" as central; cf. Alford, *Matthew*, 248; Argyle, *Matthew*, 189.

[267] Donfried, "Allegory," 420–21, notes five common themes: 1) the division motif, 2) the coming of the master and the eschatological judgment, 3) the delay of the Parousia, 4) preparedness, and 5) the theme of "the door."

268 Agbanou, *Discours*, 143, notes that "then" (τότε) joins 25:1–13 to 24:45–51 "tightly" ("étroitement"); cf. Wenthe, "Parable," 9.

269 Carson, "Word-Group," 279; Bruner, *Matthew 13-28*, 904; Schweizer, *Good News*, 466; Sabourin, *L'Évangile*, 324; BAGD, 567.

270 Note the contrast with the preceding subunit. In 24:45–51, the error of the wicked slave was in thinking that the master would delay longer than he actually did. In the Ten Maidens, the error stems from not realizing that the bridegroom would delay as long as he actually did; cf. Schlatter, *Evangelist*, 719; Grundmann, *Evangelium*, 515; Alford, *Matthew*, 249; Meier, *Matthew*, 294–95; Filson, *Matthew*, 263; Grässer, *Problem*, 127.

These two contrasting features underscore for the implied reader that the time of the Parousia is utterly unknowable. It could be sooner than one might think. It might be later. Concerning that day and hour, no one knows except the Father (24:36).

271 It is unimportant whether the "lamps" (αἱ λαμπαί) are actual "torches" (Jeremias, *Parables*, 174–75) or "lamps" held on a stick (Zahn, *Evangelium*, 669).

272 For "oil" as "good works," cf. Donfried, "Allegory," 423; Agbanou, *Discours*, 149; Bruner, *Matthew 13-28*, 896–97.

I would rather side with Carson, "Matthew," 249, who writes that the "oil" is "merely an element in the narrative showing that the foolish virgins were unprepared for the delay and so shut out in the end."

273 Some see eschatological overtones in "middle of the night" and "cry" in 25:6 and "meeting" in 25:1, 6; cf. Lövestam, "Wakefulness," 85–89; Grundmann, *Evangelium*, 518; Grässer, *Problem*, 123–24.

274 Note the parallels with Matt 7:21–23. In both passages, those who are excluded from the feast or the reign of heaven cry out, "Lord, Lord!" In 7:23, Jesus declares that he will say, "I never knew you" (οὐδέποτε ἔγνων ὑμᾶς). In the parable, the bridegroom says, "I do not know you" (οὐκ οἶδα ὑμᾶς, 25:12). Note well that the "division" that takes place is one that divides those who claim a fellowship with Jesus. The foolish maidens cry out to the master, "Lord, lord." Yet, not everyone who says to him, "Lord, Lord" will enter (cf. 7:21).

275 Beare, *Matthew*, 483, says that 25:13 is not "the natural moral" of the story; cf. Grässer, *Problem*, 86, 120.

276 Cf. Manson, *Sayings of Jesus*, 243; Filson, *Matthew*, 264; Carson, "Matthew," 514; Schniewind, *Evangelium*, 248; Sabourin, *L'Évangile*, 325.

277 Cf. Bratcher, *Translator's Guide*, 317.

278 Sherriff, "Matthew 25:1–13," 302, claims that the five themes of (1) "suddenness," (2) "judgment/division," (3) "performance," (4) "delay," and (5) "watch!" run throughout the various subunits that comprise 24:37–25:13. He is not completely correct. The theme of "performance" is absent from 24:37–42; 24:43–44; and 25:1–13. Further, the theme of "delay" is absent from 24:37–42 and 24:43–44. Nevertheless, his comment is apt enough: "In its own right the story of the Ten Maidens serves as an apt summary statement of this section" (p. 303).

279 The exact force of "just as" (ὥσπερ) in 25:14 is unclear. Some see it as the first member of a comparison, the second member of which has elided and must be supplied; cf. BDF, § 453.4; Grundmann, *Evangelium*, 521–22. Others, however, see a comparison with what has preceded. Agbanou, *Discours*, 157, says that the comparative member to be supplied is "thus is the Parousia." Meier, *Matthew*, 298–99, supplies "thus is the kingdom of heaven."

There can be no doubt that "for just as" joins 25:14–30 to what has preceded. On the other hand, the shift in thematic emphasis away from the dominant motif of the suddenness of the Parousia should also be noted.

[280] Schweizer, *Good News*, 471, asserts that one talent was the equivalent of ten thousand days' wages. Sufficient is the comment of Carson, "Matthew," 516: "The sums are vast."

[281] Peter Fiedler, "Die übergebenen Talente: Auslegung von Mt 25,14–30," *BibLeb* 11 (1970): 262–63, claims that the parable is shot through with inconsistencies and contradictions. He lists, among others, the following:

1. A rich man would have more than three slaves.

2. The master possessed only ten talents, yet later calls this trust "a little."

3. At the beginning of the parable the master possesses only ten talents. How then can he give out more to the faithful slaves?

4. The words "enter the joy of your master" speak of spiritual and heavenly realities and depart from the parable's narrative world.

5. The giving of the third slave's buried talent to the one who now has ten seems unfair.

6. The words of 25:30 violate the parable itself, as is the case with point 4 above.

7. Matt 25:29 intrudes between 25:28 and 25:30.

Fiedler's analysis is a good example of finding problems where none exist. The parable never relates that the master had only three slaves. To the contrary, the master speaks to others of his slaves in 25:28. Further, the parable never claims that the eight entrusted talents were all of the master's possessions. Indeed, the very fact that the master does refer to this trust as "little" shows that he possessed far more than this amount. Although the words "enter the joy of your master" and the sentence of 25:30 are remarkable, it is not necessary to see them as "departing" from the world created by the parable. There is no overt speech about spiritual realities here.

[282] The first slave "immediately" (εὐθέως) went out, worked with his five entrusted talents, and gained five more (ἐκέρδησεν ἄλλα πέντε) talents. Likewise (ὡσαύτως) the second slave gained two more (ἐκέρδησεν ἄλλα δύο) talents.

[283] The third slave didn't "go" (πορευθείς), as the first two slaves did; rather, he "departed" (ἀπελθών). He didn't "work" or "gain"; rather, he "dug" the earth and "hid" his master's talent. Note that the talent belongs to his master.

[284] The two historic present tenses in 25:19 emphasize that 25:19 is a transition verse. These are the only two historic present tenses in the parable. As Jesus narrates the parable, he uses aorist indicatives for all of the other main verbs. Note that here, as was the case in the parable of the Ten Maidens, it is the arrival of the master that is the turning point of the parable.

[285] The very precise parallelism involves the description of the first two slaves' approach to the master, their speech to the master, and the master's speech to them.

[286] The implied reader first detects the contrast between the first two slaves and the third slave when Jesus' words narrate the approach of the third slave. Rather than describing him as one who "received" (ὁ λαβών) a trust (as with the first slave, 25:20), Jesus describes the third slave as one who "had received" (ὁ εἰληφώς, 25:24) a trust. The perfect participle of "to receive" carries this implicit judgment: "He received one talent ... and he still had it!"

[287] The third slave's words reveal his point of view with regard to his master. The implied reader knows, for at least three reasons, that the slave's words are not an

accurate portrayal of the master's character. In the first place, the master entrusted to each of the slaves a certain amount, "according to his ability" (25:15); cf. Manson, *Sayings of Jesus*, 246. In the second place, the master has already given equal praise and equal reward to the first two slaves. In the third place, the implied reader knows that the master in the parable stands for Jesus. The master is not a "hard man."

288 The master's condemnation of the third slave is all the more severe through the technique of theoretically granting the truth of the slave's charge: "You knew that I was a hard man...." Even should that have been the case, the slave's behavior would still have brought condemnation, for he should have invested his master's talent with bankers and gained at least some interest. Those who agree that the master's reply does not constitute endorsement of the slave's description of him include Grundmann, *Evangelium*, 523; Carson, "Matthew," 517; Beare, *Matthew*, 490. Some, on the other hand, think that the master accepts as valid the slave's characterization of him; cf. Bratcher, *Translator's Handbook*, 320; Agbanou, *Discours*, 158; Meier, *Matthew*, 300 (with reservations).

The Greek of 25:27 is difficult. Some take "it was necessary [ἔδει] to give my money to the bankers" as a potential indicative, and translate, "You should have given my money to the bankers." Cf. Dana and Mantey, *Grammar*, 169; Brooks and Wynbery, *Syntax*, 116; Burton, *Moods and Tenses*, § 30.

The presence of ἄν in the second clause of 25:27, "I would have received what was mine with interest," suggests another option, namely, the elision of the protasis of a contrary to fact condition. Thus, I would translate, "It was necessary for you to give my money to the bankers. And [if you had done so, εἰ ἐποίησας] when I came I would have received what was mine with interest." Cf. Bratcher, *Translator's Handbook*, 321.

289 Agbanou, *Discours*, 158, notes the parallelism between the "double" reward for the first two slaves ("I will appoint" and "enter into the joy") and the "double" punishment for the third slave ("take away" and "throw him into the outer darkness").

290 It might be said that the parable of the Talents changes the theme of "the delay of the Parousia" into the theme of "the interval until the Parousia." Inherent in the idea of "delay" are concepts of "waiting," "vigilance," and "ignorance of the time." These latter concepts receive no expression in the parable of the Talents, further showing that the Talents has dropped the theme of "delay."

291 Some commentators join the parable of the Talents, without hesitation or qualification, to the preceding material in the ED; cf. Agbanou, *Discours*, 121; Meier, *Matthew*, 276–77; Gnilka, *Matthäusevangelium*, 2:356.

Others note the uniqueness of 25:14–30; cf. Sabourin, *L'Évangile*, 319; Zahn, *Evangelium*, 667, 671.

292 The proverbial statement of 25:29 recalls the words of Jesus at 13:12, "For whoever has, it will be given to him and it will be abounded; but whoever does not have, even what he has will be taken from him." In 13:12 the saying has to do with receiving the mysteries of the reign of heaven. To know these mysteries has been given to Jesus' disciples (13:11).

In the parable of the Talents, the emphasis is not upon the receiving of revelation, but upon the life lived during the period between Jesus' resurrection and Parousia. Yet the implied reader is a disciple because he or she has also been given to know the mysteries of the reign of heaven and, chiefly, that in Jesus the reign of heaven has come into the present time in a real, though hidden, manner.

293 The parable of the Talents is a warning to the implied reader; cf. Dodd, *Parables*, 115. Yet the implied reader is the one in whom the intention of the text finds its fulfillment, namely, to live a life of faithful service.

[294] Verbal parallels between the parables of the Talents and the Wicked Tenants (21:33–46) invite a comparison. The verb "to go on a journey" (ἀποδημέω) occurs in Matthew's Gospel only at 21:33 and 25:14, 15. Also, the combination of "take away" and "give" in the passive voice occurs in both places (21:43; 24:28–29).

The parable of the Wicked Tenants speaks of the time when the reign of heaven will be taken away from the nation of Israel and given to the "nation" that is Jesus' disciples. The parable of the Talents teaches that throughout the period of time until the Parousia, Jesus has given the reign of heaven, its blessings and its responsibilities, to his disciples. But should any disciple prove to be unfaithful in his or her use of what has been entrusted, that disciple will suffer judgment, even as Israel as a nation did. The trust will be taken away and will be given to another.

[295] Agbanou, Discours, 168, has a nice turn of phrase: "Le capital d'amour et de pardon reçu du Seigneur, doit être en retour investi dans la communauté."

[296] For an excellent history of interpretation, see Gray, The Least. For a major redaction-critical treatment, see Johannes Friedrich, Gott im Bruder? Eine methodenkritische Untersuchung von Redaktion, Überlieferung und Traditionen in Mt 25,31–46 (Stuttgart: Calwer Verlag, 1977).

[297] In 25:31–46 the heavy emphasis is upon the Parousia itself. Life that was lived prior to that event enters into the subunit only for the purpose of explaining why (γάρ, 25:35, 42) the judgment comes in the manner that it does.

[298] Those who acknowledge that 25:31–46 does not belong to the genre of "parable" include Oudersluys, "Parable," 153; O. Lamar Cope, "Matthew XXV:31–46: 'The Sheep and the Goats' Reinterpreted," NovT 11 (1969): 33; Lambrecht, "Parousia Discourse," 329; Agbanou, Discours, 178; Grundmann, Evangelium, 525; Bruner, Matthew 13-28, 914; Meier, Matthew, 302; Gnilka, Matthäusevangelium, 2:367.

Some insist that 25:31–46 is a parable; cf. Gray, The Least, 351–52; John R. Donahue, "The 'Parable' of the Sheep and the Goats: A Challenge to Christian Ethics," TS 47 (1986): 10.

[299] Marguerat, Jugement, 482–83; cf. Bruner, Matthew 13-28, 913, who notes Marguerat's work, and Schnackenburg, Matthäusevangelium 16,21–28,20, 249, who comments similarly.

[300] Gray, The Least, 255–57, in surveying only twentieth-century interpretation on the two issues of "all the nations" and "the brothers of Jesus," notes no less than thirty-two differing positions.

[301] Gray, The Least, 8–9.

[302] Many have noted that 25:31–46 offers the pinnacle of Matthean Christology. Marguerat, Jugement, 488, writes that this text "represente le stade ultime dans ce [synoptique] processus de concentration christologique." Often scholars perceive an allusion to Zech 14:5: "And then the Lord my God will come and all the holy ones with him." Cf. France, Evangelist, 311; J. A. T. Robinson, "The 'Parable' of the Sheep and the Goats," NTS 2 (1956): 229; Schniewind, Evangelium, 251; Sabourin, L'Évangile, 328.

[303] What is not clear is the precise point of comparison between Jesus' separation of all the nations and the procedure followed by a shepherd. Gray, The Least, 352, thinks that in view is the swiftness with which a shepherd can recognize and separate sheep from goats. Others think that a shepherd separates the two groups because sheep can be left out at night, but goats cannot. Cf. Jeremias, Parables, 206; Oudersluys, "Parable," 153; Schnackenburg, Matthäusevangelium 16,21–28,20, 249. Some mention the possibility that the "goats" might really be "rams," in which case the motif of "strong" being separated from "weak" is introduced; cf. H. E. W. Turner, "Expounding

the Parables: The Parable of the Sheep and the Goats (Matthew 25:31–46)," *ExpTim* 77 (1965–1966): 244; Grundmann, *Evangelium*, 526. Cope, "Matthew XXV:31–46," 37, says that the sheep are whiter and thus "more commercially valuable."

304 Sabourin, *L'Évangile*, 330, properly notes the change at 25:32 from the neuter plural "all the nations" to the masculine plural "them." This shows that individuals rather than groups (literally, "nations") are in view in the judgment; cf. Tisera, *Universalism*, 270.

305 Commentators have noted that "right and left" as a symbol for "approval and condemnation" is common in ancient sources; cf. Cope, "Matthew XXV:31–46," 37; Sabourin, *L'Évangile*, 329; Beare, *Matthew*, 494; Gnilka, *Matthäusevangelium*, 2:372. For a discussion of the diverse possibilities of metaphorical meaning for the combination "right and left," see J. M. Court, "Right and Left: The Implications for Matthew 25:31–46," *NTS* 31 (1985): 223–33.

306 Note how the repetition of "then," τότε, moves the unit forward (25:31, 34, 37, 41, 44).

307 Son of God Christology is inherent in this text by virtue of the King's designation of God as "my Father."

308 The verb "inherit" occurs in Matthew's Gospel three times and only in the future tense; cf. 5:5; 19:29.

309 The list of six acts of kindness finds parallels in the OT and other sources. Gray, *The Least*, 11, notes Isa 58:7; Ezek 18:7, 16; Job 22:7; 31:32; Tob 4:16 as possible parallels; cf. Catchpole, "The Poor on Earth," 390; Grundmann, *Evangelium*, 527; Gnilka, *Matthäusevangelium*, 2:373.

Others mention differences with typical Jewish lists of piety. Missing in the list in Matt 25:35–36 is the piety surrounding the burial of the dead; cf. Beare, *Matthew*, 494; Grundmann, *Evangelium*, 527. By contrast, Agbanou, *Discours*, 188, notes that Jewish traditions do not emphasize the visitation of those who are in prison as a work of piety.

310 Some interpreters assert that the righteous answer the King "in innocent surprise" and that this element of surprise is the key to the interpretation of the pericope; cf. Paul W. Meyer, "Context as a Bearer of Meaning in Matthew," *USQR* 42 (1988): 72; Hahn, "Rede," 124; Tasker, *Matthew*, 239. Others offer the same assertion to argue against legalism in the text; cf. Marguerat, *Jugement*, 512; Carson, "Matthew," 522.

311 It is crucial to note the force of the King's words in 25:40: ἑνὶ τούτων τῶν ἀδελφῶν μου τῶν ἐλαχίστων. It does not mean "to *only* the least of my brothers," in exclusion of other "brothers" who are not "the least." The sense is "to my brothers, including and especially the least of them." Cf. Newman and Stine, *Translator's Guide*, 809.

An exact parallel in Matthew's Gospel that supports this reading occurs at 5:19, where Jesus says, "Whoever, therefore, relaxes one of the least of these commandments [μίαν τῶν ἐντολῶν τούτων τῶν ἐλαχίστων] and teaches in this way to people will be called least in the reign of heaven." The words of Jesus are not directly against the "relaxing" of *only* the least of the commands. Rather, he warns against relaxing *any* command, *even* the least one.

312 Cope, "Matthew XXV:31–46," 39, calls 25:40 and 25:45 "the dramatic climax of the passage." Cf. Catchpole, "The Poor on Earth," 392–93.

313 Moulton, *Prolegomena*, 221, states that the perfect participle κατηραμένοι (25:41) "has the full perfect force, 'having become the subjects of a curse.' " This is the only occurrence of the verb in Matthew's Gospel, and the related noun, κατάρα, does not occur at all.

314 "Eternal fire" occurs also at 18:8 as a metaphor for eschatological judgment; for "fire" as "judgment," cf. 3:10, 11, 12; 7:19; 13:40, 42, 50; 18:9.

315 In a conversation on Sept. 16, 1993, Dr. Paul Raabe pointed out to me that on the one hand, the reign into which the righteous enter was prepared "for them," whereas on the other hand the eternal fire into which the cursed enter was prepared "for the devil and his angels." Here, perhaps, is Jesus' (and the narrator's) view of the goodness of God and the tragedy of those who are rejected on the last day! Monsarrat, "Matthieu 24–25," 71, errs in stating specifically that the eternal fire is prepared for those who are cursed.

Schlatter, *Evangelist*, 728, aptly notes that a parallel to "the devil and his angels" occurs at 12:24: "Beelzebul, the ruler of the demons." Sabourin, *L'Évangile*, 329, notes a parallel in the first-century *Life of Adam and Eve*, in which Satan speaks about "other angels who were under me" (15:1) and "me, with my angels" (16:1).

316 The absence of the word "brothers" at 25:45 is not significant. It is explained by the fact that at a number of key points, the narrator abbreviates the parallelism of this scene with the prior scene. Catchpole, "The Poor on Earth," 395, notes: "Narratives moving forward in two stages frequently show a shortening and summarizing tendency in the second part."

317 Two main interpretations have been offered:

1. "All the nations" means "all peoples, Jew and Gentile, Christian and non-Christian"; cf. Tisera, *Universalism*, 272–74; Bornkamm, "End-Expectation," 23; Hahn, "Rede," 124; Beasley-Murray, *Jesus and the Kingdom of God*, 310; Beare, *Matthew*, 493.

2. "All the nations" means "all Gentile peoples, but not the Jews"; cf. Jeremias, *Parables*, 209; Hare and Harrington, "Make Disciples," 364–65.

Gray, *The Least*, 356–57, notes the controversy over the meaning of πάντα τὰ ἔθνη in Matthew's Gospel. He lists five possible understandings of "all the nations" in 25:32:

1. Christians and non-Christians, Jews and Gentiles

2. All non-Christians, with the exception of the Jews

3. All non-Christians, including the Jews

4. All humanity, which has been converted to Christianity

5. Christian leaders

Gray finds numbers 4 and 5 "exegetically untenable."

318 Graham N. Stanton, *A Gospel for a New People: Studies in Matthew* (Edinburgh: T. & T. Clark, 1992), 212, also notes that Matthew does not expect that all the nations actually will be converted to discipleship.

319 I underscore these words because of the connection they make between the rejection of the message and the treatment afforded to the messengers who bear it. Those who reject the message will also mistreat the messengers. The missionary preachers will find themselves in situations of great need.

320 Carson, "Matthew," 521: "Presupposed is the fulfillment of 24:14." Cf. Donahue, "Parable," 26–27.

321 From a narrative-critical perspective, then, a question that has vexed commentators is irrelevant. Different answers are given to the question "Are 'all the nations' in 25:32 disciples of Jesus, or non-disciples, or a mixture of both?" From the temporal vantage point afforded by Jesus' words to the disciples on the Mount of Olives, "all the nations" are not disciples, for the mission has not yet gone out to make them such.

322 Lincoln, "Story for Teachers," 121, writes: "In 25:31–46, the disciples are given the clearest preview of what will be involved in their mission of being lowly teachers with authority among the nations."

323 Recall the tension within Matthew's Gospel regarding the timing of the Gentile mission. On the one hand, the mission begins at 28:18–20. On the other hand, according to 21:43 and 22:7 that mission will begin after the "owner of the vineyard" (21:40), that is, "the king" (22:7) punishes those who reject his "son," to wit, after he "burns their city" (22:7).

324 Those who concur in this understanding of "all the nations" include Oudersluys, "The Parable," 156; Zahn, *Evangelium*, 673; Broer, "Gericht," 292; Lambrecht, "Parousia Discourse," 334; Cope, "Matthew XXV:31–46," 34; J. Ramsey Michaels, "Apostolic Hardships and Righteous Gentiles: A Study of Matthew 25:31–46," *JBL* 84 (1965): 28–29.

325 Jesus identifies himself at 25:40, 45 with those termed "his brothers" and not those termed "the least." Accordingly, those who focus on the use of "little" (μικρός) or its superlative "least" (ἐλάχιστος) are somewhat off the mark; cf. Lambrecht, "Parousia Discourse," 337–38; Lincoln, "Story for Teachers," 121; Savas Agourides, " 'Little Ones' in Matthew," *BT* 35 (1984): 332.

326 The term "brother" refers to a literal biological brother at 1:2, 11; 4:18, 21; 10:2, 21; 12:46–47; 13:55; 14:3; 17:1; 19:29; 20:24; 22:24, 25.

327 Stanton, *Gospel*, 216, says that Matthew uses "brother" eighteen times to refer to "fellow members of the Christian family." Agbanou, *Discours*, 191–92, admits that every other occurrence of "brother" in Matthew's Gospel means "disciple." He asserts, however, that is not the meaning at 25:40.

328 I owe this insight completely to Gray, *The Least*, 354. Those who concur in seeing "the least of these, my brothers" as a group separate from either "sheep" or "goats" include Cope, "Matthew XXV:31–46," 37; Broer, "Gericht," 292; Manson, *Sayings of Jesus*, 249–50; Zahn, *Evangelium*, 674.

Those who specifically reject this view include Turner, "Expounding," 245; Sabourin, *L'Évangile*, 331; Bratcher, *Translator's Handbook*, 324. Carson, "Matthew," 522, writes: "The King could point out surrounding brothers who had been compassionately treated." This latter point is difficult to visualize. It would certainly be easier if the pronoun were the far demonstrative, "those," that is, "those over there among you."

329 Matt 19:28 offers a strong parallel to this feature of 25:31–46. There Jesus promised the Twelve that they would, at the regeneration, sit on twelve thrones and judge the twelve tribes of Israel. Just as the scope of the mission is enlarged from Israel to all the nations, so is the scope of participation of the brothers of Jesus at the judgment.

330 Many, of course, argue that the ones to whom the deeds of kindness and hospitality were done are simply needy persons of any kind; cf. Tasker, *Matthew*, 238; Grundmann, *Evangelium*, 528; Sabourin, *L'Évangile*, 331; Beasley-Murray, *Jesus and the Kingdom of God*, 310. Arguments in favor of this position include the following:

1. Jesus is "the Son of Man," and there is a corporate sense in which Jesus as "the Son of Man" identifies with all humanity; cf. Beasley-Murray, *Jesus and the Kingdom of God*, 310. Gray, *The Least*, 246, notes that this view gained some prominence in the nineteenth century.

2. The universal identification of Jesus with "the poor" is related to the first beatitude, "Blessed are the poor in spirit" (5:3); cf. Grundmann, *Evangelium*, 528; Agbanou, *Discours*, 191.

In response to number 1, it can be noted that the phrase "the Son of Man" in Matthew's Gospel does not function in a corporate fashion. There is no such emphasis that would be known to the implied reader. In response to number 2, it can simply be noted that the Beatitudes are spoken to the disciples of Jesus, and only overheard by the crowds.

Those who think that "the poor" are needy persons in general admit that their posi-
tion is one that finds little direct support elsewhere in the Gospel of Matthew; cf.
Beasley-Murray, *Jesus and the Kingdom of God*, 310; Broer, "Gericht," 285; Marguerat,
Jugement, 510.

Moreover, under this interpretation the disciples of Jesus and "all the nations," who
are not Jesus' disciples, are judged at the Parousia according to different criteria (cf.
10:32–33); cf. Marguerat, *Jugement*, 486.

[331] Those who agree in this specific understanding of "my brothers" at 25:40 include
Oudersluys, "Parable," 155; Cope, "Matthew XXV:31–46," 39; Donahue, "Parable,"
25; Court, "Right and Left," 231; Lincoln, "Story for Teachers," 121. Gray, *The
Least*, 248–49, 263, notes nine nineteenth-century and eleven other twentieth-century
interpreters who hold to this view.

A number of interpreters hold that Jesus' brothers at 25:40 are simply "all Christians";
cf. France, *Evangelist*, 264; Kik, *Matthew Twenty-Four*, 112; Gundry, *Matthew*, 513–14;
Hans Freiherr von Soden, "ἀδελφός κτλ.," *TDNT* 1:145; Carson, "Matthew," 519.

[332] Filson, *Matthew*, 130; Carson, "Matthew," 245; Argyle, *Matthew*, 79; Davies and
Allison, *Matthew*, 2:174; Garland, *Reading Matthew*, 113–14. Schnackenburg,
Matthäusevangelium 1,1–16,20, 92, nicely says: "Aufnahme der Verkündiger ist eine
Auszeichnung, weil sie mit der Annahme des Evangeliums Hand in Hand geht."

[333] Lambrecht, "Parousia Discourse," 336. Stanton, *Gospel*, 220, tellingly cites both Matt
10:11–15, 40–42, and *Didache* 12–13 as evidence that "acceptance of Christian
prophets (in this case by the Christian community, not society at large) consists (in
part) in provision of shelter, food, drink, and clothing."

For a full discussion of this theme, see Weaver, *Missionary Discourse*, 86–89.
Regarding Jesus' words in 10:15, "It will be better for the land of Sodom and
Gomorrah in that day than for that city," Weaver writes: "With these words Jesus
states directly that which was left unexplained in 10.11 and merely hinted at in
10.12–13: 'worthiness' hinges directly on the reception accorded the disciples' ministry. It is in receiving or not receiving the disciples themselves and in hearing or not
hearing their words that persons reveal their worthiness or lack of it" (p. 87).

[334] Manson, *Sayings of Jesus*, 251, writes: "It is assumed that the help has been given to the
disciples of Jesus, when they were engaged on their apostolic task, when they arrived
in a strange town, hungry and thirsty, or when they were worn out and ill through toil
and travel, when they were imprisoned for preaching the Gospel—why else should the
brethren of Christ be in prison?" Cf. Cope, "Matthew XXV:31–46," 38.

[335] Michaels, "Apostolic Hardships," 36–37, offers this excellent observation: "Jesus' disciples are not so much called upon to 'help' the poor as they are to *become* poor and
outcast themselves in the completion of their world mission." In this, one might note
that such disciples would be following in the footsteps of their crucified Master.

[336] There is another "identification" text at Matt 18:5. There Jesus is speaking in a
different, nonmissionary context. He says, "Whoever receives one such child in
my name, receives me." The context in chapter 18 is that of fellowship and the
relationship between disciples of Jesus. Within that fellowship, disciples are to
receive and care for those fellow disciples who might be regarded as the least
important, including children.

[337] Stanton, *Gospel*, 217, writes that "the closing logia of the missionary discourse,
10.40–2, foreshadow the closing pericope of the final discourse."

Michaels, "Apostolic Hardships," 28, excellently notes the following parallels
between 10:40–42 and 25:31–46:

1. Both pericopae are the conclusion of a discourse, each with a missionary thrust.

2. In both pericopae, Jesus identifies himself with certain persons.

3. In 10:42, the "cup of cold water" parallels the deeds of hospitality offered to Jesus' brothers.

4. Each pericope has what Michaels calls "two groups of the redeemed." In 10:40–42, there are "the little ones" and "those who receive them." In 25:31–46, there are "the brothers of Jesus" and "the sheep."

338 Michaels, "Apostolic Hardships," 29–36, notes a remarkable number of parallels in other early Christian literature to the theme of "care offered to missionaries by those who believe their message." Included are Acts 16:30–34; 2 Cor 11:23–29; *Did.* 4:1; *2 Clem.* 17:3.

339 Argyle, *Matthew*, 193, draws a parallel with Acts 9:4, commenting: "Note how closely Christ identifies himself with his people." Stanton, *Gospel*, 218, similarly notes Acts 22:8; 26:15; 1 Cor 8:12; Ignatius, *To the Ephesians*, 6:1; Justin, *First Apology*, 16:9–10; 63:5. One might add to the list also Gal 4:13–14.

340 Weaver, *Missionary Discourse*, 104–17, labels and analyzes the various subunits of the third major section of the discourse, 10:24–42. Her label for 10:26–33 is "call to fearless witness," and for 10:34–39, "consequences of fearless witness." Her label for 10:40–42 is "ultimate significance," and she writes: "The disciples' ministry carries the authority of God himself, and thus conveys the presence of God to those who receive the disciples. In this message lies the ultimate significance of the disciples' relationship to Jesus" (p. 118).

341 Zahn, *Evangelium*, 674, specifically notes that 25:31–46 gives great comfort to the disciples and that 10:40–42 has a similar function; cf. Brown, "Matthean Apocalypse," 18. Stanton, *Gospel*, 222, notes that the shift in function is supported by the shift in genre. The prior subunits of the ED were parables. Stanton calls 25:31–46 an "apocalyptic discourse" and writes: "Its genre ... prepares the reader or listener for a change of direction in the argument of the discourse as a whole. Since apocalyptic writings usually function as consolation to groups of God's people who perceive themselves to be under threat or alienated from the society in which they live, this is likely to be the central thrust of 25:31–46."

342 Cf. Lambrecht, "Parousia Discourse," 340; Oudersluys, "Parable," 157.

343 Anderson, "Over and Over," 194–95, writes that the general effect of "anticipations" in a narrative is "to get the implied reader to ask 'how' instead of 'what.' " Such a use of foreshadowing creates "suspense of anticipation" rather than "suspense of uncertainty."

344 Grey, *The Least*, 8, writes: "Looking at the larger context, it would seem that 25:31–46, in a proleptic fashion, is integrally related to the Great Commission that occurs a few chapters later (28:16–20) where the disciples are sent to the very same people (πάντα τὰ ἔθνη) that are to be gathered before Christ at the end of time. The two scenes have to be taken together." Cf. Donahue, "Parable," 14; Brown, "Matthean Apocalypse," 19.

7

CONCLUSION

The implied reader's understanding of the ED in Matthew's Gospel is, in a way, summarized in this book's title: *Jerusalem and Parousia*. It is the contention of this monograph that, in broad strokes, the implied reader's understanding of 24:1–26:2 is just that simple. The narrative introduction of the ED includes a double question by the disciples of Jesus (24:3). With regard to the fulfillment of Jesus' prediction of the temple's destruction, as recorded in 23:37–39 and 24:2, their first question is this: "When will these things be?" The second question in 24:3 focuses on a subject that the disciples have juxtaposed to the issue of Jerusalem's destruction, namely, the Parousia of Jesus at the consummation of the age: "What will be that which shows your Parousia and the consummation of the age?"

Jesus' lengthy answer (24:4–25:46) corresponds to and answers each of these questions in turn. The first major section of the ED (24:4–35) gives an unequivocal answer to the disciples' first question. Jesus' answer is, "These things will take place before this generation passes away" (24:34). His answer to their first question also corrects the disciples' invalid eschatological point of view, by which they have closely joined together the destruction of Jerusalem and the Parousia. He warns both the disciples and the implied reader not to misinterpret the normal tumults of history as signs of the consummation of the age (24:4–8). When false prophets and false christs appear, they are not to be believed (24:23–26). The Parousia will carry its own power of self-attestation (24:27–28). Until the Parousia, the disciples of Jesus will commit themselves to the heralding of the Gospel of the reign of heaven to all the nations (24:14).

After answering (and correcting) the disciples' first question, in the second major section of the ED (24:36–25:46) Jesus addresses their second query. This is the summary of his lengthy response: "There will be no 'sign' of the Parousia and of the consummation of the age. Therefore, be ready and live faithfully until that unknown and unknowable day. Do not, moreover, flag or wear out in the missionary enterprise, for you go out as my brothers, and those who accept you accept me."

There are no positive indications from within the story of Matthew's Gospel that the disciples, to whom Jesus spoke the ED, understood or fully grasped the import of this, the last of the great discourses in Matthew's Gospel. Such incomprehension on the part of the disciples would be no surprise. The implied reader, however, will know how to interpret Jesus' words. Even with regard to the most difficult part of the ED (24:29–31), the implied reader will be able to discern the eschatological interpretation that Jesus' words there place upon the destruction of the temple and the ensuing fullness of the mission to the Gentiles.

For the implied reader has grasped the entire eschatological point of view of the remarkable and coherent story that is the Gospel of Matthew.

It is a remarkable story in that both its narrator and its protagonist make extravagant claims about the time in which the plotted events of the narrative occur. The narrator of the story reveals the truth that, beginning with the origin of Jesus, who is called Christ (1:16), the present time is the time of fulfillment (1:17, 23), the time when the eschatological reign of heaven begins to work in the world. Already in those days of fulfillment, angelic visitations, and a miraculous virginal conception, John the Baptist proclaims the arrival of the reign of heaven (3:2). Indeed, Jesus himself echoes, in his first public proclamation, the eschatological message of the Baptist (4:17). By his exorcisms (12:28) and in his parables that speak of things to which the action of the reign of heaven already may be likened (13:24, 31, 33, 44, 45, 47), Jesus himself reinforces the narrator's point of view. Even now the bridegroom is here (9:15) and the time of the wedding feast has begun (22:1–14). Already the reign of heaven is present and at work, even though it is coming in hidden and unexpected ways (11:7–15). Further, in contrast with John's own accurate but insufficient point of view, Jesus' words and deeds reveal that the dominant purpose of his end-time ministry is not to judge the people, but to save them from their sins (1:21; 11:2–6).

The whole of Jesus' ministry is eschatological in character. But because the goal to which the story's plotted events points is the suffering, death, and resurrection of Jesus, the most dramatic eschatological colors are reserved for the portrayal of these events. I have argued that Jesus' words in 16:28 are most importantly fulfilled when in Gethsemane he obediently accepts the Father's will that he drink the cup that leads to his suffering and death (26:36–46). In this scene, which opens the door to and sets in motion the passion narrative, Jesus paradoxically shows himself as "this man coming with his royal power" (16:28).

I have further argued that, whereas James and John misunderstand their own question about sitting on Jesus' right and left in his royal reign (20:20–23), the narrator portrays Jesus' crucifixion as his "enthronement" as the true King of the Jews, and the two thieves crucified on either side as those who sit on his right and his left in his royal rule (27:27–38). The implied reader understands that the passion of Jesus is an event of eschatological import, for he or she observes the end-time signs that accompany Jesus' death and concurs with the soldiers' confession, "Truly this man was the Son of God" (27:45–54).

To be sure, the reign of heaven that Jesus' present ministry brings into the time of the story is only a hidden, even paradoxical, manifestation of eschatological power and reality. The final goal of history in the world of Matthew's story is the consummation of the age. Then, Jesus will judge each according to his work (16:27). Then, all the nations to whom the Gospel of the reign has been heralded will be gathered before this man, and he will separate them as he sits on his throne in judgment (25:31–46). As was noted above, the time of that final day is utterly unknown to the implied reader (24:36). The implied reader does not, however, expect the consummation of the age in the near future (24:14; 24:48; 25:5, 19; 26:13). He or she knows that the mission of Jesus' disciples will go out into all the world as a witness to all the nations (24:14; 26:13).

Because the time of Jesus' ministry has such an eschatological cast, the implied reader has accepted the primary corollary to that reality. This corollary is the truth that human response to the ministry of this end-time Christ also carries eschatological significance. Jesus' own words repeatedly emphasize this theme. Those who respond in discipleship already possess the reign of heaven in the present time of the story (5:3, 10), for Jesus' whole ministry brings salvation, and his atoning death procures the forgiveness of sins (26:28). These same ones who respond in obedient discipleship also will enter into the consummated reign of heaven on the last day (7:21–23). Even though Jesus' divinely ordained purpose is one of eschatological salvation, there is a dark side to this corollary of eschatological response. For many in Israel, and especially those who are its religious leaders, do not become Jesus' disciples. Rather, they oppose John and Jesus and rise up in opposition against them (21:23–32). They put to death both eschatological Elijah and the Christ, whose way he prepared (17:12). As Jesus so consistently styles them, "this generation," the generation of the time of eschatological fulfillment, will be judged on the last day as the consequence of their failure to respond in discipleship to Jesus (11:16–24; 12:31–45).

Yet judgment will not only come for "this generation" on the last day. Even as discipleship results in both final blessing and present salvation, so also does the opposition to Jesus of "this generation" result in a judgment within history against the nation. By means of the parables of the Wicked Tenants (21:33–46) and the Wedding Feast (22:1–14), as well as the controversy regarding the Sonship of the Christ (22:41–46), Jesus reveals that the nation who rejects him as the Christ will receive God's judgment already within the span of their own generation. The reign of heaven will be taken away from them. Their city will be burned. They, as the enemies of the Christ, will be put under his feet even as he sits at the right hand of God. Jesus' diatribe against the scribes, Pharisees, and the city of Jerusalem itself culminates in the prediction of desolation upon Jerusalem's house, the temple (23:38).

Such judgment possesses an eschatological character. It partakes of the same nature as the judgment on the last day. It will be manifested to the enemies of Jesus, however, "from now on," as Jesus' answer to his enemies makes abundantly clear (26:64). I have argued that, given the entire context of the Gospel's story, the implied reader will know that Jesus' words to the high priest in 26:64 find a threefold fulfillment. First, the signs at Jesus' death and especially the tearing of the temple curtain give evidence that this man is seated at God's right hand and has been invested with power by the Ancient of Days, as Ps 110:1 and Dan 7:13–14 declare. Further, the tomb guards' testimony also reveals the same truth to the obdurate religious leaders (28:11–15). Finally and most climactically, the destruction of Jerusalem's temple, which will come upon this generation (23:36), is God's judgment in fulfillment of Jesus' words to the high priest.

In similar fashion, I have argued that Jesus' temporal limitation of the Twelve's mission to Israel (10:23) is also fulfilled when the predicted destruction of Jerusalem occurs. The fall of the city will be "the coming of this man," the nearness of which must cause the Twelve to hasten through the cities of Israel. For they will not complete those cities until that eschatological judgment comes. Jesus' words in 23:34–36 repeat this solemn and tragic truth as well. There he promises this generation that he will send emissaries. As those emissaries "flee to the next city" (10:23), they will be rejected and mistreated and killed "from city to city" (23:34), so that all the righteous blood of history might come upon them. And so, in the view of the narrator and Jesus, it shall.

Accordingly, the eschatological preaching, healing, and exorcism mission to the lost sheep of Israel as a nation is of a limited duration. It will come to a premature end. This is not the case with the worldwide mission to all the nations that explodes into the time beyond the temporal boundaries of the Gospel's plotted events (28:18–20). Even though divine judgment will come upon the nation that rejected the Son of God, the missionary preaching of the reign of heaven, along with triune Baptism and comprehensive teaching of the commands of Jesus, will continue until the consummation of the age (28:19–20). The time in which the implied reader finds himself or herself is the time of mission to all the nations. Despite hatred and persecution (24:9), hunger and imprisonment (25:35–36, 42–43), Jesus' missionary brothers, beginning with the Eleven (28:10), will go in order to make disciples throughout the world.

Their proclamation will especially focus on the death and resurrection of Jesus for, by wonderful coincidence, the woman who anointed Jesus' body for burial will be known wherever that message is heralded; her story will be told (26:13). At a time known only to God, the consummation of the age will come when that heralding will have been completed. Then, the Judge will come and sit upon his throne. All humanity will be separated into two groups, owing to their acceptance or rejection, their hospitality or neglect of the missionary brothers of Jesus (25:31–46).

The world created by the narrative of Matthew's Gospel is remarkable, to be sure. Yet it is also remarkably simple, and the contours of its eschatological point of view are revealed as coherent and clear. Jesus is the Christ. He brings salvation and judgment. The time of the story has an eschatological character. So do all the days of mission between the resurrection of Jesus and his Parousia. The judgment day will come. Until then, the implied reader will, in obedient discipleship, participate in the mission to all the nations.

This is the understanding of the implied reader. Real readers of this story are invited, at least temporarily, to understand and accept this story's values on their own terms. More than this, Matthew's Gospel makes a powerful appeal, through the words of its protagonist, to every human reader. Let the one who has ears to hear hear.

BIBLIOGRAPHY

Aalen, Sverre. " 'Reign' and 'House' in the Kingdom of God in the Gospels." *New Testament Studies* 8 (1961–1962): 215–40.

Achtemeier, Paul J. "An Apocalyptic Shift in Early Christian Tradition: Reflections on Some Canonical Evidence." *Catholic Biblical Quarterly* 45 (1983): 231–48.

Agbanou, Victor K. *Le Discours Eschatologique de Matthieu 24–25: Tradition et Rédaction.* Paris: Libraire Lecoffre, 1983.

Agourides, Savas. " 'Little Ones' in Matthew." *The Bible Translator* 35 (1984): 329–34.

Alford, Henry. *Matthew-Mark.* Vol. 1, Part 1 of *Alford's Greek Testament: An Exegetical and Critical Commentary.* Grand Rapids: Guardian, 1976.

Allen, Willoughby C. *A Critical and Exegetical Commentary on the Gospel according to S. Matthew.* New York: Charles Scribner's Sons, 1907.

Allison, Dale C. "Elijah Must Come First." *Journal of Biblical Literature* 103 (1984): 256–58.

———. *The End of the Ages Has Come: An Early Interpretation of the Passion and Resurrection of Jesus.* Philadelphia: Fortress, 1985.

———. "Matt. 23:39 = Luke 13:35b as a Conditional Prophecy." *Journal for the Study of the New Testament* 18 (1983): 75–84.

Anderson, Janice Cappell. "Double and Triple Stories, the Implied Reader, and Redundancy in Matthew." *Semeia* 31 (1985): 71–89.

———. "Over and Over and Over Again: Studies in Matthean Repetition." Ph.D. diss., University of Chicago Divinity School, 1985.

Arens, Eduardo, S. M. *The ΗΛΘΟΝ-Sayings in the Synoptic Tradition: A Historico-Critical Investigation.* Göttingen: Vandenhoeck & Ruprecht, 1976.

Argyle, A. W. *The Gospel according to Matthew.* Cambridge: Cambridge University Press, 1963.

———. "Wedding Customs at the Time of Jesus." *Expository Times* 86 (1974–1975): 214–15.

Arndt, William F., and F. Wilbur Gingrich. *A Greek-English Lexicon of the New Testament and Other Early Christian Literature.* A translation and adaptation of the 4th revised and augmented ed. of Walter Bauer's *Griechisch-Deutsches Wörterbuch zu den Schriften des Neuen Testaments und der übrigen urchristlichen Literatur.* 2d ed. revised and augmented by F. Wilbur Gingrich and Frederick W. Danker from Walter Bauer's 5th ed., 1958. Chicago: University of Chicago Press, 1979.

Barth, Gerhard. "Matthew's Understanding of the Law." Pages 58–164 in *Tradition and Interpretation in Matthew.* Edited by Günther Bornkamm, Gerhard Barth, and Heinz J. Held. London: SCM Press, 1963.

Bauer, David Robert. *The Structure of Matthew's Gospel: A Study in Literary Design.* Journal for the Study of the New Testament Supplement Series 31. Bible and Literature Series 15. Sheffield: Almond Press, 1988.

Beare, Francis Wright. *The Gospel according to Matthew: Translation, Introduction and Commentary.* San Francisco: Harper & Row, 1981.

———. "The Synoptic Apocalypse: Matthean Version." Pages 117–33 in *Understanding the Sacred Text.* Edited by John Reumann. Valley Forge, Pa.: Judson, 1972.

Beasley-Murray, George. "Jesus and Apocalyptic: With Special Reference to Mark 14,62." Pages 415–29 in *L'Apocalypse Johannique et L'Apocalyptique dans le Nouveau Testament*. Edited by Jan Lambrecht. Leuven: University Press, 1980.

———. *Jesus and the Future*. London: Macmillan, 1954.

———. *Jesus and the Kingdom of God*. Grand Rapids: Eerdmans, 1986.

———. *Jesus and the Last Days: The Interpretation of the Olivet Discourse*. Peabody, Mass.: Hendrickson, 1993.

———. "New Testament Apocalyptic: A Christological Eschatology." *Review and Expositor* 72 (1975): 317–30.

Becker, Joachim. *Messianic Expectation in the Old Testament*. Translated by David E. Green. Philadelphia: Fortress, 1980.

Berkey, Robert F. "ΕΓΓΙΖΕΙΝ, ΦΘΑΝΕΙΝ, and Realized Eschatology." *Journal of Biblical Literature* 82 (1963): 177–87.

Black, Matthew. "Jesus and the Son of Man." *Journal for the Study of the New Testament* 1 (1978): 4–18.

Blass, F., and A. DeBrunner. *A Greek Grammar of the New Testament and Other Early Christian Literature*. Translated and revised by Robert W. Funk. Chicago: University of Chicago Press, 1961.

Bloch, Renee. "Methodological Note for the Study of Rabbinic Literature." Pages 51–76 in *Approaches to Ancient Judaism: Theory and Practice*. Edited by William Scott Green. Missoula: Scholars Press, 1978.

Blomberg, Craig. *Interpreting the Parables*. Downers Grove, Ill.: InterVarsity, 1990.

———. *Matthew*. The New American Commentary. Nashville: Broadman, 1992.

Booth, Wayne C. *The Rhetoric of Fiction*. 2d ed. Chicago: University of Chicago Press, 1983.

Borg, Marcus. "A Temperate Case for a Non-Eschatological Jesus." *Forum* 2 (1986): 81–102.

Bornkamm, Günther. "End-Expectation and Church in Matthew." Pages 15–52 in *Tradition and Interpretation in Matthew*. Edited by Günther Bornkamm, Gerhard Barth, and Heinz J. Held. London: SCM Press, 1963.

Boyer, James L. "Second Class Conditions in New Testament Greek." *Grace Theological Journal* 3 (1982): 81–88.

Bratcher, Robert G. *The Kingdom of God: The Biblical Concept and Its Meaning for the Church*. New York: Abingdon, 1953.

———. *A Translator's Guide to the Gospel of Matthew*. Helps for Translators. London: United Bible Societies, 1981.

Broer, Ingo. "Das Gericht des Menschensohnes über die Völker: Auslegung von Mt 25,31–46." *Bibel und Leben* 11 (1970): 273–95.

———. "Redaktionsgeschichtliche Aspekte von MT. 24:1–28." *Novum Testamentum* 35 (1993): 209–33.

Brooks, James A., and Carlton L. Winbery. *Syntax of New Testament Greek*. Lanham, Md.: University Press of America, 1979.

Brown, Francis, S. R. Driver, and Charles A. Briggs, eds. *A Hebrew and English Lexicon of the Old Testament*. Oxford: Clarendon Press, 1976.

Brown, Raymond E. "The Pater Noster as an Eschatological Prayer." Pages 217–53 in *New Testament Essays*. Milwaukee: Bruce, 1965.

Brown, Raymond, Karl Donfried, and John Reumann, eds. *Peter in the New Testament: A Collaborative Assessment by Protestant and Roman Catholic Scholars*. Minneapolis: Augsburg, 1973.

Brown, Schuyler. "The Matthean Apocalypse." *Journal for the Study of the New Testament* 4 (1979): 2–27.

Bruner, Frederick Dale. *The Christbook: A Historical/Theological Commentary (Matthew 1–12)*. Waco: Word, 1987.

———. *Matthew*. Vol. 2: *The Churchbook (Matthew 13–28)*. Dallas: Word, 1990.

Burnett, Fred W. "Prolegomena to Reading Matthew's Eschatological Discourse: Redundancy and the Education of the Reader in Matthew." *Semeia* 31 (1985): 91–109.

———. *The Testament of Jesus-Sophia: A Redaction-Critical Study of the Eschatological Discourse in Matthew*. Washington, D.C.: University Press of America, 1979.

Burton, Ernest De Witt. *Syntax of the Moods and Tenses in New Testament Greek*. 3d ed. Repr., Grand Rapids: Kregel, 1976.

Caird, George B. *Jesus and the Jewish Nation*. London: Athlone, 1965.

———. *The Language and Imagery of the Bible*. Philadelphia: Westminster, 1980.

Campbell, J. Y. "The Kingdom of God Has Come." *Expository Times* 48 (1936–1937): 91–94.

Cargal, Timothy B. " 'His Blood Be upon Us and upon Our Children': A Matthean Double Entendre?" *New Testament Studies* 37 (1991): 101–12.

Carson, Donald A. "Matthew." Pages 3–600 in volume 8 of *The Expositor's Bible Commentary*. Edited by Frank E. Gaebelein. Grand Rapids: Zondervan, 1984.

———. "The ΟΜΟΙΟΣ Word-Group as Introduction to Some Matthean Parables." *New Testament Studies* 31 (1985): 277–82.

Casey, Maurice. *The Son of Man: The Interpretation and Influence of Daniel 7*. London: SPCK, 1979.

Catchpole, David R. "The Answer of Jesus to Caiaphas (MATT. XXVI.64)." *New Testament Studies* 17 (1970–1971): 213–26.

———. "The Poor on Earth and the Son of Man in Heaven: A Re-Appraisal of Matthew XXV.31–46." *Bulletin of the John Rylands Library* 61 (1978–1979): 355–97.

Charette, Blaine. "A Harvest for the People? An Interpretation of Matthew 9:37f." *Journal for the Study of the New Testament* 38 (1990): 29–35.

Charlesworth, James H. "The Concept of the Messiah in the Pseudepigrapha." Pages 188–218 in volume 19.1 of *Aufstieg und Niedergang der Römischen Welt*, part 2: *Principat*. Edited by Wolfgang Haase. Berlin: Walter de Gruyter, 1979.

Charlesworth, James H., ed. *The Old Testament Pseudepigrapha*. 2 vols. Garden City, N.Y.: Doubleday, 1983.

Chatman, Seymour. *Story and Discourse: Narrative Structure in Fiction and Film*. Ithaca: Cornell University Press, 1978.

Chilton, Bruce. *A Galilean Rabbi and His Bible: Jesus' Use of the Interpreted Scripture of His Time*. Wilmington: Michael Glazier, 1984.

———. *The Glory of Israel: The Theology and Provenience of the Isaiah Targum*. Journal for the Study of the Old Testament Supplement Series 23. Sheffield: JSOT Press, 1982.

———. *God in Strength: Jesus' Announcement of the Kingdom*. Studien zum Neuen Testament und seiner Umwelt, series B, vol. 1. Freistadt: Plöchl, 1979.

———. "Introduction." Pages 1–26 in *The Kingdom of God in the Teaching of Jesus*. Edited by Bruce Chilton. Philadelphia: Fortress, 1984.

———. " 'Not to Taste Death': A Jewish, Christian and Gnostic Usage." Pages 29–36 in *Papers on the Gospels: Sixth International Congress on Biblical Studies, Oxford, 3–7 April 1978*. Vol. 2 of *Studia Biblica 1978*. Edited by E. A. Livingstone. Sheffield: JSOT Press, 1980.

Collins, John H. "The Kingdom of God in the Apocrypha and Pseudepigrapha." Pages 81–96 in *The Kingdom of God in 20th-Century Interpretation*. Edited by Wendell Willis. Peabody, Mass.: Hendrickson, 1987.

Cope, O. Lamar. "The Death of John the Baptist in the Gospel of Matthew; or, the Case of the Confusing Conjunction." *Catholic Biblical Quarterly* 38 (1976): 515–19.

———. "Matthew XXV:31–46: 'The Sheep and the Goats' Reinterpreted." *Novum Testamentum* 11 (1969): 32–44.

———. " 'To the Close of the Age': The Role of Apocalyptic Thought in the Gospel of Matthew." Pages 113–24 in *Apocalyptic and the New Testament*. Edited by Joel Marcus and Marion L. Soards. Journal for the Study of the New Testament Supplement Series 24. Sheffield: Sheffield Academic Press, 1989.

Cotter, A. C. "The Eschatological Discourse." *Catholic Biblical Quarterly* 1 (1939): 125–32, 204–13.

Court, J. M. "Right and Left: The Implications for Matthew 25:31–46." *New Testament Studies* 31 (1985): 223–33.

Cranfield, C. E. B. "St. Mark 13." *Scottish Journal of Theology* 6 (1953): 189–96, 287–303; 7 (1954): 284–303.

Cranmer, David J. "Digressions Introduced by 'for...' " *The Bible Translator* 35 (1984): 240–41.

Dahl, Nils Alstrup. "The Passion Narrative in Matthew." Pages 42–55 in *The Interpretation of Matthew*. Edited by Graham Stanton. Philadelphia: Fortress, 1983.

Dana, H. E., and Julius R. Mantey. *A Manual Grammar of the Greek New Testament*. New York: Macmillan, 1955.

Danby, Herbert. *The Mishnah: Translated from the Hebrew with Introduction and Brief Explanatory Notes*. Oxford: Oxford University Press, 1933.

Daube, David. "The Abomination of Desolation." Pages 418–37 in *The New Testament and Rabbinic Judaism*. London: Athlone, 1956.

Davies, W. D., and Dale C. Allison Jr. *A Critical and Exegetical Commentary on the Gospel according to Saint Matthew*. Edinburgh: T. & T. Clark, 1988 (vol. 1) and 1991 (vol. 2).

Denis, Albert-Marie, O. P. *Concordance Grecque des Pseudepigraphes d'Ancien Testament*. Louvain-la-Neuve: Universite Catholique de Louvain, Institut Orientaliste, 1987.

Dodd, C. H. "The Kingdom of God Has Come." *Expository Times* 48 (1936–1937): 138–42.

———. *The Parables of the Kingdom*. Rev. ed. New York: Charles Scribner's Sons, 1961.

Donahue, John R. "The 'Parable' of the Sheep and the Goats: A Challenge to Christian Ethics." *Theological Studies* 47 (1986): 3–31.

Donfried, Karl Paul. "The Allegory of the Ten Virgins (MATT 25:1–13) as a Summary of Matthean Theology." *Journal of Biblical Literature* 93 (1974): 415–28.

Edwards, Richard A. "Narrative Implications of *Gar* in Matthew." *Catholic Biblical Quarterly* 52 (1990): 636–55.

———. "Reading Matthew: The Gospel as Narrative." *Listening* 24 (1989): 251–61.

Ellis, Peter F. *Matthew: His Mind and His Message*. Collegeville, Minn.: Liturgical Press, 1974.

Elmore, W. Emory. "Linguistic Approaches to the Kingdom: Amos Wilder and Norman Perrin." Pages 53–66 in *The Kingdom of God in 20th-Century Interpretation*. Edited by Wendell Willis. Peabody, Mass.: Hendrickson, 1987.

Epp, Eldon Jay. "Mediating Approaches to the Kingdom: Werner Georg Kümmel and George Eldon Ladd." Pages 35–52 in *The Kingdom of God in 20th-Century Interpretation*. Edited by Wendell Willis. Peabody, Mass.: Hendrickson, 1987.

Faierstein, Morris M. "Why Do the Scribes Say That Elijah Must Come First?" *Journal of Biblical Literature* 100 (1981): 75–86.

Farmer, Ron. "The Kingdom of God in the Gospel of Matthew." Pages 119–30 in *The Kingdom of God in 20th-Century Interpretation*. Edited by Wendell Willis. Peabody, Mass.: Hendrickson, 1987.

Feuillet, A. "Le Sens du Mot Parousie dans L'Évangile de Matthieu: Comparaison entre Matth.xxiv et Jac.v, 1–11." Pages 261–80 in *The Background of the New Testament and Its Eschatology*. Edited by W. D. Davies and D. Daube. Cambridge: Cambridge University Press, 1956.

Fiedler, Peter. "Die übergebenen Talente: Auslegung von Mt 25,14–30." *Bibel und Leben* 11 (1970): 259–72.

Filson, Floyd V. *A Commentary on the Gospel according to St. Matthew*. London: Adam & Charles Black, 1960.

Fitzmyer, Joseph A. "Another View of the 'Son of Man' Debate." *Journal for the Study of the New Testament* 4 (1979): 58–68.

———. "More about Elijah Coming First." *Journal of Biblical Literature* 104 (1985): 295–96.

Ford, J. Massingberd. "The Parable of the Foolish Scholars." *Novum Testamentum* 9 (1967): 107–23.

France, R. T. *Jesus and the Old Testament: His Application of Old Testament Passages to Himself and His Mission*. London: Tyndale, 1971.

———. *Matthew: Evangelist and Teacher*. Grand Rapids: Zondervan, 1989.

Franzmann, Martin H. *Follow Me: Discipleship according to Saint Matthew*. St. Louis: Concordia, 1961.

Freedman, David Noel, Gary A. Herion, David F. Graf, John D. Pleins, and Astrid Beck, eds. *The Anchor Bible Dictionary*. 6 vols. New York: Doubleday, 1992.

Frei, Hans. *The Eclipse of Biblical Narrative: A Study in Eighteenth and Nineteenth Century Hermeneutics*. New Haven: Yale University Press, 1974.

Fuller, George Cain. "The Olivet Discourse: An Apocalyptic Timetable." *Westminster Theological Journal* 28 (1966): 157–63.

———. "The Structure of the Olivet Discourse." Th.D. diss., Westminster Theological Seminary, 1964.

Fuller, Reginald. "Jesus, Paul, and Apocalyptic." *Anglican Theological Review* 71 (1989): 134–42.

Garland, David E. *The Intention of Matthew 23*. Leiden: E. J. Brill, 1979.

———. *Reading Matthew: A Literary and Theological Commentary on the First Gospel*. New York: Crossroad, 1993.

Gerhardsson, Birger. "The Matthean Version of the Lord's Prayer (Matt 6:9b–13): Some Observations." Pages 207–20 in volume 1 of *The New Testament Age: Essays in Honor of Bo Reicke*. Edited by William C. Weinrich. Macon, Ga.: Mercer University Press, 1984.

Giblin, Charles H. "Theological Perspective and Matthew 10:23b." *Theological Studies* 29 (1968): 637–61.

Glasson, T. Francis. "The Ensign of the Son of Man (MATT. XXIV.30)." *Journal of Theological Studies* 15 (1964): 299–300.

Gnilka, Joachim. *Das Matthäusevangelium*. Parts 1 and 2. Freiburg: Herder, 1986.

Gollinger, Hildegard. " 'Ihr wißt nicht, an welchem Tag euer Herr kommt': Auslegung von Mt. 24,37–51." *Bibel und Leben* 11 (1970): 238–47.

Goodwin, William W. *A Greek Grammar*. Repr., New York: St. Martin's, 1987.

Granger, John W. "Matthew's Use of Apocalyptic." Th.D. diss., New Orleans Baptist Theological Seminary, 1990.

Grässer, Erich. *Das Problem der Parusieverzögerung in den synoptischen Evangelien und in der Apostelgeschichte*. Berlin: Verlag Alfred Töpelmann, 1957.

Gray, Sherman. *The Least of My Brothers, Matthew 25:31–46: A History of Interpretation*. Society of Biblical Literature Dissertation Series 114. Atlanta: Scholars Press, 1989.

Green, Joel B., Scot McKnight, and I. Howard Marshall, eds. *Dictionary of Jesus and the Gospels*. Downers Grove, Ill.: InterVarsity, 1992.

Green, William S. "Introduction: Messiah in Judaism: Rethinking the Question." Pages 1–14 in *Judaisms and Their Messiahs at the Turn of the Christian Era*. Edited by J. Neusner, W. S. Green, and E. S. Frerichs. New York: Cambridge University Press, 1987.

Grundmann, Walter. *Das Evangelium nach Matthäus*. Berlin: Evangelische Verlagsanstalt, 1968.

Guelich, Robert. "The Matthean Beatitudes: 'Entrance-Requirements' or Eschatological Blessings?" *Journal of Biblical Literature* 95 (1976): 415–34.

———. *The Sermon on the Mount: A Foundation for Understanding*. Waco: Word, 1982.

Gundry, Robert H. *Matthew: A Commentary on His Literary and Theological Art*. Grand Rapids: Eerdmans, 1982.

Haenchen, Ernst. "Matthäus 23." *Zeitschrift für Theologie und Kirche* 48 (1951): 38–63.

Hagner, Donald. "Apocalyptic Motifs in the Gospel of Matthew: Continuity and Discontinuity." *Horizons in Biblical Theology* 7 (1985): 53–82.

———. *Matthew 1–13*. Dallas: Word, 1993.

Hahn, Ferdinand. "Die Eschatologische Rede Matthäus 24 und 25." Pages 109–26 in *Studien zum Matthäusevangelium: Festschrift für Wilhelm Pesch*. Edited by Ludger Schenke. Stuttgart: Verlag Katholisches Bibelwerk, 1988.

Hare, Douglas R. A. *Matthew*. Interpretation: A Bible Commentary for Teaching and Preaching. Louisville: John Knox, 1993.

———. *The Theme of Jewish Persecution of Christians in the Gospel according to St. Matthew*. Cambridge: Cambridge University Press, 1967.

Hare, Douglas R. A., and Daniel Harrington. " 'Make Disciples of All the Gentiles' (MT 28:19)." *Catholic Biblical Quarterly* 37 (1975): 359–69.

Harrington, Daniel J. *The Gospel of Matthew*. Collegeville, Minn.: Liturgical Press, 1991.

Hart, John F. "A Chronology of Matthew 24:1–44." Th.D. diss., Grace Theological Seminary, 1986.

Hatch, Edwin, and Henry A. Redpath. *A Concordance to the Septuagint and the Other Greek Versions of the Old Testament*. 3 vols. Repr., Grand Rapids: Baker, 1987.

Heil, John Paul. "The Blood of Jesus in Matthew: A Narrative-Critical Perspective." *Perspectives in Religious Studies* 18 (1991): 117–24.

————. *The Death and Resurrection of Jesus: A Narrative-Critical Reading of Matthew 26–28*. Minneapolis: Fortress, 1991.

————. "Ezekiel 34 and the Narrative Strategy of the Shepherd and Sheep Metaphor in Matthew." *Catholic Biblical Quarterly* 55 (1993): 698–708.

————. "The Narrative Structure of Matthew 27:55–28:20." *Journal of Biblical Literature* 110 (1991): 419–38.

Higgins, A. J. B. "The Sign of the Son of Man (MATT. XXIV.30)." *New Testament Studies* 9 (1962–1963): 380–82.

Hill, David. "The Figure of Jesus in Matthew's Story: A Response to Professor Kingsbury's Literary-Critical Probe." *Journal for the Study of the New Testament* 21 (1984): 37–52.

————. *The Gospel of Matthew*. London: Oliphants, 1972.

Hooker, Morna D. "The Prohibition of Foreign Missions (Mt 10:5–6)." *Expository Times* 82 (1970–1971): 361–65.

Horbury, William. "The Messianic Associations of 'The Son of Man.' " *Journal of Theological Studies*, New Series, 36 (1985): 34–55.

Horsley, Richard A. " 'Messianic' Figures and Movements in First-Century Palestine." Pages 276–95 in *The Messiah: Developments in Earliest Judaism and Christianity*. Edited by James H. Charlesworth. Minneapolis: Fortress, 1992.

Howell, David B. *Matthew's Inclusive Story: A Study in the Narrative Rhetoric of the First Gospel*. Journal for the Study of the New Testament Supplement Series 42. Sheffield: Sheffield Academic Press, 1990.

Huffmann, Norman A. "Atypical Features in the Parables of Jesus." *Journal of Biblical Literature* 97 (1978): 207–20.

Iser, Wolfgang. *The Art of Reading: A Theory of Aesthetic Response*. Baltimore: Johns Hopkins University Press, 1978.

————. *The Implied Reader: Patterns of Communication in Prose Fiction from Bunyan to Beckett*. Baltimore: Johns Hopkins University Press, 1974.

Jeremias, Joachim. *The Parables of Jesus*. 2d rev. ed. New York: Charles Scribner's Sons, 1972.

Johnson, Marshall. "Reflections on a Wisdom Approach to Matthew's Christology." *Catholic Biblical Quarterly* 36 (1974): 44–64.

Josephus. Translated by H. St. J. Thackeray et al. 10 vols. Loeb Classical Library. London: William Neinemann.

Kaiser, Walter C., Jr. "The Promise of the Arrival of Elijah in Malachi and the Gospels." *Grace Theological Journal* 3 (1982): 221–33.

Kamlah, Ehrhard. "Kritik und Interpretation der Parabel von den anvertrauten Gerdern." *Kerygma und Dogma* 14 (1968): 28–38.

Kea, Perry. "The Sermon on the Mount: Ethics and Eschatological Time." Pages 88–99 in *Society of Biblical Literature 1986 Seminar Papers*. Edited by Kent Richards. Atlanta: Scholars Press, 1986.

Keegan, Terence J. "Introductory Formulae for Matthean Discourses." *Catholic Biblical Quarterly* 44 (1982): 415–30.

Kik, J. Marcellus. *Matthew Twenty-Four*. Philadelphia: Presbyterian and Reformed, 1948.

Kingsbury, Jack Dean. "The Composition and Christology of MATT 28:16–20." *Journal of Biblical Literature* 93 (1974): 573–84.

———. "The Developing Conflict between Jesus and the Jewish Leaders in Matthew's Gospel: A Literary-Critical Study." *Catholic Biblical Quarterly* 49 (1987): 57–73.

———. "The Figure of Jesus in Matthew's Story: A Literary-Critical Probe." *Journal for the Study of the New Testament* 21 (1984): 3–36.

———. "The Figure of Jesus in Matthew's Story: A Rejoinder to David Hill." *Journal for the Study of the New Testament* 25 (1985): 61–81.

———. "The Figure of Peter in Matthew's Gospel as a Theological Problem." *Journal of Biblical Literature* 98 (1975): 67–83.

———. *Matthew as Story.* 2d rev. and enl. ed. Philadelphia: Fortress, 1988.

———. *Matthew: Structure, Christology, Kingdom.* Minneapolis: Fortress, 1975.

———. "Observations on the 'Miracle Chapters' of Matthew 8–9." *Catholic Biblical Quarterly* 40 (1978): 559–73.

———. "On Following Jesus: The 'Eager' Scribe and the 'Reluctant' Disciple (Matthew 8.18–22)." *New Testament Studies* 34 (1988): 45–59.

———. "The Parable of the Wicked Husbandmen and the Secret of Jesus' Divine Sonship in Matthew: Some Literary-Critical Observations." *Journal of Biblical Literature* 105 (1986): 643–55.

———. *The Parables of Jesus in Matthew 13.* London: SPCK, 1978.

———. "The Place, Structure, and Meaning of the Sermon on the Mount." *Interpretation* 41 (1987): 131–43.

———. "The Plot of Matthew's Story." *Interpretation* 46 (1992): 347–56.

———. "Reflections on 'The Reader' of Matthew's Gospel." *New Testament Studies* 34 (1988): 442–60.

———. "The Verb *AKOLOUTHEIN* as an Index of Matthew's View of His Community." *Journal of Biblical Literature* 97 (1978): 56–73.

Kittel, Gerhard, and Gerhard Friedrich, eds. *Theological Dictionary of the New Testament.* Translated by Geoffrey W. Bromiley. 10 vols. Grand Rapids: Eerdmans, 1964–1976.

Klassen-Wiebe, Sheila A. "Matthew 1:18–25." *Interpretation* 46 (1992): 392–95.

Knowles, Michael. *Jeremiah in Matthew's Gospel: The Rejected-Prophet Motif in Matthaean Redaction.* Journal for the Study of the New Testament Supplement Series 68. Sheffield: Sheffield Academic Press, 1993.

Knox, D. B. "The Five Comings of Jesus: Matthew 24 and 25." *Reformed Theological Review* 34 (1975): 44–54.

Kolenkow, Anitra B. "The Fall of the Temple and the Coming of the End: The Spectrum and Process of Apocalyptic Argument in 2 Baruch and Other Authors." Pages 243–50 in *Society of Biblical Literature 1982 Seminar Papers.* Edited by Kent Richards. Chico, Calif.: Scholars Press, 1982.

Kümmel, Werner Georg. *Promise and Fulfillment: The Eschatological Message of Jesus.* Naperville, Ill.: Alec R. Allenson, 1957.

Künzi, Martin. *Das Naherwartungslogion Markus 9,1 par.: Geschichte seiner Auslegung.* Tübingen: J. C. B. Mohr, 1977.

———. *Das Näherwartungslogion Matthäus 10,23: Geschichte seiner Auslegung.* Tübingen: J. C. B. Mohr, 1970.

Ladd, George E. *The Presence of the Future: The Eschatology of Biblical Realism.* Grand Rapids: Eerdmans, 1974.

Lagrange, Marie-Joseph. *Évangile selon saint Matthieu.* 7th ed. Paris: J. Gabalda, 1948.

Lambrecht, Jan. "The Parousia Discourse: Composition and Content in Mt., XXIV–XXV." Pages 309–42 in *L'Apocalypse Johannique et L'Apocalyptique dans le Nouveau Testament*. Edited by Jan Lambrecht. Leuven: University Press, 1980.

Lampe, G. W. H., ed. *A Patristic Greek Lexicon*. Oxford: Clarendon Press, 1961.

Lanser, Susan Sniader. *The Narrative Act: Point of View in Prose Fiction*. Princeton: Princeton University Press, 1981.

Lattke, Michael. "On the Jewish Background of the Synoptic Concept 'The Kingdom of God.' " Pages 72–91 in *The Kingdom of God in the Teaching of Jesus*. Edited by Bruce Chilton. Philadelphia: Fortress, 1984.

Leitch, Thomas M. *What Stories Are: Narrative Theory and Interpretation*. University Park, Pa.: Pennsylvania State University Press, 1986.

Lenski, R. C. H. *The Interpretation of St. Matthew's Gospel*. Columbus Ohio: Wartburg, 1943.

Liddell, Henry G., and Robert Scott, comps. *A Greek-English Lexicon*. Revised and augmented by Henry S. Jones. Oxford: Clarendon Press, 1953.

Lincoln, Andrew T. "Matthew—A Story for Teachers?" Pages 103–25 in *The Bible in Three Dimensions: Essays in Celebration of Forty Years of Biblical Studies in the University of Sheffield*. Edited by David J. A. Clines, Stephen E. Fowl, and Stanley E. Porter. Sheffield: Sheffield Academic Press, 1990.

Lindars, Barnabas. *Jesus Son of Man: A Fresh Examination of the Son of Man Sayings in the Gospels in the Light of Recent Research*. London: SPCK, 1983.

Linton, Olof. "The Demand for a Sign from Heaven (Mk. 8,11–12 and Parallels)." *Studia theologica* 19 (1965): 112–29.

Longman, Tremper, III. "The Divine Warrior: The New Testament Use of an Old Testament Motif." *Westminster Theological Journal* 44 (1982): 290–307.

Louw, Johannes P., and Eugene A. Nida, eds. *Greek-English Lexicon of the New Testament Based on Semantic Domains*. 2d ed. 2 vols. New York: United Bible Societies, 1989.

Lövestam, Evald. "The ἡ γενεὰ αὕτη Eschatology in Mk. 13,30 pars." Pages 403–13 in *L'Apocalypse Johannique et L'Apocalyptique dans le Nouveau Testament*. Edited by Jan Lambrecht. Leuven: University Press, 1980.

———. "Spiritual Wakefulness in the Synoptic Gospels." Pages 78–132 in *Spiritual Wakefulness in the New Testament*. Lund: CWK Gleerup, 1963.

Luz, Ulrich. "The Disciples in the Gospel according to Matthew." Pages 98–128 in *The Interpretation of Matthew*. Edited by Graham Stanton. Philadelphia: Fortress, 1983.

———. *Matthew 1–7: A Commentary*. Translated by Wilhelm Linss. Minneapolis: Augsburg, 1989.

Maartens, P. J. "Mt 24–5." Pages 42–52 in *Discourse Analysis of the Greek Text of Matthew 14–28: Addendum to Neotestamentica 16 (1982), Structure and Meaning of Matthew 14–28*. New Testament Society of South Africa, 1982.

———. "The Structuring Principles in Mt. 24 and 25 and the Interpretation of the Text." *Neotestamentica* 16 (1982): 88–117.

Maier, Gerhard. *Matthäus-Evangelium*. Vol. 2. Neuhausen-Stuttgart: Hänssler-Verlag, 1983.

Mandelkern, Solomon. *Veteris Testamenti Concordantiae Hebraicae atque Chaldaicae*. 2 vols. Jerusalem: Sumptibus Schocken, 1971.

Manson, T. W. *The Sayings of Jesus*. Grand Rapids: Eerdmans, 1979.

Marcus, Joel. "The Gates of Hell and the Keys of the Kingdom (Matt 16:18–19)." *Catholic Biblical Quarterly* 50 (1988): 443–55.

Marguerat, Daniel. *Le Jugement dans l'Évangile de Matthieu*. Labor et Fides Editeurs, 1981.

Matera, Frank J. *Passion Narratives and Gospel Theologies: Interpreting the Synoptics through Their Passion Stories.* New York: Paulist, 1986.

———. "The Plot of Matthew's Gospel." *Catholic Biblical Quarterly* 49 (1987): 233–53.

McDermott, John. "Matt 10:23 in Context." *Biblische Zeitschrift,* New Series, 28 (1984): 230–40.

McKnight, Scot. "Jesus and the End-Time: Matthew 10:23." Pages 501–20 in *Society of Biblical Literature 1986 Seminar Papers.* Edited by Kent Richards. Atlanta: Scholars Press, 1986.

McNamara, Martin. *Palestinian Judaism and the New Testament.* Wilmington: Michael Glazier, 1983.

Meier, John P. "John the Baptist in Matthew's Gospel." *Journal of Biblical Literature* 99 (1980): 383–405.

———. *Law and History in Matthew's Gospel: A Redactional Study of Mt. 5:17–48.* Rome: Biblical Institute, 1976.

———. *Matthew.* Wilmington: Michael Glazier, 1980.

———. "Nations or Gentiles in Matthew 28:19?" *Catholic Biblical Quarterly* 39 (1977): 94–102.

———. *The Vision of Matthew: Christ, Church, and Morality in the First Gospel.* New York: Paulist, 1978.

Metzger, Bruce M. *A Textual Commentary on the Greek New Testament.* London: United Bible Societies, 1971.

Michaels, J. Ramsey. "Apostolic Hardships and Righteous Gentiles: A Study of Matthew 25:31–46." *Journal of Biblical Literature* 84 (1965): 27–37.

Michel, Otto. "The Conclusion of Matthew's Gospel: A Contribution to the History of the Easter Message." Pages 30–41 in *The Interpretation of Matthew.* Edited by Graham Stanton. Philadelphia: Fortress, 1983.

Monsarrat, Violaine. "Matthieu 24–25: du Temple aux démunis." *Foi et Vie* 76 (1977): 67–80.

Moore, A. L. *The Parousia in the New Testament.* Leiden: E. J. Brill, 1966.

Moore, Stephen D. "Are the Gospels Unified Narratives?" Pages 443–58 in *Society of Biblical Literature 1987 Seminar Papers.* Edited by Kent Richards. Atlanta: Scholars Press, 1987.

Morris, Leon. *The Gospel according to Matthew.* Grand Rapids: Eerdmans, 1992.

Moule, C. F. D. *An Idiom Book of New Testament Greek.* 2d ed. Cambridge: Cambridge University Press, 1959.

Moulton, James Hope. *Prolegomena.* Vol. 1 of *A Grammar of New Testament Greek* by James Hope Moulton, Wilbert Francis Howard, and Nigel Turner. 3d ed. Edinburgh: T. & T. Clark, 1908.

Moulton, James Hope, and George Milligan. *The Vocabulary of the Greek Testament: Illustrated from the Papyri and Other Non-Literary Sources.* Repr., Grand Rapids: Eerdmans, 1985.

Mounce, Robert. *Matthew.* Peabody, Mass.: Hendrickson, 1985.

Neusner, Jacob. "The Formation of Rabbinic Judaism: Yavneh (Jamnia) from A.D. 70 to 100." Pages 3–42 in volume 19.2 of *Aufstieg und Niedergang der Römischen Welt,* part 2: *Principat.* Edited by Wolfgang Haase. Berlin: Walter de Gruyter, 1979.

———. *The Mishnah: A New Translation.* New Haven: Yale University Press, 1988.

———. "The Modern Study of the Mishnah." Pages 3–27 in *Mishnah, Midrash, Siddur*. Vol. 1 of *The Study of Ancient Judaism*. Edited by Jacob Neusner. Hoboken, N.J.: Ktav, 1981.

———. "The Use of the Later Rabbinic Evidence for the Study of First-Century Pharisaism." Pages 215–28 in *Approaches to Ancient Judaism: Theory and Practice*. Edited by William Scott Green. Missoula: Scholars Press, 1978.

———. "The Use of Rabbinic Sources for the Study of Ancient Judaism." Pages 1–18 in *Text as Context in Early Rabbinic Literature*. Vol. 3 of *Approaches to Ancient Judaism*. Edited by William Scott Green. Chico, Calif.: Scholars Press, 1981.

Newman, Barclay M., and Philip C. Stine. *A Translator's Handbook on the Gospel of Matthew*. New York: United Bible Societies, 1988.

Niedner, Frederick A., Jr. "Rereading Matthew on Jerusalem and Judaism." *Biblical Theology Bulletin* 19 (1989): 43–47.

Oudersluys, Richard C. "The Parable of the Sheep and Goats (Matthew 25:31–46): Eschatology and Mission, Then and Now." *Reformed Review* 26 (1973): 151–61.

Pamment, Margaret. "The Kingdom of Heaven according to the First Gospel." *New Testament Studies* 27 (1980–1981): 211–32.

———. "The Son of Man in the First Gospel." *New Testament Studies* 29 (1983): 116–29.

Patrick, Dale. "The Kingdom of God in the Old Testament." Pages 67–80 in *The Kingdom of God in 20th-Century Interpretation*. Edited by Wendell Willis. Peabody, Mass.: Hendrickson, 1987.

Perrin, Norman. "Jesus and the Language of the Kingdom." Pages 92–106 in *The Kingdom of God in the Teaching of Jesus*. Edited by Bruce Chilton. Philadelphia: Fortress, 1984.

Pesch, Rudolf. "Eschatologie und Ethik: Auslegung von Mt 24,1–36." *Bibel und Leben* 11 (1970): 223–38.

Petersen, Norman R. " 'Point of View' in Mark's Narrative." *Semeia* 12 (1978): 97–121.

Plummer, Alfred. *An Exegetical Commentary on the Gospel according to St. Matthew*. Grand Rapids: Baker, 1982.

Porter, Stanley E. *Idioms of the Greek New Testament*. Biblical Languages: Greek 2. Sheffield: Sheffield Academic Press, 1992.

Powell, Mark Allan. "Expected and Unexpected Readings of Matthew: What the Reader Knows." *Asbury Theological Journal* 48 (1993): 31–52.

———. "The Religious Leaders in Matthew: A Literary-Critical Approach." Ph.D. diss., Union Theological Seminary in Virginia, 1988.

———. *What Is Narrative Criticism?* Minneapolis: Fortress, 1990.

Rahlfs, Alfred, ed. *Septuaginta*. Stuttgart: Württembergische Bibelanstalt, 1935.

Reeves, Keith H. "The Resurrection Narrative in Matthew: A Literary-Critical Examination." Ph.D. diss., Union Theological Seminary in Virginia, 1988.

Reicke, Bo. *The New Testament Era: The World of the Bible from 500 B.C. to A.D. 100*. Translated by David E. Green. Philadelphia: Fortress, 1968.

———. "Synoptic Prophecies on the Destruction of Jerusalem." Pages 121–34 in *Studies in New Testament and Early Christian Literature*. Edited by David Edward Aune. Leiden: E. J. Brill, 1972.

———. "A Test of Synoptic Relationships: Matthew 10:17–23 and 24:9–14 with Parallels." Pages 209–29 in *New Synoptic Studies*. Edited by William R. Farmer. Macon, Ga.: Mercer, 1983.

Ridderbos, Herman. *The Coming of the Kingdom*. Edited by Raymond O. Zorn. Translated by H. de Jongste. Philadelphia: Presbyterian and Reformed, 1962.

Rimmon-Kenan, Shlomith. *Narrative Fiction: Contemporary Poetics*. London: Methuen, 1983.

Roark, Dallas M. "The Great Eschatological Discourse." *Novum Testamentum* 7 (1964–1965): 122–27.

Robertson, A. T. *A Grammar of the Greek New Testament in the Light of Historical Research.* 3d. ed. New York: Hodder & Stoughton, 1919.

Robinson, J. A. T. "Elijah, John, and Jesus." Pages 28–52 in *Twelve New Testament Studies*. London: SCM Press, 1962.

———. "The 'Parable' of the Sheep and the Goats." *New Testament Studies* 2 (1956): 225–37.

Rolland, Philippe. "From the Genesis to the End of the World: The Plan of Matthew's Gospel." *Biblical Theology Bulletin* 2 (1972): 155–76.

Sabourin, Leopold. "Apocalyptic Traits in Matthew's Gospel." *Religious Studies Bulletin* 3 (1983): 19–35.

———. *L'Évangile selon Saint Matthieu et ses Principaux Parallèlles*. Rome: Biblical Institute, 1978.

———. "Recent Gospel Studies." *Biblical Theology Bulletin* 3 (1973): 283–315.

———. " 'You Will Not Have Gone through All the Towns of Israel, before the Son of Man Comes' (Matt 10:23b)." *Biblical Theology Bulletin* 7 (1977): 5–11.

Sandmel, Samuel. "Parallelomania." *Journal of Biblical Literature* 81 (1962): 1–13.

Sayers, Dorothy. *The Man Born to Be King: A Play-Cycle on the Life of Our Lord and Saviour Jesus Christ*. New York: Harper & Row, 1943.

Schlatter, Adolf. *Der Evangelist Matthäus: Seine Sprache, seine Zeit, seine Selbständigkeit.* Stuttgart: Calwer Verlag, 1957.

Schnackenburg, Rudolf. *Matthäusevangelium 1,1–16,20*. Würzburg: Echter-Verlag, 1985.

———. *Matthäusevangelium 16,21–28,20*. Würzburg: Echter-Verlag, 1987.

Schniewind, Julius. *Das Evangelium nach Matthäus*. Göttingen: Vandenhoeck & Ruprecht, 1964.

Schwarz, G. "Zum Vokabular von Matthäus XXV.1–12." *New Testament Studies* 27 (1981): 270–76.

Schweitzer, Albert. *The Quest of the Historical Jesus: A Critical Study of Its Progress from Reimarus to Wrede*. Repr., New York: Macmillan, 1968.

Schweizer, Eduard. *The Good News according to Matthew*. Translated by David E. Green. Atlanta: John Knox, 1975.

Senior, Donald. "The Death of Jesus and the Resurrection of the Holy Ones (Mt. 27:51–53)." *Catholic Biblical Quarterly* 38 (1976): 312–29.

———. *The Passion of Jesus in the Gospel of Matthew*. Wilmington: Michael Glazier, 1985.

Sherriff, J. M. "Matthew 25:1–13: A Summary of Matthean Eschatology?" Pages 301–5 in *Papers on the Gospels: Sixth International Congress on Biblical Studies, Oxford, 3–7 April 1978*. Vol. 2 of *Studia Biblica 1978*. Edited by E. A. Livingstone. Sheffield: JSOT Press, 1980.

Sibinga, J. Smit. "The Structure of the Apocalyptic Discourse, Matthew 24 and 25." *Studia Theologica* 29 (1975): 71–79.

Smith, Morton. "What Is Implied by the Variety of Messianic Figures?" *Journal of Biblical Literature* 78 (1950): 66–72.

Smyth, Herbert Weir. *Greek Grammar*. Revised by Gordon M. Messing. Cambridge, Mass.: Harvard University Press, 1956.

Stanley, David. "Matthew's Gethsemane (Mt 26:36–46)." Pages 155–87 in *Jesus in Gethsemane*. New York: Paulist Press, 1980.

Stanton, Graham N. *A Gospel for a New People: Studies in Matthew*. Edinburgh: T. & T. Clark, 1992.

———. "'Pray That Your Flight May Not Be in Winter or on a Sabbath' (Matthew 24.20)." *Journal for the Study of the New Testament* 37 (1989): 17–30.

Strack, Hermann L., and Paul Billerbeck. *Kommentar zum Neuen Testament aus Talmud und Midrasch*. 6 vols. Munich: C. H. Beck, 1922–1961.

Strecker, Georg. *Der Weg der Gerechtigkeit: Untersuchung zur Theologie des Matthäus*. Göttingen: Vandenhoeck & Ruprecht, 1962.

Stuart, M. "Observations on Matthew 24:29–31, and the Parallel Passages in Mark and Luke, with Remarks on the Double Sense of Scripture." *Bibliotheca Sacra and American Biblical Repository* 9 (1852): 329–54, 449–67.

Tacitus. *The Histories and the Annals*. Translated by C. H. Moore and John Jackson. 4 vols. Loeb Classical Library. Cambridge: Harvard University Press, 1937.

Tasker, R. V. G. *The Gospel according to St. Matthew*. Grand Rapids: Eerdmans, 1961.

Thompson, William G. "An Historical Perspective in the Gospel of Matthew." *Journal of Biblical Literature* 93 (1974): 243–62.

———. "Reflections on the Composition of MT 8:1–9:34." *Catholic Biblical Quarterly* 33 (1971): 365–88.

Tisera, Guido. *Universalism according to the Gospel of Matthew*. Frankfurt am Main: Peter Lang, 1993.

Trilling, Wolfgang. *The Gospel according to St. Matthew*. Vol. 2. Translated by Kevin Smyth. New York: Crossroad, 1981.

Turner, David L. "The Structure and Sequence of Matthew 24:1–41: Interaction with Evangelical Treatments." *Grace Theological Journal* 10 (1989): 3–29.

Turner, H. E. W. "Expounding the Parables: The Parable of the Sheep and the Goats (Matthew 25:31–46)." *Expository Times* 77 (1965–1966): 243–46.

Turner, Nigel. *Style*. Vol. 4 of *A Grammar of New Testament Greek* by James Hope Moulton, Wilbert Francis Howard, and Nigel Turner. Edinburgh: T & T Clark, 1976.

———. *Syntax*. Vol. 3 of *A Grammar of New Testament Greek* by James Hope Moulton, Wilbert Francis Howard, and Nigel Turner. Edinburgh: T. & T. Clark, 1963.

Uspensky, Boris. *A Poetics of Composition*. Translated by Valentina Zavarin and Susan Wittig. Berkeley: University of California Press, 1973.

Vermes, Geza. "The 'Son of Man' Debate." *Journal for the Study of the New Testament* 1 (1978): 19–32.

Verseput, Donald. *The Rejection of the Humble Messianic King: A Study of the Composition of Matthew 11–12*. Frankfurt am Main: Peter Lang, 1986.

Viviano, B. T. "The Kingdom of God in the Qumran Literature." Pages 97–108 in *The Kingdom of God in 20th-Century Interpretation*. Edited by Wendell Willis. Peabody, Mass.: Hendrickson, 1987.

Voelz, James W. *Fundamental Greek Grammar*. St. Louis: Concordia, 1986.

Vögtle, Anton. "Das christologische und ekklesiologische Anliegen von Mt. 28,18–20." Pages 266–94 in *Papers Presented to the Second International Congress on New Testament Studies Held at Christ Church, Oxford, 1961*. Vol. 2 of *Studia Evangelica*. Edited by F. L. Cross. Berlin: Akademie-Verlag, 1964.

Vorster, W. S. "Literary Reflections on Mark 13:5–37: A Narrated Speech of Jesus." *Neotestamentica* 21 (1987): 203–24.

Walter, Nikolaus. "Tempelzerstörung und synoptische Apokalypse." *Zeitschrift für die neutestamentliche Wissenschaft* 57 (1966): 38–48.

Weaver, Dorothy Jean. *Matthew's Missionary Discourse: A Literary Critical Analysis.* Journal for the Study of the New Testament Supplement Series 38. Sheffield: Sheffield Academic Press, 1990.

———. "Power and Powerlessness: Matthew's Use of Irony in the Portrayal of Political Leaders." Pages 454–66 in *Society of Biblical Literature 1992 Seminar Papers.* Edited by Eugene H. Lovering Jr. Atlanta: Scholars Press, 1992.

Weiss, Johannes. *Jesus' Proclamation of the Kingdom of God.* Edited and translated by R. H. Hiers and D. L. Holland. Repr., Chico, Calif.: Scholars Press, 1985.

Wenham, David. "A Note on Matthew 24:10–12." *Tyndale Bulletin* 31 (1980): 155–62.

———. "'This Generation Will Not Pass...': A Study of Jesus' Future Expectation in Mark 13." Pages 127–50 in *Christ the Lord: Studies in Christology Presented to Donald Guthrie.* Edited by Harold H. Rowdon. Downers Grove, Ill.: InterVarsity, 1982.

Wenthe, Dean O. "The Parable of the Ten Bridesmaids (Matthew 25:1–13)." *Springfielder* 40 (1976): 9–16.

Willis, Wendell, ed. *The Kingdom of God in 20th-Century Interpretation.* Peabody, Mass.: Hendrickson, 1987.

Wink, Walter. *John the Baptist in the Gospel Tradition.* Cambridge: Cambridge University Press, 1968.

Witherup, Ronald D. "The Cross of Jesus: A Literary-Critical Study of Matthew 27." Ph.D. diss., Union Theological Seminary in Virginia, 1985.

Wolthuis, Thomas R. "Experiencing the Kingdom: Reading the Gospel of Matthew." Ph.D. diss., Duke University, 1987.

Zahn, Theodor. *Das Evangelium des Matthäus.* Leipzig: A. Deichert, 1903.

Zaiman, Joel H. "The Traditional Study of the Mishnah." Pages 27–36 in *Mishnah, Midrash, Siddur.* Vol. 1 of *The Study of Ancient Judaism.* Edited by Jacob Neusner. Hoboken, N.J.: Ktav, 1981.

Zucker, David J. "Jesus and Jeremiah in the Matthean Tradition." *Journal of Ecumenical Studies* 27 (1990): 288–305.